The Collapse of Price's Raid

Shades of Blue and Gray Series

Louis S. Gerteis and Clayton E. Jewett, Series Editors
Herman Hattaway and Jon Wakelyn, Consulting Editors

The Shades of Blue and Gray Series offers Civil War studies for the modern reader–Civil War buff and scholar alike. Military history today addresses the relationship between society and warfare. Thus biographies and thematic studies that deal with civilians, soldiers, and political leaders are increasingly important to a larger public. This series includes books that will appeal to Civil War Roundtable groups, individuals, libraries, and academics with a special interest in this era of American history.

The Collapse of Price's Raid

The Beginning of the End in Civil War Missouri

MARK A. LAUSE

UNIVERSITY OF MISSOURI PRESS   COLUMBIA

Copyright © 2016 by
The Curators of the University of Missouri
University of Missouri Press, Columbia, Missouri 65211
Printed and bound in the United States of America
All rights reserved. First paperback printing, 2025.

ISBN: 978-0-8262-2025-7 (hardcover : alk. paper) | 978-0-8262-2332-6 (paperback : alk. paper)
Library of Congress Control Number: 2015955172

∞™ This paper meets the requirements of the
American National Standard for Permanence of Paper
for Printed Library Materials, Z39.48, 1984.

Typefaces: Minion, Adobe Jenson, and Rage Joi D

Contents

The Collapse of Price's Raid

Prologue

The Making of a Raid

The Spectre of Quindaro

As of Saturday, October 8, 1864, General Sterling Price's Army of Missouri found itself transformed from a liberating force into an oversized raiding column. As the former, it failed to take St. Louis or Jefferson City, much less reclaim the state for the Confederacy, but it had spent nearly three weeks marching through much of the Federal Department of Missouri, which had generally kept its best-trained and -equipped forces away from the Confederates.[1] That weekend, though, Price had ordered his army to bypass the state capital, and the bluecoats behind him mounted up and began what became almost daily attacks, even as the authorities on the Kansas line raised an entirely new Army of the Border. From this point, every day the Confederates could stay in Missouri would be a day less hunger and misery in the desolation to the south, where armies had regularly tramped for years, taking anything they wanted or wanted to deny the enemy. Thereafter, the Confederates would measure success by taking not the state but corncribs and stacks of grain. Perhaps without the soldiers realizing it, Price's liberating invasion became a raid.

The Confederate reappearance in Missouri had been part of a broader effort to influence the upcoming 1864 elections in the Union, a particularly critical event in that state, which the Confederacy had claimed as one of its own. Behind issues of war-weariness, which preoccupied much of the public discussion of the election, lay that of slave emancipation, which President Abraham Lincoln had proclaimed as a military tactic in those parts of the South in rebellion. Because the proclamation freed no slaves in Missouri, Unionists in the state divided between the Conservatives, who sought to save the institution, and the Radicals, who hoped to destroy it as part of a general effort to make a much more generally egalitarian and democratic society. A mistaken Confederate confidence in a broad political backlash to radicalism, particularly of issues of race, buoyed the hopes of Price and his generals to reverse the tide of Civil War as late as the fall of 1864.

Freeing Missouri

Secession had grown from the fiction that the mere election in 1860 of a president personally critical of slavery represented an attack on the rights of the slaveholders. The founders of the Confederacy had taken unilateral pre-emptive action to forestall an anticipated radicalization of the Federal Union on the subject of slavery. Acting on these unrealized fears paradoxically assured their realization.

In hindsight, it is obvious that any visions of a Confederate victory in 1864 required a serious misunderstanding of the state of the conflict. Union forces had divided secessionist territory once the previous year, along the Mississippi River, and, after securing their hold on Tennessee, made a determined drive into Georgia, seizing Atlanta and threatening to divide the eastern remnants of the Confederacy. Months earlier, the Federals had bottled up the best of the se-cessionist forces, those under Robert E. Lee, at Richmond and adjacent Peters-burg, where hunger, disease, and desertion began taking their toll.

Among the persistent secessionists, the most realistic aimed to hold out in the hope that the Union government and army might misstep in a way that could made the Confederacy look more viable abroad. The more desperate schemed to mobilize what they perceived to be massive voter disaffection with the Republicans behind Federal lines. Some had planned bank robberies in New England, the mass rescue of Confederates from Northern prison camps, or the kidnapping of the president to force the renewal of prisoner exchanges. Confederate forces in the field planned raids into Pennsylvania and Maryland, and what proved to be a terribly belated move into Tennessee in an attempt to draw the Union armies back out of Georgia. On the western border, they resur-rected the oft-discussed idea of reclaiming Missouri.

For various reasons, the smart money would have bet on Missouri. From 1862 on, both sides had systematically moved recruits from the west to the east, but Federal victories on the Mississippi River in 1863 had denied the Confederacy the option of continuing to do so. This left the Confederates west of the river with proportionately greater numbers and made the otherwise far-fetched scheme to retake Missouri seem a reasonable attempt to thwart a renewed Unionist mandate in the elections.

However, the secessionist assessment of conditions in Missouri was mostly wishful thinking. Missourians naturally chafed under the military occupation of the Federal army, but their grievances had been so pressing under the secessionists that they had risen up against their state government to ease the Union advance into the state. The Confederates had raided into the area almost continually and should have known what would greet them, but self-deception predominated. "St. Louis papers represent the State in a complete state of revolution," one of them wrote to his father. "God speed it."[2]

Confederate prospects in Missouri—or anywhere—had been at their peak in 1861. Southern whites not entirely convinced of the wisdom of secession might go along when it all seemed like a colorful, exciting, and viable way of negating Republican victories at the polls, but their new allegiances proved shaky as the guns and bloodshed started and grew worse. While Federal tactics in Missouri were severe and alienating, they were a response to secessionist methods that had been even more thuggish than those employed in the Deep South. As the Unionists advanced across entire swaths of the South, growing numbers of Confederates had to reconsider the idea of defending homes that were now behind Federal lines. As elsewhere in the border and shallower South, whites in Missouri had experienced nothing since the war's start that would convince them of the Confederate cause.

War also brought to the fore African Americans, those Southerners and Missourians who, at the start, had not figured much in the plans of either side. More numerous and larger waves of black refugees began turning up at St. Louis, Jefferson City, or other locations secured by Federal troops. Union soldiers had come to realize that slavery represented an asset of their enemies and begun harboring fugitives and encouraging slaves to run away. This continued alongside remarkable attempts by conservative officers to return slaves to their owners until a common military policy emerged. After a bit more than a year of war, Lincoln decided to issue his proclamation emancipating slaves in those areas in rebellion against the Union, making it public on the eve of the fall elections of 1862.

Unionists in Missouri and the far west had the same arguments about military necessity and the sense that slavery had been the moving force behind secession, though the proclamation never applied there. Missouri slaveholders had long nurtured grudges against illegal incursions from Kansas that freed slaves, but they now also faced determined efforts by Missouri Unionists—soldiers, militia, and civilians—to destroy the institution, root and branch. Eager to retain their assets or to avoid the disruptions of emancipation, Conservative Unionists held the line against such actions, while Radical Unionists entered politics to eliminate slavery through the upcoming 1864 elections in Missouri. While Lincoln had continually urged the army to remain neutral in these internal political disputes, it rarely did. After all, the shortcomings of the Emancipation Proclamation left it liable to continue protecting the constitutional rights of the slaveholders to their property. Then, too, commanders of the Federal army in the state generally cringed over anything that might encourage the Radicals or African Americans. Even as Union officials sought to concentrate their forces, a general could send telegrams such as: "If you have not already started the 200 colored troops to Saint Louis, do not send them." "There is a perfect little army of niggers here," complained another at Jefferson City, "and I don't know what the devil is to become of them."[3]

Until then, though, the military would have the ultimate responsibility for African Americans. Runaways and fugitives naturally clustered under protection of the army, but the peculiar status of slavery in the state created a market for gangs operating to kidnap blacks and take them south. To prevent this—and to stop the drain of needed labor—the army barred the removal of blacks from the state without a permit. This flustered the initial plans of antislavery organizations to raise money for the purchase of Missouri slaves and their movement to free states. The Ladies Contraband Relief Society at St. Louis managed to arrange some employment and, by 1863, worked to help refugees downriver as far as Columbus, Island No. 10, Memphis, Helena, and Bolivar, but forwarded 2,500 out into the relative safety of the free states. Unable to protect blacks or to resist their drive for freedom, the army moved toward its own plan to find civilian work for refugees. This did not prevent the local military authorities at places like Warrensburg or Sedalia from simply banishing blacks for things like vagrancy. Only with some reluctance did slaveholding Missouri begin raising and arming units of black soldiers.[4]

In contrast, Kansas embraced the new policies. Despite having many fewer people than Missouri with a proportionately smaller black population, Kansas had two African American regiments in the field, the newest officered by the 29-year-old Radical candidate for governor, Samuel Johnson Crawford. In 1864, local militia musters in Missouri often took the initiative of arming blacks, but the state of Kansas made specific provisions to get them to the front. The Kansas State Militia (KSM) not only raised distinct "colored" units but officially supplemented regular companies "old men, boys, and Negroes" willing to bear arms, even if technically not obligated to do so.[5]

Then, too, Kansas also had a battery of "Colored Artillery," the first active unit of the war that would actually have black officers, some prominent, such as Captain Hezekiah F. Douglas, of Muscatine, Iowa. A second was Lieutenant Patrick H. Minor, the highly educated private secretary of Colonel George Hoyt, who had defended John Brown. Stranded by events at Fort Scott, their First Lieutenant William D. Matthews took charge of raising black militia there. A "giant and coal-black negro, a Hercules in strength, unlettered, but devoted to his service" he had helped recruit the first regiment. The white officers had petitioned to get him a commission and, eventually, he got one in the battery.[6]

Confederates had resented the introduction of blacks a year earlier, and regularly killed any taken prisoner, with Federal units sometimes retaliating in kind. In the 1864 campaign, a white Federal prisoner, Samuel J. Reader, remembered how a black man in his group "excited more comment than all the rest of us put together." One of their captors demanded, "What's that nigger doing there?" with "a chorus of fierce yells" following: "Kill him, shoot him!" Periodic frustration in the fighting renewed these tirades with "fresh ferocity in some of the rebels" who, Reader wrote, "yelled like wild Indians . . . and various were the modes proposed of killing him. 'Don't shoot him! Kill him with a white oak club!' shouted one ruffian." Later, Reader got alongside the target of their abuse and "took an opportunity to advise him to escape at the first opportunity." "Yes, sir," the black man replied.[7] Yet, the longer the war went on, the broader its mobilization had to be.

In the West, Indians remained vital to the campaign. Although the Delaware had originally served in the Federal brigade of Indian Home Guards, the machinations of the high command discouraged Chief Fall Leaf and his men to the point that they just came home, but many found the best solution to the discriminatory treatment of distinctly Indian units by joining regular Kansas Cavalry regiments. Large numbers of Delaware volunteered for the Fourteenth and about 170 for the Fifteenth. Wyandottes provided many members of the Fifth Kansas Cavalry—notorious for its emancipationist policy from the war's onset—and others from both of those nations participated in the Sixth and the Twelfth Kansas Cavalry, while the Kaw or Kanza filled almost a company of the Ninth. Under the press of events in 1864, Kansas Federal commanders authorized the Agent to the Ottawas "to raise a company of Indians from friendly tribes . . . for special service."[8]

It should be noted that as the war raged on, one of the officers in the Second Colorado later reported a still more unorthodox, though clearly important, source of soldiers. Years before, George West had encountered a "girl-mountaineer" from Iowa. During gold rush at Pike's Peak, "Charlotte" found it easier to make her own way by donning male dress. She turned up from time to time in New Mexico or Colorado, working as a teamster. Returning to Iowa, she enlisted as "Charley Hatfield" and wound up alongside the Coloradoans, some of whom knew her secret. When she ran into West, she explained that she had been detailed to work as a clerk at headquarters but had volunteered to infiltrate Price's camp. "Mountain Charley" had not been the only woman campaigning in 1864.[9]

The 1864 campaign threatened to unleash just the radical dynamic the Conservatives feared. For all the damage the Second Kansas Cavalry had inflicted on Quindaro, its Captain Samuel Johnson Crawford had gone on to take command of the Second Kansas Colored, and the 1864 governor's campaign in Kansas found Crawford actively working to replace Carney. So, too, the Confederate presence spurred Radical aspirations in Missouri, where Thomas Fletcher also fought Price's army while running for governor on an explicitly emancipationist platform.

The Dynamic of Further Radicalization

Reader's Confederate guards understood where emancipation led, even if their prisoner did not. Asked why he fought, Reader cannily avoided slavery to claim that he bore arms for the Union. "You're fighting for Nigger Equality," his captor explained. "You intend to force nigger equality on the South." "We'll die to the last man before we'll submit to such a thing." After several such exchanges, Reader concluded that "our fighting to force Negro equality on the South" seemed "a bitter pill to them all." "Grant will never take Richmond in God's world," one of them insisted, "and the South will never be whipped, as long as we have a man left alive," because the alternative to fighting on would be "the horrors of 'Nigger equality,' and appealed to his Yankee auditors to imagine their own feelings, when a sooty son-in-law should invade the family circle."[10]

Spurred by national controversy over slavery, many Americans began rethinking assumptions about race. Hundreds of thousands had gone into rebellion against the dominant political and social institutions of their society. Across the region torn by the raid were clusters of spiritualists, whose Banner of Light discerned a dynamic at the war's onset toward "a Government which shall act as a paternal providence over all its subjects, irrespective or race, color or sex." A resident on the Missouri-Kansas line wrote Massachusetts to send lecturers on the subject to those who "live on the borders where rebels and bushwhackers continually annoy us." Boston spiritualists had colonized what became Kidder, Missouri, which fielded Unionist Home Guards at the war's onset. By 1864, veterans of those efforts included Major William Plumb and Lieutenant Patrick S. Kenney riding with the Missouri State Militia (MSM) against Price's army.[11]

Quindaro, Kansas, on the Missouri River demonstrated where emancipation could lead. On the eve of the war, abolitionists purchased land among the Wyandottes to provide easier access to settlers from the Free States, inadvertently founding a refuge for runaway slaves as well. Local investment came from across the river, where the Yankee-born founder of Parkville, Missouri, had lost his paper, the Industrial Luminary, to a proslavery mob. What became a flourishing mixed-race community of several hundred sustained its own newspaper, whose assistant editor, Clara I. H. Nichols, had helped launch the territorial woman's-rights organization. Its voters cast ballots for one of two local parties—the People's and the Workingmen's—and regularly hosted John Brown and his men. When the war started, Mayor Alexander Gray rode off with the notoriously antislavery Fifth Kansas Cavalry and the town imploded with the war. Thereafter, guerrillas regularly struck the area, seizing Parkville in the summer of 1864.[12]

Of course, native peoples, runaway slaves, and white malcontents had long managed to form multiracial maroon communities just beyond the margins as white settlement spread across the continent. Quindaro, however, functioned within the framework of Euro-American civilization and the market economy of its investors. Secessionists feared that the Republican insurgency would not only emancipate slaves but, ultimately, encourage the kind of behavior flaunted at Quindaro.

Secessionists had warned the ruling classes in the North that the dynamic of expropriating their property in slaves had implications for property generally. Three years of war had already pushed the genuinely pragmatic Coloradoans in that direction. In March 1864, Major James Nelson Smith wrote from Independence about the two or three hundred "old men, women and children, who are unable to get work, and thereby support themselves, consequently have to be supplied by Government with rations, wood &c." His suggestion was to seize "one or more of the deserted farms, in this vicinity, and belonging to rebels," which "would not only keep them from eating the bread of idleness, and contracting habits of vice, but would be enabled, not only to support themselves (and thereby save a great expense to Government) but would bring a revenue in to Government." His district commander referred the proposal to his superiors, who deigned to more than scornfully return it.[13]

Their pragmatism drove them to what radicals had long argued: liberty required land. "Nothing, not even the bestowal of suffrage, will so materially aid [in] destroying the effects of Slavery [as] the creation of a self-reliant independent yeomanry out of the former slaves," wrote a veteran of John Brown's band. Granting "personal freedom, secur[ing] no political or civil rights, and leav[ing] the freed class to struggle out of the slough the best way they can with the narrow plank of free labor" would merely subjugate former slaves to "the serfdom of capital."[14]

ILLUSIONS OF COMMAND

The fifty-five-year-old Virginia-born General Sterling Price would command this desperate bid to thwart such an American apocalypse. He had been the governor of Missouri, a leader of the antebellum Democratic Party, a hero of the U.S. War with Mexico, and the most prominent proponent of secession. He probably never really knew how many men served in his Army of Missouri, which he took back into the state. In September 1864, the earliest official reports enumerate over 12,000, but subsequent reports claimed to have raised 1,000 from the sparsely populated communities of the southeast. While the unprepared Federals had initially underestimated the numbers, they later talked of as many as 10,000 Confederates raised north of the Missouri. It became common to estimate that Price had from 20,000 to 30,000, with a few going to 35,000 or higher.[15] Realistically, the Confederates may have recruited or "conscripted" enough to total more than 17,000 or 18,000 men, but Price rarely commanded more than half that many.

Once this army had bypassed the large but ineffective Federal defenses in Arkansas and reached Missouri, it faced as few as 12,000 troops commanded by forty-five-year-old General William Starke Rosecrans. His Department of Missouri garrisoned key positions but had much of its force in outposts of the MSM. Diverted on its way from Louisiana to Tennessee, General Andrew Jackson Smith's infantry eventually added 4,500 men, and an impressive-sounding "Illinois Provisional Brigade" exaggerated the mere 1,500 that had reached St. Louis in time to matter. In the emergency, Rosecrans had the civilian provisional government of the state also called out the Enrolled Missouri Militia (EMM), a force that theoretically included every man of military age healthy enough for service.

The frequently mentioned figure of 20,000 EMM may have represented a later statewide total. In fact, though, as the Confederates neared St. Louis, the city had fewer than 1,500 organized and armed EMM at St. Louis, part of a small force that proved large enough to bluff the Confederates into turning west. A week later, Price's army reached Jefferson City, where some 6,000 to 7,000 armed Unionists waited with their backs to the river hourly expecting that massive Union army supposedly raised at St. Louis. Even this late, though, those thousands of Union infantry, with thousands of mostly newly mobilized EMM back at St. Louis had only ventured into Franklin County, and that only recently. Fortunately for the Federals, Price again overestimated what he faced and marched west from the state capital as he had from St. Louis.

After Jefferson City, the fifty-nine-year-old Samuel Ryan Curtis redoubled efforts to build a second Union army on the Kansas border. The New York native had won laurels in the War with Mexico before going to Iowa, where he went into banking and entered politics. The grand old man of the Trans-Mississippi war effort, Curtis had fought and beaten Price at Pea Ridge, a victory credited with forcing the Confederates to abandon their Missouri ambitions. However, October 1864 left him with perhaps 4,500 men—clusters of cavalry, along with some artillery and recruits—most at Forts Leavenworth and Scott with tiny garrisons scattered across the state.[16] Building his new Army of the Border required a tug of war with the state authorities to mobilize the Kansas State Militia (KSM). Like the EMM in Missouri, the KSM theoretically included every man of military age fit for episodic garrison duties. This call up meant much more than local service, testing the depths of the population's commitment to the war and shaping the outcome of the elections in that state.

All three of these commanders—Price, Rosecrans, and Curtis—relied very heavily on field commanders. Price, overweight, sickly, and frequently described as drunk, rode in a buggy, coach, or an ambulance, from which he could hardly manage his large army strewn out over a broad countryside. Much of the work of command in the field fell to subordinates, particularly the well-born, well-married, and well-connected Brigadier General Joseph Orville Shelby.

Shelby, a forty-four-year-old plumed cavalier, embodied as much of an aristocracy and Southern chivalry as Missouri could have sustained in 1864. Born in Kentucky of an old Virginia family, intimately involved in the settlement and government of Tennessee and Kentucky, Shelby grew up as one of the entitled youth of the Lexington elite. After he came of age and got the trust, he headed west, settling on a hemp plantation near Waverly on the Missouri River, where he also ran a thriving rope business, and dabbled in real estate and slaves. When the troubles with Kansas erupted a few years later, few had more to lose than Shelby, who became one of the most popular of the misdescribed "Border Ruffians," often young men from some of the best families in the state. When war came in 1861, Shelby quickly embraced the secessionist state government, particularly after Federal troops had driven it from Jefferson City. The captain of a Waverly company, he led from the front and attained an outstanding reputation in the early battles. Throughout, the Federal hold on Missouri remained incomplete enough to permit recruiters to return and organize units and march them back to Confederate lines.[17] If there had been no Jo Shelby as history remembers him, someone would have been sorely tempted to invent him.

In many respects, this is precisely what his adjutant, Major John Newman Edwards, did. The twenty-five-year-old Virginia-born newspaperman had arrived in Lexington, Missouri, as a youngster at the onset of the troubles with Kansas. He excelled at a kind of journalism that translated the sectional tensions into a romantic crusade of heroes and villains. On the eve of the war, he became the editor of the secessionist *Expositor* but did not take up writing until the summer of 1862, when then-Colonel Shelby returned to the area to recruit a full regiment, Edwards readily joined him. Shelby, who hated writing reports, found Edwards relished doing so, pouring his purple prose across pages of otherwise dry documents. Not happy with this, one of Shelby's superiors uttered "an impious expletive," and quipped, "Why, Shelby is a poet as well as a fighter!" "No," answered another officer, "but his Adjutant is a born poet." The war Edwards actually saw bore no resemblance to the heroic glories of Sir Walter Scott or Homer, but it never kept Edwards from presenting it as such.[18] A war worthy of Edwards's imagination required some vigorous fictions, and he rarely balked at telling a whopper if it made the story better.

Rosecrans's Department of Missouri had found no way of ending the rather horrendous partisan war. He, like Price, had found his most useful days as a commander behind him, but, unlike Price, felt no compulsion to relive them. The War Department sent him, the highest-ranking Catholic general in the Federal army, to help anchor a vital constituency of Unionists. Rather unexpectedly, though, the former Cincinnati businessman had consistently used the most reactionary policies he could, deploying the army to break strikes and to stop emancipationist Radicals, a course that also led Rosecrans to dissolve troublesome EMM units that had been freeing slaves, a solution that effectively disorganized the defense of parts of the state on the eve of the Confederate invasion. Nothing came of Major General U. S. Grant's suggestion to Secretary of War Edwin M. Stanton that Rosecrans's removal might best serve "a proper regard for the present and future interests of the service." However, his superiors must have wondered when he stalled sending his first report to General Edward R. S. Canby, Federal commander in the Trans-Mississippi "until the movement of Price was developed."[19] According to Rosecrans, this had taken three weeks.

Rosecrans's superiors likely counted on the judgment of his chief underling, Major General Alfred Pleasonton. The son of the man who had saved much of the government archives from the British in 1814, the forty-year-old Washington-born functionary could not remember when he did not have an inside track to government service, having followed his older brother through West Point. Consistently exaggerating his service and ceaselessly campaigning against "foreign" rivals, he rose to command the cavalry corps of the Army of the Potomac, famously bypassing peers in favor of "boy generals"—Elon J. Farnsworth, Wesley Merritt, and George Armstrong Custer. Before Gettysburg, Pleasonton had failed in his assignment to locate Robert E. Lee's army but translated the ability of his men to hold their own against the legendary Confederate cavalry of J. E. B. Stuart at Brandy Station into a public relations victory. Pleasonton later claimed that, at that point, he had then been offered command of the army but turned it down owing to his criticisms of emancipation. In the spring of 1864, Grant came east with his own cavalryman, Phillip H. Sheridan, and Missouri suddenly seemed a conveniently distant and relatively quiet place for Pleasonton. In hindsight, he might not have been the best choice for a state whose Unionism depended so heavily on Germans and the foreign-born and where emancipation had become the touchstone of its internal politics. Then, too, the September 1864 arrival of the Confederates back in Missouri found Pleasonton in a Fifth Avenue Hotel in New York.

Despite his age, Curtis proved to be a far more active officer than Price or Rosecrans, but he found himself regularly hobbled by the same political divisions among Unionists in Kansas, amounting at times to conservative mutinies. When not simply denying developments in Missouri, the governor, the business interests, and much of the militia command placed priorities on real or imagined threats to Kansas. The same day Price's army entered Missouri, Confederate Cherokee raider Stand Watie captured a supply train at Cabin Creek—just below the Kansas line. Over the next few weeks, rumored armies of Indians plundered the region; some 5,000 of these fictional warriors threatened com-

munities near St. Louis. Meanwhile, Radicals such as Senator Jim Lane, Lieutenant Colonel George H. Hoyt—old John Brown's lawyer—and Charles R.
Jennison proposed suspending all business at places such as Fort Scott and putting "all, black and white, between the ages of sixteen and sixty, under arms at
once."[20] To a great extent, Curtis used such Radicals to take the heat for such in-
novations, even as he had to keep the Conservatives placated.

This essentially left field command largely in the hands of thirty-eight-year-
old Maine-born doctor, Major General James Gillpatrick Blunt. He had apparently briefly attended the Ellsworth Military Academy before going to sea and
returning to study medicine. After moving to Ohio, he had become active in the
new Republican Party but moved on to Kansas, where he found himself fighting
alongside John Brown, James Montgomery, and other Free Staters. At the war's
start, he had joined Lane's Kansas Brigade, winning a brigadier generalship in
early 1862 and proving himself an aggressive and daring cavalry commander. In
November and December, at Cane Hill and Prairie Grove, he defeated Confederate forces that had included Shelby's men, but Edwards acknowledged him to
be "a grand soldier in every way, and a grand man besides." Blunt also remained
an ardent proponent of abolition and the recruitment of black and Indian soldiers, and one of his old comrades, William A. Phillips, took command of the
Indian Brigade in the territory. The year 1863 saw Blunt's little tri-racial army
win victories at Honey Springs in July, and, by September, secure Fort Smith as
part of a new Union line running along the Arkansas River.[21]

In all of this, Blunt and the Radicals benefited greatly from the almost inex-
haustible pen of Richard Josiah Hinton. In contrast to Edwards and the Homeric
terms he used to recount the tale of Shelby and his army, Hinton strove for the
clinical prose of frontier journalism in discussing the activities of Blunt and
Curtis. Born only a few years after Blunt, Hinton was the son of a London stone
mason and became a young Chartist, active to broaden the British suffrage, a
movement in which he attained his first military experience. In America, he
naturally joined Wendell Phillips and the abolitionists at Boston. After helping
in the rescue of a runaway slave, Hinton went to New York, where he learned the
newspaper business before going to Kansas, where he wrote while fighting for
the Free Staters. He shared the views of James Redpath "that slavery should be
abolished, by political parties, if possible—if not, then by armed parties of in-
surrectionists."[22] Hinton had joined gubernatorial candidate Crawford in trying
to launch a Second Kansas Colored when Blunt lost his command after barely
escaping an October 1863 ambush near Baxter Springs, though enemies other
than the guerrillas made the change.

All but the most tough-minded and principled of the white officers had found
themselves drawn into very well defined practices in dealing with the Indians.
For a generation, army officers, Indian agents, and politicians made fortunes

buying and selling to the military and managing the Office of Indian Affairs (OIA), the most lucratively corrupt pursuit in the antebellum government. Among other things, the Indian agent oversaw the distribution of the annuities to the tribe and, of course, the preliminary deduction of whatever the Indians owed the trader licensed by the U.S. government to exercise a monopoly over doing business with them. For a generation before the war, southern Democrats monopolized the patronage, and corruption became endemic to the institution's function. Despite the intentions of some Republicans, institutional dynamics prevailed, and war generated newer opportunities for those eager to facilitate the movement of OIA assets and military contracts.

General John M. Thayer at Fort Smith and Colonel Charles W. Blair and Captain David S. Vittum at Fort Scott cooperated in a "ring" that rustled Indian cattle to supply the army, which kept the Union Indian soldiers charged with protecting the cattle dismounted and undersupplied. William Phillips's determination to fight this landed him in arrest at Fort Smith. Although Blunt awarded contracts to friends and allegedly got large kickbacks from the OIA agents and "the ring," he found himself on the outs when Governor Carney elbowed his way into the lucrative business and began getting his political enemies out of it.[23]

What the powers-that-be had demanded of Blunt as a demonstration of his loyalty had been his participation in the war against the native peoples threatening the Santa Fe Trail. He brought Kansas troops into the area, while other columns acted under Brigadier James H. Carleton—the pious Colorado architect of the Sand Creek Massacre—and Kit Carson in New Mexico. On September 22, Blunt's men set off from Fort Larned in the District of Upper Arkansas for the Cimarron Cutoff. Three days later, they found "a large group of Cheyenne and Arapahoe warriors" closing in on a detachment of the First Colorado Cavalry along the upper Walnut Creek." Blunt not only drove them off but pursued them ruthlessly for two days.[24] At that point, the message from Curtis arrived, recalling him to aid in the emergency mobilization of Kansas to meet the Confederate incursion.

To Curtis's credit, he knew that victory needed the muted and compromised radicalism of Blunt more than the militant entrepreneurialism of Carney. On October 10, he brushed aside the governor to put Blunt in charge of the District of South Kansas, replacing Major General "Tardy" George Sykes, who had come west after losing command of a corps in the Army of the Potomac after Gettysburg. Realizing that southeast Kansas faced no immediate threat, Blunt had Blair pass command to Vittum and march "all the mounted troops of my command in the direction of Kansas City." Blair managed to cobble together bits of regiments garrisoned in the area with some local KSM, a company of scouts, and Lieutenant D. C. Knowles's section of the Second Kansas Battery to organize a column of "about 1,000 men." Across the state, military necessity opened the door for all sorts of radical influences unsavory to the Conservatives.[25]

The dynamics of war have always been complex. Power accrued quickly to an executive branch eager to secure the cooperation of the business community and, in this case, to a regular army command that shared little of its politics. For three years, the authorities had built a massive military from relatively small numbers, incurring an unprecedented debt with neither an adequate regulatory process nor much public oversight. The problem proved particularly troublesome in the West, where patriotic desperation and self-interest merged to create major financial scandals in the Union headquarters at St. Louis. Even farther removed from the sources of supply, Kansas proved worse, and the management of occupied Arkansas proved even more lucrative. The stresses of civil war carried the already unbelievable level of antebellum corruption in Indian affairs to unimaginable levels. Public attention rarely focused on financial irregularities, and, when it did, those responsible for the corruption found it easy to blame subordinates such as the quartermaster sacrificed in the Department of Missouri early in the war.[26] These systemic issues complicated and compromised Federal military responses from the first appearance of Confederates back in Missouri.

The immense distances in the West naturally placed a tremendous importance on the region's railroads. Still, while the Confederates had targeted and would continue to target them, Union commanders placed remarkably low priority on defending them. Indeed, even as the troops maneuvered against each other, the Federal authorities exercised a remarkable largess using its resources to repair the railroads. The legions of private citizens whose homes, farms, and shops benefited from no similar assistance may not have appreciated the importance accorded business and development, but it would hardly matter.

The age of modern war had begun.

One

The Raid and the Pursuit

1

Of Liberation and Occupation

Boonville, October 8–13

As the Confederate Army of Missouri turned away from the state capital into the countryside, it relied ever more obviously on Brigadier General Jo Shelby and his column. Shelby and his men, including hardened veterans of the partisan warfare that had plagued the state, had led the advances on St. Louis and Jefferson City, but they remained, by temperament and experience, hard-riding cavalry raiders who truly came into their own as the goals of the army changed into those of a raid. Once Price's men bypassed Jefferson City, Shelby's cavalry took the advance into the countryside, hoping now not to retake Missouri so much as to stay there as long as it could. Paradoxically, the Confederates never quite realized that they could not easily eat off the land without consuming the support they needed.

General William S. Rosecrans's Federal Department of Missouri with its much touted cavalry general from the eastern armies, Alfred Pleasonton, had essentially left the risky defense of Jefferson City to four Missouri militia generals. They had deflected the Confederates from the capital and immediately thrown everything they had into the pursuit of Price's army to the west of Jefferson City. Shortly after, Pleasonton arrived to take charge, even as the Confederates had settled into a secure position in what had been a secessionist stronghold in the state. The logistics of the Federal pursuit proved as much dependent on internal Unionist politics as on the movements and threats of the enemy.

FROM RUSSELLVILLE AND CALIFORNIA TO BOONVILLE

The Federal plan to concentrate its forces to defend Jefferson City left the militia to garrison central and western Missouri with minimal coordination from superiors. Meanwhile, those forces at Jefferson City had expected Major General Alfred Pleasonton to show up with thousands of reinforcements, and, when he did not, Brigadier General Clinton Bowen Fisk—the senior of the four district commanders—commanded the defenses at the state capital until the Confederate army veered west on Saturday, October 8. The impressive fortification had kept bloodshed minimal, but the cost of the town's defense became increasingly apparent as Price's army trailed off and the residents began filing their claims for the damages, the owner of the Jefferson City *Examiner* in the lead. The defenders had seized thousands of feet of rail fences, demolished structures, and cut hundreds of fruit trees to provide a clear field of fire approaching the defenses.[1]

After Jefferson City, though, Fisk provided a standing embarrassment to these assumptions, as well as lacking appreciation for the brilliance of his superiors. "I cannot believe that Price would be permitted to march leisurely for twenty-five days within the borders of our State, and then sit down at Boonville and deploy his rebel horde on the river counties of my district." It seemed to him "a melancholy fact" that the Confederates had attained this much success. "I censure no one, but it seems to me that somebody is to blame," he added. Fisk expected "Bloody Bill" Anderson and other guerrillas to rampage across northern Missouri. "Towns will be plundered and small detachments of troops captured and disarmed."[2]

Another of the district brigadiers at the capital, John B. Sanborn, organized the small mounted force available at Jefferson City into three small brigades under Colonels John F. Philips, John L. Beveridge, and Joseph J. Gravely to pursue the retreating Confederates. This initial force of about 3,500–Pleasonton gave its number as only about 3,000–expected Price's army to continue west through Russellville, Versailles, and Warsaw, after which it would either take the Springfield Road to immediate safety in the desolation of the South or the northbound roads into "the Great Bend" of the Missouri River. Saturday night, the Federals under Philips and Gravely bivouacked along the Moreau with those of Beveridge on Gray's Creek, ten miles west of Jefferson.[3]

On Sunday, October 9, Sanborn's men covered another four miles and faced "lively skirmishing" just two miles shy of Russellville. There, the Second Arkansas from Gravely's brigade and the Ninth MSM Cavalry from Beveridge's emerged from heavily timbered country east of Russellville into the waiting Confederate force of Colonel Colton Greene's Third Missouri Cavalry of Brigadier General John B. Clark's brigade. Major William B. Mitchell's Seventh Provisional EMM led skirmishers forward, as Lieutenant Richard G. Chitwood's squadron from the Eighth MSM Cavalry drove in the pickets, and Colonel Colton Greene reported that they "engaged the enemy warmly for forty minutes," ordering Lieutenant Jonathan W. Graves to lead a desperate countercharge. In the end, the Confederates fell back some two miles to the southwest of Russellville toward the Versailles Road. Lieutenant Philip Smiley's Battery

H of the Second Missouri Light Artillery landed a few shots before Lieutenant Riley B. Riggs of the Sixth MSM Cavalry lost his life in attempting to flank the Confederate position. In the end, the Federals pushed nine miles west toward Versailles, reaching High Point before turning north toward California, some twenty miles away.[4]

In fact, the advance of Price's army had already reached that town and, "not halting a moment," hurried north towards Boonville, leaving California to Colonel Jeff M. Thompson. Although called the "Swamp Fox" for his earlier raids in the bootheel of the state, Thompson found it disturbing that so many of Shelby's officers and men came out of a long experience as guerrillas, preoccupied with random looting and violence. He found that Colonel Moses W. Smith's advance had "helped themselves pretty freely" to whatever they personally wanted, missing the obvious military targets, such as the new depot and other railroad property. Thompson "did not allow the men to break ranks, and no disorders were committed while I remained in the town." Yet, it must have seemed peculiar to many residents when Price himself caught up and declared that "he desired to make friends, not enemies, and that the depredations he had committed were done as military necessity."[5]

After Thompson and Price had moved on, General John S. Marmaduke's division had taken over and were ripping up the train tracks either side of town when, between 4:00 and 5:00 p.m., Philips's Federals broke through the timber onto the open prairie southeast of town. The Confederates under Colonels Greene and Robert R. Lawther, together with those of Lieutenant Colonel John F. Davies, formed a battle line and began blasting the bluecoats with two pieces of Captain Henry C. Hynson's Texas Tenth Light Artillery. Philips dismounted the Fourth MSM Cavalry behind the crest of a ridge running east and west, about half a mile south of the town, with the First, Fourth, and Seventh MSM Cavalry extending their line, with some of the First Iowa Cavalry beyond the road coming from Russellville to cover the deployment of Captain Charles H. Thurber's guns. More artillery under Lieutenants Albert Wachsman and Philip Smiley turned up by the day's close. By then, the Federals had swept "the last straggling rebel" from the town. Philips reported three casualties and the Confederates "much greater," though noting only five dead behind them.[6]

With much of Price's army bivouacked up the road on the Moniteau near Pisgah, Sanborn sent his own men into camp at California. In the darkness, Commissary Sergeant Robert Weeden stumbled about with Joshua Lorring in search of Weeden's horse, which had been left behind when the Federals dismounted. There he encountered a dozen others stumbling around in the dark, one of whom asked, "Is our boys in town?" Alerted, Weeden got the questioner to identify himself as a member of Colonel William Ferguson Slemons's Arkansas brigade. Then, "as quick as thought," Weeden and Lorring began blasting away with their revolvers. Though Lorring's pistol jammed, Weeden was said to have killed three or four and mortally wounded one. Afterward, noted Philips, Weeden "returned to camp, and in his coolness and modesty, scarcely considered his adventure worthy of mention."[7]

Even as the fighting sputtered back at California, Shelby's cavalry reached Boonville, some thirty miles away. As they had in eastern Missouri, the Federals had left clusters of a few hundred militia mobilized in the path of the entire Confederate army. A prosperous river town of over 3,500 on the eve of the war, Boonville's propertied whites tended to be from Southern backgrounds, and the town experienced serious fighting in every year of the war. Yet, the threat of guerrilla attacks provided the greatest danger, and many Confederate sympathizers participated in the Unionist militia system to maintain order in the area. In the fall of 1864, Captain Horace Shoemaker brought together the three local militia companies, two of which claimed later to have enrolled with an understanding that they would only fight bushwhackers but not Confederate regulars. All three turned out as the dust of an approaching column inspired rumors that "Bloody Bill" Anderson would strike the community.[8]

Shelby sent Colonel Benjamin Elliott's battalion downstream from town and Lieutenant Colonel D. A. Williams upstream, "rendering all attempts to cross the river by the ferry-boat abortive." Beyond this, as one scholar noted, accounts become "confusing and conflicting," but, more than this, the Confederate accounts contradict each other. Shelby's column did include guerrillas, and some announced, on the outskirts of town, that they hoped to burn out "the Dutch," and killed some two dozen Germans, "nearly all in cold blood." Meanwhile, Major John N. Edwards's initial report stated that the town's "oldest and most respected citizens came to me with information that inside of the fortification was one company of Southern men and boys, impressed into service by the iron hand of despotism." Shelby sent in a flag of truce offering for the town's surrender "a guaranty on my part of that protection accorded to prisoners of war."[9] However, there is no evidence of this.

Another account by Edwards declared that Captain Arthur C. McCoy and others "struck the Federal pickets this evening at about an hour by sun," with the "whole brigade" hitting Federal "heavy reserves" and having to wage "a thirty minutes' fight" before being held "within thirty feet of a heavy and strong fortification," where they were "held at bay until the artillery could come up." Shelby had expected "100 to 800 Federals," but they captured only 300 Federals, albeit "with new cartridge-boxes and belts."[10] The "heavy and strong fortification" consisted of a barricade across the street before Thespian Hall.

Thompson came off the road just in time "to receive and take charge of the prisoners." He complimented "the soldierly and courteous manner" with which Lieutenant Colonel William H. Erwin took the surrender. Meanwhile,

Thompson took his own brigade into camp, noting that "we had marched forty miles this day, the last four of which was at full speed, and the men and horses were both much fatigued."[11]

Boonville

Monday, October 10, when Price and his staff headquartered themselves at the City Hotel on Morgan Street, his army had successfully squelched any likely signs of opposition, and he may have believed his own report that "my reception was enthusiastic in the extreme. Old and young, men, women, and children, vied in their salutations and in ministering to the wants and comforts of my wearied and war-worn soldiers." For his part, Price told them what he had told everyone since entering the state. The Confederates had returned to Missouri to stay, he declared, but they would be able to do so only if the population rallied to their support and defense. With Thompson's brigade camped a few miles west of town, the rest of Shelby's division arrived, with Sidney D. Jackman's men settling in south of town as a rear guard, while the divisions of Marmaduke and James F. Fagan finished their march from the Moniteau near Pisgah to reach Boonville.[12]

Confederates had not passed through a town of comparable size for days, and residents of all political stripes later talked of its "plunder." The sheer numbers Price had to feed and equip explain the losses one merchant claimed of 10,000 sacks of flour, the stripping of the shoe and boot stores, and the seizure of everything of any use from the surrounding farmland. On one level, such necessity might even explain the loss of a thousand gallons of Catawba wine. Later estimates placed total losses near $60,000 in the town, not counting looting of private homes and taking of horses. However, the troops also broke into the stores and carted off hoopskirts, dresses, ribbons, dry goods, and all sorts of things that could have been of little use to most of them, as well as the regalia of the Masonic and Odd Fellows lodges. Worse, conscription and the means for its implementation replicated the impositions of the Federal occupation in an even more brutal form.[13]

Governor Thomas Caute Reynolds, the South Carolina–born head of the Confederate state government-in-exile, had understood the difficulties of winning the hearts and minds of civilians by robbing or bullying them. He had objected to the plundering of eastern Missouri towns, including strongly Unionist communities. By Boonville, he wrote Price that "in an expedition designed to re-establish the rightful government of Missouri the Governor of the State cannot even purchase a horse or a blanket, while stragglers and camp followers are enriching themselves by plundering the defenseless families of our own soldiers in Confederate service."[14]

Reynold's politics and Price's war had fathered the career of a twenty-five or twenty-six-year-old Confederate officer who rode into Boonville wearing several sets of six-guns and brandishing human scalps on his bridle.[15] The son of a hatter who had abandoned his family to go to California in search of gold, William Anderson had moved to Kansas in 1857 with his reunited family, which made a good living. The ascendant Free State authority warred on horse thievery, which pushed its practitioners, such as the Andersons, like Quantrill, beyond the law, making them pragmatic allies of the secessionists, particularly as the Federal army occupied Missouri. After Quantrill's massacre of the inhabitants of Lawrence in August 1863, the authorities tried to relocate civilians from western Missouri and incarcerated relatives of guerrillas. On August 21, the Kansas City building that held Anderson's three sisters collapsed. As the guerrillas wintered in Texas in 1863–1864, Anderson broke with Quantrill, returning to Missouri as "Bloody Bill" to wage an even more vicious war; he rarely spared prisoners and often mutilated the corpses of his victims.

Anderson reportedly wrote to a Lexington newspaper the following summer: "I have chosen guerrilla warfare to revenge myself for wrongs that could not [be] honorably avenged otherwise." He claimed to have been targeted for death because he "would not fight the people of Missouri, my native state," after which the Federals "revenged themselves by murdering my father, destroying all my property, and have since that time murdered one of my sisters and kept the other two in jail [for] twelve months." About two weeks before Boonville, Anderson's men massacred roughly 150 Unionists near Centralia.

The butchery continued. They killed Captain Shoemaker, the captured commander of the surrendered militia himself, apparently grabbing the paroled officer off the street. Fisk heard rumors they had hanged him, and other accounts said they had fired seven bullets into him and cut his throat. Shelby—actually Edwards—wrote that to maintain his reputation "as a soldier and officer of honor" he had to report that "some persons in nothing save the name of Confederates" had taken the officer from his guards and killed him. "That he deserved death no one denies; that he met it thus every good soldier must lament and deplore."[16] While writing that they deplored the murder, they did nothing to seek out and identify—much less punish—the guilty parties.

Residents fared poorly, particularly west of town, where Thompson had Shelby's original brigade camped. As the raiders plundered his home, Johann Ludwig Staebler hid in the safety of his chimney, and local lore kept him there for three days. The bodies of John Godfrey Boller and Jacob Henry Neef later turned up on their farms, and citizens found the body of a dead African American male who had been caught hiding in James M. Nelson's corncrib. A few days later, the body of Boller's wife turned up with that of her son.[17]

Whatever short-term advantage the Confederates got through guerrilla tactics, the strategy engendered a confusion that could hurt both sides. On October 11, the telegraph operator from Sedalia tapped Rosecrans the story that Price's advance in Tipton had captured blue-uniformed persons who "escaped by pretending to belong to George Todd's gang of bushwhackers." Their captors had accepted the story but taken them back to Boonville, from which the men escaped and reached Sedalia.[18]

On Tuesday, October 11, as those escapees reached Sedalia and Sanborn's Federals approached Boonville, Pleasonton remained at Jefferson City, assuring Rosecrans that their various militia groups had "about 800 at Sedalia, 300 at Warrensburg, and 300 at Lexington." Although he had "no means of communicating with either Lexington or Boonville at this time," he told Rosecrans that they "will delay the enemy north of the railroad." Meanwhile, he would send Fisk with reinforcements and concentrate Colonel Theodore A. Switzler's tiny militia with artillery from Columbia to Boonville, ensuring control of the Missouri River and the Federals' ability "to send and get troops from Kansas." He added that he had kept the railroad safe by holding Sanborn's horsemen "south of the rebels" and had put to work the infantry of Major General Andrew J. Smith—"always opposed to red tape, and always in favor of fighting"—repairing the railroad as far as the Lamine (sometimes formerly spelled La Mine) bridge, which open the line "all the way through to Warrensburg."[19] In short, Pleasonton had available infantry repairing the railroad, coupled to the baseless absurdity that a tiny militia force would hold back an army at Boonville, which had actually fallen to the Confederates two days before.

More realistically, Sanborn, with his men in the field, hoped only that the comforting environs of Boonville would help keep Price there. Rather than move directly on Boonville, he advanced west along the line of the railroad from California toward Tipton. Once the Union horsemen had established a series of outposts along that line, they began probing north to within ten miles of Boonville.[20]

That Tuesday, Colonel James McFerran's First MSM Cavalry crept north toward the Bell Air and Boonville road. The men encountered and drove back Confederate pickets, and Major Alexander W. Mullins led two squadrons that drove about a hundred rebels on their way to Boonville. "No casualties on our side; loss of the enemy not ascertained." Philips and the rest of the brigade arrived to find McFerran battling "several bands, a hundred strong in some cases, chasing and firing on and wounding quite a number and capturing some horses and arms." Philips used his brigade to secure their position, and, even as darkness fell, used two battalions of the Fourth MSM Cavalry to keep the firefight going until 2:00 a.m., though one wonders at his report that "the remainder of the command slept quietly beyond range" before falling back to the Tipton road at 4:00 a.m. [21]

At the same time, Beveridge's brigade moved in on another part of the camp. The Confederates began "putting rails on fires." This drew members of the Seventeenth Illinois Cavalry into the sights of riflemen hidden in the shadows, but James Butler "Wild Bill" Hickok, another famed gunman, "discovered the trap and warned them back. Later, he located one of the Confederate gunmen: 'One died there, but it was not Wild Bill.'" In the end, Price decided to bolster Marmaduke's line by deploying Fagan's division in support "about half a mile from the river." For Shelby, the news "rudely broken in" on "the bright hours of pleasure and enjoyment," and his division moved to protect the possible line of retreat to the west. Jackman, planning "to leave a force of observation where he was," encountered the Federals as they were withdrawing "about dusk," and his brigade held its position through the night in expectation of renewed fighting the next day.[22]

In the predawn hours on Wednesday, October 12, Boonville residents in the Federal Fifth MSM Cavalry began an aggressive drive on Jackman's brigade. Colonel Joseph A. Eppstein sent Major John B. Kaiser with two dismounted companies across Shoemaker's Bridge on the Saline Creek to strike the Confederates of Lieutenant Colonel Charles H. Nichols, "about 300 strong." Kaiser's men formed "a skirmish line on each side of the road," and "a vigorous fight" ensued for half an hour. Nichols's men fell back—300 yards according to Confederate reports or "about one mile" in the Federal account—to where Colonel DeWitt C. Hunter's men held a "very formidable [line], consisting of barns, stables, and rail breast-works on a very commanding ridge." The Federals resumed their advance until they encountered Lieutenant Colonel John A. Schnable's men and had engaged most of Jackman's brigade, including Lieutenant Jacob D. Connor's section of Collin's artillery. Believing his men outnumbered "ten to one," Eppstein fell back about a mile to the junction of the road to Tipton, after which Colonel John L. Beveridge, commanding the brigade, ordered Eppstein to rejoin him at California. Jackman described a tough fight "of an hour's length, after which I succeeded in driving the enemy back along the road over which we had but a short time before retreated. [23]

Early that same morning, Colonel John F. McMahan led his Sixth Provisional EMM from Pisgah toward Boonville until they encountered "a picket of 100 men" under Captain David G. Hicks of Colonel John Q. Burbridge's regiment, killing one and capturing another. McMahan's men dismounted and engaged the enemy "warmly for two hours," losing two enlisted men with four wounded, with one officer. Colonel Gravely began to turn up near the Lamine Creek with the Second Arkansas Cavalry, Sixth Provisional EMM, and a squadron of the Eighth MSM Cavalry, facing a Confederate line that seemed to Gravely to have "several thousand men" back toward Boonville. Lieutenant John A. Gideon's company actually entered "the outskirts of the town and entered, and for a short time occupied two or three houses for protection to his men." By 10:00 a.m. Major William B. Mitchell's Seventh EMM Cavalry battalion moved with them from the bridge over the Lamine, as Major William Plumb's command thwarted a move against their right flank. The Sixth EMM and Colonel John E. Phelps's Arkansans got within "three miles from the city." Around 5:00 p.m., when the Confederates brought up artillery, Gravely called a halt. These aggressive Federals had outrun their own supply line and had to fall back "to bivouac beyond Saline Creek" so they could backtrack to California for rations the next day.[24]

For his part, Jackman decided the Federals had 1,000 to 1,500 men with "three pieces of artillery," based on information from "intelligent citizens." By 8:30 a.m., he reported "some damage—a good many men and horses wounded and some killed." As the day wore on, though, the Federals slipped down the lower Tipton road, though he still 'heard heavy musketry to the right after dark. I have sent a scout to ascertain the meaning of it. Not knowing the whereabouts of General Shelby, and being uncertain as to the disposition of the enemy's force, I have determined to await at this place for orders or remain until morning." [25]

Reports from both sides caution against bureaucratic exaggeration of successes. Facing an enemy that fell back to be resupplied, Jackman reported that they had "retired before General Shelby succeeded in reaching their flank, tearing up the bridge after them. They gave way before Colonel Slemons and I had the time to make an attack." Colonel Colton Greene reported that the "retreat left his dead and wounded in our hands," and Lawther also reported "driving them back" at a cost of but two wounded. Jackman's description of keeping up with the Federals as they were pulling back became an account by Shelby—actually Major Edwards—of how the brigade "attacked and drove" the enemy back across the Saline. The withdrawal of the Union cavalry to be resupplied became, in Price's report, an account of how the foe had been "pursued . . . a distance of twenty-one miles from Boonville with heavy loss." They found two members of the Seventeenth Illinois Cavalry stumbling around in the dark, one of them toying with flight, muttering quietly, "Now for a race, bullets or no bullets. We don't want to go to Andersonville."[26] (Had they a clear idea of where they were, they would have known that Andersonville was no option.)

Shelby's report praised Jackman, for "this brilliant fight stamped him a fine cavalry officer, brave and skillful in action, with everything requisite to make him a dashing commander." Eppstein thought Kaiser's advance faced "about 800 or 900 men," and Jackman described having about 600 of his men engaged, though part of Fagan's command arrived in support. Jackman's description of the distance over which his men fell back also became a longer distance when his men pursued the Federals over exactly the same ground. Confederates also reported their pursuit of a withdrawing battalion as the driving back of "a full brigade." Eppstein reported inflicting serious losses on the Confederates; "The enemy must have been seriously damaged from appearances; the extent I am not able to state." Jackman said he lost only four killed and twenty wounded, including a Captain King. Then, too, Shelby described the Union losses as "heavy," which Eppstein enumerated as two killed and four wounded, one mortally.[27]

Both sides obscured their losses. The Confederates had fifteen killed, and twenty-eight so severely wounded that they could not be moved, while taking with them a large number of wounded, including a colonel, according to one rumor, although they seem to have left more than the twenty-eight behind. A few days later, the Federals found twenty-eight Confederate wounded in Thespian Hall, with more in private homes, mostly Jackman's men. "The secesh ladies of Boonville overflow with kindness to these men, which is not so very improper, but a poor wounded union soldier died in this hospital and there were scarcely found kindly hands to close his eyes." One claimed Federals were taking charge of the hospital to poison the Confederate wounded and expected Bill Anderson to retake the place. Unionists countered, "A more detestable set of wretches never disgraced the human race than the secesh of Boonville."[28]

Logistics of Pursuit

This truncation of these operations underscored the problems of moving, supplying, and feeding impromptu armies, a conglomerate of small units with different training and experience. The more militia, recruits, or armed civilians mobilized, the more eccentrically armed and equipped they became. When the Federals needed to supply less than 2,000 men south of Kansas City, they needed "equal proportions of .54, .58, and .69" caliber cartridges. The Department of Missouri found "the tubes of many of the Austrian rifles issued to the new one-year Missouri regiments are defective," forcing a decision of whether to issue new tubes or determine whether "it may be necessary to issue other arms." One regiment of MSM Cavalry had the Smith breech-loading carbine, and one of the regular cavalry outfits carried the Henry repeating rifle, weapons that one Confederate complained "poured a rapid and scathing fire into our commands, which far exceeded any firing we could do from our muzzle-loading Enfield rifles." Confederates carried everything from Enfields imported from England through Mexico to old flintlocks or smoothbore "Kentucky pea-rifles," while others had shotguns. Artillery varied from one six-foot-long piece, "invaluable for picking off individuals at long range," to Southern-cast breech-loaders with Captain Richard A. Collins's battery, the best in Price's army, some firing a single leaden ball as far as three miles.[29] After turning his infantry to working on the railroad and deciding to concentrate the rest of his forces at California and along the line west, Pleasonton did not have enough to resupply those of his men engaged at Boonville.

On Wednesday, October 12, Pleasonton described the actions below Boonville as ending with "Sanborn's retreat," though he did not note that this resulted from his failure to supply them. Meanwhile, Colonel Edward Catherwood's Thirteenth Missouri Cavalry had shown up, the first of General A. J. Smith's corps, so he sent Catherwood to keep an eye on Boonville. Pleasonton now had a mounted force of about 4,000 to cover the withdrawal of those troops that had been engaged there. He reported more—those under General Joseph A. Mower's command— to join him Thursday, though much of his infantry trailed behind, as far east as Washington.[30]

So, too, the westward pursuit by the Enrolled Missouri Militia from the St. Louis area had stopped almost as soon as it began. However, the Federal authorities continued to face problems in the wake of Price's army. Samuel Hildebrand and Dick Berryman had recruited large bands of irregulars and kept them active in southeast Missouri. Fights took place from Tyler's Mill down to Ponder's Mill on the border.[31] More important, perhaps, earlier mistakes had led to the burning of railroad bridges that needed to be repaired.

At the onset of the campaign, Rosecrans had ignored warnings about the invasion until they came from a "reliable citizen," a railroad and mine owner. After the Confederates had destroyed the bridges on the Iron Mountain Railroad to Pilot Knob, particularly the bridges on the Big River, the South Big River, and near Mineral Point, the department made them its top priority. Indeed, Rosecrans kept the reinforcements who were supposed to have been on their way to help save Jefferson City back near St. Louis for days. As fighting began at the state capital, he sent Republican gubernatorial candidate Colonel Thomas C. Fletcher to personally supervise railroad repair by the EMM at Pacific and Moselle, while other crews went to work on the bridges over Boeuf Creek, the Gasconade, and the Osage. Shortly after, he tried to persuade the 100-day Illinois volunteers to pitch in on the work. It remains unclear the number of men and the value of their labor that the army put to work for the railroads, but the EMM commanders assured St. Louis that, despite rumors of "rebels and Indians,"

"We will keep at work at the bridges until we hear definitely."[32]

Closer to where the priority on pursuit made even more sense, Pleasonton had set his forces to work on that bridge over the Lamine west of Jefferson City. General A. J. Smith dutifully and cooperatively had his men at work, but by October 15, he pressed his subordinates to get the job finished "so as to cross a train in twenty-four hours." "Let us have a connection with Sedalia as soon as possible," he wrote an underling. Three days later, Rosecrans's headquarters still issued orders to keep Smith's men at work on the repairs.[33] One can only imagine how they thought that the already slower-moving infantry would be of any use against a retreating mounted force when delayed a week for such purposes.

Meanwhile, the Army of Missouri took advantage of being left alone by starting on the move again. Part of Shelby's cavalry headed west toward a camp along the Blackwater, though various detachments fanned out across the countryside. One, under Lieutenant James Wood of Colonel Elliot's battalion, probed south to the line of the Pacific Railroad, burning the bridge at Otterville. Another, under Lieutenant Jesse McCaleb of Burbridge's regiment, probed as far south as Laclede County, where he reported capturing and paroling a lieutenant and twenty-eight men. Colonel A. W. Slayback took a larger force southwest to locate and test the strength of the Federal pursuit. The main Confederate march from Boonville had been roughly along the south bank of the Missouri River west, then following its bend north toward Arrow Rock. In the course of this, Price claimed to have added "between 1,200 and 1,500 men, mostly unarmed" to his army before heading on to Chouteau Springs, eleven miles from Boonville.[34]

This need for the Union horsemen to backtrack for supplies lost the better part of two days. "The rebel army has left Boonville and is reported to have moved off on the Georgetown road. Their rear is reported to be but a short distance." Sanborn had "no doubt that the enemy has moved to Lexington" with the goal of striking at Kansas. For this reason, he later explained, he hoped to bog down the Confederates "in or near Saline County until the Kansas troops were organized and on the border." By Thursday, October 13, the nature of the Union pursuit had changed. Major Francis Malone's detachment of the Seventh Kansas had joined in, as had Catherwood's Thirteenth Missouri.[35] Of course, the more Union troops came up, the more acute the problems of supply became.

On the very day Sanborn reported this movement to headquarters—the first day in four that Confederates were not actually in Boonville—Rosecrans got word to General Samuel R. Curtis of Kansas that "Price's main force was at Boonville this morning with most of his forces. We are rapidly concentrating and will soon move on him, and if he is not careful we will pass to his rear." Curtis believed that Rosecrans "had taken the field."[36] In fact, Pleasonton remained at Jefferson City, and the head of the Department of Missouri himself had only just left St. Louis, and their plans to move "soon" continued to get postponed.

Rosecrans also described Sanborn's movement west toward Georgetown in terms of protecting the line of the Pacific Railroad. Sanborn's own reports indicate that part of his forces followed the Confederate movements to Marshall, Arrow Rock, and Waverly more closely, but the cavalry, infantry, and support reaching California on October 14 had been earmarked for other purposes. Nothing was done to provide supplies to Sanborn and his men in the field, and those four-days rations they and their mounts had retrieved at California on Thursday would not be replaced for six. The local EMM in central and west-central Missouri, however, found themselves facing the invasion with very little in terms of a chain of command to their department.[37] Two weeks after the first major fight at Pilot Knob and a week after the Confederates had threatened St. Louis, the Department of Missouri remained ponderously slow and easily distracted in its most essential operations.

In part, the slow responses seemed to grow from an unnecessarily confused discussion of Confederate goals. Generals, governors, and the press spoke of Price's "salient disappointment" at failing to take Jefferson City, though he had clearly opted not to make a serious attempt to take the state capital. Unable to draw conclusions from this, the discussion simply shifted as to whether Price's new goal "may be Leavenworth or some place in the vicinity in Kansas." However, the *Missouri Democrat* very correctly discerned Confederate goals as being "to re-furnish and re-stock the naked and famished rebel population in his trans-Mississippi domain, out of the comfortable homes and teeming granaries of Missouri." In Franklin County alone, the Confederates had taken two thousand horses and looted two-thirds of the homes along its route of march.[38]

In fact, Price and the Confederate command remained remarkably flexible, a reflection of the confidence they had in their grasp of their opponents' fears and foibles. At about this time, Price caught wind of "a large number of arms" (amounting to 5,000) stored in the city hall at Glasgow. He sent General Clark, of Marmaduke's division, with his own brigade and 500 of Jackman's, with orders to cross the river at Arrow Rock and attack the place the next morning at daylight and capture it, at the same time sending Shelby with a small portion of his division and a section of his artillery to attack the town from the west side of the river at the same hour, to divert the attention of the enemy and protect the infantry's advance under the cover of the fire of his artillery. In addition, Price ordered Thompson to take "a force of not less than 800 or 1,000 men and a section of artillery to Sedalia by way of Longwood." He would attack the garrison there "if he should deem it advisable and prudent."[39] In the face of what he believed to be a larger pursuing Union force, Price sent two detachments, organized around a couple of his best brigades, the one striking north at a vital community on the Missouri River and the other hitting south against the railroad.

2

The Railroad

Sedalia to Warrensburg, October 14–18

General Sterling Price assured supporters around Boonville that he had brought his troops back to Missouri to stay. Almost immediately, though, his failure to begin fortifying the town made it clear to everybody there—and to the Federals as far away as the St. Louis press rooms—that he planned to move on. "Price will catch merry thunder before he leaves the State of Missouri," declared the *Missouri Democrat*, "if he is so fortunate as to get out at all."[1] Yet, mid-October delivered important victories to his forces.

The Confederates straddled the two major east-west routes across the state: the Missouri River and the Pacific Railroad, which reached its western terminus at Warrensburg. On the very same day, the Confederates dispatched forces to strike respectively at Sedalia on the railroad and Glasgow on the river. Both of these alerted and informed the organization of the Army of the Border in Kansas. The loss of Sedalia and still more assets of the Pacific Railroad provided yet another demonstration that the Department of Missouri had not only failed to mobilize and organize an effective defense of the state, but could not even protect what it had already determined to be its most important priority. The importance of this setback on the department provided a great contrast with that impact on the mobilization of Kansas.

THE MILITIA ISSUES AND THE VOLUNTEER PROBE

To the west of Price's march, Generals Samuel R. Curtis and James G. Blunt hastily assembled an Army of the Border that planned to meet the Confederate army in the vicinity of Kansas City. The war had swirled about Kansas City and its 3,800 residents on the southern bluffs of the Missouri River. The entire city, at the time, clustered west of Holmes Street, with its southeast corner near Eighth and Locust and the southern limit around Eleventh and Central. The country road that became Twelfth Street ran east toward the Big Blue River and Independence beyond. What would be Troost Avenue ran south through the timbered countryside to Brush Creek and beyond. A road zigzagged up from the bluffs to Westport, which had long been the most important town in the area, the head of the Santa Fe Trail.[2]

Jackson County's rather nasty little guerrilla war had periodically lapped at Kansas City. When the war broke out, the city had been a bastion of commerce in a slaveholding agricultural region. As Missouri's secessionist government had sought to mobilize the Missouri State Guard against the Federals, the local editor and politician Robert Thompson Van Horn had, with the assistance of Kersey Coates, assembled a Unionist Home Guard that supplied the Federal cause with one of the few armed bastions beyond St. Louis. By the fall of 1864, Coates commanded the local EMM at work on the earthworks running east and west south of the town. In the absence of guidance form the Department of Missouri, the EMM relied heavily on General Curtis and the Kansans, who later sent the KSM to help Missourians defend their homes.[3]

Riding as much as any between the commands of Curtis and Major General William S. Rosecrans, Colonel James H. Ford's Second Colorado Cavalry concentrated at Pleasant Hill. The Coloradoans had a strong record in the field, fighting alongside blacks and Indians in the previous year's campaign to protect Fort Gibson in the Indian Territory. However, they also proved to be popular and effective garrison troops in Missouri, having none of the history of the Kansans in the minds of white Missourians. Only a few days before—on September 29—Rosecrans had transferred the regiment to Curtis, who placed them at Pleasant Hill, roughly twenty-five miles southeast of Hickman's Mills. They would monitor any attempt by the Confederate forces to slip back south, though Ford, who likely knew the terrain better than any of the Kansas officers, thought the best forage and water would draw Price's army on a course north of Pleasant Hill and south of Independence, heading directly toward Hickman's Mills. He took the initiative to adjust his position.[4]

Curtis and Rosecrans discussed catching the Confederates between them. Rosecrans sometimes talked of Price moving to the south but declared he would place his infantry under Generals A. J. Smith and Joseph A. Mower to the south near the Osage "and hurt him." However, Colonel Charles W. Blair at Fort Scott reported only bushwhackers, like those who had burned Lamar. However, their best information, from prisoners and deserters, indicated that Price would stay in the fertile fields of Missouri as long as he could and then push west. Even the Confederate general's son, Edwin, talked rather freely about his father's stated intentions to take Leavenworth. For this reason, General Clinton B. Fisk, technically in charge of North Missouri, fretted that the garrisons of Lexington and Boonville "will be gobbled."[5]

Unlike Rosecrans, Curtis responded very quickly, albeit with mixed results. Politics in Kansas later exaggerated to 15,000 and 20,000 the numbers of patriotic citizens in the KSM taking up arms and moving to the front. In fact, Governor Thomas Carney and the conservatives worried that the mobilization would bring James H. Lane, Blunt, and the other Radicals to prominence on the eve of the election. Too, Carney—the richest man in Kansas, as well as the governor—complained of its impact on commerce, particularly that martial law closed businesses in Kansas while their competitors in Missouri still functioned. The grudging nature of his cooperation encouraged KSM General George Deitzler to drag his feet, creating a sense of impatience among the men who had left "their homes and business to the care of the women, the old and decrepit, thereby incurring heavy losses and great inconvenience," and wanted "to end the campaign as soon as possible." Conservatives also found suspicious "the mystery surrounding the movements of the enemy, and the uncertain and conflicting information."⁶

Understandably, the Radicals, in turn, had little sympathy with Curtis's diplomacy and thought that he simply coddled the business interests with their conservative predilections. Colonel Samuel J. Crawford, the Radical candidate for governor, thought the general could have turned things around quickly if he "had arrested a half-dozen politicians in the Militia camps and sent them to Fort Leavenworth in irons." Less seriously, he thought it would have helped to have "shot one or two Militia brigadiers from the cannon's mouth." With such obstacles removed, Crawford thought Curtis could have had "an invincible army of fifteen thousand men—infantry, cavalry, and artillery."⁷

Without such measures, parts of the KSM showed signs of "restlessness" as they brooded along Turkey Creek, at Shawneetown, and at other gathering points. Even after the fighting west of Jefferson City, the Democratic and conservative press regularly minimized the size of Price's army or simply reported it as southbound through Missouri or even already back in Arkansas. Or they circulated rumors that Confederate Indians had entered South Kansas. In the absence of cooperative state authorities, U.S. Senators Lane and Samuel C. Pomeroy personally came forward to assist in supplying and moving the militia. The politics of the mobilization became even touchier as it became increasingly obvious that the only way to keep the Confederates out of Kansas involved crossing the state line and meeting them in Missouri, which went beyond the understanding of what a militia was supposed to do. Radical editor John Spear told Curtis that the men "either want to go into Missouri or go home," and Curtis began to move troops cautiously across the border only as far as the Big Blue, with Blunt taking charge of the small force at Hickman's Mills.⁸

Curtis personally scouted the terrain, riding from Kansas City to Independence and south to Hickman Mills before returning to Wyandotte. By then, he had his engineer, Captain George T. Robinson, surveying a possible fifteen-mile line of defense from the Big Blue at the Missouri River south toward Indian Creek. In addition, militia and civilian crews set to work on a second line before Kansas City, with a fallback position north of the Kansas River at Wyandotte.[9]

Blunt himself reached Hickman's Mills Thursday morning, October 13. The mobilization of the KSM had freed a hodge-podge of small cavalry detachments to join him, with the First Colorado Battery and bits of the Fifth and Tenth KSM. He also expected nearly a thousand mounted men and six pieces of artillery coming up from South Kansas under Blair, who had left only 800 men to protect Fort Scott, knowing that the KSM would take up much of the slack. By Friday, the reinforcements had reached Paola, only a day's march from Hickman Mills, and Colonel Charles R. Jennison had showed up with more men. Blunt also reported that Captain Andrew Allen, with 150 of the Seventy-seventh EMM had garrisoned Pleasant Hill, Missouri, which freed the well-mounted and experienced Coloradoans for scouting. Major Nelson Smith with a detachment of those Coloradoans had just returned to Independence from a scout to the east.[10] All told, Blunt counted enough for a major reconnaissance deep into Missouri.

On Saturday, Blunt made a bold decision. Convinced that Price's army had not turned south, he determined to find where the Confederates were, but this meant bringing the KSM into Missouri. Already heartily disliked by the conservatives, he tried to break the impasse with his General Field Order No. 2, reorganizing everybody in his district into three brigades under Jennison, Thomas Moonlight, and Blair, a reorganization that placed 471 members of Colonel G. A. Colton's Fifth KSM, 530 of James D. Shoddy's Sixth KSM, and 751 from William Pennock's Tenth KSM under Blair. On the one hand, this gave the brigaded KSM the same access as volunteer units to supplies like the "blankets or overcoats, of which many of them are very destitute." On the other hand, Brigadier General William H. M. Fishback denounced Blunt's move as "contrary to the spirit of the militia law of Kansas" and a personal insult. Deitzler told Fishback to "obey all lawful orders issued by General Blunt" but to ignore those of Blair.[11]

Fishback seized upon this as a justification to disobey Blunt's order "to cross the state line," where "their rights as Kansas men and Kansas militia would there no longer be respected." Pretending "no definite information of Price or his whereabouts," he sent Shoddy's regiment back into Kansas. Blunt then sent part of the Fifteenth Kansas Cavalry with a howitzer to stop them only a few miles from camp, where they disarmed and arrested Shoddy. As the militia elected new officers, Blunt sent Fishback back to Paola with Shoddy. The Sixth KSM replaced Shoddy with Colonel James Montgomery. Fishback later claimed to have repented his position and agreed to go where Curtis wanted him but filed a tirade over the issue in lieu of a report. Over the next few days, though Deitzler helped get the First, Second, Third, Fourth, Thirteenth, Fourteenth, Twentieth, and Twenty-first KSM across the state line to the Big Blue. Curtis even coaxed him into sending the Twelfth and Nineteenth KSM as far as Independence. From there Lieutenant Colonel Samuel Walker's detachment of the Sixteenth Kansas joined Smith's Coloradoans for another ride "about twenty-nine miles on the Lexington road, and making a circuit toward Snibar and Lone Jack, returned by Hickman Mills, but saw no enemy."[12] With KSM settling in, Blunt's work of locating Price could begin.

SEDALIA

Notwithstanding Rosecrans's solicitous concerns for the railroads, his decisions still continued to leave it vulnerable. To concentrate the troops at Jefferson City, the Department of Missouri had stripped the garrisons, leaving the towns along the western stretch of the rail line to their own devices. Left in charge at Sedalia, Colonel John D. Crawford of the Fortieth EMM had earlier asked Brigadier General Egbert B. Brown for specific instructions, adding that his men had "no ammunition; nothing to eat." "Keep all your force," Brown ordered, adding that they should press the work on the fortifications and be assured that supplies were on the way. However, the arrival of Price's army west of Jefferson City left towns like Sedalia cut off.[13] In the absence of a clear chain of command, these Missouri outposts naturally turned to Curtis in Kansas, then desperately seeking any information that might bolster his position with the KSM.

What happened around Otterville and the Lamine bridge alerted Kansas as well as Missouri. Even as Price's army bypassed Jefferson City, Captain George Todd and over a hundred men followed the railroad west, burning the water tanks and depots, and damaging the Lamine bridge. When they also burned some houses at Otterville, the postmaster there hurried to Sedalia, reporting that guerrillas had "completely skinned the town, shot two white men and killed three negroes." More raiders turned up the next day, October 9, and the Sedalia garrison sent twenty-five men with a locomotive east and dispatched scouts. A year before, Lieutenant James Wood of Colonel Benjamin Elliott's battalion in Jo Shelby's division had destroyed "the large and magnificent bridge" at the Lamine, and they returned to make a third raid into the area, where they "charged upon it in the dim dawn of a dusky morning and woke the tardy sun by a mingled mass of flame and smoke, and crackling and splintered timbers, and crumbling arch and abutment."[14]

Rosecrans made up for these shortcomings by misleading Curtis as to the condition of his troops. He told the Kansas commander that Major General Alfred Pleasonton's cavalry had been pressing Price's columns northwest of Georgetown, as they moved west of Boonville toward Lexington. On October

14, he assured Curtis that General Smith's infantry "shall occupy Sedalia" the next day and suggested that Curtis needed to take his new and unorganized army east through Hickman Mills and Pleasant Hill, or through Independence to Lone Jack.[15] In fact, Rosecrans himself sat at Hermann, Pleasonton at Jefferson City, and Smith with his men working on the Lamine bridge.

Even as Rosecrans made these helpful suggestions, General Jeff Thompson began quietly moving Shelby's old brigade toward Sedalia. Colonel Alonzo W. Slayback already had scouts that direction. On Thursday night Shelby informed Thompson that Price wanted much of his brigade—"not less than 800 or 1,000 men and one section of artillery"—to slip through Longwood to Sedalia. Their goal would be to sweep up the cattle and mules said to be there, and to "attack the Federal force at that place if he should deem it advisable and prudent." Before sundown, Thompson moved 1,200 men and Lieutenant S. S. Harris's section of Captain Richard A. Collins's battery headed toward Longwood, with tentative plans to reach Sedalia around 3:00 a.m. They took a larger force than suggested because the brigade had begun to shed soldiers. Shelby told Price "about 600" had already gone off to "their homes . . . many with leave and many without." Thompson also used many of his men to establish a chain of relays for his couriers every six or seven miles and assured Price that he would not act without orders or risk defeat. While on the road, Thompson met a courier from Slayback warning of "a large body of Federal cavalry" to the south.[16]

Saturday morning, one of Thompson's relay riders reached Price with news from two Union stragglers "well known to our men," because they had "belonged to our army and been captured by and compelled to join the Federal Army." Reading between the lines, the deserters had to talk fast and credibly to save themselves. They told Thompson that the Union cavalry force that Thompson had skirted had been Brigadier General John B. Sanborn's three brigades with 2,500 men and eight pieces of artillery on their way through Georgetown to Lexington. As well, the prisoners told Thompson that General A. J. Smith's infantry had moved into the area with "not less than 10,000, but are called from 12,000 to 18,000." And, they said, "a large force is being massed in Kansas City via the Hannibal and Saint Joseph Railroad and Platte County Railroad." Although only three miles from Sedalia, Thompson balked at risking the time needed to do his business there. He chose instead to pursue the rear of Sanborn's cavalry. Meanwhile, Captain John L. Jenkins's scouts ventured "within speaking distance" of talkative Federals near Syracuse, some of the thousand members of Smith's infantry actually there.[17]

Thompson finally chose to take Sedalia, after finding the Federal cavalry far too distant to harass and the nearby Union infantry nowhere to be seen. Back at Sedalia, though, Crawford's Fortieth EMM caught wind of the massive Confederate force nearby, and they well knew that no large Federal force marched or rode near enough to save them. By some accounts, he had "at least eight hundred men, and two hundred and fifty rounds of ammunition to each man," but Crawford opted either to evacuate the town or found that his men "broke for the brush, after firing a few skirmish shots, though he had excellent entrenchments." The story told was that a Mr. Henry of the Sedalia House watched the militia flee and approached Thompson, whom he had known before the war. "See here, Jeff. I am a strong Union man," he said, "but my wife is a strong Secessionist, and she wants me to tell you for her, to come into the town and behave yourself."[18] Remarkably, given the course of this campaign, Thompson did so.

As was often the case, though, not everyone in the town agreed with the decision. They realized that the depot would go and it was "a great, wooden structure, against which a number of the store buildings backed, and to burn the depot was to burn the town." "Colonel" William Bloess and "Major" William Gentry—both actually privates in Crawford's Fortieth EMM—decided to resist, as did some of the residual personnel of the old garrison, including Private George Sparks of the First MSM Cavalry. They had a "little band" that "hurried to the trenches and prepared for defense." Thompson's men faced only "the handful of citizens in the ditches." After half an hour's cannonading that left Sparks dead, the home guard surrendered, and Thompson's men rode into town.[19]

Thompson's account described something very different. He wrote that they found the town "in the midst of a vast prairie, and the only manner to surprise it was by a direct and rapid march." The Confederates found the town "defended by two redoubts at opposite angles of the town, and continuous lines of rifle-pits all around." Elliott's regiment in advance got "within pistol-shot" of the Federal pickets before they were identified, and the Confederates charged "over the intervening open prairie between the lane and the town friend and foe alike rushed for the lines of the Federals." Thompson described a charge at 3:00 p.m. that carried the town in a few minutes. When Elliott and his men leaped the rifle-pits behind the fleeing pickets, the Federals there immediately surrendered, but Thompson hesitated in order to form the rest of the brigade and deploy the artillery, during which time "the enemy recovered from their first panic and drove Elliott out of the lines." The Confederates actually needed to continue firing "some shells and shot into the forts as the flags were flying, but we soon found they were deserted." Not until 8:00 p.m. did the Confederates have possession of the captured property.[20]

What actually had happened proved even more confusing. After the defeat of the militia, Captain Oscar B. Queen and Lieutenant Reuben T. Berry turned up with a patrol from the Seventh MSM Cavalry, which had ventured from Sanborn's column in search of ammunition. They rode almost directly into Thompson's men, and, assuming the local militia was still in control at the "forts," Queen's men occupied "the improvised defenses" and began "fighting gallantly" only to find themselves "instantly surrounded [and] 27 of [the] company were taken prisoners."[21]

Thompson also reported his efforts to keep order. He placed Gordon's regiment, under a Lieutenant Colonel Y. B. Blackwell in formation to protect the artillery, which covered the railroad. Thompson "used every means in my power to control the men, to prevent pillage, and also to secure as much valuable material as was possible for the army; but in spite of every effort there was considerable plundering of the stores, but I am confident the private houses were respected." Assigning Slayback's command as a provost guard, Thompson complained that others had been "broken in their charges, were less manageable, but still I am proud to say no outrage or murder was committed." A later reminiscence of the raid recalled the post office "pretty well overhauled, and but little remained after the examination was over in the shape of letters or valuables of any kind." They robbed two locals, Mat Offield and Theodore Shelton, at gunpoint.[22]

Confederate claims as to the number of prisoners taken proved as inconsistent as usual. Thompson had "no printed paroles with me, and the time not allowing me to write them, I was compelled to take verbal paroles." He saw three categories of prisoner: what he called several hundred "home guard"; 75 EMM; and 47 MSM and volunteers. He sent the first group home "unconditionally," and gave the verbal paroles to the remaining 125, larger than the Federal accounts indicate. Shelby—or rather Major John N. Edwards, who wrote his reports—rounded the number to 200, a number Price repeated in describing a "bold and daring assault" upon a "strongly fortified and well garrisoned" bastion.[23]

Later, a defender of the surrender insisted that the account in the *Missouri Democrat* had been wrong. Colonel Crawford and Lieutenant Colonel John L. Parker had held the place on their own for two weeks with "considerably less than 500 men" in "slight and short ditches" suitable for dealing with bushwhackers. What Thompson brought against them had been "a larger and overpowering army," not the reported 1,000, but 1,500 "with a reserve a short distance from town" numbering nearly the same. Everybody feared the Confederates would treat an armed defense by destroying the town, and "the burning of the depot would have been the destruction of the town." Even so, a local man named Frank McCabe did lead an armed resistance by "a little squad" that had actually fought until they were surrounded. At about 10:00 p.m., the departing Confederates did send parties to burn the water tank and the depot. "The ladies from Captain Henry's hotel (the Parker House)" reportedly put out the fires.[24]

Another account said that "the ladies of Sedalia banded themselves together to the number of about 50 and waited upon him with a prayer not to destroy the depot and the town." Thompson said he had to obey his orders, but would wait until 5:00 a.m. Sunday and "hinted to them that if the old barn happened to be green and didn't burn up the fault would be theirs." At the scheduled hour, "a bucket brigade of ladies" waited at the depot, and the Confederates torched the depot and left. The women "promptly extinguished the flames." Another account had it that Mrs. Henry not only expostulated against the burning of the depot, but, with her daughters, "stole the matches from the soldiers."[25]

Thompson's report indicates that they left 100 men behind, as the column rode off to the northwest, hoping to reach the area of Cook's Store by sundown. However, rumors of large Federal forces to the west and at Brownsville turned the Confederates north. In the fanciful world of Major Edwards, "great masses of the enemy came looming up to see what bold intruder had broken in upon their quiet sleep of years, but the wary Thompson, true to his well-won sobriquet, fell back fighting before them in splendid style after destroying everything owned by the United States Government."[26]

Only about thirty miles to the west, Blunt's scouting party, under Major Martin Anderson of the Eleventh Kansas, reached Warrensburg, at the terminus of the Pacific railroad, where it got wind of Sedalia's capture. Left to their own devices, the defenders of Warrensburg decided not to await their fate quietly. Although disabled by earlier wounds, Major Emory S. Foster got Captain George S. Grover to pull together companies of "Johnson County Citizen Guards," technically part of the Fortieth EMM. After gathering all the available muskets and 5,000 rounds of ammunition, they barricaded the roads into town and brushed aside the many objections in this conservative community to arm "thirty or forty negroes" from the local "contraband village in the suburbs of the town." They found one of the self-described Unionists who opposed "a war for the nigger," shirking militia service by hiding "under a negro bed—showing that though he was opposed to fighting with negroes, he was not opposed to skulking with negroes." Determined organizers raised money to ensure they would have the new Martin-Henry breech-loading rifles. Although the Fortieth EMM had lost one company at Sedalia, its preparedness at Warrensburg had kept a nearby concentration of several hundred Confederates at bay until Major Anderson and 300 Kansas Cavalry arrived.[27]

When Anderson and his men had reached Warrensburg on Sunday, they found the telegraph still in order, but "great excitement about Sedalia," where the operator tapped out a tale of their attack by 5,000 Confederates. Anderson later heard from Jefferson City that the operator at Sedalia had left, and that Confederates had also raided Knob Noster, so he and his men turned their horses back toward Pleasant Hill.[28]

News from the field also frustrated the efforts of Foster and Grover to reestablish contact with the Department of Missouri. On their behalf, Lieutenant Ashley L. Reavis of the Fifty-Second EMM headed east and actually got within thirty miles of Sanborn's column near Marshall but returned with a realization of their isolation. Grover and his men then decided Sunday night to ride west to find Kansas troops. On Monday morning, Blunt and Senator Lane found them along Big Creek just east of Pleasant Hill, and took them back to Holden. Blunt then sent them back to Warrensburg, where they found that Thompson had rejoined Shelby.[29]

At this point, Blunt had a clear idea of where to find the Confederates. Price had not taken his army south nor marched it west from Sedalia to Warrensburg, which meant that he was almost surely headed toward Lexington. Blunt also knew that Sanborn's cavalry had concentrated somewhere near Dunksburg, and had Rosecrans's assurances that he had a large body infantry "within supporting distance." Blunt sent couriers to Sanborn "urging upon him the propriety of uniting our forces and promptly commencing an offensive movement against Price." Meanwhile, he knew he had enough authority to race to Lexington ahead of the Confederates ostensibly "with a view of saving the Government property." Doing so might also force the hand of Curtis and Carney in terms of bringing the KSM into action. Blunt telegraphed Curtis to send those parts of the Sixteenth Kansas Cavalry and Second Colorado Cavalry east from Independence while he himself would head that direction from Hickman Mills.[30]

Department of Missouri

The appearance of a large Confederate army on the Missouri River gave everyone north of the river with a vested interest in destabilizing Federal military authority an opportunity to do so. For two weeks, Union officials stripped their garrisons of volunteer and MSM units, replacing them with a general mobilization of the EMM. Two years earlier, the provisional state government and the army had mandated the enrollment of all male citizens of military age for mandatory local service for strictly limited periods of time. North of the river, many of those enrolled into the militia had sympathies with the Confederacy or, at least, few with the Union. When pressed, they could either not show up for service or make entire units less than reliable.

On October 10, Pleasonton had sent Colonel Theodore A. Switzler's regiment with four pieces of artillery to Boonville by boat, and General Fisk reached Rocheport with detachments of the Thirty-ninth and Forty-ninth Missouri Volunteers and one section of Thurber's battery on the steamers Sioux City and Hattie May. They had left the previous day for Glasgow in the hope that they might implement Pleasonton's scheme of using them to keep Price's army from taking Boonville. Lucky for them, the low river levels stopped them before they could steam into serious trouble. Fisk "met citizens fleeing from Boonville" at the Rocheport wharf, and scouts confirmed the present of Confederate camps that "extend six miles down the river from Boonville on the south side," with fifteen pieces of artillery and "considerable of a cavalry force on the north side of the river." Their presence had inspired "a general uprising of the disloyal element, and such as do not voluntarily enlist with them are being conscripted, both white and black." Fisk's column constructed a bridge to cross the guns over a creek hoping "to relieve the beleaguered city and garrison" twenty miles away at Glasgow.[31]

Price sent the guerrillas that met him at Boonville back into north Missouri with the railroad there as their most obvious target. "Bloody Bill" Anderson had special orders from Price to strike east as far toward St. Charles as he could. Democratic Congressman James S. Rollins, of Columbia—who had nearly lost his life to Anderson earlier at Centralia—joined the Radicals in requesting the return of Fisk, his troops, or both to the region north of the river. Formally and informally, Federal officers across the district warned of the "murder and destruction" about to descend upon them. However, Pleasonton reassured Rosecrans that Price had only sent across the river "from 1,500 to 2,000 cavalry to pick up horses and conscripts, but I don't think he intends crossing."[32]

The reporter for the *Missouri Democrat* wrote that Pleasonton "seems to be making a more vigorous campaign against our poor Missouri Brigadiers than against General Price," especially Fisk. The radical who had defended Jefferson City remained the only successful Union commander since Ewing had defended Pilot Knob. Fisk wanted desperately to get back to his district in North Missouri to deal with the escalation of guerrilla war and Confederate recruitment there.[33]

Pleasonton seemed to have learned remarkably little from Sedalia. His cavalry pressed as far as Cook's Store in Lafayette County. By Sunday, Colonel John E. Phelps's two hundred Arkansas Unionists with a hundred from the EMM trailed Thompson in his escape from Sedalia, but Rosecrans fretted that Thompson might double back on them. On the way back Sunday from a scout to Waverly, Colonel James McFerran's First MSM Cavalry had to detour to the west to avoid a clash with Thompson's Confederates. Lieutenant Colonel Joseph Eppstein's Fifth MSM Cavalry also had a brush with Thompson but had to backtrack themselves, like other of Pleasonton's force, to Cook's Store and the Blackwater, "where we drew three days' rations" and returned to the field.[34] This fallback for supplies to Cook's Store—like the earlier one from Boonville to California—meant that the pursuers had to cross over roads not once but three times.

Nevertheless, by Monday October 17, Lieutenant Colonel Thomas Theodore Crittenden had gotten his force to Sedalia with Lieutenant Philip Smiley's section of Captain William C. F. Montgomery's battery. However, Smith's infantry, which Rosecrans had located near Sedalia days earlier, actually remained near Lamine bridge, though many of them had only just passed through Jefferson

City. Rosecrans and Pleasonton discussed keeping south of Price without press-ing him until the infantry came up.[35] This had, of course, been their plea since St. Louis, where they waited for two weeks for Joseph Mower's infantry to walk out of the Ozarks where they had been sent to chase mounted Confederates.

Too, Rosecrans and Pleasonton became preoccupied with the idea that Price's army could turn back on them, or get behind them. Indeed, at every point he had a choice, Price had headed away from concentrated Union troops rather than toward or anywhere near them, and there was no reason to suspect he would change his mind. However, the Confederate guerrilla activities that con-tinued in the wake of the Federal armies challenged the illusion that the Union forces could protect the state if not their vulnerable lines of supply. Rosecrans could not forget that as his men fought near Boonville, they also had armed enemies back across the state. His subordinate at St. Charles happily noted "capturing a lot of desperate bushwhackers, amongst them a certain Lennox" active in northeast Missouri and facing "grave charges."[36]

More frightening, though, "Bloody Bill" Anderson and fifty heavily armed men slipped back north of the river from Boonville into north central Mis-souri with orders to cripple the railroad back to St. Charles and Hannibal. At Williamsburg, they heard information that distracted them from their orders to destroy the railroad bridges back around St. Charles. Local authorities had decided to shift the county seat from Danville, and the small militia garrison had moved from the old blockhouse on the southeast corner of the square to the railroad. This left a rumored $50,000 of the county treasury temporarily in the Watkins and Drury Store. On Friday night, October 14, the guerrillas thun-dered past a startled local at the edge of town on the hill just west of Loutre Creek. Two miles from town, they invited themselves into the home of Benja-min White, a Southern sympathizer, who lost his watch, his money, and other household items, while they tore up the yard and threatened his family. [37]

When they galloped into town, the guerrillas opened fire on some militia on the square near the store, instantly killing Sergeant Michael A. Gilbert of the First Provisional EMM (formerly of the Sixty-seventh EMM) and Private Henry Diggs, from a provisional company of the Sixty-Ninth EMM. Dr. Sam-uel Moore, at the south end of town near the Danville Female Academy, heard the shooting and, expecting no more than a small band, ran up the street and unhorsed one of them before half a dozen others shot him down and beat him to death near the stable. On the east end of town, they shot a twelve-year-old as he watched from his doorway. A man shot at home crawled into his yard as flames consumed his house. Flames soon rose from the disused blockhouse on the square.[38]

At the Danville Female Academy, Anderson's men told the young ladies that their neighbors were burning alive—a story that reached the New York press—

but almost all the locals, including militia, had found safety in the woods, one of them having mortally wounded one of the raiders. The guerrillas naturally ransacked the printing office, the store of Watkins and Drury, and most of the homes. Many of the screaming and crying students desperately threw their trunks down the stairs to save what they had, and made a flag of truce by tying an undergarment to a pole. Most fled to the woods in their nightclothes, but those who remained probably saved their school by calling to the attackers, "We are rebels!" The fortunate schoolmaster, David S. Robinson, formerly of the Sixty-seventh EMM, had gone to nearby Washington, and his wife refused to turn over the keys for the chapel to torch-bearing partisans, even at gun-point. At that critical turn, one of the officers passed by and ordered, "Take that pistol from that woman's breast." Fifteen-year-old Laura Draper said, she "never saw such distress in my life as I saw that night."[39]

Around midnight, the guerrillas left, promising to kill anybody leaving town before sunrise. On the outskirts, they stole a buggy for their wounded, and Arch Clements killed one of their hostages, the schoolteacher Merrill Simons, though another, blacksmith William Ellis—possibly a member of the militia—somehow survived. Soon after, the Vermont-born postmaster Silas A. Thompson—though discharged after having been wounded at Gettysburg—frankly informed the garrison at Warrenton that the raiders had killed five people and left one wounded and that he could stay only at the risk of his life. He urged posting a company to protect the town.[40]

Meanwhile, Anderson's men continued east into the predawn hours Saturday. At New Florence, they found Union uniforms on the platform at the railroad depot, intended for troops at Rhineland. Donning these, they gutted the town's stores. Sunrise found them at High Hill, sacking more stores and burning the rail depot and the water tank. However, they balked at an attack on Warrenton, some fifteen miles further east, where Lieutenant Colonel Frederick Morsey of the Third MSM Cavalry estimated that he needed 100 men to "drive these rebels out of the country. I have nothing here but raw militia and $20,000 of Government property to protect, which would be of great advantage to the rebels." Colonel Cornelius H. Canfield of the Sixty-seventh EMM reported guerrilla bases came in from Wellsville near Danville. Later that Saturday, Lieutenant Colonel A. G. Hequembourg with a large contingent of the Fortieth Missouri wounded some of the guerrillas near High Hill, killing fifteen and capturing their horses. By 11:00 p.m. Sunday, they were poised to restore the telegraph and clear the railroad as far as Mexico. Lieutenant McIntire led a force two miles south from Florence after hearing of High Hill. Meanwhile, Canfield of the Sixty-seventh EMM got the drop on Anderson, killed thirteen of his riders on the spot, and captured six horses. "Not a man of ours received a scratch. Gilbert in Danville had been "hung and scalped." "Do assist them as soon as possible in clothing and food."[41]

Price claimed that, after Boonville, Anderson's men "did effect some damage to the roads, but none of any material advantage, and totally failed in the
main object proposed, which was to destroy the large railroad bridge that was
in the end of Saint Charles County." The greatest damage, though, came with
the news that "Bill Anderson is north of the Missouri River." The realization
rattled the nerves of those communities recently devastated by the passage of
the Confederate army, and commanders such as Lieutenant Colonel George
Klinge at Hermann faced rumors of "a force reported to be marching down
on him from the north side of the river." Similar rumors had Anderson moving on Warrenton and St. Charles "with 400 men [and] two pieces of artillery,"
and that Confederates had retaken Washington. In response, subdistrict commander Brigadier General Thomas Ewing could only reassure all and sundry
that Anderson could not be near them, and, if he was, he would have no artillery. Fear of Anderson's raid inspired plans to bring militia down from Iowa to
protect the railroad.[42]

As war did its business on the railroads, Glasgow on the Missouri River braced
itself. The more farsighted Federal officers understood that the town could be
the gateway to North Missouri, though the farsighted grew fewer as one looked
up the chain of command. Pleasonton took Fisk's large boats and sent him one
smaller steamer, *Isabella*, and he continued on with 250 "picked men" with two
pieces of artillery to Providence where Switzler's column joined him. Although
the men remained concerned for Fayette, Glasgow, and Huntsville, Pleasonton
sent them orders Thursday to countermarch overland back to Jefferson City with
the idea that they would then join Smith's infantry column at California. Still,
as Smith remained at Jefferson City, Fisk's men remained there, where they had
started in the first place.[43]

Fisk asked for orders to march the twenty miles cross-country upriver to
Glasgow where he hoped to thwart Confederate activities in north Missouri.
The town had a serious cache of quartermaster and commissary stores, but Fisk
likely felt considerable responsibility for having sent Colonel Chester Harding Jr.
with his new Forty-Third Missouri down from Saint Joseph on the *West Wind*.
On the morning of October 11, Fisk sent an officer to make his personal appeal
to Pleasonton at Jefferson City. At the same time, he got word from Captain
John E. Mayo at Glasgow that the Confederates had taken Boonville and begun "conscripting every man and boy between the ages of sixteen and sixty in
the country." Mayo knew that 150 of Price's men had crossed the river and got
"as far as Boons-borough, about eleven miles from here." Fisk thought 5,000
newly recruited Confederates threatened North Missouri, of whom "4,990 were
doubtless cheerful volunteers."[44]

3

The River

Glasgow and Beyond the Missouri, October 14–17

Jo Shelby greeted the gray dawn of October 15 opposite the town of Glasgow. The sun was rising over the western bluffs just where the Missouri River bends sharply south. Bear and Gregg Creeks pour into the river along the northern and southern edges of town. To the south, the bridges of the Boonville and Fayette roads cross the Gregg over a mile apart from each other, and another road crosses the Bear near the Missouri River before forking toward Keytesville and Huntsville. An old plank road also enters the town from the west. The Federals had breastworks and rifle pits on the high ground of the courthouse square.[1]

Kansas General Samuel R. Curtis needed all the arguments he could muster to persuade Thomas Carney and other conservatives of the need to mobilize the state and cooperate fully with his plans. This made it so essential to locate Price's army that he cooperated with a plan of the isolated members of the Department of Missouri around St. Joseph to take a boat downriver to Jefferson City. By the time that they reached Glasgow, however, the Confederate army had swept up between them and the capital and had begun to move against their tiny garrison. The appearance of Confederates north of the Missouri River continued for days afterward, further confusing efforts to locate, much less effect, the movement of General Sterling Price's army.

THE FLOTILLA

With the Confederate invasion, the Department of Missouri chose to concentrate garrison troops across the center of the state at Jefferson City. Colonel Chester Harding Jr. at distant St. Joseph had one of the most difficult tasks. He commanded the new recruits of the Forty-Third Missouri, many not yet mustered or prepared for a desperate battle, and they had to get to the capital over a much longer distance. At the same time, General William S. Rosecrans's uncertainties about the location and scale of the enemy army in his department increasingly frustrated General Curtis in Kansas. He sent his son, Major Samuel S. Curtis, to Leavenworth to seize the steamer Benton; it together with the *West Wind* provided the possibility of a joint flotilla downriver. In addition, a number of officers without command, including Second Lieutenant Georg F. Simmonds of the Sixty-second U.S. Colored Infantry also reported to Harding, sometimes with small contingents of men.[2]

Early on, it became apparent that it would be no simple cruise. Submerged trees formed "snags" quickly and predictably, and sandbars formed just as easily. For this reason, steamboats anchored generally at night rather than to risk traveling in the dark. The lower river level made this particularly vital. They had to get down the river to Independence and Liberty, then the ports of Camden and Wellington to reach Lexington. After that, they would pass Brunswick and Cambridge to arrive at Glasgow. Then Harding would have to negotiate Arrow Rock, Boonville, Rocheport, and Hartsburg to fulfill his orders by landing at Jefferson City.

They reached Camden without trouble. When they anchored there the first night, locals warned them of guerrillas only seven miles further, at Wellington, within striking distance of government stores at Lexington. The next morning, the two steamboats approached Wellington, and Harding's men cleared the town. They opted to cover the fifteen miles to Lexington on foot, arriving before dawn on Monday and awaiting the arrival of the boats a few hours later. Fearing the guerrillas would seize the large amount of supplies at Lexington, they quickly moved them onto the *Benton*, and continued downriver.[3]

A Unionist civilian signaled them from the south bank about fifteen miles above Brunswick, warning that Bill Anderson and two hundred guerrillas waited just downstream. The boats continued cautiously and, as the channel brought them near the shore on the bend, the soldiers fired into the brush with their muskets and the six-pounder. When these failed to draw a response, they decided that they had best clear the rebel base within striking distance of the river. Further along, mounted guerrillas approached the shore as Harding's men ducked below the rails. When they rose to fire, about thirty to forty mounted guerrillas scattered. Captain Oscar Kirkham of the Fifth MSM Cavalry and other officers claimed the pilot, a former rebel soldier, had signaled the guerrillas, but skirmishers under Simmonds of the Sixty-second USCT filed ashore and secured the town. The rest of the little expedition followed and encamped. Requisitioning fifty horses, they scouted for four or five miles about the area before determining that it would be safe to spend the night.

At 10:00 a.m. Tuesday, October 11, the boats approached Brunswick. By this point, if not sooner, what the expedition faced ceased to be bushwhackers and came to be advance units of Price's army, sent upriver far in advance of the main army. A guerrilla named Ryder had been there the previous day with a force of about 100 men, but had left the same evening. Then there was Captain Joseph E. Kennedy of the Fourteenth Partisan Rangers Cavalry, an unbrigaded unit in General John S. Marmaduke's division, with about eighty men, "most of whom he had raised in the place the preceding day." Harding's men filed off at the mouth of the Grand River and surprised "forty or fifty of the confederates posted in a strong log and earthwork." The Federals killed two and mounted about fifty of their own to pursue the Confederate recruits and dissolve any force that might "concentrate near the river bank downstream and attack their passing boats."[4]

On Wednesday morning, the two Union boats ran aground just above Cambridge. While there, the officers heard that "rebel conscripts and about 50 of Shelby's men" held the town. A message also got through from Captain John E. Mayo at Glasgow, reporting that he had lost contact with General Clinton B. Fisk and Jefferson City and asking for assistance. Yet, the boats remained stranded until Thursday afternoon, after which they "ran by Cambridge without stopping," the men on board firing into the woods near town to scatter any attempted ambush, and reaching Glasgow on the evening of October 13.[5]

That Thursday, the Federals found Glasgow's leading citizens at the landing alongside Mayo and his officers. Mayo had a motley group of defenders, consisting of bits of his own Sixth MSM Cavalry, but members of the Ninth MSM Cavalry under Captains James Adams and S. A. Hunter with a few from the Thirteenth Missouri Cavalry and the Seventeenth Illinois Cavalry. A former officer of the Twenty-Fifth Missouri, Captain George C. Bingham—no relation to the contemporary artist George Caleb Bingham—brought in about sixty militia from Saline County. Captain Clayton Tiffin of the Fourth Provisional EMM had twenty from Ray County with Captain John Vance's company of the Forty-Sixth EMM, and his colleague, Captain Samuel Steinmetz commanded a company of Glasgow enrollees ready "to hold the place as long as possible." Harding's officers could actually enumerate 481 officers and men from volunteer and MSM regiments, with a total of at least 150 militia and citizens, which they elsewhere added to a force of 550, but the actual numbers ran nearer 650. They had pits large enough for about 40 men on the hill around the Herreford's house. Mayo had detachments scouting the country in every direction on both sides of the river.[6]

Mayo's last orders had been to hold the town, though the generals had assured him that he would surely face no attack "other than from irregular troops" or the Confederate conscripts near Keytesville, Roanoke, and Fayette. Despite the presence of Price's army at Boonville, the Federal command convinced itself that they "had no steam or other ferry boat with which to cross any large body of men with or without artillery." However, Harding realized that his force would no longer be needed at Jefferson City and could be no real help to the vast Union force they thought would push west from the state capital and likely reach the Glasgow area shortly.[7]

Major Curtis, on the other hand, had accomplished his mission of verifying the location of the Confederate presence in central Missouri. Curtis realized that the westbound Confederate army had yet to get artillery upriver from Glasgow, which should make it safe to get back to Kansas City and warn his father. The master of the *West Wind* decided its deeper draft and the falling water level made it unusable for this, so Curtis took the *Benton*. He reported that they got "about twenty guns on board, and barricaded the pilot-house as well as we could, and built very serviceable breast-works of cord-wood around the boiler and main decks."[8] On Friday morning, October 14, Curtis left Glasgow.

Saturday's Battle

Harding deployed what he had wisely. He placed the half dozen companies of the Forty-Third south and east of the square on a ridge between the northern and southern approaches. Mayo took command of the troops at the bridge over Gregg Creek on the Boonville road; they were removing its planks. Captains James A. Adams and Samuel A. Huntershad their men of the Ninth MSM Cavalry at the opposite end of town, overlooking Bear Creek, near the home of Ben. Lewis. In addition to deploying more scouts and strengthening the picket squads, Harding sent Bingham and the Saline County militia east to repair the telegraph lines toward Jefferson City. Near dark on Friday, they galloped back into town, after having run into a force of 250 Confederates.[9]

The most immediate danger moved through the night toward them on the far bank of the river. An hour before dawn, Shelby arrived with 125 men and two guns of Captain Richard A. Collins's battery opposite Glasgow. As prearranged, they greeted the sunrise about 5:00 a.m. by blasting "the sleeping Federals, the silent town, and the rough and rugged fort." The noise drew Rev. William Goff Caples onto his front porch. Local Unionists viewed Caples as an unrepentant old secessionist who had regularly and materially aided Shelby's recruiters. A shell from Collins's artillery screamed onto his porch and ripped away the fleshy part of one of his legs, mortally wounding one of the biggest secessionists in North Missouri.[10] Tragically, Brigadier General John B. Clark did not have his men in position to begin the attack.

However, in the absence of the Boonville ferry, the Confederates faced real delays crossing at Arrow Rock, and the attacking force was still three miles from Glasgow when the men heard the sound of Collins's guns. This left Harding's sharpshooters free to open "a merciless fire" on the battery and its infantry support. Clark succeeded "after considerable difficulty, in crossing my command, but not as early as was expected." Forty members of the Saline County militia found themselves cut off but managed to avoid enough of Clark's brigade to make it to Macon. Late that morning, "Captain Holloway's colored servant" escaped the net and found his way apparently to the railroad and thence to St. Joseph. Those scouts that could did gallop back to Glasgow with the hope that at least a thousand Confederates approached and not far behind them.[11]

Harding immediately dispatched reinforcements. Major Benjamin K. Davis added three companies of the Forty-Third to Gregg Creek, and Captain Andrew Dusold's company of that regiment together with Captain Steinmetz's militia hurried to the main bridge. By 9:00 a.m., Colonel Sidney D. Jackman's brigade had reached town, and they found the first of Clark's soldiers on the high ground half a mile from the creek. Jackman's men hurried to the left and threw their skirmishers forward. As they advanced, Collins's guns resumed their fire from across the river, Union Captain Holloway deciding that their purpose had been to keep the Federals from reaching the *West Wind* or even to use safely the streets. As the shells damaged the buildings near the fortifications, Shelby even sent Captain Arthur C. McCoy and a Captain Carrington in a boat across the Missouri to see whether it was feasible for Shelby to join the direct attack on the garrison. They returned, "the bullets plowing and hissing in the water all around them."[12]

As more and more Confederates arrived off the road, they extended their line beyond the flanks of those Federals at the creek, who had, thus far, held their positions "manfully." By 10:00 a.m., Colonel Colton Greene, in temporary command of Clark's brigade, had extended the Confederate formation to the northeast with the regiments of Colonels William L. Jeffers, Solomon G. Kitchen, and John Q. Burbridge and Greene's own men. Greene saw the Federals in their works visible half a mile to his front and brought up a gun under Lieutenant T. J. Williams of Captain S. S. Harris's Fourth Missouri Light Artillery. Harding watched this persistent advance.[13]

Shortly after, Colonel Robert R. Lawther's men scurried further north, beyond Greene's, and made escape impossible. Captain Hunter's eighty-five men of Ninth MSM Cavalry covering the north entrance to the town managed to stop Lawther's advance, holding them for the day. By then, Harding had committed the entire of his tiny reserve. Firing flared along the entire line, and several Confederate attempts to mount an assault mired only because of "houses, fences, &c. The militia and citizens in the rifle-pit aided materially in repelling the assaults referred to."[14]

Step by step, though, the Confederates backed the Federals into their rifle-pits and fortification "designed to hold about 250 men" along the crest of the bluffs over the river. Union sharpshooters in the upper floors of the brick buildings, notably Lewis Brothers' Tobacco Works and the schoolhouse, anchored the Federal positions. As Simmonds tried to lead a detachment of sharpshooters into position, Confederate fire killed him, as well as Steinmetz. Dusold fell, bleeding from a head wound initially thought mortal, responded to the news that he would live with the comment, "Well, by Gott, den I fights 'em again." Captains George M. Brown and Oscar Kirkham of the Forty-third led a countercharge that disoriented part of Jackman's line. Still, some of Jackman's men got "within forty yards of the works" before Clark ordered them to hold their position. Later, he visited Clark, "urging him to move at once upon the fort."[15]

Confederate success isolated men under Major Lewis and Captain Hunter cut off from the fort and in Lewis's tobacco factory. They continued to fight for twenty minutes after the surrender, "of which fact they were ignorant." The enemy had hailed with flag of truce and told them, but they refused to see it until they were allowed to send a messenger to ascertain the truth. Captain Woodruff of Lawther's regiment demanded the major's name: "I know you. You're black as Hell. Hand over that watch and damn quick, too!" The officer threatened to kill him and would have had Colonel Lawther not intervened. Lewis was sent to the house to stay until called for. Woodruff called him and threatened to kill him, but Lawther saved him again. At nightfall, he fled with others to the brush, at which point "drunken guerrillas entered and sacked the unprotected home."[16]

Around 11:00 a.m., the firing slackened, and two citizens bearing a flag of truce approached the Federal position. They told Harding that he faced 4,000 men under Clark "in my front and on my flanks," with the entire of Shelby's division across the river, preparing to cross by steamboat. "As these gentlemen brought me no message from the rebel commander I had no answer to send." Meanwhile, Collins's guns continued to sweep the streets leading from the river east and from the positions north of town.[17]

Fighting intensified northeast of the rifle pits, and Greene reported taking a critical building from the Federals. After this, Harding acknowledged that the Confederates held "every available shelter" and could cover the piecemeal advance of their skirmishers. Finally, Clark reported "a heavy force within from thirty to fifty yards of us." And, "My line was so thin that it could be pierced anywhere," complained Harding. Holloway's positions "separated by only the width of village lots, our boys sheltered by the front fences and the enemy firing from behind those in the rear." The Federal officers decided "to capitulate, if honorable terms could be obtained, in order to save the lives of [their] men and of the citizens as well as to save the city itself, which would have been sacked and destroyed had it been taken by assault." Around noon, Harding "become convinced that [he] could not hold the place if the enemy chose to make an assault." He sent Major John R. Moore, to burn "about 50,000 rations," but nobody could reach the stores along the waterfront," including "about 1,000 suits of cavalry clothing." While the Federals did not know that Jackman and Clark planned an assault, they saw the Confederate guns rolled up "to short range so as to tell upon the houses where we were sheltered; they would soon be untenable." Harding and his officers rightly decided that any such attack "would have proved very disastrous to the tired and hungry men and a resistance avail little or nothing."[18]

Harding heard the Confederate terms as Holloway consulted the regulations on surrender. At 1:30, Harding agreed that the garrison would march out with its arms and colors, their officers keeping their horses, sidearms, and private property; the men keeping their belongings; and "private property of citizens to be respected." Both officers and men had been under constant fire for nearly eight hours, and their conduct apparently unexceptionable." Harding noted that, though he had not agreed to this, one of Clark's officers subsequently swore the Federal prisoners "not to take up arms against the Confederate States during the war and not to give aid or comfort to the enemies thereof."[19]

Almost immediately, the contenders began generating misestimates of the losses that became subsequently incorporated into the historical literature. Union reports of having 550 reflect the official convention of simply not counting militia with any concern for accuracy. Confederate accounts run as high as 1,000, with Price opting for "between 800 or 900 prisoners." The actual number likely ran to 650 actual participants, with a certain portion of civilians taken in the course of the battle as well, and the consistent unconcern with militia counts probably explains the improbably low reports of eight to eleven killed with up to thirty-two wounded, both low for eight intensive hours of fighting. Even accepting the count of roughly a dozen killed, a reasonably conservative estimate would place the wounded nearer four dozen, and one suspects that the proportion should not have been lower than for clashes lasting longer than a day.[20]

The toll the Federals had exacted on the attacking forces had been severe. "The enemy's loss was much larger," wrote Holloway, "several officers having been killed and many officers and men wounded." Based on what he heard among them, Harding guessed that "as many as 67" had been killed or mortally wounded on both sides of the river with more than 200 sustaining lesser wounds. Clark acknowledged "considerable loss in gallant officers and men in crossing the open fields and before we could get under cover of the houses around the fortifications, the loss in this action being__killed and__wounded." The blanks as to numbers awaited fuller reports from his subordinates who never fully reported, though the most heavily hit regiment, Greene's, admitted to the loss of seven killed, including two officers, and forty-six wounded.[21] The losses reflected more than a decimation of a force of 1,800 to 2,000 engaged.

Clark's Confederates took a day or so recrossing the Missouri River with a remarkable booty that included, according to Price "about 1,200 small-arms, about the same number of overcoats, 150 horses, 1 steam-boat, and large amounts of underclothing," though at least one report claimed "about 2,000 stand of small-arms." Burbridge commanded the last regiment to leave Glasgow, and he complained, "The understanding relative to the distribution of captured property up to this time was that all should be equally divided among the regiments engaged in the capture. Yet on this occasion, though a large quantity of horses and arms were taken, my regiment obtained none of either, though at the time I had over 100 unarmed men in my command."[22]

McKerr, a noted copperhead near Glasgow, told Clark after the battle. "You must not expect us to leave our homes and follow you; but we have done the best we could—we went over and helped you take Glasgow." "These men will be at the polls on two weeks from next Tuesday to vote for McClellan." After following the Confederates to Glasgow, Sam Cobbage hung around until Colonel Forbes's EMM retook the town and captured him. Cobbage bragged on killing two citizens. "You ought to have seen how quick the damned Radical son of a bitch turned black after he was."[23]

Despite the surrender terms, the victors did seize the property of civilians in Glasgow. Two days after the battle, the local banker, W.E. Dunnica, had the sense to remove $32,000 from the safe and bury it in his yard. Nevertheless, when two of William C. Quantrill's men seized him and took him over to the bank, they got $21,000, the richest haul of guerrillas in the war. A few days later, "Bloody Bill" Anderson turned up, fresh from his plundering at Danville and the northeast to visit the Virginia-born Benjamin Lewis. Although the richest man in town and related by marriage to both Price and Clark, Lewis had voluntarily freed his 150 slaves and been an ardent Unionist. After threatening his family and raping one of his former slaves, Anderson beat Lewis into permanent debility to extract information as to where he kept his money.[24]

Those tending the wounded behaved with remarkable heroism. Dr. John Q. Eggleston, not yet mustered in as the surgeon of Harding's regiment, and a civilian Doctor Todd from Brunswick helped Major Frank Gibson Porter, medical director of the District of North Missouri maintain the hospital over the course of the battle. Todd and Porter remained after the battle, "faithfully at their posts after the regular Confederate forces left, during the days when Anderson and Jackman and their gangs of murderers and fiends had possession of the place."[25]

The paroled officers made their way quickly back to Federal lines. After being paroled, they rejoined their men to be marched across the river to the Lamine, where a Confederate escort turned them over to Captain Henry S. Glaze, acting on behalf of Fisk, who took them on to the Union troops who had retaken Boonville. Yet, they noted that "many citizens and non-combatants joined us in our march from rebel rule." Nevertheless, wrote Harding, "We were treated with courtesy and kindness by General Clark and nearly all of his officers whom we came in contact with," and the other Union officers, including Glaze agreed. Fisk rightly fretted over the enlisted men captured at Glasgow, warning his comrades to expect their return "exhausted and starving. Do all you can for their comfort. If rations fail to reach them from Jefferson City cook yours for them and I will order an issue to cover them."[26]

Rosecrans specified that "every comfort" be given to the Confederate officers "with forty enlisted men, bearers of flag of truce." However, he wrote Price that some had been "clothed in our uniform. I have always adopted as a rule, necessary for my own protection, that soldiers of your army captured in our uniform, should be treated as spies." He had no objection to their wearing captured clothing "provided its color is changed so it cannot deceive me." He warned Price that permitting them to wear unaltered Federal uniforms "exposes your men to the rigorous punishment demanded by military prudence as a protection against surprise." He added a protest against Price's association with guerrillas "whose record is stained with crimes at which humanity shudders." "You and I, general," he told Price, "have tried to conduct this war in accordance with the highest dictates of humanity and the laws of war among civilized nations. I hope the future will make no change in this respect."[27]

Major Samuel Curtis, who had left Glasgow before the attack in hopes of reaching Kansas City, encountered no Confederates until Brunswick and faced no hostile action until Miami City. Several miles above Waverly, they veered the boat to the north bank to avoid Confederates and wound up running aground and "for about half an hour a brisk fire was kept up on both sides." A more dangerous encounter awaited at Lexington, where they grounded for ten minutes while under fire and "very liable to capture, but fortunately escaped." This continued for miles as Confederates only fifty feet away tried to stop the boat, hitting the pilothouse about seventy-five times. In all, Curtis thought "3,000 or 4,000" shots were fired at them, with "about 600" actually striking the boat. Nevertheless, he reached Kansas City on October 16 at 4:00 p.m.[28]

His father the general quickly contacted Harding's superiors in the Department of Missouri, but the best available information on Glasgow included such outdated assurances as "only very small parties of rebels are on north side of river. He says there are no columns moving on north side of river." Curtis had already warned "commanders and owners of steam-boats and ferry-boats on the Missouri River" to keep their vessels out of Confederate hands. Once news leaked out of the attack, rumors proliferated that Glasgow would be the prelude to a full-scale invasion of north Missouri, reports even crediting Marmaduke with having sent columns east to Macon and another west. A resident of Macon reported that Harding had 2,500 men who had fought and beaten Shelby and had begun to pursue him.[29] Nevertheless, locating and getting some measure of Price's army justified Curtis's declaration of martial law not only in Kansas, but into parts of Missouri, even as he gathered what he called the Army of the Border.

The River Communities: Paris to Missouri City

Glasgow dramatized the vulnerability of communities along or near the river. Having moved the most experienced and best armed and organized troops from the garrisons in the District of North Missouri, the department referred stories of "the depredations of guerrillas in Audrain, Pike, and Lincoln Counties" to the beleaguered command structure attempting to maintain order with their poorly organized and equipped militia. "What disposition have you made of your forces to meet them? Can't you put a scouting party in that part of the country at once? Answer at once."[30]

Price capped a series of speeches as his army moved into increasingly sympathetic communities. On October 15, the general made a direct appeal for his former constituents "to throw off the shackles which have bound you for nearly three years. It is unnecessary for me to recite the wrongs you have suffered; the remedy for them is now in your own hands. You can relieve yourselves and serve your country by joining the army I have brought for your redemption."[31]

Meanwhile, the Confederates told themselves that thousands of Missourians, eager to free their state from Federal authority, joined up, and some of the Federal officers agreed. "Of the 5,000 rebels who went to Price from this district," complained Fisk, "4,990 were doubtless cheerful volunteers, and they and theirs, and all who aid, comfort, feed, conceal, and inform them, should go out from among us, and all the loyal people will say amen." More realistically, General Curtis noted that the Confederates treated Missouri as one of their states and had been "conscripting every man fit for military duty. He had possession of the steam ferryboat at Boonville, which was in serviceable condition."[32]

One must wonder whether the Confederate army recruited enough to make up for the many disappearing from its ranks. The reasons for those disappearances ran the gamut from simple desertion to their disintegration into bands of plunderers. Major J. Nelson Smith informed his superiors that "most of the recruits enlisted by Captains Rathbun and Bedinger, as well as most of their conscripts, deserted and returned to their homes."[33] In the short run, though, the recruits and hangers-on opened many communities to attack.

Within hours of the Saturday attack on Glasgow, other Confederates had seized Paris. The Federals knew that Major Elliott Majors had been in Monroe County for some time and was "said to have recruited 1,500 men besides the force with which he captured Paris; there are numerous small bands all over the country who will be flocking to him." Confederates "charged into the town with wild yells at about four o'clock, surrounding Captain William E. Fouke's garrison, reported fifty-five of the Seventieth EMM and ten from Ninth Missouri State Militia. Absent but feeling responsible, Fisk reported that Fowkes "with 100 men" faced Confederates "to the number of 400." By 8:00 p.m., the garrison had surrendered. "Officers and men were sworn not to bear arms against the rebels; horses, arms, and private property were stolen and carried away." As the parolees began marching to Shelbina, officials learned that Colonel Washington McDaniel commanded the Confederate force. A subsequent scout to Paris skirmished with the enemy but found that McDaniel and Majors had crossed.[34]

That weekend, Confederates under Lieutenant James N. Chiles hit Ridgely and Smithville in Clay County, just across the river from the Kansas City area. On Sunday night, they "captured and plundered" Ridgely. They "robbed people of about $2,000." This constituted "a considerable force of rebels, some dressed in Confederate uniform" engaged in "robbing the county of horses, cattle, and everything else they can get, even to household goods. Send troops quickly if possible. Answer whether you can send them." The following day, Monday, the same group gave the same treatment to Smithville, then burning the town. In addition, reports identified other guerrilla or recruiter parties under Captain Paul F. Thornton of the Fourteenth Missouri Partisan Rangers Cavalry and Captain John Thrailkill passing through Clay into Platte and Buchanan Counties.[35]

Other Confederate detachments threatened more of the downriver garrisons under the broad subdistrict command of Colonel John H. Shanklin at Chillicothe. On October 13, "200 of Shelby's command" crossed at Waverly, gathering strength as it swept through nearby towns until Major George Deagle at Carrollton thought that he faced 400 to 500 advancing on his 150 to 160 of the Sixty-fifth EMM. Shanklin ordered him to hold on to the town "unless an overwhelming force approaches it." On Saturday, they captured two of Deagle's pickets, releasing one of the wounded to inform Deagle that Colonel B. Frank Gordon had advanced on the town with 600 men and "that it would take them fifteen minutes to place the artillery after which the town would be shelled." In reality, Major Jeremiah C. Cravens and Capt. Williams had raised a modest force of new recruits and indeterminate size, and their reports later attributed the victory to Williams's bluffing, though they also doubled the number of men involved on both sides, repeating their claim of 600 and numbering the federals as "about 300." The Confederates paroled Deagle and the officers but disregarded the terms to execute six prisoners for allegedly having killed Colonel William Peery and two other recruiters. They sloughed off the responsibility by claiming that they had merely turned the men over to "Bloody Bill" Anderson, who was actually on the other side of the state.[36]

The Confederates stayed in Carrollton until October 17 then left for better pickings, a large body heading for Richmond in Ray County. The garrison commander there, an officer of the First MSM Cavalry reported having 300 of the Fifty-first EMM under Major John Grimes. Civilians and patrols encountered individuals at Turkey Creek as well as on Shoal Creek, Compton's Ferry and other points near the river as well.[37]

Shanklin also monitored developments at Brunswick, some fifty miles southeast of his headquarters at Chillicothe and through Chariton County. The Federals had to abandon their garrisons at Fulton, Sturgeon, and Huntsville. To secure Macon City, they had to evacuate Fayette. A small detachment of the Third MSM Cavalry formed the core of the local EMM defending Columbia. As Price's army moved from Boonville, a column of 800 Confederates reached Keytesville, and 200, associated with Shelby's division, showed up at Brunswick, these Chariton County towns being, respectively, twenty and thirty miles even further up the Missouri than Glasgow. One Federal officer passed on the assessment of a Unionist from the area: "The rebels now hold Chariton County." As well, an organized body estimated as a hundred left for Price's army from Moberly, roughly thirty-five miles northeast of Glasgow. Large groups of partisans hit Spencerburg, and Paynesville, while panicked citizens destroyed the stores at Milton. Observers found parts of Randolph County "about depopulated of the adult male residents, who are in the rebel or the union army, or are citizen refugees."[38]

That same day, hundreds of Confederates appeared at Missouri City on the north bank of the river, just below Kansas City. Soldiers at Liberty heard that 500 rebels had taken Missouri City on the north bank of the river just below Kansas City. "A rebel gang under Chiles, Todd, and Anderson, 400 or 500 strong" supposedly crossed there. Rosecrans assured them that only Jackman's force had crossed the river, and those "not more than half armed. All you have to do is to fight hard and don't be afraid. Let enemy come close and shoot low. No surrender." Old Rosy correctly insisted that no such force could have been in Missouri City without having been spotted by Curtis's men, but remained himself ignorant of the fact that Curtis's son had seen "near Richfield, or Missouri City, is Todd, Taylor, and others, 400 or 500 strong. They were still there on yesterday, threatening Liberty." When Confederate squads turned up near Stewartsville near St. Joseph, officers of the Eighty-seventh EMM asked about rumors that "Liberty is being cannonaded" and a force of 4,000 rebels bore down on them, placing them in "infinite peril unless speedily re-enforced."[39]

The situation rightly concerned every responsible officer in the field. Brigadier General James Craig told Fisk and his superiors in St. Louis that, despite his rank, he commanded "less than 500 troops in the district, no artillery, and small-arms exhausted." This had not been enough to save Glasgow and Carrollton, prevent the plundering of Ridgely, or stop the "500 armed Confederates and guerrillas" said to be rampaging through Clay County. The same headquarters that had depleted his forces advised: "Don't shut yourself up in the towns, but protect them by taking the offensive. . . . Let the citizens dig rifle-pits and protect their towns, while you attack the enemy." When Brigadier General J. B. Douglass complained, St. Louis officials muttered among themselves that Lieutenant Colonel Alexander G. Hequembourg of the Fortieth Missouri at Mexico acted more effectually than he."[40]

South of the river, Rosecrans and General Alfred Pleasonton had Sanborn's cavalry nipping at the heels of Price's army as they waited for the reinforcements being shuttled up the Missouri to Jefferson City. Tellingly, perhaps, the generals moved much of Colonel Edward F. Winslow's cavalry by land, even as they moved the bulk of General A. J. Smith's infantry by steamboat. This kept the largest possible forces together but slowed the arrival of the most rapidly moving units from getting to where they could be of use until October 16, only a day ahead of the infantry.[41]

Pleasonton chose this point to reorganize the entire operation yet again. Walking among them with his riding crop, he made no particular secret of his contempt for Germans and his sense that service in Missouri represented a real step down from the Army of the Potomac. John F. Philips, John L. Beveridge, and Joseph J. Gravely had commanded three small brigades in Sanborn's Provisional Cavalry Division. With the arrival of "about 2,000" more cavalry under Winslow, Pleasonton took charge of a new Provisional Cavalry Corps, in which Winslow got his own brigade and the district commanders—Sanborn, Brown and John McNeil—took the other three, leaving Fisk predictably out of the picture.[42]

"I shall move forward the balance of the command immediately upon ascertaining that the enemy continues his march toward Lexington," suggested Sanborn. "If he moves in any other direction I shall endeavor so to move as to intercept his column." Rosecrans agreed that "everything depends upon knowing if Price has gone to Lexington or not. To find that out quickly, with as little fatigue to the animals as possible, is of every importance." Rosecrans had the uncanny knack for flashes of genuine insight and brilliance coupled to an inability to act upon them; "it may have been well to send troops to Boonville, but I think not to Lexington." "I don't consider Lexington worth our attention," he wrote, adding wisely. "What we want is to gain time while the enemy stays north of the railroad. Our troops ought to make Sedalia and Clinton while the cavalry harass them farther north."[43]

The Confederate movement west from Boonville placed Lexington in the crosshairs. Price ordered his army to begin concentrating once more, and he sent Shelby to "push forward the whole command under you and General Clark without delay, so as to get to this point some time to-night. You will watch well your left flank for any approach of the enemy from that direction." Captain Rathborne had captured Lexington the day before, with a hundred men, representing themselves as part of Price's advance. Also in the report for that day: "Price's main body was retreating south through Warrensburg, in Johnson county." Clark was on the north side of the river, but said to have occupied Brunswick and be moving on Keytesville.[44] The Army of Missouri headed west.

Two

The Third Army

4

Arrival of the Army of the Border

To Lexington and Beyond, October 17–20

The Second Colorado remained the most important force in the field in the immediate path of General Sterling Price's actual line of march. The Confederates generally detested the Kansans and viewed the Missourians opposing them as traitors, but they had developed a grudging respect for the Coloradoans. One of these adaptable westerners later recalled how they had turned an old guerrilla tactic to their own advantage, dressing up to "'play bushwhacker' on some disloyal harborer of the gentlemen of the brush." They had two companies mounted on white chargers, and Price's men called them "that damned White Horse Regiment." One Confederate noted that the guerrillas had been "doing pretty much as they pleased along the Kansas border until the Second Colorado came." When the Coloradoans struck a trail, they "followed it to a funeral."[1]

Unlike the militia, such units had the experience, numbers, supply, and artillery support to challenge the large Confederate army, which had spent most of a month going pretty much where it chose, with the decisive exceptions of Saint Louis and Jefferson City. General James G. Blunt, hoping not only to locate Price's army but to goad the rest of the Federal forces into decisive action, gathered everything he had available to ride out and meet it at Lexington. What happened there brought part of General Samuel R. Curtis's tiny new Army of the Border into action for the first time, with surprising results.

IN THE PATH OF THE CONFEDERATE ADVANCE

As Price's army had bypassed Jefferson City, some of the Coloradoans had reestablished a garrison at Independence, only about nine miles east of Kansas City. The roughly 1,500 inhabitants of Independence had always been mostly Southerners. A considerable proportion of them detested what they saw as a military occupation, and some eagerly supported the partisan cutthroats who had seasonally operated nearby. The garrison determined it could hold the town against 500, but the location of Price's army acquired a new urgency as the telegraph lines to the east went down, and guerrilla forces became thicker, skirmishing with the Federals at Round Prairie.[2]

On Wednesday, October 12, news that the Confederates had started west from Boonville drove most of the few remaining Unionists from Independence. The next morning, guerrillas torched the railroad bridge near town, and the small garrison of Coloradoans under Captain Thomas Moses briefly slipped away until they heard reinforcements would join them. In the early hours of Friday, they returned, unnerved and exhausted, to the town square where they unexpectedly encountered those reinforcements. Used to blue-clad guerrillas, both detachments drew their weapons and prepared to blaze away at each other. Later, "a thrill of horror chilled the blood of the entire command, as they shuddered to think how nearly fatal had been their mistake."[3]

The coolheaded Major James Nelson Smith quickly organized a large scout to the east, beyond the Little Blue River, to find Price's advance. They returned with rumors of all sorts, indicating the passage of some Confederates north over the Missouri, and more threatening stories that 8,000 of them had veered south toward Warrensburg. Smith's horsemen veered in that direction, making their way toward Hickman's Mills. One of them recalled that "the clouded sky, betokening a storm, soon made the way very dark, augmented by the heavy timber and dense underbrush through which we passed, over rocky cliffs, and deep ravines, frequently obliged to proceed in single file for miles, the path not being wide enough to admit more than one passing at a time." At points along the dark route, they had to backtrack to regain the path.[4] With little respite, they then backtracked to Independence, where men from the Fourth, Twelfth, and Nineteenth KSM had secured the town.

Meanwhile, about thirty-five miles to their east, Captain James D. Eads of the First MSM Cavalry had a tiny garrison of eighty men at Lexington; they were cut off from the rest of General William S. Rosecrans's department and periodically skirmishing with some of the reported 500 to 1,500 Confederates nearby. Eads had turned to Curtis for reinforcement on October 12. Shortly after, even as the local telegraph operators had headed out to look for the Confederates, the agent of the stagecoach line reached Independence with news that the growing guerrilla presence had persuaded Eads to move his tiny garrison across the river to Richmond. By Friday morning, October 14, small bands of guerrillas had briefly taken Lexington. The press reported "the cold-blooded massacre of thirty Germans and other citizens in Lafayette county, and that the murderers openly declare their motto to be 'Spare no Union man.'"[5]

On Monday, October 17, Majors Smith and James Ketner of the Sixteenth Kansas Cavalry led about 300 Coloradoans and Kansans from Independence to Lexington. They had found telegraph line far too broken to permit repair so they simply hurried east to Lexington, where bushwhackers had killed some civilians and begun firing at boats on the river. "The most extravagant evidences of joy were manifested by the union citizens of that place on the arrival of our troops," reported the Federals. Initially, they found "very few citizens in the streets, and they all women and children, but as soon as they learned that Federals occupied the town what few male citizens there were left commenced crawling out of their holes, and the citizens generally commenced swarming around us, some in tears, some in smiles, and some in rags, and generally appeared much rejoiced at our arrival, and offered us the hospitalities of the town, inviting us to their homes, and acted as if they felt that they could not do too much for us." The bushwhackers had subjected the town to "a reign of terror, both loyal people, McClellan people, and rebels," leaving "many poor families very destitute." [6]

Federals reconnoitered the area and uncovered groups of bushwhackers and Confederate recruiters nearby. Scouts also located several hundred Confederates clustered about six miles to the south and a "large force of the enemy" eight miles east at Dover, with the advance of Price's army a little more than twenty miles farther downriver at Waverly. At Lexington, the Coloradoans "captured 30 double-barreled shotguns brought by the enemy to Lexington to arm their conscripts with; also 1,000 rounds of ammunition, all of which [they] destroyed, as [they] had no transportation to carry them away." Lacking the supplies necessary to remain, Smith ordered his men to return to Independence, though the locals offered to "feed my whole command as long as I chose to or could stay there." Smith got Eads's militia back into the town from Richmond and left "well satisfied that he could hold the place if he chose to." [7]

For their part, the Confederates proved to be even less well informed, thinking that about 2,500 Federals had occupied Lexington. In the wake of successes at Glasgow and Sedalia, Price sent troops that direction. His men were "said to be moody, and discouraged, but desperate. The Missourians who accompanied him say they may as well fight it out here as any where,—they have come home to stay." [8]

"State lines and State sovereignties greatly embarrass military operations," complained Curtis when the KSM continued to balk. Curtis strove to get the KSM clustered at the Kansas, or Kaw, River to the Kansas City area and to reward them with arms and mounts, "at a time when red tape was at a discount." Conservative papers had been "denouncing the whole thing as a fraud or fallacy and expressing a belief that Price had left the country." Under severe pressure to make no mistakes, the general filtered a great deal of rumor. A "Mr. Graham" near the scene of the fighting at Sedalia reported that, at that time, General John Sanborn had "10,000 mounted men and two batteries" at Georgetown, a few miles north of Sedalia, as well as General A. J. Smith's "6,000 or 7,000 infantry and two batteries" at Otterville, and a force under Brigadier Generals Thomas Ewing and John McNeil on the Missouri River with five boatloads of troops chasing Price.[9] In such an equation, Curtis needed as much direct information on Price's army as he could get.

Blunt, with his mix of volunteer units at Hickman's Mills, decided to make a reconnaissance in force into Missouri. Both Charles R. Jennison and Charles W. Blair had scouts riding into Missouri to check, among other places, fords on the Osage River, which the Confederates "would naturally cross going south." Senators James H. Lane and Samuel C. Pomeroy had already visited Blunt, and the former decided to join the planned reconnaissance east to Pleasant Hill, with the idea of reaching Warrensburg, adding, "The route toward Sedalia seems our most likely way to strike Price, viewing matters as we now have them presented."[10]

"No place in Missouri has suffered more in former times than Pleasant Hill," reported the *Missouri Democrat*. Quantrill had earlier half-burned the town, but, in contrast to Lexington, the local militia refused to abandon the place. For this reason, after Jefferson City and Warrensburg, Pleasant Hill became "only the third town of any size this side of Saint Louis that has not been desecrated by rebel feet during this raid." After the garrison of Coloradoans got orders to pull back toward Independence and Kansas City, Captain Andrew Allen of the Seventy-Seventh EMM mobilized the local company, brought in more from Harrisonville, and armed "nearly all the males of Pleasant Hill, old and young." They did locate Confederates operating a few miles away, "mostly bushwhackers, who used to live here," in addition to Poole, Dave Lard, Cook, Hays, Carter, and four brothers named Hall. Also "a man named Reynolds, professing to be an officer in the C.S.A., a very desperate character was also here. Not one of them but claimed to belong to the Confederate army." At 7:30 a.m. on Sunday, October 16, Captain George S. Grover's "Johnson County Citizen Guards" of the Fortieth EMM had passed through from Warrensburg with news that Sedalia and possibly Knob Noster had fallen.[11]

That the rest of Price's army had not followed those columns through these towns meant that the bulk of the Confederates remained up by the river. Blunt explained this to his officers and ordered everyone with a mount to converge on Lexington, adding, "You cannot be too hasty in moving." The Coloradoans, who had just gotten back to Independence, found themselves right back in the saddle and headed for Lexington. Sergeant David C. Nettleton of the Second Colorado had avoided the first ride because he had been sent as a courier to Blunt and then found himself "detained and attached to his bodyguard." Smith's column encountered bushwhackers about eighteen miles out of Independence. "It being quite dark, my command and their horses being tired and worn out, I did not think it advisable to pursue them. I here had my telegraph operator tap the wire so that I might communicate with you, but he reported that he could get no circuit and I had to abandon it." Just before dawn, Smith sent patrols to locate the rebels and continued on toward Lexington.[12]

Around 10 a.m. Tuesday, October 18, after "a small body" of KSM and Captain Grover's EMM turned up just southwest of Lexington, the first of Blunt's 1,100 men formed into Lilliputian brigades under Jennison and Thomas Moonlight. The advance chased off the "bushwhackers" under Dave Poole, "killing and wounding some and taking several prisoners." As the rest of the Federals filed into camp near the fairgrounds and the college, Blunt declared martial law over Lafayette County, instructing "all able-bodied male persons between the ages of fifteen and sixty years of age (white or black)" to report to Major Smith by 2 p.m. for labor on the fortifications: "Each man is required to furnish himself with a spade or pick." Then, too, Moonlight sent detachments southeast toward Warrensburg and east toward Dover, a hamlet about halfway to Waverly. Around noon, Grover's militia found themselves with Lieutenant J. L. Thornton's company of the Eleventh Kansas out on the Dover road, where they skirmished "through corn fields and heavy timber, on the banks of the Tebo, with what seemed to be a constantly increasing force of the enemy."[13]

The Confederates who had been at Lexington had been requisitioning supplies, "and executing the conscript laws of the so-styled Confederate States." Meanwhile, Price had gotten word of Smith's earlier scout to Lexington about the time he heard of the capture of Sedalia. By Tuesday, Thompson's brigade, back from Sedalia, and Clark's brigade of General John S. Marmaduke's division, back from Glasgow, joined Jo Shelby's division at Waverly. They had earlier covered the rear guard against General Alfred Pleasonton's cavalry and had passed west and taken the lead. In short order, they had one column moving off to the left, cutting off the road to Sedalia and any easy communication between Blunt at Lexington and Pleasonton's horsemen on the Blackwater. On Wednesday morning, a Union reconnaissance of 100 to 120 men encountered Shelby's advance. Filing on the general's behalf, Major John N. Edwards exaggerated "a heavy force of Federals under General Blunt five miles from Lexington, on the Salt Pond road. Immediate battle was given."[14] In fact, neither had that many men involved, though they would shortly.

THE BATTLE

Early on Wednesday, October 19, Jennison had sent more scouts toward Sedalia, Berlin and Dover roads; the last group was Grover and a detachment of his Warrensburg militia. Around 11 a.m. couriers galloped into Lexington from two directions. One from Curtis declared that he could send no reinforcements because "of the embarrassments thrown in his way by the Governor of Kansas and others relative to moving the militia out of the State." The other came in from a patrol and reported two Confederate columns were advancing on the town, one from the Salt Pond road to the southeast and the other from Dover to the east. One Union veteran identified the latter as led by "Wild Bill" Hickok. A later account described their stand: "in the face of such overwhelming force," an estimated 2,000 Unionists faced an estimated 35,000 Confederates. Nettleton of the Second Colorado recalled that the rebels "came up in plain view and extended their flanks till they nearly surrounded us."[15]

Shelby's old brigade under Thompson formed fast and hit hard. Colonels B. Frank Gordon and Benjamin Elliott reported Blunt's men as "stubborn at first and handled their artillery well, but Thompson gave them no breathing time." In their ranks, the Virginia-born Maurice M. Langhorne had grown up in Lexington, where he had learned the printing trades in a local newspaper office before leaving for the West before the war. With its outbreak, he had returned and joined Shelby's men, in contrast to the family friend and fellow Missourian who shared his trade, name, and residence—Samuel Langhorne Clemens—who had, at the start, tasted more of war than he wanted and headed west.[16]

Moonlight's line formed at the edge of a cornfield before a wide meadow, but it did not hold long. Sergeant Archer S. Childers recalled Moonlight's standing in the skirmish line and "encouraging the men to stand firm" as the Confederates rushed to position only seventy-five yards from them, unleashing a volley that killed their orderly. As the Confederates called out to surrender, Childers turned to find the Union line had pulled back beyond a fence at the edge of the cornfield, leaving him alone in front of the rebel line with only Lieutenant William V. Philips in his line of sight. In one of those oddities of combat, Childers ran back to the new position without any of the Confederates taking a shot at him.[17]

Blunt and his staff had prepared Jennison's line as a fallback position. Senator Lane recalled that the Confederates struck that formation at 1 p.m. to their left on the Waverly road. Jennison complimented the work of Captain William A. Johnson in directing the Federal skirmish line, which flushed out an estimated 400 Confederates in "a spirited contest [that] was commenced with small-arms, the single howitzer being used occasionally with excellent effect." Jennison's men then held a position "running through the camp, and immediately south of the Fair-Grounds." Lieutenant Colonel George Hoyt had "troops and artillery . . . advantageously posted in the streets" to cover any attack on the Camden road, with Lieutenant James Burton Pond's detachment of the Third Wisconsin Cavalry to the south. Blunt personally placed two companies of the Fifteenth Kansas Cavalry with their howitzers "southeast of the city, facing a section of open and undulating country, with cultivated fields extending from one to two miles in our front, with the Independence road in our rear, upon which I designed to fall back whenever it became necessary."[18]

Once beyond Jennison's brigade, Moonlight's men re-formed "in a deep cut close by the Fair Ground." Childers watched the Union howitzers throw some shells over their heads without needing to be closer to aim, "for by this time the whole plain in front was filled with horses and men. I could see them scatter as the shells fell in their midst." In an unusual position for a U.S. senator, Lane displayed a Sharp's carbine on the skirmish line. "By the stubborn fighting and skillful management of the troops," wrote Lane, "General Blunt held the enemy for five hours." The arrival of rifled Confederate artillery defined most of the last two hours of this as "their long-range guns opened a brisk fire in my front, to which my short-range howitzers could not reply with effect."[19] On the other hand, the aggressiveness of the Confederate onslaught broke much of the Federal chain of command. Many of those off scouting found themselves cut off, and Captain Orren A. Curtis's troopers were briefly stranded in town. Meanwhile, Robert Simmons of the Seventeenth Illinois Cavalry, after several days as a prisoner in Price's camp, slipped away with Blunt's guns "doing good execution among the Johnnies."[20] Both he and Curtis eventually rejoined their units.

By all accounts, though, Blunt had handled his forces brilliantly. A deserter supposedly later told the story, oft repeated by Blunt's admirers, that Shelby later encountered a group of his officers discussing who commanded the Union troops in the town. "Well, gentlemen, I've only one thing to say," Shelby supposedly commented. "It was either Blunt or the devil." Blunt and Shelby had faced each other before, at Cane Hill and Prairie Grove.[21] Interestingly enough, Shelby had used similar tactics in the Boston Mountains nearly two years before, but Blunt clearly had learned them well.

By dusk, men under Jennison rallied for a final time near "a cross-road leading to the main highway from Lexington to Independence." He used three companies of the Fifteenth Kansas Cavalry as a rear guard, "until the entire command was safe beyond successful pursuit." In moving one of the howitzers through the dark over the uneven road, the crew accidentally broke its limber, and the entire column passed before it could be repaired. However, Lieutenant Murphy of the Fifteenth and Sergeant Patterson of the Fourteenth stayed with those repairing the piece and "succeeded in bringing it off in the very face of the enemy's pursuing columns."[22] Jennison reported that his brigade got away with no further incident.

Moonlight's brigade had a more difficult time of it, though he took personal command of their retreat. He repeatedly directed the placement and fire of their four mountain howitzers and moved the Eleventh from post to post "in a gallant manner." Several times, they fought until flanked, then used the artillery fire to cover their retreat to a new position. Perhaps describing the same incident as Jennison, Moonlight reported that "the howitzers here did good service, but on leaving the field the tongue of one of the pieces got broken, so that it was necessary to lash the limber and piece to other pieces in order to save them, which was done in the very face of the enemy and under his fire."[23]

One of the last of these encounters came as Confederates moved on both flanks. "When I heard their bugle sounding the charge and saw the rebel line come sweeping down the hill right on us, yelling like demons, my hair almost lifted my hat off of my head," recalled Childers, "and I looked around to see what the rest were doing." They had "revolvers popping away as fast as they could pull the trigger; and, strange to say, we only had one man wounded in this charge"; that man was James Thomas, whom the rebels mistakenly left for dead. Moonlight held his company in ambush long enough to get his skirmishers from the lane and close the gate. "By this time it was so dark we could see but a few steps."[24]

Those stranded on patrols likely had a still harder time, though most seem to have been lucky. East of town, Grover's Missouri militia heard the artillery back in town behind them, but Jennison's courier recalling them to Lexington arrived when part of their force had already engaged enemy patrols. Grover sent a messenger to recall them and waited, but what seemed like a Confederate regiment showed up "on the brow of the hill about three hundred yards away, to the east and the officer in command rode down towards us to ask to identify." Just before an attack, the men Grover had recalled turned up on their own; the messenger had been killed before reaching them. Together, they wheeled and rode straight for the Confederates, turning unexpectedly right up a side street to the Wellington road and galloping west with the enemy in close pursuit. Twice, they had met rebels at intersections "but rode through them." By then, Blunt's retreat had a long lead on the Missourians, and Grover did not catch up until after midnight.[25]

Nettleton recalled that the Confederates "pressed us heavily till dark when we set fire to a bridge and we saw no more of them." At some time after dark, another Coloradoan, Captain George West, rode up with an escort of thirty men to try to deliver dispatches for Blunt. They supposedly nearly rode into the arms of the rebels at Lexington but, by chance, encountered Curtis's men as they were trying to make their way back to the rest of the Union forces. Moonlight reported that the Confederates pursued the rear of his column "for several miles." He wrote that "long after dark we were compelled to fight him on every piece of ground favorable for making a stand."[26]

Confederate reports confirmed this, though they exaggerated the "great haste and confusion" of the Federal retreat. Thompson's "uninterrupted success" left him west of the city, and his men trailed after Blunt's column "until the darkness of night rendered further pursuit impossible." In the aftermath of battle, Shelby's men went into camp near town, gradually joined by Marmaduke's. Dr. J. H. Baker "examined the battle ground" and the town and enjoyed the rations and the cool weather.[27]

They did not spend much time finding casualties, such as the severely wounded and immobilized Kansan left for days "stripped naked" and "ridden over several times by the rebels." The one man Grover's militia had lost in town, William Talbot, had fallen with "a small rifle ball striking him squarely in the center of the forehead, and coming out just above the base of the skull in the back of the head, equi-distant from the ears." Left for dead and untreated, he turned up later, though "partially demented ever afterwards." The laconic Richard J. Hinton quipped that such treatment had been "not such as to materially improve the reputation for chivalry of which they boast so hugely."[28]

Both sides scrambled to define the meaning of the battle. Reflecting the assessments of Curtis and Blunt, Hinton declared the Unionist goals "successfully accomplished," in that the Federals had defined the location and strength of the Confederate forces "for the first time since Price had left Pilot Knob." Conversely, Shelby called it "the first real indication of the immediate presence of a concentrated force in our front, and I knew now there would be heavy work for us all in the future."[29] If so, one wonders what the Confederates expected of their old enemies on the border or how many times the Federals needed to learn such lessons about a force that had been rampaging through Missouri for a month.

Nevertheless, neither side really learned that much about the enemy's numbers. Blunt's force of about 2,000 had faced a similar number of Confederates at the start and perhaps no more than 6,000 to 8,000 actually arrived in time to join the fight, though Federal reports claimed to have faced "the whole of Price's army." Blunt and Moonlight estimated Price's numbers as 20,000; Moonlight claimed they had "outnumbered us more than ten to one, so that they were enabled to flank us, as well as press us in the rear, thereby making our position a warm one and giving us lively work." Lane thought they had faced 25,000, and others gave even larger Confederate numbers, and Price claimed to have met and beaten "between 3,000 and 4,000 Federals."[30]

Given such incorrect estimates of the numbers involved, casualty estimates merit severe skepticism. The actual reports offer the numbers of killed and wounded in the single digits, and one Kansas paper placed the total at twenty, and "a gentleman who participated in the advance of our force under Blunt" told another paper that after two missing companies turned up, Union losses ran "about forty killed, wounded and missing." Perhaps the disconnect between descriptions of the fighting and such numbers moved Curtis to estimate "about 50."[31] These seem minimal as well, and the casualties for the attacking Confederates would have run twice as high.

After Lexington

Blunt's exhausted men moved all night through a chilling rain. Around 2 a.m. on Thursday, October 20, they reached the covered bridge over the Little Blue and passed over onto the bluffs west of the river. They needed rations and rest, but there seemed little prospect of the latter. Blunt sent a courier the eight additional miles to Independence to telegraph Curtis. Convinced that Pleasonton's cavalry could not be far behind, Blunt claimed "a strong natural position for defense on the west side of that stream" and wanted Curtis to send Colonel James H. Ford's Second Colorado forward from Independence. Blunt wanted to hold Price's army on the Little Blue until the Department of Missouri could catch up with them.[32]

Curtis had already sent Captain George West and fifty Coloradoans from Independence to find Blunt. When the column turned up, the general sent Major Thomas I. McKenny with orders in person. "I have no time to explain," wrote Curtis, but they needed "united councils as well as a strong position," and much of the KSM had still balked at going farther into Missouri than the Big Blue. Politics, rather than generalship, selected that line to fortify and provision. By 9 a.m., Blunt had most of his force back at Independence.[33]

Nevertheless, as Curtis suggested, Blunt left Moonlight with a couple of howitzers "and, say, 400 men at the Little Blue." Curtis wanted that rear guard "not to fight a battle, but to delay the rebel approach, and fall back to our main force." Blunt used the vagueness of the order to instruct Moonlight to burn the bridge "and to make such resistance as he could" until Blunt could be notified. Curtis also left a larger number of men, including what they had of the Eleventh Kansas Cavalry and part of the Fifteenth. One story had West's Colorado patrol looking for Blunt but finding Captain Curtis with his men of the Fifteenth, who had cut their way out of Lexington on their own. As they were without orders, these lost cavalrymen stayed with Moonlight.[34]

Meanwhile, General Curtis had pulled the Fourth and Nineteenth KSM back from Independence to the Big Blue, and Ford's Coloradoans closed the road from Independence to Kansas City to allow for the speedy extraction of Blunt's forces. Curtis also sent Captain Absalom Hyde and some of the Sixteenth Kansas Cavalry steaming downriver on the *Tom Morgan* with orders to turn back when it encountered artillery. Captain W. D. McLain brought up his battery of Independent Colorado Artillery to Independence should it be needed. Pressed, Curtis even agreed to let Blunt "feel" the enemy when it turned up on the Little Blue, though the general still did not intend—and actually forbade—bringing on a battle at this point.[35] Standing orders required everyone, when pressed, to fall back to the Big Blue.

In this no-man's-land between the generals, some of the exhausted officers tried to unwind in an Independence hotel. Jennison "and some kindred spirits" played poker in a nervous insomnia, while H. G. (George) Ward occupied a room across the hall and tried to sleep. He recalled that, at one point, Major Smith of the Second Colorado "came to my room and wanted to know if it would disturb me if he did some writing there." The two had spent much of the previous year fighting together in the Indian Territory and in Arkansas, and Ward "felt proud to class him among my personal friends." Ward recognized Smith's depression, so he "joked him and tried to laugh away his blues. I shall never forget the way he looked, nor his manner, as he came and stood over me and asked if I believed in forewarnings of death." Smith could not brush away a feeling that he would not survive the next day's fighting, and Ward remembered that he spent most of the night pacing and writing.[36]

Remarkably, the news from Lexington actually shook Governor Thomas Carney and the conservatives. They had continued to scoff at reports of Smith's earlier scout, and Carney had bypassed the military in Kansas to contact Brigadier Thomas Ewing in the Department of Missouri to ask "whether Price is still in a position to threaten Kansas" and to open channels for Rosecrans "to communicate to him confidentially." Carney complained that Curtis had "the whole arms-bearing population of the State . . . in the field at an enormous public expense and sacrifice of private interests." After Blunt's foray to Lexington, though, even such skeptics in the KSM as George Deitzler realized the scale of the threat. Blair had no problem getting his "brigade of mixed troops" to the Big Blue, and U.S. Senator Samuel Pomeroy arranged the release of KSM General William Henry M. Fishback in return for his cooperation.[37]

Lexington had a different impact in the Department of Missouri. Colonel John F. Philips surely recorded rumors common among its officers that the Army of the Border had failed miserably when he wrote, "Old Pap drove Blunt, with his Kansas Mamelukes, back and gone on by Lexington." Rosecrans's officers in north Missouri even told the *St. Joseph Herald* that "Price whipped Blunt yesterday evening; captured nearly all his artillery."[38]

Rosecrans and Pleasonton later claimed to have known about Lexington only through Curtis in Kansas. Just before these developments, some troops of Pleasonton's men camped only eight miles from Lexington and had scouts that direction, and Blunt sent scouts miles in their direction from the town. Certainly, the detachment Blunt had sent earlier to the EMM at Warrensburg found that Major William C. LeFever of Sanborn's staff had turned up, assuring them that Pleasonton had a large force at Dunksburg about ten miles above Knob Noster, itself only ten miles east of Warrensburg. Too, Pleasonton's horsemen had reached Sedalia only another twenty miles east, and General A. J. Smith's infantry was concentrated another ten miles on, at Otterville.[39] Yet Pleasonton claimed to have missed a major fight only a few miles beyond his advance.

Despite the time-consuming complications, channels of communications existed between Curtis and Rosecrans. "Our forces are in constant communication with Gen. Rosencrans," declared the Kansas City *Journal of Commerce*, "and all are acting in conjunction and harmony." Sharing his hopes to hold Price on the Big Blue, Curtis frankly urged the department troops to "come up in his rear and left." In particular, he hoped Rosecrans would push on to link up with the Army of the Border near Hickman's Mills, and "we will bag Price."[40]

Rosecrans would later claim, alternately, that he had "heard nothing from Curtis" and that they had discussed moving on Lexington. He told Smith that they would move by "a forced march to-morrow," and some of Pleasonton's men started north only hours after Blunt's departure. However, McNeil got no orders to head for Lexington until around 2:00 p.m. on Thursday, and the first of his men only got there seven hours later. Lieutenant Robert M. Meager of the Second Missouri Cavalry caught seven of the hundred or so who lagged behind after the last Confederates left town. Parts of the Fifth MSM Cavalry met two separate groups of rebels on the edge of town. By then, though, the weather had "turned awful cold—raining—like to froze."[41]

The reason for this fourteen-hour delay between the first movement of Pleasonton's horsemen and the orders to move on Lexington had been a fear he and Rosecrans shared: that Price's army might double back on Jefferson City. Rather than drive on Lexington, they gave the Confederates another day's grace by moving instead on Waverly and Dover. At sunrise on Thursday, two squadrons of Colonel John E. Phelps's Arkansas Federals surprised a group they claimed to be 500 or 600 Confederates at Dover, killing or wounding two or three and taking thirteen or fourteen prisoners, mostly stragglers or deserters, four or five of whom were officers. Consistent with this movement against a nonexistent Confederate force said to be backtracking against Jefferson City, Rosecrans advised Curtis to expect only diversionary feints west of Lexington toward Wellington or "at farthest" the few miles to the west at Napoleon.[42]

As Hinton later wrote, "Had it been possible to have, at this time, extended our right by way of Lone Jack, and thus united with Rosecrans' left, throwing the main portion of the Army of the Border, with that of Missouri, on the east and south of Price, leaving sufficient to the west to check him temporarily, it is certain that we should have succeeded in bagging the prey, and bringing him to grief." He added, however, that "the character of the main portion of our force precluded this." Blunt and others thought this the most likely way to capture Price's entire force. "I consider it of the highest importance that we mass our forces on a line south of Price's position, and then it matters little whether he

[Price] moves east or west, we can cut him up." Without Pleasonton and Rose-crans pressing vigorously, Price could "make his retreat through Kansas."[43]

In fact, Rosecrans had never been in a hurry to pursue Price's army. Hinton offered only mild criticism: "An obvious criticism on General Sanborn's move-ments" had been the inexplicable failure to keep his supplies coming forward, though the line ran through secure Federal roads. Brigadier General Egbert B. Brown's men were spending day and night "without forage or food (except a day's rations of hard bread), and, as shown in my report, part of the time fight-ing on foot."[44]

Meanwhile, Rosecrans and Pleasonton had continued to deploy reinforce-ments coming up from Saint Louis and Jefferson City to work on the railroad. On October 21, they finally found a place for General Clinton B. Fisk, who had commanded the defense of Jefferson City, which was "take command of all troops at that point and on the railroad from California to Warrensburg," which meant railroad repair. "The labor performed by troops in the reconstruction of destroyed bridges, the opening up and maintaining lines of communication, the pushing forward with promptness troops and supplies to the army at the front, is too frequently overlooked or forgotten in the recapitulation of services rendered in important campaigns."[45]

For their part, the Confederates never understood this dynamic among their enemies. When a Union prisoner at Glasgow had told Confederate Brigadier General John B. Clark that he would be overtaken by Pleasonton's cavalry, the general thought the suggestion absurd. He joked that the trouble with the Fed-erals had been that they "carried boarding-houses about with them."[46] It was a standard army quip about newcomers coming to war overburdened, but the experienced Union command, weighed down by preoccupations with jurisdic-tions and lines of authority, had hobbled the advance of its forces.

Price's men, though, had troubles of their own. By then, the westbound Confederates had covered the twenty miles from Lexington to Fire Creek Prairie and Wellington, one of them noting that the weather had turned "Cold + misty." One of Price's underfed men noted that he had never even been paid but irregu-larly and that in worthless Confederate money—and he had seen none of that for more than a year before marching back into Missouri. Arkansas Confeder-ates who had missed the battle at Lexington and the rich pickings there reported marching for days on a diet of corn and meat without salt. Colonel Archibald S. Dobbin had to take risks in order to seize and grind flour. General James Fa-gan told Price that "hundreds of my men are without the necessary clothing to be at all comfortable, even in the mildest weather at this season in this climate." He reported his hungry men prone to illness that came with the "vicissitudes of weather—such as catarrh, bronchitis, pneumonia, rheumatic affections, and glandular swellings." The Arkansans remained "much dissatisfied and complain a good deal."[47] Clearly, the military's power of life or death over such men became increasingly essential to the survival of the army as discontent in the ranks smoldered into stories that "Old Pap" had taken to the bottle.

The experience of two of the KSM scouts along the Little Blue supports none of those allegations against Price. George Todd and his men found Samuel Fry and J. H. Glathart separated from their comrades and lost, but Price had clearly issued orders on the subject. "I never took a Kansas man a prisoner in my life," said Todd, "but you shall not be hurt, I will turn you over to Gen. Price." They found Price resting on the ground and noted that he apparently did not know Todd. Price asked about the deployments of Blunt, Lane, and Jennison, but this had been changing so much his prisoners could provide no information. The Confederate commander then asked about numbers, and the scouts bluffed "that when we left we thought they would number 28,000," including about 17,000 militia. Price challenged them, saying that Kansas was "too new a state" to be able to field that many militia, but Fry assured him that, on paper, the KSM had 20,000 men subject to being called up. "Where do you think they will fight me?" asked Price. The two men were not sure but guessed the Federals would stand at Independence and then on the Big Blue, but rumors brought many reinforcements. Price declined to parole them immediately because Rosecrans had told the *Missouri Democrat* that he would not respect the parole of any prisoner unless he had been held at least ten days.[48]

Regardless of his earlier choices, Price had begun to ask all the right questions and to pick the best general options he had left himself available. The countermarch east, which Rosecrans and Pleasonton feared, made no more sense than a right turn into the Missouri River. Price's men faced poor roads and sparse forage to the south and expected a massive Union army in that direction. Price reasonably thought the more rapid-moving horsemen moved "parallel to my line of march," cutting off his retreat south, while the "heavy column of infantry—in all about 30,000 strong" followed behind him. More, that course would take his army back through well-foraged terrain to the homes of his homesick veterans, youthful volunteers, and reluctant conscripts and back toward what he thought to be "a heavy force under Generals A. J. Smith, McNeil, Sanborn, and others," which was following "as fast as the impaired state of the roads would admit."[49] Given the options he thought he faced, Price might well be forgiven for wanting a drink.

5

From the Little Blue to the Big Blue

The Fight for Independence, October 21

Friday, October 21, began the Götterdämmerung that had been shaping up for weeks. The light snowfall of the previous evening had melted away, leaving a "chilly and unpleasant" morning. A succession of Federal officers provided most of the information we have about what took place during the next three days of a mostly moving battle. This leaves much doubt as to Confederate operations, and Union officialdom never resolved the inconsistencies among the reports or firmly associated times with specific events.[1] In part, the impending end of the war rendered completion of the paperwork less important, but there seemed to be an agreement not to challenge conflicting accounts that has smudged much of the fighting to a blur with a few instances of crisp clarity.

By Wednesday and Thursday, there remained little doubt that the Confederates would not backtrack to the east, leap the Missouri River to the north, or head south into the sparse resources of the already well-plundered Ozarks. They rolled west from Lexington and would cross the Little Blue near Independence and continue west until something stopped them, either General Samuel R. Curtis's army to their front or being forced to meet attacks from the south by General Alfred Pleasonton. In the hope of catching the Confederate forces between them, Curtis tried to slow their westward advance. In the end, though, his decision had been to hold the Confederates back along a defensive line established west of Independence, on the Big Blue River.

THE LITTLE BLUE

Colonel Thomas Moonlight's Kansans tried to cover the likely crossings of the Little Blue but lacked the local knowledge of the Missourians they faced. Major Martin Anderson commanded the main body of pickets at the covered bridge, onto which they had pulled a hay wagon. Captains James E. Greer and Joel Huntoon covered other outposts, a ford downstream and another four miles upstream, respectively. The shooting started early in the morning, as Captain David R. Stallard of General John S. Marmaduke's staff directed the advance that drove in the Federal pickets east of the river and began an irresistible press. Anderson's men torched the wagon but saw, to their horror, that Brigadier General John B. Clark's brigade had stormed toward the far side of the bridge. The Kansans hurried off before they could nurse the fire enough to consume the bridge. Along the way, they ran into Greer's men, who had also fallen back "without firing a shot." They likely saw the Confederates saving the bridge, which would serve them well.[2]

The blast of Confederate artillery from a hill east of the river had already startled some of Moonlight's exhausted men. Without a proper meal for several days, soldiers sat down to some hardtack, bacon, and coffee brought up from the rear. They had already begun rolling their flour "into thick dough, rolled on sticks ready to bake before the fire, and our cups of coffee on the coals to boil, when shizz! Went the bullets and rebels were upon us." One Federal sergeant hurried his men into a skirmish line down at the timber as soon as he "saw the smoke rising up from the bridge."[3] In short order, though, Moonlight had his 600 men with four twelve-pounders on a ridge overlooking the river.

The Fourth and Tenth Missouri Cavalry under Lieutenant Colonel William J. Preston and Colonel Robert Lawther spearheaded the advance of Clark's Confederates, but the Kansans hit Lawther's advance before his troops secured their position at a stone wall. By the time Stollard had brought up 150 of Colonel Colton Greene's Third, he found Lawther's men routed and the Kansans well covered. Still, a strong Confederate line formed and T. J. Williams's three-gun battery of Harris's artillery likely rolled over the unburned bridge into position west of the river behind them. Greene subsequently reported driving a superior force back from the field on his own, but the Kansans actually flanked him and sent his men back with those of Lawther. In short order, Lieutenant Colonel Robert C. Wood's Fourteenth Missouri Cavalry Battalion of Jo Shelby's division arrived to stabilize the Confederate right. Colonel Sol G. Kitchen's Seventh Missouri Cavalry also got there early.[4]

Moonlight's men naturally gravitated to the high ground to the left of the road to Independence overlooking the floodplain, a position that also offered the cover of "stone walls, fences, and houses." Their early acquisition of this position accounted for "the few killed and wounded on our side, compared with the enemy, who suffered terribly." The Federals also used their howitzers well, though a secondhand account by one Kansan recalled a Confederate officer who was "finely mounted on an iron gray horse" while taking his men through waist-deep waters to get at one of their howitzers. With his eyes focused on the guns and not even turning to his men, he shouted, "Close up, God damn you." Still, while Moonlight reported that "the object for which I was left [was] accomplished," he and his men could, from their position, see the Confederates using the bridge the Federals had failed to destroy.[5]

Wishful thinking also infused Confederate reports, which focused on selective events and smudged their timing. Sterling Price acknowledged Marmaduke's "critical condition," which required Shelby "to march rapidly to his relief," but his claim that Marmaduke had faced "far superior numbers" was absurd. More troops and artillery arrived over the intact bridge, and Shelby's old brigade under Jeff Thompson arrived, dismounted, and hurried to Clark's left. Thompson claimed that, from this point, they pushed the Federals "from position to position, several of which were very strong and well defended," which conflates a great deal of time. At first, though, the Confederates made little progress against the Federals behind their stone walls and would not until the rebels got enough of their own artillery into place.[6]

The fight wore down Moonlight's troops. "Our boys were hungry, tired and worn out," recalled one of them, "yet they gave the enemy such a reception as they hardly expected." Several officers fell, and the brigade began "a slow retrograde movement, taking advantage of every fence and wall to check the rebel onset by deadly volleys of small arms and rapid canister firing." The last part to be pulled back did so "cheering lustily, and occasionally breaking into the stirring refrain of 'Rally round the flag, boys.'" By 10 a.m., though, they had "held the enemy back for hours," part of them holding their position "without any ammunition, supplying its place with lusty and defiant cheers."[7]

At this point, Generals Blunt and Curtis turned up with "less than 2,000" to join Moonlight against the divisions of Marmaduke and Shelby. Blunt's persistence had persuaded Curtis to reverse his earlier position to mount a more aggressive resistance. They had cobbled together what they could at Independence and hurried east toward the sound of the fighting. The reinforcements arrived just in time. The Third Wisconsin and Fifteenth Kansas from Jennison's brigade hurriedly extended Moonlight's line on the right. Four hundred men of the Second Colorado from Colonel James H. Ford's brigade rushed there as well, while "about 200" of the Sixteenth Kansas Cavalry under Lieutenant Colonel Samuel Walker and Major James Ketner went to Moonlight's left. McLain rolled into position two guns that successfully blasted back a Confederate attempt on the Federal flank, but Curtis had Major Robert Hunt roll them back to a less exposed position. Hunt also got the two howitzers associated with the Fifteenth Kansas Cavalry at a clump of trees "in shelter of a friendly house." Curtis got word to Washington from the field: "I have been fighting Price three hours on the Little Blue with my cavalry. We have a strong position fifteen miles in the rear, where I intend to make a stand."[8]

Curtis later described this, oddly, as "giving permission rather than order-ing" the advance, and Blunt certainly took responsibility for the force that ar-rived. "Dismounting," recalled Dick Hinton, "we advanced immediately into the timber." Other accounts described the "coolness and skill" of Moonlight's conduct, called Jennison "a 'perfect brick,'" and referred to Lieutenant Colonel George H. Hoyt as "the dashing soldier he is." Captain William D. McLain fell wounded as he manhandled the "new rifled pieces" of his Colorado battery. Walker and Ketner of the Sixteenth Kansas were said to have "held the whole Rebel force in check all day." Most of all, they praised Blunt. Senator Jim Lane called him "the bravest of the brave . . . constantly under fire, directing move-ments, and inspiring by his own example his greatly inferior force," and Hinton described him as "the animating spirit of the battle."[9]

In reality, Curtis fully lived up to his old reputation as well. He sent future Kansas senator Edmund Ross to lead Moonlight's reequipped men back to an increasingly untenable Union position and slipped into a new position, near the four howitzers between Ford and Jennison. As the Confederates massed for another attack, the Eleventh began singing "Rally 'Round the Flag, Boys." The Confederates rode into a hornet's nest, and Marmaduke himself lost two horses. However, the numbers proved large enough; Colorado sergeant David Nettleton noted that "their lines were too long and came up around our flanks." Ford also thought the numbers "too overwhelmingly large" to resist, having a particularly "large body to our right, which compelled the right to give slowly back.[10]

Blunt had brought fewer men but more firepower, as he had at Prairie Grove and Honey Springs. "We had Martin-Henry breech loading rifles," recalled Captain George S. Grover, "so that we could fire sixteen shots before reload-ing, while the enemy were armed with Enfield rifles, a long single barreled, un-wieldy muzzle loading gun, wholly unfit for cavalry use." Lane had a Sharp's carbine, but Price's men had a better match with their artillery. At one point, they focused both their own batteries and musketry on Hunt's howitzers and two horses fell at their first volley, as the sergeant in charge, a reputed bully from Leavenworth, fled. Though hit in the head by a shell fragment, Hunt helped Major Edmund Ross of the Eleventh and Percy H. Bloomer of the Fifteenth cut the harness from the dead horses and get their guns to safety.[11]

After George Ward got Moonlight's men to the ammunition train, he saw Major James Nelson Smith where Captain George West had led the Colorado skirmishers forward. Smith looked worried as he passed the Warrensburg men. "Grover," he said to their commander, "I had a strange dream last night, and believe I will be killed today about ten o'clock." As "the heavy battalion of John-nies [were] charging across the bottom towards us," Ward heard Smith order the bugler to sound a recall to West's skirmishers. Abner C. Jones delivered a message from Moonlight, and, as he and Smith began fumbling for a pencil and paper, a large shell spooked Smith's horse, which lurched "into a very exposed position." When Jones joined him, Smith began digging in his pocket for a pencil, and several balls hit him simultaneously, one piercing his left lung. He slumped over onto Jones's shoulder and fell to the ground. As West scrambled back with his skirmishers, Captain Uriah B. Halloway grasped his knee and exclaimed, "My God! there goes poor Smith!" "It was hardly necessary to take the second look," said Ward. "Intuitively I knew that the Major's premonition was not an idle fancy, and there amidst the hurtling bullets and crash of battle, I bade all that was left of him a final adieu." Grover said he checked his watch and noted it to be five minutes after 10 a.m.[12]

At about the same time, Shelby's men made their move. Just as the battle began, a party of new recruits turned up from Carrollton with a reported 600 men ready to fight. For nearly an hour, they had faced "rapid and continuous firing in my front." With artillery support, their dismounted men pressed forward, with Captain George Todd and a cluster of guerrillas at the fore. The Coloradoans, who knew Todd well, noted that he had three times led an attempt to flank the Federals and failed. At this point, though, Lieutenant Colonel Charles H. Nichols's mounted regiment charged the Federals' left.[13] What followed were the first steps of an embattled seven-mile Union retreat.

The Federal Withdrawal

The Confederate onslaught rolled the Federal line back half a mile west of the stone walls. McLain's battery to the left of the road checked the Confederate advance, and Blunt threw the Eleventh and Fifteenth Kansas with the Second Colorado into a countercharge. Wood's cavalry battalion inflicted severe casualties on the countercharge but ran low on ammunition and gave way, until Kitchen's Seventh Missouri and J. F. Davies's battalion arrived to stem the tide of the retreat. The Federals kept the Confederates at "a respectful distance" at a cost. Some officers lost horse after horse. The Union plan involved holding a position until "compelled to retreat, but fighting every inch." "Inch by inch, was the entire road to Independence, (a distance of 7 miles,) sternly and bravely contested by our little force, protecting the rear, and holding the impetuous enemy in check, allowing a safe, and perfectly orderly retreat of our entire force."[14]

Blunt rallied his forces at a still stronger position about two miles from the Little Blue on an elevation near a farm that one participant described as "the Massey house." The land dropped sharply down toward the river and had a particularly heavy stone wall there. Under heavy Confederate fire, Pond "rode thru the gap in the wall and along by the side of the wall putting his hand on it, in order to induce his men to come on down the slope and take the position, and this they soon did." His detachment of the Third Wisconsin dutifully came forward. The Sixteenth Kansas and Second Colorado joined them, but Thompson's brigade pressed forward and once more began to flank the Federals. Todd was once more mentioned prominently. At a certain point, Blunt sent the Eleventh Kansas back to establish another position, and the entire Federal force gained enough space to fall back. The Second Colorado Cavalry and Sixteenth Kansas, "assisted by a portion of the Eleventh Kansas Cavalry," covered the retreat. Ford wrote that he formed "half of my command in line across the road on some favorable spot, and while that was engaging the enemy formed the remainder of the force in a similar manner in their rear, and when the first line became too hotly engaged marched it back by companies to the rear of the second line."[15] The Coloradoans provided the cover the Federals needed to successfully slip back through Independence.

Such continued movement—and so many officers running about giving orders—posed considerable problems. At times, General Curtis himself moved his artillery and gave more orders that naturally found his officers at cross-purposes, as when a young staff officer ordered Grover's Missouri militia to fall back to the rear of a battery. When they did so, Jennison protested that they had abandoned the guns and needed to go back. Subsequent praise from Moonlight, Blunt, and Curtis for his quick action left Grover no less frustrated. As always, the weight of the confusion fell to the enlisted men. A spent ball hit William A. Timbocher of the Eleventh Kansas above his right eye and knocked him unconscious just as his regiment retreated. When he recovered and caught up with his company an hour later, his surprised captain exclaimed, "The dead is alive!"[16]

About halfway back to Independence—or about four miles from the Little Blue—Curtis or his bodyguard picked another position, and the general himself hurried back to his main line. When the Federals saw Confederates congregating in the shelter of a house about 600 yards away, howitzers "dropped several shells in their midst." Prisoners later confirmed that two crashed through the roof and exploded in the house. Colonel Walker of the Sixteenth covered the withdrawal of the guns.[17] The Confederates seemed to have been disorganized enough to give the Federals some time.

One of the Kansans, Benjamin F. Simpson of the Fifteenth, rode back to what he described as the Saunders's house, where he met a friend, Major Preston B. Plumb, along with Ford, Moonlight, Blunt, and other officers who were wrestling "to decipher a dispatch or order which had just been received from General Curtis." Exhausted, Simpson collapsed as did some of the other officers. Before they could steal much of a nap, though, scouts arrived with the news that Shelby's men had re-formed and were on the way.[18]

The Federals fell back another mile or so toward Independence before getting another dispatch from Curtis warning that the Confederates could cut off their line of retreat. "Don't exhaust our troops," he told Blunt, "but fall back to this place with the least further effort. . . . Let Price have Independence. It is easily flanked, and his force, it is said, large." The column stopped, and Simpson fell asleep until Blunt woke him an hour later. Still hoping to persuade Curtis to fight at Independence, Blunt intended to send Simpson to report in person, but Lane suggested that Curtis "stood much on military etiquette and would be apt to resent the sending of so young a man as Simpson." Blunt suggested that Lane himself go make the case to the general.[19]

The Union line re-formed about two miles east of Independence. Simpson had scouted the site where the road seemed to run between two elevations; that to the south was timbered. They parked McLain's battery on the other side, covering the open ground to the right of the road, though the Confederates steadily pushed the Federals east through the timber, until Blunt directed the Colorado guns to open on the woods "with canister and case shot." When the Confederate musketry slackened, the Federals countercharged through the woods, the Eleventh finding and using another of those ubiquitous stone walls, until Walker's Sixteenth arrived to cover their withdrawal and that of the artillery. By 3 p.m., though, this position, too, had become entirely untenable, and Blunt decided to use the brief respite of Confederate disorganization to move into a final rearguard position at the town.[20]

Throughout the day, the citizens of Independence received the wounded. Help also came from "a considerable number of the rebel ladies who resided in the place" but showed up at Major Samuel B. Davis's Federal field hospital. When they got word to evacuate the town, Davis gathered all the wounded who could ride or walk at his field hospital in Independence. When James P. Erickson, the surgeon of the Sixteenth Kansas, remained with "thirty-one of the wounded," Davis "sent an ambulance, and got from the commissary stores, which had been ordered to be destroyed, sufficient subsistence for those in hospital for several days. I also left a good supply of medical and hospital stores."[21]

At some point, Simpson hurried back to destroy the remaining army supplies. He had a score of men from the Fifteenth, though "two or three more joined" along the way, as did Lieutenant William V. Phillips of the Eleventh. As they reached the barn, someone began taking potshots at them from the doors and windows of the town. Whether Confederate sympathizers or Unionists fearful of blue-clad guerrillas or simply residents who wanted to keep the supplies for their own use, they kept the saboteurs from using the street. Once inside the barn, the men kicked over the flour and broke barrels of vinegar over them. They also "knocked in heads of molasses barrels to have molasses run over bacon." As the detail finished and headed on toward the Big Blue, they saw some men at the bridge and "captured three citizens, who said they were returning from Independence to their homes."[22]

As the main body of the Federal force scurried back through town, they heard that, two days before, General Phillip Sheridan's army had beaten General Jubal Early's Confederates at Cedar Creek in Virginia's Shenandoah Valley. Anyone who had followed the war realized that this would permit the war effort in the region to focus on extending and strengthening the Union stranglehold on Richmond and Petersburg. Curtis had announced the news from the saddle in the town square of Independence and sent notice to his officers. Meanwhile, the Sixteenth Kansas protected the last of the Union troops slipping through Independence, though a secessionist townswoman shot a lieutenant of the Second Colorado, which had come up in support. Colonel Levi S. Treat, a fifty-year-old Connecticut Yankee commanding the Twelfth KSM and the local EMM left town reluctantly. The resupplied Eleventh Kansas covered its retreat through the streets to the railroad bridge on the east.[23]

The Confederates sought to overwhelm the very last of the Federals who were pulling back from the town square. George Todd led the charge, then "placed the reins in his teeth, firing his revolvers over his shoulders until a Union bullet struck his throat." Later tales reported that he and Major Smith had killed each other, but Smith had already died. Grover saw three shots from the Fifteenth Kansas almost simultaneously from the barrels of Lieutenant Colonel Hoyt of the Fifteenth, Sergeant William R. Caldwell, and "a private soldier of that regiment." Grover thought the last most likely because it "seemed, to me that his was the first shot, though the two others followed in quick succession, and Todd fell headlong from his horse, at the first fire."[24]

At Little Blue and Independence, Missourians and Kansans fought side by side for the survival of the Union. The latter shouted "Remember Lawrence!" while the battle cry of the former, "Remember Lexington!" seemed appropriate for those, some of whom had fought there in 1861 as well as two days before. Former sergeant Frank Gould of the Second Colorado had decided to stay in Missouri after he had served his time and found himself an officer of the EMM at Kansas City. Opting to go back into battle with his old comrades, he continued to cheer them on, as he bled out after a shell "almost literally tore his shoulder away." One of the wounded Warrensburg men shouted, "Hurrah for old Johnson!" to his comrades, as they carted him back.[25]

The fighting sputtered into the night, particularly around the railroad bridge east of town. Thompson boasted that Shelby's men pushed the Federals "until nearly night, and entered the town in line of battle just at dark, having fought dismounted for seven miles." "A skirmish was kept up in the streets of Independence and as far as the railroad bridge," reported Moonlight, "when the enemy abandoned the pursuit; it was then dark."[26]

As the Federals fell back, the Confederates followed. The divisions of Shelby and Marmaduke remained at the front, the latter camping on Rock Creek, two miles west of Independence. As of 10 p.m., the Federals had pickets "within two miles and a half of Independence, and within sight of the enemy, as seen on the following morning." "The enemy's camp-fires show at the present time for a distance of six miles," wrote Jennison.[27]

The shooting had continued from sunup to past sunset, but Hinton estimated the battle lasted about eight hours. Moonlight's force of 600 had held back the Confederates for "the first three," while 3,000 Federals spent the next five hours battling "over six miles of ground, against an enemy increasing in numbers, until the three divisions of Price's army were developed, thus outnumbering us ten to one." Sergeant Francis Gordon thought the Federals had 4,000 men against 30,000 for Price. Simpson believed their force "did not exceed 4000 men and perhaps not 2500." He thought it disheartening not to have brought the forces at Kansas City into action at Independence, but Hinton believed they had held back the Confederates until Pleasonton's forces had gotten "within striking distance."[28]

The losses for the Federals, who usually got to pick the ground on which they would fight, could have been far worse. Blunt estimated them at "about two hundred," with half among Moonlight's men and about sixty from Ford's brigade. However, another estimate said a single regiment of the latter, the Second Colorado, lost "about 100 killed wounded and missing—probably not more than 15 or 20 killed." With some losses in the other brigades and the presence of militia units, which Blunt did not include, the Federal casualties may well have run as high as 300 men that day.[29] Given the scale of the forces, the engagements on the Little Blue came close to decimating the very core of his army, which Curtis had hoped not to exhaust.

The attacking Confederates would have lost more. A Federal prisoner in Price's camp reported that "our forces killed about 300 men, among them Capt. Todd." Hinton heard that, with the wounded, the number reached "not less than five hundred." Price's army had been hemorrhaging men across the state, but those who had intentionally gone missing during Friday's fighting would have been minimal. "That night," reported one Union prisoner, "the rebels seemed low-spirited." Yet, by all accounts, Price's men prepared to push their way through to Kansas City Sunday "and dine in Leavenworth the next day."[30]

Barring an immediate retreat to the south, Price's army had only one viable option. While Marmaduke protected the immense supply train against the threat of capture by Pleasonton, the divisions of Shelby and James Fagan would assault Curtis's formidable line on the Big Blue. The fords tended to be deep and muddy. The Federals felled trees across the roads on either side, which would have delayed any attackers until they could bring axe men forward to clear the way for the artillery and the supply wagons.[31]

In response to those expectations, Curtis established his headquarters at the Little Blue "on the main road leading from Independence to Kansas City." Reports that the Confederates hoped to reach and seize the riches of Kansas City had been so universal that the Federals almost surely believed that to be the case. One officer from that community "brought an ambulance to take wife and son back South," and the Confederate ranks still "expected to winter in Kansas City."[32] Curtis positioned his men accordingly.

The Line on the Big Blue

During the night, Curtis moved his volunteer units into positions to reinforce the KSM, but many who had been "without subsistence for several days" found that their supply trains remained back in Kansas City. Moreover, Curtis's chosen line ran more or less continuously, according to danger from the Missouri River, to the crossing of the Blue, near Hickman's Mills, a distance of fifteen or sixteen miles. He did not expect to hold a concentrated drive by Price's army, "but to engage it till Pleasonton's [sic] forces should attack in the rear."[33] Still, Curtis would find himself spread thinly, having nothing like the numbers he had expected.

Later accounts ascribed 15,000 men or more to the Army of the Border, but the full mobilization of the KSM had not yet taken up arms, much less positions, along the river. By this time, Governor Thomas Carney of Kansas had fully realized the threat to his state. "The enemy are reported to be close at hand and advancing. The danger is imminent. The militia of Kansas will have to stand the brunt of Price's whole army." "Not a man can be spared from military duty, and not a moment should be lost in this crisis. Rally, one and all! Your brethren in arms, your Governor, your General appeal to you."[34]

When it really mattered, the record of the KSM proved complicated. A member of the Twenty-First KSM wrote the *Kansas City Times* that "the boys are all anxious to have a conflict with old Price and his hordes of devils that are infesting Missouri; destroying property and carrying off what he can, to feed the miserable cannibals that infest the caves and mountains of Arkansas and Texas." However, the Jefferson County regiment of the KSM started from Olathe with 480 men and arrived in Kansas City with only 90. "A good many of their officers finding they could not induce the men to move forward, threw away their swords, and taking up muskets in their stead, bravely joined the ranks, and with the heroic little band, followed their gallant leader, to meet the foe." The Twenty-Third KSM also brought depleted numbers into action.[35]

Price, who always exaggerated the numbers he thought he faced, believed the Federals had "between 6,000 and 8,000 men" holding "a position strong by nature and strengthened by fortifications, upon which all their art had been exhausted." Most likely, the Army of the Border had about 5,000 men, a large portion of whom had just been through the previous day's decimation, and the entire army could only have been spread thinly. Worse, once he got south of the road from Independence to Kansas City, Curtis had the numbers to allow for only small concentrations, leaving even key fords "not strongly guarded, only a small force being stationed at that point."[36] The persistent problems with the KSM also left the chain of command remarkably confused.

Within these limits, Curtis made his assignments. He "assigned General Blunt to the command of the right wing, including all south of the road, and to General Deitzler the left wing, which includes all north of it." In fact, though, the organization and chain of command had remained much more muddled and mixed than this implies. Most of what Curtis later described as Deitzler's militia actually served under Charles W. Blair, who functioned more as brigade commander under Blunt.[37]

Curtis's defenses relied on the thick woods, steep banks, and muddy bottom of the Big Blue to prevent any attempted crossing where no road forded the stream. Curtis rightly doubted the Confederates would make a serious attempt to ford nearest the city, where the Big Blue entered the Missouri River, making for the deepest and least forgiving of the fording points. Here a small steamboat and about 250 of Colonel A. C. Hogan's recently arrived Nineteenth KSM, anchoring the Union left, covered the ford farthest downstream to the north. The main body of Hogan's regiment held a position three miles upstream.[38]

The considerable, if apparently uncounted, Kansas Colored Militia spanned the line to the fords farther upstream. Captains James L. Rafferty and Richard J. Hinton (Hinton was both a journalist and a Union Army officer) brought what little cohesion the barely organized force enjoyed.[39] Still farther upriver was Colonel James Montgomery's Sixth KSM; thorough accounts also mention small detachments of the Second and Fourteenth Kansas Cavalry.[40]

Curtis had a dozen pieces of artillery placed in nests cut out expressly to give them a good field of fire at the main roads to the west. Half of these weapons belonged to Captain James H. Dodge's Ninth Wisconsin Light Artillery and the other half to Captain H. Ford Douglas's Independent Colored Battery. Blair, commanding the Third Brigade, also executed much of the preparations here, felling trees to obstruct fordable places in the stream.[41]

Along the next two miles south, to their right were Colonel G. A. Colton, Fifth KSM, and Lieutenant Colonel George Eaves's Twenty-fourth KSM, also called the "Bourbon County battalion." As Blunt's forces crossed the Big Blue, he sent Simpson to organize that part of the Jefferson County KSM that had not begun disintegrating at Olathe. However, when Simpson and his squad found "a good supper spread on the top of a box for Colonel G. A. Colton," they started to eat it, and made "considerable inroad on it" before the colonel returned.[42] Everybody needed food as well as ammunition, including the two guns at the next ford, under Lieutenant Daniel C. Knowles's Second Kansas State Artillery, which was supported by Colonel William Pennock's Tenth KSM.

The road running west from Independence toward Westport and Little Santa Fe crossed at Byram's Ford. At the flank of Blair's militia brigade, Colonel W. D. McCain's Fourth KSM covered the site, regarded as naturally defensible. Attackers from the east would have to descend across a relatively open area, wade breast-deep waters, negotiate the felled trees, and then face a steep and increasingly muddied western bank into three hundred yards of level bottomland dominated by a high hill.[43]

Blunt's brigades under Jennison, Moonlight, and Ford held the shallower, more vulnerable, stretches of the river to the south, but they were liberally supplemented by a sprinkling of KSM, some under the episodically uncooperative Deitzler. From these, squadrons of the Second Colorado Cavalry patrolled, probing, east of the river. About two miles upstream from Byram's, Colonel Moonlight covered Hinkle's Ford, or Simmons' Ford. Ford had McLain's battery on the right of Moonlight's brigade at the brow of the bluff immediately west of the Blue. The Second Colorado Cavalry and Twelfth Kansas State Militia were formed in line on the left of the Second Brigade, with the exception of six companies Second Colorado Cavalry, "which I was ordered to take across the Blue as skirmishers." This battalion remained skirmishing with the enemy until late in the afternoon, taking some prisoners, and did not report back to the brigade until the next morning.[44]

Colonel George W. Veale provided about 500 men, mostly the Second KSM at the Moccabee farm, which overlooked the rock-bottomed Russell Ford. Sergeant P. I. Bonebrake recalled being there with "lawyers, doctors, preachers, farmers, and others, some of who had never fired a gun." They spread out along a lane with a fence "eight or ten rails high, staked and rendered and in good repair," where the road sloped southeast to the Big Blue. Dropping these large numbers of men with minimal rations caused problems even before the battle. Mrs. Moccabee complained of missing chickens, and the men broke into a nearby storage bin "and soon re-appeared with their pockets and haversacks filled with apples. A line was formed, and I doubt if a single apple was left for 'Old Pap Price' on the morrow."[45]

Samuel J. Reader reported these men freely shared their premonitions of death. One "earnestly repeated his conviction, that he would be killed." Another reported a prophetic dream of his own death two nights before. "We are going to get in a fight today, sure!" said a Missouri refugee among them, because he had "dreamed it all out, three different times. We're going to have a battle, and I'll be killed!" He added impressively, "My dreams never fail me."[46]

Finally, far to the right, Brigadier General Melvin S. Grant had several hundred members of the Second and Twenty-first KSM above Indian Creek at Hickman's Mills, including one brass howitzer under Captain James T. Burnes of the Second. On Friday night, a reported force of several hundred Confederates surprised a company of EMM near Hickman's Mills.[47] The farther south one went, the less the line looked like any defensive position at all.

Behind them, in Kansas City and Westport, Colonel Kersey Coates's EMM manned the fallback position in the works before that town, though he had a few guards posted at Westport and other points. Major Davis had organized a hospital there in preparation, and Senator Pomeroy and others worked diligently to bring up more KSM as they became available, positioning "one company of Delaware Indians that I found in camp near to Pratt's Mission, numbering 140 men." Captain Gustavus Zesch got an available force of mounted militia from Kansas City to Westport, and a small part of the Fifth Kansas Cavalry under a Captain Young—probably Lieutenant John F. Young, who left the regiment a few days before—waited on the state line to watch the guerrillas. The Leavenworth Battery was designated as part of this force, but as stated elsewhere it abandoned the field and returned home.[48]

That night, Mountain Charley Hatfield volunteered to infiltrate Price's camp in "female disguise." Colorado Captain George West remembered Charley as an unfortunate woman drawn into the territories by the prospect of a marriage that never happened. Donning male garb for self-protection, she became a determined fighter "always armed with a revolver or two in her belt and a long sheath-knife in her boot-leg, she seemed perfectly able to protect herself in any emergency." Sometime after enlisting in the army, she became a clerk at the headquarters of Curtis, and, with Shelby's brigade on the bluff over the Big Blue, she donned the dress of a farm girl and crossed downstream from the main ford, avoided pickets, and prepared to play the lost farm girl. Captain Arthur McCoy of Shelby's staff found a sobbing white woman trapped between the lines and took her to headquarters. She did allegedly retrieve some information before getting back to Big Blue, floating downstream, and emerging on the western bank chilled to the bone.[49]

General William S. Rosecrans later complained that he "heard nothing from Curtis." However, Curtis had telegraphed Rosecrans that he remained "confident I can stop Price at this crossing, and hope you will come up in his rear and left. He cannot get out by Hickman Mills. If you can get that position we will bag Price, if I succeed, as I hope to do." Rosecrans marched his infantry to Independence rather than Hickman's Mills, a movement that ensured that Price would not be able to turn on Rosecrans but also left an opening for Price to the south that he should not have had. Rosecrans acknowledged the communiqué in passing its contents to General Alfred Pleasonton with orders to "make your dispositions accordingly. . . . If Curtis is in good position of course Price will do nothing but demonstrate in his front and move south, and your cavalry movements should be made with that in view."[50]

In short, Curtis had positioned his men based on the expectation that Rosecrans was about to bring the wrath of the Department of Missouri down on Price's army. Curtis thought Pleasonton's mounted force waited poised to engage the Confederates so closely as to deprive them of much maneuvering room. He was expecting the attack on Kansas City and might not have extended his long thin line of KSM down to Hickman's Mills were it not for the belief that part of Rosecrans's column was moving directly on that hamlet to cut off Confederate retreat to the south.

All this was too little too late. Rosecrans had already moved—or allowed Pleasonton to move—the cavalry north to the Missouri River as well. The previous day, rather than press the Confederates, it had actually swept back east before moving into Lexington, where it had arrived only in the morning. Pleasonton sent Brigadier General John McNeil's brigade to attack Price's rear guard at Wellington while complaining that Price's westbound army had been "pushing Curtis before them" and mentioning that he had hanged three Confederates "captured in our uniform . . . firing on our troops." Rosecrans later claimed that, as the Union cavalry reached Fire Creek Prairie, he had thought McNeil would follow the Confederate rear, while Pleasonton "with the other three brigades" would veer south toward Hickman's Mills. When Pleasonton responded that he had moved "too far advanced on the Independence road" to backtrack, Rosecrans dropped the matter. Meanwhile, rumors swept through the Kansas City area that Brigadier General Egbert Brown's brigade of Pleasonton's division had already linked up with outposts of the Army of the Border at Hickman's Mills."[51]

Pleasonton, meanwhile, suggested that he had thought General Andrew J. Smith's footsore infantry had been earmarked to march to Hickman's Mills. That is, he claimed to have believed that the infantry, moving up from his rear, would bypass his cavalry and move more quickly to close off Price's line of retreat to the south. "I left a staff officer to communicate with you," he told Smith, "and supposed you would use your own discretion as to following farther than Lexington without General Rosecrans directed it, as the enemy was so far in advance." Having passed the buck, Pleasonton continued, saying that Price's army would most likely turn south, and "I cannot see how you can overtake the enemy with the start he has."[52]

So it was that the much-discussed trap for Price's army never quite materialized.

6

The Big Blue and the Reprise

From Independence to the Kansas Line, October 22

Politics had created and shaped General Samuel R. Curtis's Army of the Border, and his large entourage reflected the nature of the coalition he had built for the defense of Kansas. Governor Thomas Carney and U.S. Senators Jim Lane and Samuel C. Pomeroy rode with the headquarters staff. Colonel William Cloud, and Colonel Samuel J. Crawford—then also running for governor of Kansas—attended the general as did John Ritchie of the Second Indian Home Guard and Lieutenant Colonel John J. Sears of the Eighteenth U.S. Colored Troops (USCT). Curtis relied particularly heavily on Majors Chapman S. Charlot, Thomas I. McKenny, Theodore J. Weed, and the general's own son, Samuel S. Curtis, along with Captain Dick Hinton and Lieutenant Cyrus M. Roberts of the Seventy-eighth Ohio. Volunteer aides included the surgeon Samuel B. Davis, and others attended the headquarters staff until there would be wounded to handle.[1] Most of what was written about the events that transpired over this weekend came from the pens of these Federal officers.

First light found General James G. Blunt checking on the Union positions along the Big Blue, which he correctly feared they simply could not hold. As the fighting began and raged along that line, the troops of the Federal Department of Missouri to the east engaged the Confederates, who faced serious fighting on two fronts for the first time. The success of the Confederates in pushing toward Westport obscured their failure to extricate themselves from their unenviable position between hammer and anvil.

Byram's Ford, the Big Blue, and Beyond

Saturday dawned with "a scarcely perceptible breeze from the west; the sky was cloudless, and the air just cold enough to make overcoats comfortable." The morning brought a "clear, still and frosty" day with muskets popping along the line of the Big Blue. Captain Edwin I. Meeker of the Signal Corps had observers to the far right and left, and Lieutenant Colonel Sears of the Eighteenth USCT dispatched couriers to Blunt on the right and Brigadier General Melvin S. Grant on the far right at Hickman's Mills. Some Confederates had already ambushed the first courier to Grant's far-flung position, slaughtering all but one of his escort of twenty-one. Elsewhere, the Federals captured some of Price's men who had strayed through a line stretched to invisibility in places.[2]

Shortly after 8 a.m., Jo Shelby's skirmishers drove in the Union pickets from east of the river. General George Deitzler, commander of the KSM, reported "demonstrations at several points in front of my position." During the next hour, couriers galloped along the line, urging subordinates to remain vigilant, keep scouting east of the river where possible, and check in with Curtis every thirty minutes. Fretting over the tenuous connection he had to Grant's distant position at Hickman's Mills, Curtis moved his field headquarters near the intersections of roads leading that way. About 9 a.m., small bodies of mounted men approached the ford near the main road to Kansas City, on the far left of the line, but these seem to have been feints to cover more serious troop movements.[3]

Between 9 and 10 a.m., the major Confederate effort centered on Byram's Ford, and Blunt moved his base of operations in that direction. Colonel Charles R. Jennison held them at bay, but Blunt, brushing aside earlier issues about his authority over the KSM, tried to diplomatically nudge militia that direction. While Charles W. Blair complied, Deitzler ignored him. Gradually, though, Shelby's men crossing upstream and downstream from Byram's threatened the Federal flanks, forcing the Union to fall back "to a good position on the prairie," where Colonel Thomas Moonlight arrived with his brigade to stop and reverse the Confederate gains, at least temporarily. They forced them "from the field, with the loss of about 200, our loss being only inconsiderable, not exceeding 15 wounded, all being brought off and cared for." Jennison thought the fight "a handsome one" that left his men "elated and in high spirits" but low on ammunition.[4]

Around 11 a.m., Jennison needed the reinforcements from the Fifteenth Kansas Cavalry and its howitzers under Second Lieutenant Henry L. Barker. Below them, Confederate General Jeff Thompson sent waves of Confederates across the river, only to be driven back. With the fate of the army at stake, however, they patiently scurried from tree to tree, individually and in small groups, into ever better positions. By noon, Jennison needed Major Samuel Walker's Sixteenth Kansas Cavalry, and the EMM likely contributed the "independent company from Independence." At about this time, Major McKenny asked Deitzler why he had not sent reinforcements and was told that Blunt had already sent the Fifteenth and Sixteenth Kansas, "besides 150 infantry, also some odd troops, with four guns."[5]

By 1:30 p.m., Shelby's men had found several makeshift fords to use upstream. At one of these, he issued orders that were particularly aggressive, even for him. "Move forward immediately, Colonel," he told Sidney D. Jackman, "and attack anything and everything before you wearing a blue coat." Jeff Thompson had similar orders and, once he had "lodgment upon the west bank," more and more of his men followed. When Colonel B. Frank Gordon's regiment got over the Big Blue to the side of the ford, the flanked Federals once more fell back to the bluffs. This time, though, the rest of Shelby's division had been poised to pour across. As it did so, Jackman's brigade moved forward, to the left of Thompson's brigade. "Many unarmed soldiers were rushed into battle," wrote a Confederate doctor. "Bad management from some source."[6]

Observers probably recorded different times for the Confederate breakthrough at Byram's Ford because it happened in stages. Curtis thought the breakthrough came at 2 p.m. and Jennison about 3 p.m. Between 2 and 3 p.m., though, the Confederates had "succeeded in crossing considerable bodies, both above and below" the ford, accumulating the numbers and momentum to push Jennison and Moonlight back from the river. By 3 p.m., Colonel James H. Ford with a portion of his regiment and the Twelfth KSM arrived to reinforce Jennison. On their way to Hickman's Mills, Major McKenny and Lieutenant Roberts rode right into the chaos as Jennison tried "slowly falling back" before a wave of Confederates crossing the Big Blue and a particularly "large body of men on his right flank." Grover's Missourians arrived after having been "under fire on the hill near Raytown road" until Blunt sent for them. Wrote Grover, "We got there in time for the last round," just as the breakthrough came, and their repeaters helped to cover the retreat.[7]

At this point, the Confederates had Jennison's troops backed up to the ridgeline overlooking the river. Indeed, as one end of his line backed up, it had to scramble around a rocky ledge, creating a gap that exposed Moonlight's flank. When the Confederates struck that point, though, two Union companies wheeled and blasted several volleys to drive them off, but the line could not be restored without falling back toward Westport, its right covered by Lieutenant Colonel G. M. Woodward and part of the KSM. Later, Blunt told Moonlight to "pass around the right flank of the enemy and keep in between him and Kansas." Somewhat unfairly, a Colorado soldier reported the KSM's "having ingloriously *fallen back* beyond the Kaw river, crossing at Wyandotte."[8]

By this time, Curtis and Blunt ordered everybody to fall back. In this case, Deitzler complied with Blunt's order, perhaps because Curtis sent him a similar order. The KSM general "quietly withdrew [his] command in perfect order," as did Brigadier General William H. M. Fishback with the Fifth, Sixth, and Tenth

KSM. Ford got his Coloradoans onto the bluffs and away from danger as well, though Blair's KSM downstream got no clear orders to withdraw until around 4 p.m.[9]

In that part of the field—downstream near the Missouri—other Confederates rushed the KSM as it sought to withdraw. Colonel Hogan's Nineteenth KSM reported that a number of Sterling Price's men, who were "concealed in the brush to his front," waded across the "creek, [and] pushed through and over the abatis of fallen trees clear up to Hogan's line." Wrote Blair, "After a short, sharp little skirmish, some twenty of them were taken prisoners and the rest driven off." Deitzler claimed he had ten prisoners and left a dozen Confederates dead.[10]

Grant's KSM at Hickman's Mill faced a real disaster. Curtis sent one of those understated warnings superiors sometimes send their subordinates: "A column of the enemy has been seen passing up the Blue on the opposite side, perhaps designing to cross below you. . . . Look well to all sides of you." By this point, the garrison at Hickman's Mill realized that General William S. Rosecrans's men would not come in from the east to reinforce them, and Grant began cautiously falling back.[11]

Colonel George W. Veale, a former resident of Quindaro, had to cover this withdrawal by holding his Second KSM at Russell Ford. When they heard the gunfire to the north from Byram's ford, one of them laughed nervously and quipped, "Boys, I'd rather hear the baby cry!" Another, a veteran from Missouri, warned them to watch the muzzle of any enemy cannon. "If you see a blue streak, keep your place, for you are in no danger from that shot," he said. "But if you see no blue streak, then you get out of that mighty quick, for the cannon-ball is coming straight at you."[12]

Veale realized the vulnerability of Captain Ross Burnes's little squad, which was wrestling its brass twenty-four-pound howitzer and got 250 to 300 members of the KSM into place to support the piece. Shelby's nephew, apparently mistaking Veale for a blue-clad Confederate officer, rode forward and became a prisoner. Only 300 yards to the front of Burnes's squad and the KSM men—just beyond the reach of the canister and shells of their howitzer—a strong Confederate line formed quickly and "without hindrance." Because of a "generous sprinkling of the blue army overcoats among them," the Kansans waved their flag, in response to which "a shower of bullets came / whizzing about our ears like a swarm of angry hornets." For forty minutes, the militia held its own under heavy fire and its canister cut down the Confederate color-bearer, leaving the flag on the field as the rebels retreated. Samuel J. Reader concluded that the Federals "had whipped them, and that they were seeking safety by a hasty retreat." Meanwhile, Grant's garrison passed behind them, expecting Colonel

Sandy Lowe's Twenty-first KSM to strengthen Veale's position. Over on the Confederate line, Shelby turned to his brigade commander. "Jackman," Shelby asked about the howitzer, "do you hear that gun? I'm tired of its damned noise. Go over there and take it!"[13]

After a lull, Reader heard "the quavering notes of a bugle call from over the prairie, directly in our front. But we could see nothing." Then, from a depression beyond "a swell on the prairie" 250 yards to their front, Confederate Major George W. Nichols and Lieutenant Colonel John A. Schnable led "a long line of horsemen" that rose into view, as they broke into a trot and then a gallop, raising "a wild yell . . . that resembled a scream, rather than a cheer." Yowling "the Rebel Yell," they crashed down on the Kansans "like an approaching tornado." Reader recalled that a comrade called the charge "one of the grandest sights he had ever seen. No doubt it was a magnificent spectacle, but I suffered the disadvantage of being on the wrong side, to thoroughly enjoy it." With the line broken, Reader looked around and tried to break for cover, but "everything seemed a chaotic mass of confusion and uproar." He had long thought Andersonville would be a worse fate than death, but, when the moment came, Reader found himself "in no mood for martyrdom" and surrendered.[14]

"The fiercest part of the enemy's charge was centered on the battery consisting of about thirty men," recalled Sergeant P. I. Bonebrake. Jackman's men overran the battery, which surrendered, but the Confederates shot down twenty-four of them. They cut the throat of the black teamster Ben Hughes and apparently also murdered Moses Banks, a black man from Indianola.[15]

Behind them, Lowe's Twenty-First KSM came up, and Lieutenant Roberts encountered Major John M. Laing's detachment of the Fifteenth Kansas Volunteer Cavalry. He sent the militia forward to slow the Confederate sweep, expecting Laing to follow. As he reached "the brink of the hill descending to the Big Blue we saw right ahead of us, as far as the eye could reach, clouds of dust along the road, and knew it must be the main column of the enemy advancing." They drove off the first small group that approached them "but in a few minutes came forward with a yell." The militia unleashed a volley and fell back to where Laing's cavalry had been, only to find it had turned back toward Kansas, leaving Roberts and the militia officers drawing their revolvers to keep the KSM in line. After less than half an hour, a short breather came, and they remounted and hurried off. They got about a mile before being overrun.[16]

The responsibility fell heavily on Laing. Roberts blamed the disappearance of his cavalry for "destroying the courage" of the militia. Apparently, Laing's officers and men "did not wish to turn back, but were eager to assist and thought it very strange that he did not help the militia." Grant, too, charged Laing "for the most of my loss," and Curtis ordered Laing's arrest until "upon explanations, and in consideration of his gallantry elsewhere, I directed his release." Yet such seemingly futile gestures by the KSM permitted Grant and most of his force to make good their escape to Olathe.[17]

Later testimonies from survivors of the Second KSM contributed much to the atrocity stories of the day. The Confederates captured a doctor, stripped him, and shot him twice. "He would have been killed but for the interference of an officer." After the battle, people recalled the corpses of the men left on the field. A memorable body, shot in the head, had "the most startling appearance," his eyes "wide open, and turned upward in their sockets until nothing but a narrow portion of the iris was visible." Many had been "shot down in cold blood after surrender." The blacks in particular had been butchered.[18]

THE LITTLE BLUE AND INDEPENDENCE

Around 5 a.m., Brigadier General John McNeil's brigade of General Alfred Pleasonton's advance drove in the Confederate pickets on the Little Blue. Since crossing, the Confederates had destroyed the bridge, which Moonlight had not, so Pleasonton's force waited for daylight to throw a temporary structure across the river about half a mile from the destroyed bridge. By 10 a.m., Captain William C. F. Montgomery's artillerymen had their guns west of the Little Blue. Shortly after, Confederate artillery opened on McNeil's men, who spent the next two hours driving off what seemed like lightly protected Confederate outposts. By 1:30—about the time Shelby's men had broken through to the bluffs over the Big Blue—Pleasonton and his staff had covered three miles from the Little Blue, nearly halfway to Independence.[19]

The Arkansans under Brigadier General William Cabell faced the Federals. The Arkansans needed to slow the Federal advance from the Little Blue to Independence not only to break through on the Big Blue but to move the supply wagons west to safety. Nevertheless, Pleasonton's Federals sometimes moved so quickly that they overran Confederate detachments as they prepared their breakfasts, "which we hastily grabbed and ate as we went on fighting."[20]

The Confederate troops had breached the Federal defenses on the Big Blue long before Union forces got to the outskirts of Independence, but the supply train would not be able to cross until the fords were cleared. Painfully aware that "the rear of the train was only a short distance in advance," and that Price's army was fighting "both in front and rear," Brigadier General John B. Clark Jr. placed his brigade in position at Independence. The smaller brigade of Colonel Thomas R. Freeman joined the line, which would be strengthened by Cabell's retreating men. As the Federals came into view, Captain J. H. Pratt's section of Captain Henry C. Hynson's Tenth Texas Light Artillery lobbed shells toward them.[21]

"A perfect shower of tree tops and large limbs came down among us," recalled one of the attackers. Nevertheless, Phillip Smiley's section of Montgomery's battery got into position to respond, and Lieutenant Colonel Joseph Eppstein's MSM Cavalry deployed the two howitzers of its Lieutenant Adam Hillerich under the Confederate guns at Independence. Meanwhile, Brigadier General John B. Sanborn's brigade, some using their new carbines, came up on the right of McNeil's line. Colonel John E. Phelps's Arkansans took the lead, as Lieutenant Colonel John F. McMahan's Sixth Provisional EMM began to flank the Confederate left, with the Sixth and Eighth Missouri MSM Cavalry under Colonel Joseph J. Gravely and Major William Plumb in reserve. The Federals soon got their skirmish line within a mile and a half of the city.[22]

A volunteer from Topeka, Daniel W. Boutwell, did reach Pleasonton. A former member of the Sixth Kansas Cavalry, he had been enrolled in the Second KSM, serving under Deitzler. After the brief communications between Blunt and Sanborn around Lexington had broken down, Boutwell had offered to slip through to Pleasonton. He left Kansas City by skiff and, though fired on by the pickets, made it into Confederate lines and through Independence. There he met a handful of Missouri militiamen who had fought at the Little Blue and been trapped behind Confederate lines. Reaching Pleasonton's headquarters, Boutwell asked if the officers "would receive a verbal message from a muddy man" and proceeded to report. After enough questioning to convince himself that Boutwell was who he claimed to be, Pleasonton replied "that he had been ready to attack for several days, and not having heard any thing from above, and realizing that it was slow business to organize militia, feared that they were not ready for him to move." With the news from Boutwell, he opted to do so.[23]

By midafternoon, Pleasonton ordered Sanborn and McNeil to take Independence. At "almost exactly 3 o'clock," Sanborn's brigade advanced on foot with Phelps's Second Arkansas Cavalry moving on the double-quick in the lead. Halting to fire one great volley ahead of them, they moved among the easternmost houses of town, although streets and buildings broke up their lines. Still, their rapid rate of fire drove the Confederates back. Others rode up and dismounted behind them, hurrying across streets, ditches, enclosures, and lanes, "abreast, if not ahead, of any other troops."[24]

At a critical point, McNeil's brigade made a mounted charge into Independence. Colonel E. C. Catherwood's Thirteenth Missouri Cavalry fell "on the enemy's rear, saber in hand," with the Seventh Kansas and Seventeenth Illinois Cavalry "charging in close order" with revolving rifles and Spencer carbines. A nearby shell unhorsed Lieutenant Randolph B. Kelly of the Thirteenth "but injuring neither horse nor rider." "Much credit for our success in that charge is due to a patriotic old lady who lived at the point where we entered town," recalled one veteran. "She seeing our charging column coming, loosed a large chain which had been stretched across the street off the ground high enough to trip the advance horses. It could not have been seen, on account of the heavy dust." He added that even though the Confederates still held the town, the woman flew the Union flag from her window. The way cleared, the line of the Seventeenth leaped a rocky ravine, heading directly for the Confederate guns.[25]

The onslaught from both mounted attackers and foot soldiers unnerved the hard-pressed Confederates. After Union fire killed or disabled every horse in the team of the Confederates' battery, the artillerymen fled on foot, bringing others with them. Federal horsemen swept behind them, cutting off part of Cabell's brigade, capturing the colonel commanding the rear guard, and nearly seized Cabell himself, who had to spur his horse and leap over a gun to escape. In the process, he dropped his sword, which one of McNeil's cavalrymen picked up. Cabell's hasty departure left in Union hands two rifled brass six-pounders, Federal Parrott rifles the rebels had seized at Pleasant Hill in Louisiana.[26]

Nevertheless, at 4 p.m., Clark's men still contested the Federals' passage through Independence. They knew that, only a few miles behind them, hundreds of axe-wielding soldiers under Captains J. T. Mackey and J. T. Hogane struggled to clear Byram's Ford and other crossings, so the Confederate supply wagons could make it to safety. The fate of Price's entire army required slowing Pleasonton for just a bit longer. Fortunately for Clark and his men, around 5 p.m., they got word that the wagons had begun crossing.[27] As they backed west out of Independence, garrisoning the town fell to the detachment of Third MSM Cavalry under Lieutenant Colonel Henry M. Matthews, some of whom had been fighting Price's army since it had entered the state a month earlier.

Pleasonton moved the brigades of Brigadier General Egbert B. Brown and Colonel Edward F. Winslow past the exhausted men of McNeil and Sanborn to get fresh troops into action against Clark's determined rear guard action. Colonel James McFerran's First MSM Cavalry of Brown's brigade pushed the Confederates from three successive strong positions, but the narrow road had kept Winslow's men from deploying until two of Brown's three regiments ran "entirely out of ammunition." McFerran's men faced "a largely superior force for three-quarters of an hour," before Colonel Nelson Cole moved his artillery aside to allow Winslow's brigade forward to cover McFerran's flanks. Together, they drove the Confederates "about two miles on the Westport road," after which McFerran's men, too, ran out of ammunition. Sunset left Winslow's men—the Third and Fourth Iowa Cavalry with detachments of the Fourth and Tenth Missouri Cavalry—continuing the fight.[28]

On the Confederate side, Clark described the Federals' rushing them through "the almost impenetrable darkness of the night." "The dark obscurity that enveloped friend and foe alike was only relieved by the bright flash of our guns," wrote Colonel John Q. Burbridge, "and the deathlike stillness that reigned in

the forest around us was only broken as volley answered volley from the con-
tending forces." General John S. Marmaduke reported that by 8 p.m. they had
backed to the west bank of Sponge Creek, near the Big Blue. The Confederates hung on there until somewhere near 10 p.m., when the last of the wagons
rumbled over the Big Blue.[29]

During this unusual night combat, the defenders had real advantages. Winslow's brigade entirely superseded Brown's, which had run out of ammunition;
one of his men, the eighteen-year–old private Henry Townsend, described the
fight: "It being dark they had the advantage of us. They would lay in line until we got within 30 or 40 feet of them then fire and raise and run. Sometimes
they would stand 15 or 20 minutes then we would shoot and talk to them at the
same time." He added "that they wanted to get at the Militia, etc., etc., [and] we
continued to drive them until 12 o'clock when we were relieved and there was
no more fighting that night."[30]

Although Brown's brigade had been slated to resume the advance, McFerran's exhausted men "lay upon the road during the remainder of the night,
holding their horses, both having been without food since the night previous,
and suffering for water." Colonel John F. Philips complained, too: "We were
up all night, dragging and sleeping along on our horses and by fires, no feed,
crackers for men, worn out." Regardless of official reports, Pleasonton complained after midnight to Brown, "As your command has as yet done no fighting, the General expects you to push them vigorously to-day." He would "accept
of no excuse for the non-fulfillment of this duty, but will hold you responsible."
Despite the orders, as of 1 a.m., Brown still had not been resupplied with ammunition.[31]

The day's losses on that front are a little more clear. By nightfall, Pleasonton
correctly reported the Confederates had "left 40 killed and many sick and wounded in my hands," with other wounded having escaped. Although they had missed
taking General Cabell in the town, they had netted the colonel commanding the
Forty-fifth Arkansas and a lieutenant colonel from Jackson county, two majors,
four captains, and ten lieutenants, which included the members of three brigade
staffs. Pleasonton claimed 400 prisoners, and Price reported "300 or 400 men"
lost. McNeil's mounted charge suffered the most losses on the Federal side.[32]

THE ARMY OF THE BORDER

The Union troops driven from the Big Blue quickly became, quite literally,
an Army of the Border. After driving them from Byram's Ford, Shelby's division
continued to press its advantage, making it impossible for Jennison's men to
stop and fight without risking a flanking operation. McKenny also placed Fishback's KSM "in line of battle in the edge of the timber, with directions to hold

their ground and retard the enemy's progress." As the Confederates pushed them to the Kansas line, part of Jackman's brigade veered northwest toward Westport and Kansas City. When returning from near the state line with "a squad of about 100 men," Jackman found that the regiments of Colonels De Witt C. Hunter and W. O. Coleman had joined his men, who faced "a considerable body of Federals, who had appeared from the direction of Westport." General Thompson brought up his brigade around dusk, placing Colonel William H. Erwin's regiment to cover the road from Westport. Behind them on the field, a Confederate surgeon learned Charley Hatfield's secret while treating her for a gunshot wound in her leg and saber cut in her shoulder.[33]

At Westport, as in much of Missouri, people were divided over the issues of the war. At the onset, someone put up a secessionist flag, and despite the angry talk it did not get removed but soon had to coexist with the Stars and Stripes, which also waved "for a season" before being stolen. By 1864, residents of all sorts had "an arms length policy towards any man in uniform. No one wanted a battle. The attitude seemed to be that of stoicism—what couldn't be helped would have to be endured." A Union officer, stopping at a grocer's on his way to the Big Blue, noticed the grocer's little girl and began sobbing with concern for his own daughter. Residents with pianos contributed what they could to morale, as the area of the village rang with some familiar tunes "La Paloma," "Barbara Allen," "Sweet Kitty Maguire, Come Home." "The Confederates might overrun the town by morning. Yet there was no panic, no exodus, no loading of family chattels on wagons and scurrying for a safer area."[34]

Curtis sent his bodyguard, Major Robert H. Hunt, with his own escort—a company of the Eleventh Kansas Cavalry—to help hold the KSM. At that point, Jennison sent word that the Confederates were quickly backing him into Westport. Hunt took his company, bolstered with two howitzers and Hoyt's detachment of the Fifteenth, "to keep the enemy out of town." They "met the enemy square in the face" and were likely those bluecoats described as having "attacked the right of the Confederate column, turned his flank, and punished him quite severely." Some of the KSM joined in this desperate rear guard fight. After its success, Hunt turned over command to Captain Granville Llewellyn Gove and hurried over to help Moonlight rally his men near the state line. The force at Westport claimed to have driven back Confederates "in confusion to the cover of the timber some two or three miles distant, closely followed by our forces, until, as the sun went down, not a vestige of the rebel Shelby's division beyond its dead and a few wounded was to be seen upon the field." In later years, Shelby insisted that only Hunt's unexpected attack had saved Westport. Meanwhile, Hunt retired to Westport, where he found everything in chaos and, around 10 or 11 p.m., retired for the night at the Gillis house in Kansas City.[35]

Curtis's order had been "to withdraw within the lines of the fortifications at Kansas City," and most of his forces joined Kersey Coates's EMM there. Coates sent scouts east of the town. To defend the city, the guns of the Second Kansas Artillery covered the main road to Independence, those of Dodge's Ninth Wisconsin with the section of the Colored Artillery under Lieutenant Minor on the elevated ground, covering roads to the north and west. The Fourth and Tenth KSM stayed just south of Kansas City, while the Twelfth KSM and the Second Colorado covered McLain's Battery on the hill, covering the road to Kansas City.[36]

This "unreasonable fear" of losing Kansas City terrorized the town. Local women baked bread and prepared food for the soldiers, who ate by relay. Rev. Jonathan Fuller, who had just arrived as pastor of the First Baptist Church on Eighth Street, had heard the artillery since 3:30. "A little before dusk we could hear apparently not more than two miles south of us the cracking irregular fire of a smart musketry skirmish," he added. "Things began to look exciting, but darkness came and everything settled down for the night." He noted the arrival of large numbers of Union troops into the works before the city around 8:30 and realized that Curtis had "few or no federal troops between us and the rebels. So after taking a last look at the Rebel watchfires burning below us a few miles on the prairie, I went to bed in the rather uncomfortable conviction that the first glimmer of daylight would find the Rebels in our streets." The local *Journal of Commerce* reported, "Price said to expect [him] to be in Kansas City Sunday night."[37] One account placed only 3,000 to 4,000 Federals with artillery to defend Kansas City.

Frustrated officers found in Kansas City that their provisions and ammunition often remained upriver at Wyandotte, a situation that robbed many of sleep they would need the next day. Blunt's friend Blair complained that Deitzler had been so eager to get the KSM out of the area that he had to spend most of the night near the Wyandotte bridge running down the horses of his men, which had been taken across the Kaw. Moonlight and Jennison also had trouble locating their supplies and horses. Simpson located rations and military stores stranded in the old convention hall on the levee in Wyandotte, and he found a steamboat available but with a captain unwilling to retrieve the rations. Hearing that the man was a Confederate sympathizer, Simpson sent a squad to "go up in the pilot house and put a pistol against the pilot's head and make him take the boat after the provisions or kill him." In two hours, they got their rations, and others worked through the night to get ammunition and other supplies where they were needed. As another measure of the chaos that prevailed, Hinton noted that word of Pleasonton's presence reached them around 6 p.m., and Major Chapman S. Charlot noted hearing the news an hour later. Yet, as late as midnight, Lieutenant George T. Robinson, who had supervised construction of the defensive works, thought Curtis "had no precise knowledge as to where Major-Generals Rosecrans and Pleasonton were" and did not want to count on their help "to keep the enemy in check."[38]

Eventually, bits of the Eleventh, Fifteenth, and Sixteenth Kansas Cavalry, along with the Second Colorado, settled in some miles beyond the city to the south, in the fields near Westport and within view of the Confederate campfires running for miles to the right and left to the south. Because of Curtis's initial orders, the presence at Westport took place under the rubric of "throwing out strong pickets in the direction of the enemy" or, as Lane described it, "a sufficient force . . . for observation." Many who camped there later claimed to have been too exhausted to continue into Kansas City.[39]

Night found morale among those who had failed to hold the Big Blue in better shape than their enemies'. Reports that Federal casualties were twenty-five killed and seventy-five wounded did not include the KSM, said to have lost "from 100 to 150 in killed, wounded and prisoners," though the Moccabee farm alone counted for more, and nobody offered a guess at the numbers of missing. One Confederate account reported, "In one ghastly heap upon the lone prairie [lay] 217 dead Jayhawkers," and one of the more homicidal Confederates noted taking 207 prisoners "though they deserved instant death." Deitzler thought the attacking Confederates had considerable losses, and one Unionist counted forty enemy bodies around him, though some Confederate sources acknowledged only slight losses. In response to such fictions, one participant mused, "Where all the bullets, shot and shell went to is a puzzle, for there is no room for doubt that the firing in every form was incessant."[40]

Then, too, the Federal forces, however badly mauled, had fared better than the Confederates, who had essentially fought two battles against two armies. Without counting the hundreds of KSM who had refused to cross the state line, the missing men of the Army of the Border would probably have brought Confederate losses to 500 or beyond, and the Department of Missouri likely had 100 men taken out of commission. In contrast, the Confederates acknowledged having lost 400 against Pleasonton's attack, and those fighting Curtis's men would have suffered casualties—more when assailing the positions along the Big Blue and fewer, of course, when they had the Federals on the run. The day probably saw about 600 casualties on both sides.

Certainly, the fighting had not engaged the entire Federal force. The battle had been, as the surgeon Davis noted, "confined to our right." Colorado sergeant David C. Nettleton wrote his sister that, when all was said and done, "we had but little fighting on our part of the line." They closed the day wondering at "the campfires of the rebels, which gleamed menacingly from the woods, as if mocking the anxiety which prevailed throughout our lines. But as the darkest hour is said to be just before day, so the darkness of that night foreshadowed the dawn of final victory, and the relief of Kansas from apprehension of rebel invasion."[41] In contrast, the Confederates came out of the day with no reserves and no real idea of what Price and his staff planned.

Recalling the view from the heights overlooking Brush Creek, Major John N. Edwards could not restrain himself:

> All over and in front of Westport the glad bright sky spread a tearless mantle; the wind blew itself to silence, and sweet sleep put its sickle in among the soldiers and reaped tenderly soft harmonious dreams. Imagine this great leader Shelby; he slept in the open field without a tent; without a cover, but wrapped in his overcoat sought rest for the great battle of tomorrow. It was not a "sound of revelry by night," but the sound of sleeping heroes that were all around him. Imagine the thoughts of this man who knew that he had to fight an enemy five times as strong and with every advantage in the selection of positions, etc. As Shelby gazed toward Westport over that beautiful scene, over that beautiful prairie that was soon to be baptized with blood of his valiant soldiers. What a resolution must have passed through that man's mind to fight that battle—to do or die. He asked no better quarters; he asked no better fare than those of his men. No wonder his men loved him; no wonder that where he went they followed.

"Towards night," recalled one Confederate soldier, "Westport loomed up dimly across the great, bleak prairie." Price spent the night in the Boston Adams house not far from Byram's Ford, where his men had dealt with Curtis and expected to deal with Pleasonton the next day.[42]

More realistic views of the tensions among Federal officers survive. Curtis told his council of war in the Gillis House hotel on the levee in Kansas City that they should fall back across the Kansas River to Leavenworth, leaving Pleasonton's larger force to deal with Price. Crawford, Blunt, Lane, and "every officer present" other than Curtis "felt absolutely certain that even without Pleasonton's division, we had men enough to meet Price on the open field or anywhere else." They also argued they had Price all but on the run, for, had he actually hoped to take Kansas City, he would have struck at the fords nearer the city and lower down the Big Blue than Byram's Ford. This indicated that Price had wanted to skirt Kansas City and Westport to retreat to the south, and B. F. Simpson found Blunt doing the same: "He had a particular manner of walking when in trouble which Simpson recognized at once." Blunt sent Simpson to Ford with an order to start shooting at daylight "and then to forget that he had ever had any such order." "You ought to have been in that room at the hotel and heard that shaking old coward," Ford, referring to Curtis, later told Simpson. Ford, who had an informal agreement with Shelby not to fight in the dark, sent word to him that they would resume the battle at daylight.[43]

The disputes continued until around 2 a.m., when the arguing became unbearable to Crawford and some of the others. Leaving Lane to occupy Curtis, they took Blunt aside to suggest that he "place General Curtis in close arrest and assume command." When Blunt warned them about the seriousness of such an act, they replied that it would be "not so serious as for this army to run away like cowards and let Price sack Kansas City and devastate Southern Kansas."

"Will the army stand by me?"

"Yes, and we will stand by you while making the arrest."

When they returned to Curtis, the commander saw their determination and allegedly said, "General Blunt, I will leave the whole matter to you. If you say fight, then fight it is." At some point that evening, Sergeant P. I. Bonebrake turned up at the Harris house after having escaped the Moccabee farm into Kansas; he had spent a long circuitous day working his way up the state line to Westport.[44] Behind them all lay the massacred price of bad decisions.

Everybody seemed to forget the real reason for the Army of the Border's defeat—or they realized that talking about it would resolve nothing. They had overextended their line to Hickman's Mills in the expectation that the westbound troops of the Department of Missouri would move through Pleasant Hill to that point, cutting off Price's line of retreat. Although Rosecrans was nowhere near there, he had reaffirmed this intention at 1 p.m. when he offered Curtis the perspective "from Pleasonton's headquarters, three miles west of Little Blue." In fact, Pleasonton had ridden directly toward Price's army at Independence, informing Rosecrans of this at every stage, after which the commanding general offered yet judgment that must have been maddening. "You have doubtless exercised your best judgment," he wrote Pleasonton, "but I still think to have threatened at the Little Blue and to have moved south with the remainder of your command to the Independence and Warrensburg road would have been better." Placing themselves south of the Confederates would have made their retreat "a necessity," he wrote, "and with the infantry south of you and always behind you could have swung around in safety."[45]

Three

October 23

7

Brush Creek

From the Mists

"Nature never formed a grander battle-field than that around Westport," wrote a contemporary chronicler. Farms with pastures and cornfields broke the rolling wooded terrain south of the Kansas City fortifications and the village of Westport, from which the Santa Fe Trail meandered into the Southwest. The farther from the town one rode, the more one saw those old-fashioned heavy stone fences. Hardly more than a mile south of Westport, Brush Creek ran east toward the Big Blue river between sometimes densely wooded margins as wide as a half a mile. Two major roads crossed Brush Creek and climbed the wooded bluffs to the south with a third road farther west, the dirt military road that ran roughly along the Kansas line. From that dirt road, another climbed the plateau on a ruggedly diagonal east-west route past an old cemetery just west of the Ward farm before joining the nearer main road that ran past the Wornall house. At about this point, the trees gave way to a prairie that rolled for several miles with few breaks to the tree line of Indian Creek.[1]

An indeterminate portion of Confederate General Sterling Price's army awaited the Federals behind those stone fences on the higher ground above them. Jo Shelby's division occupied the terrain overlooking the bridge and fords coming south from Brush Creek that were nearest to Westport. To their east, up to and along another little country road, waited James Fagan's men, less William Cabell's battered brigade, then detailed to cover the supply train moving to the south.[2] Still farther east and facing that direction, General John S. Marmaduke's forces prepared to block Pleasonton's crossing of the Big Blue.

Federal Failures out of Westport

At 3 a.m., the Federals began moving their troops in the hope of crossing Brush Creek and engaging the enemy at the first light. Through the predawn hours, Charles W. Blair's KSM and other troops trudged from Kansas City into the fields south of town. Charles R. Jennison and James H. Ford moved to the roads crossing the creek, with Thomas Moonlight to the right, but neither Moonlight nor Ford was in position when, after a hardworking and sleepless night, James G. Blunt squinted through the gray murkiness at "the enemy in force on the open prairie directly south of Westport and about two miles distant."[3]

Remarkably, the Army of the Border went into battle with yet unresolved issues about command. On paper, Major General Samuel R. Curtis commanded the army, in which Blunt both commanded a provisional division and served as an overall field commander. Some sources indicate he commanded the KSM brigades of Jennison and Blair (Fourth, Fifth, Sixth, Tenth, and Nineteenth KSM with the Ninth Wisconsin Light Artillery and Lieutenant Patrick H. Minor's Colored Battery). However, Major General George Deitzler had overall command of the KSM, and Brigadier General William Henry M. Fishback took an active role in directing them as well. Some later accounts also credit Jennison as field commander of the entire operation. Blunt indisputably coordinated Moonlight and Ford, who informed Shelby that their informal truce would end at daylight.[4]

The first shots may have fired as early as 6 a.m., but Major Samuel Davis gave the time the battle started as 7 a.m. When the shooting started, Curtis galloped from Kansas City to Westport, contrary to his orders, and joined Blunt and others on the roof of the Harris house at 7:30. The general sent Major Chapman S. Charlot to find Blunt and end the gunfire. Near the line, Charlot snarled when Benjamin F. Simpson told him to find Blunt where he should be, at the front. Simpson thought the officers knew the score and "would not tell him where Blunt was." Curtis and his staff watched the brigades of Blair, Deitzler, Ford, and Jennison enter the timber along the north side of Brush Creek as well as the Confederates opposite them. Moreover, they saw "the enemy could be seen on the other side of the Big Blue, and moving rapidly in a southwesterly direction."[5]

By 8 a.m., the brigades of Ford, Jennison, Blair, and Moonlight formed the Federal line from left to right and began pressing Shelby's men. The Confederates held firm and 300 of them, under Captain Henry J. Vivian, held on at one of the easternmost fords over Brush Creek, most likely the one that later became Troost Avenue. In the confusion, Vivian's men clung to their position, even as Union troops crossed on either side. Jennison's brigade made its way through the "severe and incessant fire of small-arms" until the Confederate reinforcements turned up "and succeeded in temporarily pressing us back beyond our original position." Confederate Colonel Sidney D. Jackman reported how his men "soon rallied, and turning drove him from the field." Still cautious, Curtis feared his men faced "overwhelming odds" and withdrew them. "Our troops fought desperately and sometimes repulsed the enemy, but gradually fell back to the north side of Brush Creek." Colonel Samuel J. Crawford of Curtis's staff found the Fifteenth Kansas Cavalry on the right had been pushed back toward the state line, and he took them back to Shawnee Mission to reorganize. Between 8 and 9 a.m., a Federal battery in the lane opened fire and one rebel gun on the right began replying.[6]

Once Jennison's brigade had engaged the Confederates, Moonlight's moved in from the right, climbing the high ground from Kansas into Missouri. Chasing in the pickets, Moonlight reported that "the enemy were driven back for over a mile after a stubborn resistance." Though not part of the initial advance, Blair's KSM crossed Brush Creek, dismounted, and advanced to support Moonlight but faced a "considerable force and strongly posted behind a stone fence, which formed an admirable cover." Captain Richard J. Hinton arrived to find the colonel deploying the Eleventh Kansas with the Fifth Kansas and the Second KSM. For half an hour, they clung to the sloping ground along with Moonlight's men but "did not know whether our flanks were cleared or not." Blunt praised the brigade but noted that the time it took to come up from Kansas City left the odds so "severe and unequal" that Blunt ordered them back to the north of the creek, their right protected by Lieutenant Colonel G. M. Woodward and part of the KSM.[7]

Then, too, the Federals moved up the road to the Wornalls'. Ford's men sent forward his Second Colorado, and supported by Colonel Levi S. Treat of the Twelfth KSM they pressed beyond Brush Creek and occupied a secure position on the road as it emerged into the high prairie, but the Confederates who drove back the advance of the Federal center occupied "a small copse to the right of my brigade and commenced a flank fire upon me." Jeff Thompson's brigade engaged in this "very spirited" fighting, supported by part of Jackman's force. The Federals opposite Colonel Frank Gordon's regiment got "behind a stone fence that could not be charged on account of intervening fences." However, Confederates under Colonel Alonzo Slayback and Johnson "with their recruits" drove Ford's men back across the creek to the north and the protection of Captain William D. McLain's battery. Then, too, Captain Vivian's stubborn defenders still held the easternmost ford.[8]

The piecemeal nature of the Federal withdrawal presented the Confederates with the chance to strike north of Brush Creek around 9 a.m. Some sources indicate that Price actually ordered Shelby to attack and capture Westport, and Thompson's report indicated that Shelby had ordered him to do so. Blunt acknowledged that, while the Federal withdrawal continued to restrain the Confederates, "a small force . . . approached through the timber to attack my left flank," and Sergeant David C. Nettleton recalled being "forced back within half a mile of Westport." However, Blair had sent the Fifth and Nineteenth

KSM of Colonels G. A. Colton and A. C. Hogan to the front, where they "stood up to [the rebels] like veterans, pouring in their volleys as regularly as trained infantry practising." Their countercharge pushed Shelby's men back south of Brush Creek.[9]

Meanwhile, Shelby had Captain Richard A. Collins roll his guns to McLain's old position. In the fierce artillery exchange with the Colorado battery, then on a hill north of Brush Creek, one of the Confederate guns burst. In addition, Union artillerymen made two remarkable shots against Confederate guns that were 600 to 800 yards to the southeast. Major Robert H. Hunt, the chief of the Kansas Artillery, carefully aimed one of Eayres's guns at Captain R. A. Collins's Missouri Battery. The shell struck the muzzle of the Confederate gun as it was being loaded. The blast shattered the carriage and dropped the cannon to the ground. It also ripped off the hands of one of the gunners and inflicted half a dozen other casualties among the men and horses. Collins's men quickly limbered their remaining guns and began falling back.[10]

In Kansas City, Mrs. H. S. Millett stirred into action when she heard the guns, hurrying to Dick Van Horn's home. Van Horn had gone into the field, but his wife joined Millett by the fortifications on Twelfth Street "to see the soldiers coming and going and to get the news." Returning to Union headquarters, they watched Milt McGee distributing whisky to the men from a bucket with a tin dipper. "Each soldier got a dipperful."[11]

FURTHER ATTEMPTS

One Confederate later claimed that, at this point, they drove the Federals "from fence to fence, through a skirt of timber, and into Westport beyond." The Army of the Border recoiled but had not abandoned Westport. Nevertheless, Price later responded to criticisms that he had not been sufficiently aggressive by coupling these exaggerations to the claim that he had ordered Shelby to capture Westport. Indeed, without mentioning the earlier Federal advance south of the creek, Price reported that "Brigadier-General Shelby immediately attacked the enemy, assisted by Major-General Fagan with two brigades of Arkansas troops, and though they resisted most stubbornly and contested every point of the approach, drove them six or seven miles into Westport." However, Kansas City was that far from the creek, while Westport was scarcely more than a mile. For one account, this became "the high-tide mark of Price's entire invasion . . . the last aggressive advance made by any of Price's men in the line of his original goals of Kansas City and Fort Leavenworth."[12] This, even though neither had been Price's "original goals."

By about 9:30 a.m., though, the Federals decided on a second "general advance of my entire line, which was promptly executed." Blunt explained that this effort would include the militia, "having all arrived on the field," and the rapid movement of artillery to keep up with the advance. The Kansans bore the brunt of this attempt, and Deitzler's men tried to manhandle the howitzer batteries across the stream and uphill through the opposite timber but found the slope too muddy and steep, and the resistance to this move was so sharp that General Blunt and he sent word to General Curtis in Kansas City that they could not take the hills under the existing circumstances.[13] The weight of the sources, though, does not support more than two unsuccessful attempts to take the bluffs.

Federal accounts had their own kinds of falsifications, of course. Deitzler said that his men arrived, formed, and helped secure a position south of Brush Creek, an oversimplification that amounted to dishonesty. On the other hand, a later account, promotional of Jennison's reputation as a commander, asserted that "the same ground was won and lost a third time by Jennison's men, the field being literally strewn with dead and wounded."[14] Most evidence, though, implies two failed efforts.

After this second attempt, the Confederates did not pursue the withdrawing Federals toward Westport but pressed down the slope to the Kansas state line. In a woods nearby, they planted "one section of a Parrott battery on the Line road, rendering our position one of extreme danger." A shell spooked the horse of one of the Kansans wounded the day before, and his regimental commander, watching the horse throw him, quipped, "They are after Timbocker again to-day, and I guess they have got him this time." The captain sent a man to work on Timbocker until he regained consciousness. Jennison reported that his brigade fell back once more, "almost to suburbs of Westport." Several Confederate shells crashed in the area of Westport, one exploding in Shawnee Street, north of the old Harris house.[15] A temporary threat and removed quickly.

By this time of the morning, Curtis had personally ventured out to confront Blunt. He found him between the Harris house and Brush Creek and "ordered Blunt to cease firing. Blunt said he would not order any retreat under fire, and told General Curtis if he wanted to take that responsibility, he could order the firing to cease and retreat to be made." Curtis reminded him of the order. Blunt shrugged, saying that "the engagement [was] on before the order could be carried out, and that it was too late to retreat."[16]

Curtis sent a hasty dispatch to Henry Halleck: "The enemy turned upon us and commenced a strong assault upon my advance this morning, and a hard battle has been progressing for two hours. I am deploying re-enforcements of militia, and the enemy now seem to be retiring."[17] Between 9:30 and 10 a.m. Curtis came to the front himself.

The commander arrived to take his place with "the heroic Jennison, as he rode far in advance of his line, straight at the enemy's long gray columns." Present when they "deployed in an open field, beyond the trees, it was an inspiring and never to be forgotten sight," wrote a soldier, "to see our gallant little army, led by Gens. Curtis and Blunt, in person, forming for its last charge in disorder, owing to the rapid and well directed fire upon them by our two batteries of eight twelve-pound guns, at short range." Jennison attacked around 10 a.m. and drove the enemy "for a distance of four miles over the open prairie."[18]

By 10 a.m., the KSM pressed in a remarkably well-organized support. "Our boys commenced and soon the whole woods resounded with loud and long continued cheer after cheer as we drove them and pushed them from the timber. Our batteries are now hurried through the corn-field, followed by the militia, who are supporting them. Here we have punished them severely; their dead are numerous and lie on the field unburied. Our loss compared with theirs is trifling." Only an hour before, Deitzler had turned over command of the militia at Kansas City to Brigadier General Byron Sherry and headed south to join the battle.[19]

The Federals may have made yet another unsuccessful attempt to move through the bluffs, but this may have been no more than the delay of a general Union advance. As part of that advance, Deitzler's KSM pushed the Confederates "from the timber southwest of town, where a small body of them had taken position."[20] These may have formed part of the group described as Jennison's men, who gained the cover of stone walls and rail fences, thanks to the unexpected arrival of artillery support on their left.

At this point, Curtis emerged from the timber with big guns. George Thoman farmed to the east of the Ward family's brick farmhouse. The previous evening, some of Shelby's men had taken one of Thoman's mares, though she was about to foal. Good horsemen, the Confederates knew better but had no interest in accommodating anyone who spoke with a "broken German accent." When the shooting started Sunday morning, Thoman went dutifully in search of his mare and witnessed the unsuccessful Federal efforts to secure a position on the bluffs. Unable to locate the rebels who had stolen his horse, Thoman decided to get help from the Union army, pointing out a usable ford with an associated pathway angling up the bluffs. Curtis found him "an old man, a Missouri patriot of seventy-five years," but Thoman proved to be just what the general needed.[21]

Curtis himself came out of the timber to see Jennison's men—"our line, extending far away on my right, emerging from the dark forests of Brush Creek." Behind him, Major Hunt, chief of artillery, and Adjutant James Aikens helped get Captain James H. Dodge's Ninth Wisconsin Battery up the increasingly muddy course, with a vigorous little Welsh artillery officer, Lieutenant Edward Gill, goading other men and beasts pulling the two mountain howitzers. "On reading the prairie beyond the timber," recalled Major Theodore J. Weed, "our artillery was opened on the rebel line, distant about half a mile, with such effect as to cause its dispersion in less than half an hour.[22]

As Moonlight's brigade shifted to the west, Blair's KSM left every sixth man to hold the horses back at the creek but plunged into the timber, through the creek, and up to the front. They faced "a heavy fire . . . opened on us from a corn-field which stretched from our right front, and which seemed filled with skirmishers, and from a large brick house in an orchard just beyond, in which a party of sharpshooters was stationed." "Our militia continued to come swarming out of the forest," wrote Curtis, "displaying a length and strength of numbers that surprised me. Their movement was steady, orderly, and gallant."[23]

By this time, General Deitzler had joined General W. M. H. Fishback in the line of the KSM. The latter reported that "our men stood up nobly to their work and maintained their ground like veterans, and, seeing their advantage, were eager to pursue." They gave "loud and long-continued cheer after cheer" as they pressed the Confederates. More realistically, perhaps, Hinton called it "not an orderly, but a very effective fire."[24]

African Americans certainly moved to the center of the fight. Colonel Montgomery placed "a number of colored soldiers" into position on the left of McLain's battery, where Major Thomas I. McKenny reported they "behaved gallantly under a hot fire." Along with them rolled Minor's "colored battery." Secretary of War Edwin Stanton had personally intervened to force the army finally to accept his order of two years before that it actually commission black officers, three of whom had command in the field. Conservative officers in the Department of Missouri continued to sneer at the presence of abolitionists and blacks "et sui generis" among the Kansans.[25] The Confederates, however, found the very prospect terrifying.

By 11 a.m., Ford's brigade had finally gained the bluff in another attempt, forming the left of "a steady, unbroken front." The Federals manhandled the guns of McLain's battery into roughly the same place from which it had been driven. Lieutenant George S. Eayres's two guns in that battery helped to slow the Confederate formation of a battle line with double-shot canister; soon out of ammunition, he yielded the position to Lieutenant Melancthon Sayre Beach's guns. By then, Shelby's division had recoiled under pressure into a tighter position, but Fagan's Arkansans—less its largest brigade—also moved onto the field.[26]

The Turning Tide

Recognizing the desperation of the situation, the Arkansans made one of the most dramatic gambles of the battle.[27] Colonel James McGhee's lead regiment of Dobbins's brigade made a sweeping charge on the Colorado battery, but Captain Curds Johnson of the Fifteenth Kansas Cavalry joined Captain Green with two Colorado squadrons in a countercharge with sabers drawn that met the Arkansans head on in the narrow road and adjacent fields. In this engagement, Captain Curtis Johnson dashed at McGhee, the two men galloping toward each other with revolvers blazing. Sources disagree on the outcome, but a Confederate bullet severely wounded Johnson in either the foot, the left arm, or perhaps both, but Johnson kept firing until he felled McGhee, although he did not shoot him "through the heart, dropping him dead from his horse upon the field."

Meanwhile, dismounted Coloradoans came up "to the right of the battery, just in time to give the most deadly fire I ever saw." The Federals captured thirty-three men who had "lost their horses and could not get off the field. I don't know how many were killed but the road was lined with them" and "in half [a] mile, the col. That led that charge was killed." Still under fire, Private James Ross tried to bring in three prisoners, when one wheeled his horse about and tried to escape; when Ross turned to shoot him, he found himself shot. He brought in the other two prisoners before collapsing and died the next day. Private Iker emptied his carbine and both revolvers before charging forward, wielding his carbine as a club, knocking one Confederate "dead from his horse, and immediately fell dead himself, pierced by a rebel ball."

The Kansans lost fifteen men, but the Confederates broke and rode off, leaving nearly 100 to fall prisoner. Most of Fagan's casualties remained beyond the Confederates' reach, though. "I never saw such havoc," wrote Sergeant Nettleton, "the lane was strewed with dead and wounded men and horses." Up the road, moreover, the Arkansans left a score or more fearfully wounded men near the Wornall house. Not far behind, the countercharge of the Kansans swept up the lane.

Eight-year-old Frank Wornall watched the battle from his parents' home. After the previous year's raid on Lawrence, Kansas, Union authorities had forced his father, a slaveholder living in a countryside frequented by guerrillas, to stay in Westport. Left to their own devices, Frank and his mother "stayed in the cellar while the battle raged around us. Every once in a while a cannon ball would strike in our yard with a thud that shook the house. North of the house was the grove of locust trees that still stands. I could hear the cannon balls cut through those trees with a loud swishing noise, severing limbs and tearing trunks of trees." Later, when they ventured out, the boy watched "soldiers streaming past from daylight until after noon. They were galloping this way and that and I wondered what it was all about." As the fighting got closer, the Confederates built a "temporary breastwork of rails and fir[ed] from the stone walls and cornfields" nearby and took the house as a hospital. "Several died in our house," remembered Frank. "While the surgeons worked mother boiled water to wash the wounds and helped with the bandages." The boy drew water to wash the wound of "one man who was terribly wounded in the face," who sat at their cistern before just walking away.[28]

Decisively, though, the Federals had managed to get thirteen howitzers and eighteen brass Parrott guns into action. With the guns of Dodge and McLain anchoring the Federal left and center, Lieutenant Eayres had a section of that battery moved to the right, near the guns of Hickes and Patrick Minor. Curtis called it "artillery enough to represent an army of 50,000" and "a display of force that backed the Confederates south while we steadily advanced all arms over a beautiful prairie, where both armies were in full view."[29]

The Union guns made some of the "deeds of marksmanship and daring: on the field. Confederate sharpshooters again climbed the occasional trees that dotted the prairie and from these points of vantage used their rifles in picking off the Federal officers and men." Dodge of the Ninth Wisconsin Battery and Hunt, the artillery chief, saw the exposed position of one of the Confederate cannons but knew Douglass's Colored Light Artillery had the best position from which to make the shot. Lieutenant Minor courteously gave them the use of one of them, and the shell shattered the carriage of a Confederate gun and dropped the piece to the ground.[30]

These guns blasted the Confederates back "to another elevation on the broad prairie and operated their artillery and cavalry to their utmost ability in a vain attempt to check our general movement." A member of the Second KSM, who had narrowly missed being massacred the previous day, had made it to Westport, "wandered on in the rear of the Colorado Battery," and watched his fellow militia members participate in driving the same units that had behaved with such savagery toward his comrades. "On reaching the open prairie, about three miles west," wrote another, "I found that the attempt of the enemy to turn our right had completely failed and he had withdrawn all his force from that part of the field. I immediately informed the commanding general of this fact, when a charge through the timber south of town was at once ordered and promptly executed."[31]

The Federals pressed up the road against the right of the Confederate line amid "the wild picturesqueness of a battle field." Lieutenant Colonel George H. Hoyt and Captain John L. Thompson of the Fifteenth gathered some of their men, with others from the Sixteenth Kansas and Third Wisconsin Cavalry, to charge and dislodge Confederates behind the stone walls. Nearby they noted the broken and dismounted gun that bore "the mark of a Texan foundry." One of their shells had struck the muzzle of this gun while the crew had been loading it, and the bursting of the gun took off the gunner's hand and killed half a dozen others, along with some horses.[32]

Meanwhile, General Curtis determined to make contact with Major General Alfred Pleasonton's Union forces, known to be somewhere to the east. Scouts from the Sixth KSM checked as far down Brush Creek as the timbers of the Big Blue to check on the progress of Pleasonton's attack. Major Samuel S. Curtis had crossed the Big Blue downstream from Byram's Ford with Captain Ezra W. Kingsbury's squadron of the Second Colorado in the hope of making direct contact with Pleasonton at Independence. Finally, Colonel William F. Cloud's detachment of the Second Kansas Cavalry scouted that direction. A confident Curtis had already telegraphed Henry W. Halleck, the Union commander in chief and chief of staff, at Washington "and my anxious friends in the rear that the victory was ours."[33]

At about the same time, Blunt returned from the field to bring up the entire of his command. He found "a small column of rebels" threatening an unsupported howitzer in the dooryard of a farmhouse a little to the left of the road, and in the edge of the creek timber, seriously threatened by a small column of rebels advancing from the east. The howitzer was without support, but the gallant squad in charge, under direction of a sergeant, was actively engaged in double-shotting it with canister and firing into the compact rebel column. Blunt and his staff defended the howitzer with their pistols, until his bodyguard—Lieutenant William B. Clark's detachment of Company E, Fourteenth Kansas Cavalry, and Captain John Wilson's independent scouts—drove off the Confederates. Federal accounts later thought this was a force "driven and separated from the main rebel army by the advance of Pleasonton on the Byrom's Ford road." "Behind us to the right," recalled Hinton, "the militia still poured." The Confederates fell back beyond reach of the Union artillery, though the guns rolled quickly on in pursuit.[34]

Decades later—in 1912—Simpson repeated a strange story he remembered about Daniel Boutwell's turning up back in Curtis's lines. Dressed "in a buckskin suit, which was wet as he had just crossed the river," the volunteer from Topeka hunted down Blunt. Simpson saw him approach the general and say "something which seemed to anger Blunt or surprise him, and he said 'Get a rope and I will hang this man.'" "Just a moment, General," said Boutwell, who then whispered something. Blunt then said he would go with him to see Pleasonton. "They went down the line about a half a mile when the scout saw General Pleasanton [*sic*] on an elevation and waved his hat, which was answered by the general, and the salutation was returned by General Blunt." Blunt approached and Pleasonton asked what the situation was. Blunt replied. Pleasonton asked "where he could be of the most service with his men." Obviously, on the left, Blunt said and suggested "a general advance ought to be made at once." Pleasonton said he would do so as soon as he got his men into a position and that Blunt should do so as well.[35]

Simpson's account is surely garbled. The Confederates had little or no guard at the fords down the Big Blue to the north, and Boutwell, Pleasonton, or anyone else likely could have made their way across. However, given Pleasonton's reactionary politics and his apparent mistrust of his army's abilities, it seems doubtful he would have ventured a dramatic fording ahead of his forces to chat with one of the most reputedly radical generals in Curtis's ranks. Blunt may have been talking with one of Pleasonton's staffers who had accompanied Boutwell. Or Simpson may have been discussing a conference that took place a day or so later.

Whatever the details, the two Union armies gradually became aware of each other on the field. Curtis had already received the dispatches from General William S. Rosecrans and Pleasonton. He anticipated that they would be driving that part of Price's army to the east, driving them "almost due west. Everything goes on gloriously; my troops are doing splendidly; we are taking many prisoners. Pleasonton took two guns from their rear yesterday." "At this time," recalled Hinton, "a heavy column of cavalry could be seen emerging from the timber, and deploying about a mile to the east, and advancing towards the rebel right."[36]

Perhaps in the chaos of the battle, few noticed that Pleasonton's move on Independence left any attempt to cut off Price's retreat entirely dependent upon General Andrew J. Smith's infantry. Rosecrans had written Curtis, Pleasonton, and Major General Edward R. S. Canby to assure them that he would send Smith's infantry marching west to Pleasant Hill with the intention of reaching Hickman's Mills and cutting off the Confederate line of retreat to the south. For weeks, though, Rosecrans had been preoccupied with getting Price's army out of his jurisdiction, and Pleasonton reflected this in his triumphal boast that "the enemy are now out of Missouri." The previous day, though, Pleasonton had assured Curtis that "Smith's infantry is well on the way to Pleasant Hill to-night, and can beat Price's cavalry moving," after which Rosecrans advised Smith about "the importance of moving at once on Independence. Take the shortest practicable route."[37] As events unfolded, it became evident that neither Rosecrans nor Pleasonton had ever envisioned bagging Price's army.

8

Byram's Ford through Bloody Hill

The Late Morning

As the fighting around Westport began, Major General John S. Marmaduke prepared to defend the same positions the Federals had failed to hold the previous day. The rebels' general line, draped along the bluffs overlooking the Big Blue, was centered on a steep hill about 300 yards square, part of which had the additional protection of a difficult rocky ledge. Below, they looked over a broad open field sloping down to Byram's Ford, an expanse with enough stumps and rocks to create obstacles without providing much in terms of cover. Some of the detritus of the previous day's unsuccessful defense of the terrain still littered the ground, providing food for thought to the more pensive of Sunday's defenders. Before them, the bluecoats were moving through the brush at the little river, preparing for their advance.[1]

Between 4 a.m. and 5 a.m., General Alfred Pleasonton's division went into action. One of his four brigades pressed toward the Big Blue, with another coming up in support and still another in reserve. He had sent his fourth far to the south of the Confederate flank, where General Samuel R. Curtis had been led to expect all the department's forces.[2] Although the day's fighting at and above Byram's Ford proved especially intense, developments farther south proved to be decisive to the outcome.

Pleasonton's Predawn Reorganization

In the night, Pleasonton had ordered Brigadier General Egbert B. Brown to "close your command at once on Colonel Edward F. Winslow, and keep closed up, and at daybreak relieve his brigade and push yours to the front." At 4 a.m., Pleasonton told Brown "to move his brigade forward and attack the enemy at daylight and keep pushing him vigorously, as he would be well supported." He had noted that "your brigade has yet done no fighting"; Brown later objected, pointing out that, since Jefferson City, no brigade "had done more fighting . . . and killed and wounded more rebels." Rather plausibly, Brown also claimed he did not get the order until 5.30 a.m. and then found Captain Charles H. Thurber's battery blocking the road forward. Pleasonton also ordered Brigadier General John B. Sanborn's brigade to advance in support.[3]

These orders placed two brigades with artillery on a narrow road. Worse, though, Pleasonton already had Winslow's brigade at the head of that road and, at 6 a.m., ordered it to resume fighting rather than clear the road. Winslow had apparently reminded Pleasonton that Brown was to relieve his brigade and asked where Brown's brigade was. Pleasonton told him to resume the attempt to force the passage of the ford. They then included a regiment of MSM Cavalry from Brown's brigade, along with Captain George D. Knispel's detachment of 100 men from the Fourth Missouri Cavalry and a battalion of the Fourth Iowa led by Captain Doe (probably Captain Edward W. Dee, Company E), and "ordered a charge upon the enemy on the other bank."[4]

Confederate Brigadier General John B. Clark Jr. reported his brigade was "attacked at an early hour by the same enemy and with the same spirit as before." The brigade of Colonel Thomas R. Freeman also formed in support. Colonel J. F. Davies reported "a short and bloody fight and [we] were compelled to fall back." Colonel Solomon G. Kitchen fell wounded in the process. "Almost three companies, being partially surrounded," complained the Union colonel Edward F. Winslow, "would have been captured from the enemy but for awkwardness or negligence on the part of some militia officers."[5] The outcome, though, found Winslow and his cavalrymen licking their wounds back on the east side of the ford.

Within minutes, Brown found himself arrested after being "on the road thirty hours without forage or food (except a day's rations of hard bread), and, as shown in my report, part of the time fighting on foot." A description of events that most likely came from Pleasonton's headquarters described Brown's attacking and having his skirmishers repulsed, after which Pleasonton asked, "What do you intend doing?" Brown was improbably said to reply, "I don't know, sir!" This then provoked the commander's order for Brown to "go to the rear, immediately, and consider yourself under arrest." A more straightforward account ascribed the arrest to Brown's having been "dilatory and disobey[ing] orders in not attacking the enemy as directed."[6]

Colonel John F. Philips—one of the young men who had studied law in the office of General Clark's father—recorded what happened in his diary. Philips noted that, as Brown's cavalry tried to cover the several miles to reach the Big Blue, Winslow's brigade and artillery had clogged the narrow road. Philips arrived to find Brown and the other officers discussing the logistics of taking the ford. Expecting a hard day that would involve little riding, Philips sat on the ground to replace his cavalry boots with army shoes.[7] Within minutes, fate dropped on his head.

"General Pleasonton galloped up," recalled Philips. "He always rode with a cowhide whip in his hand and he had it with him."[8] Philips had fought halfway across Missouri for the general but now saw him for the first time, as he "stopped in front of General Brown and shook the cowhide whip in his face and cursed him and demanded to know why he had not obeyed orders and advanced." Brown pointed out that the road had been too narrow for him and his men to pass Winslow's brigade, but none of that mattered to Pleasonton. "You are an ambulance soldier and belong in the rear," snapped the general, who made sure that Brown would get there by placing him under arrest and sending him off. Adding that Colonel James McFerran's First MSM Cavalry had been straggling along the right of the road, Pleasonton also arrested him. Pleasonton then turned to the other officers around him and demanded, "Who is next in command here?"

"Colonel Philips is," someone said.

"Where is he?" Pleasonton demanded.

Still unshod and sitting on the ground, Philips called out, "Here I am, General."

"Well, what are you doing down there?"

"I am getting ready to push my men into that fight down there, where they have already gone."

The wording of the general's response is remembered differently, but Pleasonton in effect told Philips that, if he and his men wanted a fight, they would have it: "You take charge of this entire brigade and go down there and put those people out." After having brigade command dropped on him, Philips took charge. He left his own Seventh MSM Cavalry in the charge of Lieutenant Colonel Thomas Theodore Crittenden and turned McFerran's First MSM Cavalry over to Lieutenant Colonel Bazel F. Lazear. Philips soon got the brigade down road "to the high bank of the Blue River at Byram's Ford."[9]

The Federal officers saw that the previous day's Confederate attack over that ford had already cleared the river of the fallen trees Curtis's men had placed there, but obstacles remained between them and the muddied embankment as the Confederates had "materially strengthened" the defenses. Philips sent for axe men to clear the way, with Lazear's and Colonel Edward C. Catherwood's men providing cover. At 8 a.m., Major George W. Kelley's Fourth MSM Cavalry and Lazear's First rushed the ford by column "in the face of the galling rebel fire and despite the obstacles in the creek." Meanwhile, Crittenden's men bore to the left of the road, while Kelly's swung to the other flank. The Confederates fell back 200 yards to the range of low hills extending through an open field to the left and along a densely treed bluff to the right.[10] Dominating these sat the hill that loomed over the ford.

Once the Federals cleared the area around Byram's Ford, the Confederate guns began an intense fire upon them.[11] Philips realized that the wooded terrain on either side would confine any mounted action to the road, where it would meet a "storm of bullets and shell sweeping from that hill." As Philips rode ahead, a shell struck the horse behind him and "blew horse and man to bits. The sight sickened me." Twice, they tried and failed to advance up the road, fighting "one of the fiercest and most sanguinary conflicts of the engagement," but the Confederates tried to secure their position in "the timber on the crest of the hill," even as "the ammunition of [Philips's] command began to fail." The fire became so thick that Union officers "expressed their wonder that any of their men ever survived."

Clark's men "occupied not only the ground, but the very tree-tops as well," according to one officer's report, and Confederate sharpshooters were climbing into trees and picking off Federal officers "with deadly accuracy, not less than seven line officers and one field officer being shot at this point." With his back to a large oak, Second Lieutenant James L. Combs told Philips, "Colonel, I am shot to death." Philips dismounted and lifted Combs's head "to drink from his flask which a friend had filled with peach brandy." Lazear and Kelly lost their horses, the former also "shot through the boot," while the latter "for a time . . . almost inhaled lead [but] his lion heart never failed him."[12]

POTATO HILL, OR "BLOODY HILL"

The Federals reached the Harrisonville road without taking what had been called Potato Hill but would afterward be called "Bloody Hill." Crested by a high rock ledge and a log house that provided the Confederates good cover, the eastern slope down to the Big Blue was covered with stumps. The Confederates had batteries in support and even placed sharpshooters up trees. A 1912 newspaper account recommended a Decoration Day hike up "the very sod up which the Federal soldiers crawled, and having reached the crest of the ridge, stand there where three hundred of Marmaduke's Confederates fell; and you may place your hand even now upon the gnarled knots that cover wounds made by cannon balls in the trees of the ancient wood thereabout, and, maybe, kick up with your boot heel a minie ball or an old brass button from the uniform of some luckless fighting man who fell there."[13]

Several failures and the lack of ammunition kept Philips's men clinging to whatever cover they could find behind the stumps and rocks, and they began to answer the enemy with their rifles, carbines, and Colt revolvers. At this moment Philips was dismayed to find that his men were running out of ammunition. Brown had complained to Pleasonton that he had not gotten resupplied with ammunition, and Philips now complained that Brown "had not given out ammunition enough for the day." In turn, Philips sent Major Kelley back for ammunition and reinforcements, receiving the answer from Pleasonton "to hold [his] position without ammunition."[14]

When an orderly hurried to Philips's side to report Crittenden had been shot, Philips rushed to where his friend gasped for air. A quick search for the wound found only a serious bruise in Crittenden's side and the Confederate bullet in his pocket. The ball from a sharpshooter fired from a tree had struck a rock on the ground about twenty feet in front of Crittenden, and the ricochet had hit a roll of shinplasters in his waistcoat. His fellow officers thought he had been shot through the body, and Colonel Philips gave him a drink of the same peach brandy he had given Combs before determining the wound was not serious.[15]

Reinforcements came in the form of Colonel Winslow's brigade. One of his officers later described an understanding of the situation common among them, that the militia had been ordered to charge but "they hadn't the sand in their craw." Winslow told Pleasonton that he could take it, and dismounted two regiments, leaving a reserve under Captains Charles P. Knispel of the Fourth Missouri and Edward W. Dee of the Fourth Iowa. Winslow's men advanced "upon the main position of the enemy. Their line was formed in the edge of a long piece of timber, just on the brow of the rising ground, while in front was a fine open stretch of clearing descending gradually to the river." His charge started "about 400 yards from that of the enemy."[16]

Philips and his men, who hugged the ground for cover, did not stop, even to consult. "Don't try to go in there, Colonel!" shouted Philips. "No man can live there!" Winslow may not have heard and certainly did not heed those words but continued heroically onward for another 100 feet. There, Confederate fire knocked Winslow from his horse, a rifle ball in his leg. Winslow said this happened "just as the enemy turned to run," so he reported his movement to be "perfectly successful, though the enemy held their position." Although Pleasonton reported that Winslow had, despite the wound, continued to command his men, authority had actually fallen to Lieutenant Colonel Frederick W. Benteen.[17]

Winslow's assault also faltered, so Sanborn's brigade crossed over and formed on the left of Philips, with Colonels J. E. Phelps's Second Arkansas Cavalry and Joseph J. Gravely's Eighth MSM Cavalry in the advance. Winslow mistakenly timed the attack for 7 a.m., but Sanborn correctly described his men as "hotly engaged with the enemy." His brigade crossed over and formed to the left of Philips. Phelps noted the Confederates, "protected by stone structures (fences), had formed a double line in order to conceal and protect the maneuvers of their artillery. Here also they had burnt wagons." As soon as the artillery of Phelps's Arkansas was planted anew, the unit made another attempt, with both sides falling back to support their artillery. Phelps saw Confederates on both sides enfilading the road, the other division on open ground in advance and to the right of the artillery. Winslow's men, too, found the terrain impossible for cavalry attack, though in their reports they consoled themselves with having punished the rebels, as "the road beyond, strewn with dead, ammunition, wagons, and horses, testified it amply."[18]

A general advance across the line followed, though Winslow's brigade—under Benteen—had the largest numbers on the field. Benteen sent Major Benjamin S. Jones's Third Iowa Cavalry to the fore. As they approached one of the log houses, 200 or 300 of Philips's men were already in place nearby, though they had been pinned down in one of the earlier charges. Together, they dashed forward. Reported Jones: "We charged them, killing and wounding many of their men (Company A captured one stand of their colors) and completely routed them from their strong position, but suffered a considerable loss in wounded." Pleasonton's officers later spoke of passing "about two hundred men of Brown's Brigade, who were sheltering themselves in disorder from a very hot fire the enemy were pouring on them from the woods at the western edge of the field."[19]

Among the Union prisoners, Confederate Captain Garret S. Van Valkenburg may have been looking furtively around him. The brother of Congressman Robert Van Valkenburg, a New York Republican, had joined the Confederate army. While not well known for his deeds on the battlefield, Captain Van Valkenburg attained some reputation for what happened afterward. He later boasted of having been "captured five times and was successful in making his escape four times," although critics suggested that he actually just accepted paroles and ignored their terms.[20] If so, Van Valkenburg had real reason to want to get away before being recognized.

Philips claimed it as "a splendid victory won by bravery over numbers," but the Federals also had far superior weapons. His own Seventh MSM Cavalry had Smith breech-loading carbine, and at least one regiment of Winslow's brigade carried the Henry repeating rifle, the .44 caliber predecessor of the later Winchester lever-action repeater. Confederate general William L. Cabell later wrote that such troops "poured a rapid and scathing fire into our commands, which far exceeded any firing we could do from our muzzle-loading Enfield rifles."[21]

Decades later, Philips clambered up the hill with a Kansas City newspaperman, pausing to point out where he had seen one or another of his men that day, having fallen obedient to his orders. One section of Battery H of Captain Charles H. Thurber's command of the Missouri Light Artillery, operating under Lieutenant Philip Smiley, fired almost incessantly, with canister and at short range, from eight o'clock till after eleven. At the time, Philips decided the path might be clear enough to permit a bayonet charge. Kelley's men formed to the rear of the Seventh and dashed forward over the felled trees and abatis their comrades had erected earlier in the week. The Confederates remembered the "great fierceness" of the attack as the men closed on each other with sabers and revolvers. Marmaduke's men held the log cabins on the hill, firing through the windows until they were overpowered or shot down by the swarming Federals. An officer later estimated 5,000 hits on one cabin at the crest of the hill. [22]

The heaviest losses suffered by both officers and men in the battle occurred in these brigades and at this point. Had these forces not arrived on the field south of Brush Creek where Curtis and his men were engaged with Jo Shelby and James F. Fagan, the result would have been far different. The Federals had seized Bloody Hill at the cost of 114 casualties. Up this slope was fought the Battle of the Blue—the Big Blue—in which 114 Federal soldiers and eight Federal officers were killed. Upon the crest 300 Confederates died. [23]

Benteen saw the serious limits of this victory. Federal numbers and artillery had simply persuaded the Confederates to fall back. As Marmaduke's men moved "beyond our reach," he and the other Union commanders took little time to organize a pursuit. Sanborn thought the rebels had fallen back as far as three miles, but others estimated lesser distances before engaging the Confederates again. At least in part, this may have reflected the disorganized state of Marmaduke's division. [24]

With the Fourth Iowa Cavalry deployed as skirmishers, Sanborn on the left, Philips in the center, and Benteen on the right moved forward. The defenders did have time to take a strong position to meet them. The Union forces "advanced across the open field at the double-quick to the woods beyond." Once more, Marmaduke's men fell back. Another mile, Philips recalled, "brought us in view of the enemy formed on the prairie." Pushing west, they saw "that that portion of the enemy's force which had been engaged with General Curtis at Westport, in the forenoon, were falling back, making a connection with the force in our front." Philips's audacious charge on the rebel guns forced Marmaduke's men to fall back to protect them while Fagan's and Jackman's fell back to the south before Curtis's army. [25]

Clark described the movements differently. He guessed that they had fought Pleasonton's men for two hours—so probably until around 10 or 11 a.m. At this point, Marmaduke ordered him to withdraw toward the supply train "and protect its left flank from a threatened attack from cavalry." By then, he heard "the booming of Fagan's and Shelby's guns" behind them. Clark's brigade, the strongest in Marmaduke's force, had exhausted its ammunition and had to fall back before the foe. His brigade "repulsed the enemy several times. Falling back through my brigade the enemy came upon me in the full enthusiasm of pursuit, and though my brigade contended nobly with the foe for two hours and strewed the open field in our front with his dead, our ammunition exhausted, we were forced to leave the field again to the enemy, our dead in his hands." The results, however, left the brigades of Philips and Benteen, with Thurber's guns twisting what was left of Marmaduke's line, "nearly at right angle" to the positions of Shelby and Fagan.[26]

The ferocity of the Federal attack had broken part of Marmaduke's division. Back on the plateau south of Brush Creek, General James G. Blunt and his staff occupied the far left of Curtis's line, along what became Wornall Road. From there, they sighted a small column of Confederates moving through the woods where they were not expected to be. They were perilously close to an unsupported Federal howitzer placed before the doorway of a farmhouse. Blunt and his circle dismounted and rushed forward with revolvers blazing, followed by his personal escort, Company E of the Fourteenth Kansas Cavalry, which rushed past the desperate staff in a countercharge that secured the piece.[27] Although none realized it at the time, the Confederates were likely the first members of Marmaduke's division straggling onto the field from the fighting along the Big Blue.

Even over the noise of the immediate battle, Curtis and his men heard the sound of these guns approaching from the east. The Kansans realized, as the sounds grew louder and nearer, that Pleasonton's long and often tediously slow pursuit from St. Louis had arrived on the field at the critical moment. Curtis thought that he heard Pleasonton's guns around noon and felt so sure of what it augured that the general sent a messenger to Kansas City to notify Colonel Kersey Coates that he and his EMM would not be needed and asked him to telegraph General William S. Rosecrans that the day was as good as won.[28] At that point, though, the battle took a decisive turn several miles farther south.

Curtis also jotted a short note to General Henry W. Halleck at Washington, D.C. "We have driven the enemy seven or eight miles south of Westport," he wrote. "He now seems to be moving due south, but some of his lines may have retreated west into Kansas." He added that the guns of the Department of Missouri could be "heard on my left, and our forces will soon join. Our success is glorious. We are still in hot pursuit."[29]

The Train

In lieu of some of the maneuvers that Rosecrans had been discussing from time to time, Pleasonton had ordered General John McNeil at midnight to take Montgomery's Battery L of the Second Missouri Light Artillery toward the junction of the Independence and the Little Santa Fe roads to head off the expected attempt at escape of Sterling Price's wagon train. Pleasonton sent word to Rosecrans at 10.30 a.m. "that he has effected a crossing of the Blue after a very stubborn fight." He added his note that McNeil "may strike their train, which is making for the military road."[30]

When McNeil's brigade received its midnight orders, it had gone for "two days and nearly two nights without forage." The troops started around 1 a.m., hoping to cover the eight miles south and west to block the Confederate retreat to the south. Making their way through the tangle of traffic that tied up all of Pleasonton's forces near Byram's Ford, McNeil's brigade moved south along the eastern bank. At about 4 a.m., it passed "a large camp" of Confederates on the opposite bank. By 10 a.m., McNeil's troops had covered nearly four miles toward Hickman's Mills. The Federals saw hundreds of wagons heading south, "apparently under heavy escort, accompanied by thousands of horsemen."[31]

The Federals' emergence from the woods only two or three miles away startled the Confederates, who quickly formed a line of battle. McNeil sent the Seventh Kansas and Second Missouri Cavalry as skirmishers and deployed the three-inch Rodman rifles of Captain Montgomery's Battery. They "most gallantly pressed up to the main line of the enemy's centre." According to Price, he and his escort helped form "the unarmed men, which were present to the number of several thousand," into a line of battle, throwing forward as skirmishers the "about 200" armed recruits to Colonel Charles H. Tyler's new brigade. When Cabell arrived with his brigade around noon, he deployed his men as well, and had Colonel Thomas H. McCray's brigade in advance of the train. Price noted that the Federals responded by falling back "a considerable distance on the prairie."[32]

Cabell never filed a report (though he wrote a later account, published in 1900), but Confederates left their own version of what happened. Clark, though not present, reported McNeil "advancing upon the flank, but [he] halted without coming to an engagement." Marmaduke, who also was not present, said that "had McNeil attacked at this time they would have lost their whole train." According to the rebels, McNeil hesitated to attack for fear the Confederates would execute him for his involvement in the earlier reprisal executions at Palmyra. Ingenious Confederates, though, backed McNeil down when their small escort of the train extended its line with unarmed recruits and set fire to the long prairie grass. Jenkins's later account accepted the idea that McNeil faced a line, of which "by far the greater number" were unarmed, and that this "ruse" kept the Union horsemen at bay "throughout the entire day, never coming to closer quarters, and the train made good its escape, for that day and the next at least."[33]

Then, too, in addition to the illusion of facing Confederate lines three deep, they "actually surrounded me on three sides," McNeil wrote, and Cabell's brigade remained the largest and one of the best in Price's army. It had howitzers and other armed units, notably Colonel John Q. Burbridge's regiment, which moved into "different positions to protect the train." Even among just the armed men present, the numerical advantage would have been heavily with the defenders. Nevertheless, McNeil's initial response to encountering the train had been to advance, with Captain John F. Austin taking two companies of the Seventeenth Illinois Cavalry forward as skirmishers and bringing Montgomery's guns up to fire on the train. Merrill's Second Missouri Cavalry also advanced.[34]

McNeil thought that Confederate guns had a much bigger impact. When Price got batteries in three different locations, they opened a cross-fire on the Union guns, forcing McNeil to pull them back "some four hundred yards to the left" and reposition the brigade on higher grounds. "I determined to hold this position at all hazards," he reported, "in hope that the remaining brigades would come up." Afterward, they found "about forty of their dead on the field."[35]

The outcome remained to be seen. The officers of Winslow's favored brigade told each other that the failure was not only McNeil's: "McNeal and Sanburn [*sic*] should have been on the South but failed to get there." In reporting his version of the battle, Rosecrans said overall losses numbered only about 200, inflicting "some 49 killed and wounded and taking 2 pieces of artillery complete, including drivers and a number of prisoners." Regarding his department's job as finished, he suggested, "Can General Steele's command do some mischief either to him or General Magruder before they reunite, in case we do not overtake and scatter them, of which I think there is considerable hope."[36]

Once Price realized that the supply train threatened his modest claims of success, he sent couriers to his commanders ordering them "to fall back to the train as soon as they could do so with safety, which I would attempt to defend until they arrived." Fagan, whose division had been spread out from Byram's Ford south, had already begun to fall back to avoid being flanked, and large parts of Marmaduke's division also had begun turning up to help defend the train.[37]

What former governor Price actually watched that day was the utter collapse of the aristocratic white republic he had once governed. So, too, Jo Shelby saw the beginning of the end for the kind of mounted warfare at which he excelled, as did his counterpart, James G. Blunt. From their respective lines, Governors Willard Preble Hall of Missouri and Thomas Carney of Kansas watched the fighting, as did Thomas Reynolds, the Confederate governor of Missouri.[38] All three watched as events began to sweep them from power.

9

Across the Prairie to Indian Creek

The Afternoon into the Night

Around noon, General Jo Shelby's hard-pressed Confederates on the partly timbered plateau just south of Brush Creek got their orders from Sterling Price to fall back. Purporting to quote Shelby, Major John N. Edwards recorded his complaint that General John S. Marmaduke "had fallen back before the enemy—although he had never notified me of the fact, or I never saw his couriers." Although remnants of Marmaduke's force and a fragment of General James Fagan's Arkansans remained, the part of the Army of Missouri that had been able to hold its ground would soon have an entirely new, second Federal army entering the area behind it and to its right.[1] The tide of battle had turned, and the most able Confederate commander in the army knew that they stared defeat in the face.

The Confederate retreat ended the major fighting around Kansas City. The nature of the withdrawal of Price's men from the field proved gratifying enough to the relieved Unionists that they hesitated to address directly the tensions in their own commands. These, however, festered and their subsequent surfacing informed how one of the largest engagements in that corner of the war would—or would not—be remembered.

CONFEDERATE WITHDRAWAL

The hero-worshipping Major Edwards described Shelby as pontificating poetically—if madly—in the face of the enemy, quoting him as saying: "Tell General Price I can not fall back now. If he would help me he must send me reinforcements. Every man shall die at this wall before I leave my wounded or give up a single piece of artillery."

"But, General, you will be surrounded and cut to pieces," Edwards remonstrated.

"Leave that to me—I will save this army yet."

"If our safety can be attributed to any one man," recalled one Confederate veteran, "Jo Shelby wears the laurel."[2]

Yet Edwards's penchant for fanciful fictions aside, Shelby did exactly as ordered and dutifully sent word to his brigade commanders to fall back. He sent Colonel Sydney D. Jackman's brigade to the right to defend the road the supply train had taken south. General Jeff Thompson, too, noted that "as soon as we were supplied with ammunition and prepared to move forward orders were received for us to fall back, and we did so in line of battle under a heavy fire from the enemy's batteries." Shelby and his immediate circle saw to the rear guard for much of this initial retreat, clustering about a tree, "and were not driven off until eighteen of their troopers lay dead."[3]

Colonel Henry J. Vivian claimed later that he remained in position at the ford over Brush Creek until "the Federals were on every side of us, with the exception of one small space on the south." On his own initiative, he abandoned the ford and moved back to the top of a hill "about half a mile east of the Wornall homestead." They continued retreating south, even as Union horsemen rode by them "thinking we were Federals." Farther along, he and his men rejoined the Confederate line. "Where in hell have you been all this time?" Shelby demanded. "Right down there on the ford where you ordered me to go and stay until you sent a courier for me to return," said Vivian. Shelby replied that he had sent a courier, adding, "I suppose the Federals killed him; if they didn't, I will have him court-martialed and shot."[4]

Although observers differed a bit on the time, it seems most likely that Shelby's division began falling back around noon. After dispatching Jackman from his right to reinforce Fagan, Shelby pulled back his left, opposite the KSM, and began slowly giving ground. The rest of the line, using the stone fences well, may not have shifted until closer to 1 p.m. or even later. In the attacking force, Ben Simpson watched helplessly as "a fine boy" from Paola fell dead near him, but he and his men pressed the Confederates into "a complete rout, their broken lines flying in disorder." Back at the Wornall house, young Frank Wornall watched as a soldier came in and took his wounded brother away. "The surgeons said he must not be moved, but the brother insisted. He said he would not leave him there to be killed by the Yankees. He put him on his horse in front of him, but they went only a little way when the wounded man died."[5]

As the Union troops pushed south, they heard a growing noise toward the east. Captain George S. Grover spied "the head of a column of cavalry deployed from the timber, about a mile to the left, and advanced upon the rebel right flank, and as they swung into action, the smoke lifted, and we saw their guidons, and blue uniforms." At first, Sergeant David C. Nettleton and his comrades thought "that the Rebels were outflanking us on the left," but when they saw the gun smoke, they knew that Pleasonton had come up, and "a shout arose that made the welkin ring." General James G. Blunt saw the new line "at right angle with mine" moving west. Even from the far right of General Samuel R. Curtis's troops, Brigadier General George Deitzler of the KSM saw that both armies had come into "full view of each other on the open prairie, presenting one of the most magnificent spectacles in nature."[6]

At that same moment, some of the troops of Major General Alfred Pleasonton hit the first obstacle on the prairie after coming up the bluffs from Byram's Ford. Brigadier General John Sanborn had been driving General John S. Marmaduke's Confederates rather steadily back to the Harrisonville road. Another Confederate force—probably Arkansans—stalled this process with a cavalry charge against the right of Sanborn's brigade. Observers said that it shook the Federals considerably for a bit. Pleasonton quickly brought up Colonel John F. Philips's battered brigade. "Pleasonton, it seemed, wanted to get me killed and the M.S.M. destroyed," he wrote. He hoped that the general thought "better of myself and the MSM since the fight."[7]

To the north, Colonel Frederick Benteen had come up from the valley to find no Confederates to his immediate front. Unable to find Pleasonton, he "took the responsibility upon myself to halt my command in a large corn-field and take a few minutes to feed." At that point, though, the Confederates noisily clashed with Sanborn and "and some of our troops ingloriously [were] falling back." Benteen and Young tried to rally the troops and sent the Tenth Missouri Cavalry countercharging "in gallant style, turning the rebels and driving them."[8] As Marmaduke's men moved south, Fagan's tried to hold what he had of his Arkansas division.

In the course of this, Fagan reportedly stopped Jackman's brigade on its way back to the Moccabee farm, "the point where the gun was captured the evening before." Jackman wheeled his brigade at a gallop to find "the entire prairie in his front was dark with Federals." Dismounting his men, he ordered them "to withhold their fire until the Federals were in point-blank range." They came "in a swinging trot, and when within eighty yards at the command a destructive fire was poured into them, killing and wounding a large number of men and horses, and causing their line to reel and break." Confederate officers reported that the Federals reeled, scattered, and fled, but those on one flank had gotten within thirty paces of his line. Major John N. Edwards's account describes Jackman's dismounting "with almost the forlorn determination of Cortez, who burnt his ships, resolved to conquer or die," leading the reader to expect the next line to be about Jackman's ordering men to shoot their horses or take some comparable action. Instead, Jackman remounted them before "fresh lines of Federals" and "fell back after the train, fighting hard."[9]

As the battle backed over the low rolling swells of the prairie, the rest of Shelby's division, also backing south, grew closer, and Captain Richard Collins from Thompson's brigade brought the last gun of his battery to bear on the attackers. It "poured in double charges of grape and canister" at the Federals, who were said to have been "routed and driven back." Even from the most distant part of the Federal army, Major General George Deitzler of the KSM noted the Confederate artillery was firing there. Shortly after, observers from as far away as Westport could see Pleasonton's "flashing and thundering" guns.[10]

As the Confederates unleashed "a galling artillery fire" upon the Federal horsemen, Captain Charles H. Thurber's battery deployed. Pleasonton paced among them, brandishing his riding crop. "Rebels, Rebels, Fire, Fire, You damned Asses!" Their double canister blasts created an "almost instant demoralization!" Part of Curtis's army began pressing the Confederates as well. Around 2 p.m., Pleasonton's men rode forward, though their regiments had no specific directions for where to strike.[11]

On the southern end of Sanborn's line, Major Henry Suess of Pleasonton's staff sent the Sixth and Eighth MSM Cavalry to take the house on a prairie ridge near Collins's Confederate artillery. Colonel Joseph J. Gravely reported the Confederate force was "much larger than ours, but gave way," partly, the prisoners explained, for fear of losing access to the Harrisonville road. Although the Federals seized a number of wagons with some ammunition and supplies, the Confederates managed to get Collins's gun to safety.[12]

Between 2 and 2:30 p.m., the two Union armies came into alignment "until the two battle-fields were practically one." This happened, paradoxically, because Shelby managed to extricate all of his division from the jaws of destruction. His old brigade, then under Thompson, had been the last to pull back, and withdrew "with much difficulty, for he was hard pressed." As he reached the rise on the prairie, he found it "covered almost by a long line of troops, which at first I supposed to be our own men. This illusion was soon dispelled, and the two great waves [were] uniting."[13]

This juncture represented the apex of the battle of Westport. Several accounts suggest 30,000 combatants faced each other "on a field between three and four miles square." Some actually break this down, giving Curtis 15,000, Pleasonton 6,500, and Price 9,000. In fact, these greatly exaggerate the Federal numbers. Curtis actually had about the same core of 2,500 to 3,000 volunteers with the addition of a slightly larger force of the KSM that had crossed into Missouri. Without the brigade he had sent south, Pleasonton probably had 4,000 to 4,500. At this point, Price probably had little more than Shelby's division remaining on the field, which placed no more than 12,500 to 16,000 in action at that juncture. Then, too, there existed "no comprehensive view of the battle. It was seen only in little unrelated segments and the viewers were left to draw their own conclusions as to the significance of each."[14]

THE ROUT

The drama of what happened next required no exaggeration. What Marmaduke had kept on the field had fallen back from the Federals toward the east side of a high rise of ground, leaving Shelby's men to the east. "Not a tree or bush was to be seen for weary miles and miles, and no helping army could be seen anywhere. I knew the only salvation was to charge the nearest line, break it if possible, and then retreat rapidly, fighting the other." Thompson formed a line facing east and, as the Federals approached, got the order "to charge the enemy then in our front. Our line was not complete, but the regiments that were formed bravely threw themselves against the foe." Colonel Alonzo Slayback's broke the Union skirmish line, which Edwards described as leaving Pleasonton's force "much scattered." However, as the Confederates reached a small swell, they saw not only the enemy cavalry to their front but, to their left and rear, the large force of Federals whose artillery opened with "terrific effect."[15]

From the Federal positions, Blunt had his line "within about 800 yards of the left of the rebel line, and when they were about to charge General Pleasonton's line," Blunt got his artillery blasting "a raking fire into their flank, which threw them into confusion and stampeded them, with the main column of the retreating enemy." Shelby reported, "The column which followed me from Westport came down at the charge, and nothing was left but to run for it, which was now commenced."[16]

Then the brigades of Philips and Benteen also met Thompson's charge. As Collins's crew struggled to reload, Thurber's battery "galloped into short range . . . firing on the re-retreating Confederates with double-shotted canister." As the Confederate general Thompson later wrote, "Then for the first time in this campaign Shelby's brigade turned its backs toward the foe." Despite claiming the Federals had scattered, Shelby's report described them as "furiously, yelling, shouting, and shooting, and my own men fighting, every one on his own hook, would turn and fire and then gallop away again." Thompson left several of his regiments in the rear as support, but "as we rushed back the stampede seemed to become contagious." In the end, he found his command "in wild disorder with the enemy charging at our heels. It was impossible to rally the men as a body, but many brave fellows took advantage of positions to delay the enemy and let the others escape."[17]

Roughly a mile back from where the Federals overwhelmed Thompson's brigade, some stone walls offered cover to these particularly stubborn clusters of his men. "Up from the green sward of the waving grass two miles off," reported Major John N. Edwards, "a string of stone fences grew up and groped along the plain—a shelter and protection." Slayback, Frank Gordon, Yandell H. Blackwell, and Ben Elliott may well have used the cover to rally their men. They did not, however, "turn like lions at bay" and make their "bullets sputter and rain thicker upon the charging enemy," driving back the Union army. Based on this account, Price, too, reported that Shelby's men had "rallied, repulsed the enemy."[18]

These locations indicate that Edwards not only doubled the distance to the wall but surely overstated everything that happened there. Ben Simpson, a Union soldier, remembered this as "a stand on the high prairie" near what he called the Majors farm. He saw Lieutenant Colonel Preston B. Plumb organizing the line of the Eleventh Kansas for a charge there. Simpson later said that the Confederates had not been driven off "until after dark."[19]

Nevertheless, nothing that happened on the farm kept the general Union advance from pressing the retreating Confederates to their south. Grover described the two Federal armies as pushing the Confederates until their position folded "up like a jack-knife, while the newcomers charged simultaneously, breaking the rebel rear, in their front, in wild disorder, causing the rebels to leave their strong position and scatter through the timber of Indian Creek, with scarcely the semblance of an organization, dropping guns, cartridges and blankets in their reckless flight." One of Benteen's men recalled that the charge against Thompson "continued through farms and over the prairie for five or six miles, breaking his lines, and completely scattering his men in every direction, and inflicting severe loss upon him in killed, wounded, and prisoners."[20]

After the collapse of Thompson's brigade most of Shelby's line beyond the Majors farm disintegrated into "a run for life." The rout left "dense volumes of smoke, emanating from their burning of the prairie hay, grain stacks, &c." Periodic pockets of resistance so annoyed the KSM that Colonel Charles W. Blair complained "it was as much as my dismounted men could do to keep up with the artillery." George Deitzler acknowledged that, over "about four miles," the Confederates made "several attempts to stand, but . . . never succeeded in rallying and forming their men to offer any considerable resistance." The retreat "formed a scene never to be forgotten by any who witnessed it." Jim Lane relished watching "beaten, disheartened, and flying" Confederates running from "the resistlessness of our troops, and terror-stricken from the sound of artillery in their rear, turned their faces southward and fled precipitately."[21]

Events moved quickly. Between 2:30 and 3 p.m., depending on the account, the Union generals met at the farm of the Thomas family near Indian Creek, about five miles beyond where Shelby's holdouts were supposedly holding back the Federal army. Pleasonton and his staff had already reached that point when Curtis and his staff rode up. Both sent messages to General William Rosecrans, who remained missing, but Governor Thomas Carney, Senator Lane, and Generals Blunt, Sanborn, Deitzler, and William H. M. Fishback attended the impromptu strategy meeting that decided to press on to nearby Little Santa Fe on the Kansas state line.[22]

Federals encountered some small numbers of Confederates trying to anchor but "they broke as we reached them, reformed, and again we rode them down." All accounts indicate that the Union pursuit had been prompt and relentless. The KSM participated in this pursuit over the open fields, "firing volley after volley into the flying rebels, killing and wounding large numbers, who were left in our hands." Had they encountered more stubborn pockets of resistance, the Federals would have left some of their number to contain and break it down, while the wave itself continued sweeping south.[23]

In the wake of the Union sweep of the field, nothing really hindered movement across what had been a battlefield between the Thomas farmhouse and Westport. Couriers carried messages to and fro, and everything had moved too quickly for Major Samuel S. Curtis to have established communications between the headquarters of the armies. As he made his way through the dusk settling over the field behind the armies, he saw "but one white man, who appeared to have been a Federal soldier, and two negroes" in search of Sanborn's camp shortly after dark. Much of the KSM also crossed the field. Nor did enough Confederate holdouts remain to trouble the reporters getting their stories back over the fifteen miles to the telegraph.[24]

Shelby and the force he had hoped to rally never amounted to much and found themselves isolated and pinned by part of Thomas Moonlight's brigade. Well protected by their stone wall, the rebels managed to survive efforts to dislodge them until nightfall. At that point, they slipped off to make their way south. "We will never forget the impression made upon our minds," continued Edwards, "when we saw General Shelby coming out of the fight at Westport without a hat on his head, his sandy locks streaming in the wind, his six-shooter in his hand and his gallant division, after three days of hard fighting, overpowered and cut to pieces, but still not whipped, gathering around their beloved chieftain and ready to turn at a moment's notice on the rapidly advancing enemy." The image proved so compelling that a Confederate veteran, who was writing about it but probably was not present, covered it by simply quoting Edwards.[25] The collective self-delusions of war outlast its fighting.

Even Shelby and his men dared not reflect too intently on their prospects. They had been among the first to enter the state a month before, probed most quickly toward St. Louis, and broke the first line of Union defenses before Jefferson City. Whenever Price's army had needed its strongest forces in the advance, or as rear guard, it had turned to Shelby. Even the dullest of them must have known that what they had experienced before Westport made it all for naught.

The drift of Price's army to the Kansas line naturally left the Union troops at the western end of the battlefield closest and in the fore of the pursuit. Blunt's cavalry generally pressed the Confederates "until dark, followed by the cavalry of General Pleasonton's command." While Moonlight left some of his men, probably bolstered by some KSM, to deal with the Confederates behind the stone wall back on Majors's farm, he took most of his brigade off to Olathe to keep the Confederates from turning into Kansas.[26]

Price's retreat, with portions of the Fifteenth and Sixteenth Kansas Cavalry and Second Colorado Cavalry on its heels, hit the road from Hickman's Mills to Little Santa Fe and headed west toward the state line. With Shelby's men disorganized, Fagan's Arkansans remained to meet and slow the Federal advance. With a large force—said to be 6,000 but surely no more than half that—the Arkansans rallied a desperate rear guard action several miles to the south of Little Santa Fe. Bolstered with three rifled guns, the Confederates had firepower Charles R. Jennison's men could not match. The Federals fell back through the darkness, beyond artillery range, and waited for the rest of their army. Some miles farther on, Price pulled his shredded army into camp.[27] In its fitful sleep, it sought to dream that the forces large and well enough organized to have beaten them so thoroughly would not be so large and well organized on the morrow.

Most Confederates had enough sense to have lost their faith in the possibility of victory, without which the will to fight fades. For three hours, they had remained in harm's way not to save Missouri but to hang on to a train of stolen farm wagons and livestock. Gone was the illusion of retaking the state and a permanent reunion with friends and family. Gone was the hope Missouri would rise and free itself with a mighty shake from the yoke of Federal authority. The only goal that remained to them now would be simply securing a filling meal and an undisturbed night's sleep.

Most got neither.

Their opposite numbers pressed for reasons of their own. The Kansans faced their long-standing foes with the ferocity of those whose homes, families, and friends had been threatened, and the Missourians alongside them battled for redemption of their honor and reputation in the eyes of the rest of the Union. No tears would be enough to wash the experience from the field, not for those who had experienced the day or those for whom the sacrifice had bought the time to forget, to misplace the yellowed scribbling or the faded photograph.

In the Wake

As the fighting moved south, residents of the battlefields began emerging from their cellars and shelters to see the aftermath. Well before dark, newspaper writers and a few curious residents of Westport and Kansas City joined them.

By 5 p.m., a reporter for the *Leavenworth Times* and Rev. John Fuller with four friends wandered among the dead horses and human corpses to gawk at such sights as the Confederate cannon dismounted by the Union shot, reading into it the story of the human wreckage. One local had a half-cocked musket taken from the hands of a dead man who, in the noise and panic, had not realized that it had misfired and put a second charge down the barrel only to have a Union bullet pass under the hammer, graze the stock, and strike him in the chest. Along the way, they encountered those living their last—those "too severely wounded to be moved"—at places like the Wornall house or men shot through the bowels or bleeding out through a gunshot in the neck.[28]

At Little Santa Fe, Pleasonton sent Rosecrans a quick report. They had left the Confederates "badly punished and demoralized" and his own force ready to resume pursuit the next day. He passed along the estimate of casualties from his surgeon, Ferdinand V. Dayton of the Second New Jersey Cavalry, who had accompanied Pleasonton's transfer from the Army of the Potomac earlier in the year. Dayton reported "our wounded in to-day's fight count upward of 200 enlisted men and some 10 officers." The indications are that Pleasonton lost as many just in the breakthrough on the hill over Byram's Ford, and he gives no totals for the dead or missing.[29] If Pleasonton lost 200 to 250 wounded, the usual proportion implied 50 to 65 dead and a score of missing, for a total of perhaps 275 to 350.

The Army of the Border did not suffer as badly. "Our losses are inconsiderable," Curtis told Washington. "We lost one gun yesterday and took one to-day." Although we know less about the state of his men than his artillery strength, Curtis, unlike Pleasonton, did not respond to stalemates by turning up with a riding crop and goading his officers to order a charge. It took three tries to get across Brush Creek and secure a position on the bluffs to its south, and the initial reports indicated that loss "not so heavy on our side." The fighting did become quite intense when the Confederates attempted to take the Union artillery near the Wornall road, but Blunt's command preferred to rely heavily on those guns. In killed, wounded, and missing, Curtis's volunteer force may have lost 100 to 150, with a similar number in the KSM. This would have totaled 475 to 650 Union casualties for the day, a loss "heavier than we first supposed."[30]

Confederates were in denial when they wrote their reports. Despite everything his brigade had experienced in the field, Jackman acknowledged only a few more than 100 killed and wounded and said nothing of the much larger number of missing. Most of these reports invest disproportionate words in discussing the fate of high-ranking officers killed, wounded and missing, presumed captured. Losses were given piecemeal, as 300 dead and wounded around Byram's Ford, 100 in the Union countercharge along Wornall Road, and similar losses against Marmaduke near the Harrisonville road or where the two Union armies slammed into Thompson's brigade. Then, too, an army broken and driven from the field, particularly if rigorously pursued, would have lost much more than its pursuers. Given that the "missing," those who disappeared from his army—though many turned up in later hours and days—seem to have included most of entire units.[31] A reasonable estimate of the total Confederate dead and wounded would have to run at least 700 to 1,000, with thousands having gone "missing" for at least the duration of the battle.

To be sure, accounting for such numbers of dead and wounded remains a problem, but those who saw the field testified to the carnage. George "Fish" Davis, who had been emancipated the year before, followed events on "as pretty a morning as you ever laid eyes on; by afternoon you couldn't see the sun for the smoke from the artillery. After the battle, the hills were covered with dead men. It was terrible. Terrible."[32]

Observers came out to the field almost as soon as the shooting stopped. A short distance from a fork of the Harrisonville road, one observer noted a body with the top of his head shot off by a cannon. He seemed "the very image of a bushwhacker, and had on *three pairs of pantaloons*" and a gold ring on one of his fingers. Others apparently tried to get it but did not have the time. Another corpse was dressed in "a fine suit of new clothes, evidently the plunder of some store or house." Union artillery seemed to have performed "the main execution."[33] However, the observation may have been deceptive, since the bodies of those relatively intact disappeared quickly.

People began burying those bodies almost as soon as the fighting moved on and even sooner in some cases. Confederates borrowed a spade from the Wornall family and likely did the same at farmhouses across those fields, which meant they buried numbers of their dead near where they fell. Those who actually lived on those farms had no reason to wait for the Federal authorities to do something with the corpses scattered for miles across the landscape, and there existed no requirement of reporting such things with any precision. The day after the battle, one local pointed out the site where he had seen thirty-two Confederates hastily buried.[34] The numbers of projected Confederate dead could have easily disappeared into the fields from Brush Creek and the Big Blue to Indian Creek.

The Confederate wounded were regularly told that the Federals would kill them, and later accounts describe them as literally crawling into the woods to escape detection; some would have been doing so at Westport as well. Most had family and friends to assist in removing them from harm's way. Still, reporters, rather than military reports, noted the several score of Confederates "lying wounded out on the Blue, with but one surgeon and a single nurse to take care of them." The Federal armies had quickly moved on to other, more pressing, concerns. And the Confederate wounded who reached hospitals often received remarkably lenient treatment. "Most of the rebel wounded were mere youths—one not more than 15 years of age—and are believed, from the best accounts, to have been conscripted in Missouri."[35]

The Federals took large numbers of prisoners. As they were being marched back to the town, one of them quipped to his friend that they had surely beaten Price to Kansas City. His comrade retorted that he "wished Old Pap was along with them." Not long after the battle, the Kansas City *Journal of Commerce* complained about Confederate officers' being "allowed about the streets, as a Captain was yesterday, who boasts of having escaped twice already." (One cannot help but wonder if this was Captain Garret S. Van Valkenburg.) However, the paper's particular concern was for bushwhackers among the prisoners, murderous men who had already demonstrated their contempt for the rules of war. However, the Confederate conscription of every white man of military age they could find meant that many of those who had fallen into Union hands got remarkable consideration.[36] Indeed, in a matter of days, the press reported that the army would release large numbers of prisoners upon their taking an oath of allegiance and posting bond for their future loyal conduct.

On the Union side, record keeping in the region remained unbelievably more lax than in the East. A list of the wounded in the Kansas City hospital ran only to roughly 160, but there are also mentions of thirty-five at another location in the city, where several such hospitals had been established in churches and private homes. Another forty, mostly Kansans, suffered at the Harris House in Westport, but the campaign dropped these kinds of numbers into temporary hospitals from Independence into Kansas and from Wyandotte down the state line.[37] More important, of course, was that those Union soldiers who were close to home would have likely been sent there if possible.

As these arrangements indicated, the army had little or no mechanism for dealing with such things. Civilians, particularly women, took up the slack. Priorities varied, of course. As the battle closed, an exhausted Mrs. H. S. Millett had spent the day assisting in the city and recalled that "a young lady who was very fond of dress" told her, "The rebels are going to burn us out and I am not going to lose my silk dresses, so I am going to Kansas with them." Yet Mrs. Millett and the other "ladies of Kansas City" worked tirelessly to deal with the wounded. Mary Haverty's select school for girls in Westport dutifully held its classes but ended the day by riding to the battlefield to assist the wounded of both armies. So did "the ladies of Westport" who supplied bandages and lavished their attention on the wounded.[38]

However, Smith had clear orders from Rosecrans about "the importance of moving at once on Independence. Take the shortest practicable route." Past midnight, Rosecrans told Pleasonton that "Smith has been ordered to march to Independence by the shortest line. Delay a general engagement until he arrives, if possible. Try to keep as much to Price's south as possible, so as to communicate easily with Smith, who will probably be up by this p.m. at latest." Smith dutifully replied around 4:30 p.m. that he had reached and stopped at the Little Blue to "await the arrival of my whole command, feed, get supper, &c." He requested further orders, saying that, without them, he would resume his march at 1 a.m. Shortly after—at 5 p.m.—Rosecrans replied with little urgency.[39]

By the evening, though, Rosecrans described that the movement of Smith's troops had been "a contretemps." Smith took it on himself to send a courier to Hickman's Mills in response to rumors that Confederate General John B. Magruder had marched up from Arkansas. Only after the fighting had already swept the Confederates to Little Santa Fe and beyond did Rosecrans order Smith to "move by the shortest route to Hickman Mills, and thence to Little Santa Fé, in Kansas, where you can get forage." Rosecrans wrote to Smith: "a profound disappointment placing your infantry thirty-six hours behind time. The best thing you can do is to move down the Line road as rapidly as possible. The enemy is fully thirty-five miles ahead of us." Rosecrans claimed to have "placed a courier line on the road yesterday, but could not communicate with you. You ought to have communicated with me."[40]

During the next few hours, the supply train continued on to the military road and turned south toward Little Santa Fe. About four hours after the initial contact—probably about 2 p.m.—McNeil decided to shift "some 400 yards to the left [and] recall my skirmish line, and occupy the new position." Major Curtis, who had taken Captain Ezra W. Kingsbury's Company of the Second Colorado to Independence, had tried to reach Pleasonton but missed him and wound up continuing south, where he met McNeil with only 1,800 men engaged in this artillery duel, though Price estimated his numbers as "some 2,000 or 2,500 strong." He found it "drawn up in line of battle on a ridge, with a number of dismounted men in the valley in front of them. On the opposite ridge to the south about three-fourths of a mile distant the enemy were deployed and still deploying. Some artillery firing was progressing when I came up, which continued for several minutes thereafter, but as the enemy continued to deploy troops and was endeavoring to flank us on both sides, General McNeil ordered the command to fall back about half a mile."[41] If McNeil had indeed balked at risking defeat, he had simply followed the excellent example of his superiors, but it had been enough.

Convinced that he had "fought the entire force of Price yesterday afternoon to this point on the prairie," McNeil took his brigade into camp at 4 p.m. Although they remained in "good fighting trim," they had no replacement mounts, no rations, and little water. For the next five hours, their pickets continued to report the movement of small groups of Confederates around them, most heading from toward Little Santa Fe. McNeil's brigade waited in expectation "for the arrival of General Smith, unless otherwise ordered."[42]Despite this colossal change in what he had protected, Rosecrans told Curtis that the infantry would be "reaching Little Santa Fé to-morrow evening, and perhaps farther." "I regret Smith did not get your dispatch in time," adding that he still expected that Smith would "probably reach Little Santa Fé at the same time with you." Rosecrans said he "will probably be at Hickman Mills myself to-morrow night." Rosecrans later reported that Smith's infantry had shown up at Independence, and he had "ordered a forced march to Hickman Mills, hoping it would strike the enemy in flank while passing that point." Moreover, Rosecrans informed McNeil that "General Smith will be with you by 10 a.m. at latest. Watch the enemy's motions during the night."[43]

"If Smith gets to Pleasant Hill to-day he should strike at once for the military road, but from the way the rebs are traveling I think he will be too late." Rosecrans also reported that had Smith been "ordered and marched" there rather than to Independence, the Confederates would have faced 9,000 Union infantry and five batteries. At best, his infantry could be "support in case of possible reverse to us or re-enforcements which were constantly reported on their way to meet the enemy." Rosecrans arranged to get a telegraph operator to Pleasant Hill.[44]

Of course, Pleasonton had not left such a small defensive force and pushed his faster, mounted force to Hickman's Mills. In his own defense, he claimed that the Confederate general "intended to take Kansas City," and the results left Pleasonton's army "nearer to [the Confederate general] than I could get by any flank movement of my whole force." Most important, he had sent McNeil "to get on the military road ahead of them, if possible, or on their flank, if in motion."[45] McNeil, in turn, seemed to have been expecting Smith's infantry to come up behind him in support.

Yet there would be plenty of responsibility to bear—or shift to the underlings. "I arrested General Brown and Colonel McFerran to-day," reported Pleasonton, "the first for disobedience of orders and gross neglect of duty in face of the enemy, and Colonel McFerran for permitting his regiment to be broken up and straggle scandalously." Pleasonton had "heard nothing of McNeil to-day; he was ordered to be at this point at daylight this morning."[46] The axe would fall in his direction, too, but not quite yet.

Rosecrans had entirely failed to deploy troops where he knew they needed to be. And he shared none of this with Curtis but suggested, "If you can possibly harass the enemy's rear guard strongly and firmly, and pass the main part of your command to the south of him, General Smith will come up and destroy him." With the maddeningly facile charm of obliviousness, Rosecrans added, "Don't fail to do this."[47]

"The charge was made, and the rebels broke disordered upon our right and centre," Captain Richard J. Hinton recalled. "Again our lines were advanced. Everywhere in front, were seen the general officers, cheering and encouraging, greeted with the enthusiastic shouts of the men, while twice the rebel columns had broken and re-formed. Both lines were now deploying upon the open prairie, ours still having the advantage of some fields and fences."[48]

Four

Union Victories

10

Flight and Pursuit

Indian Creek to the Mounds, October 24–25

Exhausted and begrimed, Union officers tumbled from their saddles and grabbed for their maps, as they reached the timber fringing Indian Creek, a mile or so south of the expansive prairies above Westport. The Confederates had followed their long supply train through Little Santa Fe, the hamlet only a mile or so toward the southwest, on the military road. Ominously, roughly eighty miles to the south sat Fort Scott, the defenses of which had been virtually stripped to constitute the Army of the Border. As Dick Hinton put it, "Next to Leavenworth, the post of Fort Scott is the most important in Kansas."[1] That gave the Federals their common marching orders to secure one of the largest government supply depots in the West, unchangeable by anything that had taken place at Westport.

Many on both sides knew the border south from Little Santa Fe. About thirty-five miles south, a small Union garrison had long held an outpost at Coldwater Grove. Another ten miles south was the small crossroad at West Point, and roughly another ten would take the riders to the hamlet of Trading Post and the nearby ford over the Marais des Cygnes. Only a bit beyond that came a crossroad near Mine Creek, which was only about twenty miles from Fort Scott.[2]

NIGHT OF THE GENERALS

General Samuel R. Curtis reported the Union victory had been "most decisive." "We did not stop to count our losses or bury our dead in any of these conflicts," he wrote. "In killed, wounded, and missing it was probably 500. The enemy's loss in killed and prisoners was not larger, but their men scattered." Nearly two months after the battle, General George Deitzler thought the losses of the KSM "comparatively slight" but declined even to present an estimate of "the number of militia in the field, of men killed, wounded, and taken prisoners, nor of particular acts of gallantry and daring of members of the militia which deserve honorable mention." One boy recalled that his father "gathered up the saddles from dead horses on our farm and put them near our woodpile. There were hundreds of them." For decades after, they "plowed up bushels of bullets, shells, cannon balls, sabers and pieces of muskets."[3]

A reporter for the Kansas City *Journal of Commerce* rode over the field, composing graphic descriptions of the dead. Near the Wornall house, he found "seven dead rebels lying; side by side, and near them an officer," misidentified as Colonel James McGhee. Some corpses had clothes worse for the wear and others wore the fruits of plundered stores and prisoners whom they had encountered and robbed somewhere in the hundreds of miles behind them. Noting "a rebel cannon, broken to pieces by a shot from one of our guns," the newspaperman encountered the "dead horses, saddles, blankets, broken guns and dead rebels." A Union soldier had tried to get the gold ring from one of the bodies that still had it, along with three pairs of pants, though missing the top of his head. Eager to reclaim their farms, locals had already began to put the bodies into the ground near where they fell. Here and there, those shot in the stomach or the neck or the head gasped out their last breath.[4]

Major Samuel B. Davis and other army surgeons sent ambulances "to every accessible part of the field" to gather the wounded that could be moved. Many of the worst Confederate wounded remained at the Wornall house, but the Federals brought others in to a temporary hospital at Westport, ultimately leaving dozens of the more severely wounded there temporarily. Others clustered at Shawneetown, Hickman's Mills around Westport near Brush Creek, or anywhere the fighting had been particularly intense. When the Union cavalry had retaken Independence, they retook most of the thirty-one wounded members of Curtis's army who had to be left behind when Sterling Price's army seized the town, and the army sent a boat to bring them back. The surgeons, chaplains, and even such officials as Senator Samuel C. Pomeroy spent the aftermath tending the wounded, getting those who could be moved by ambulance into Kansas City. There, a doctor went door to door to get Mrs. H. S. Millett and other women to the Southern Methodist Church on Fifth Street, where they "put the pews together to form couches and they lay there and on the floor. Some died soon after they were carried into the church." Millett recalled seeing an Indian there. "The next day we got together all the quilts we could and converted the church and the dance hall into comfortable hospitals."[5]

Riding back and forth between responsibilities, Hinton encountered forty or fifty prisoners under guard near Westport. He described some looking like bushwhackers and others "like 'good quiet farmers,' who had lately joined the expedition for plunder." Although many seemed to be "mere boys," they shared "the stolid, ignorant, degraded appearance of the whole of them," confirming his sense that they fought a war "of intelligence, enlightened and Christian civilization against barbarism." Yet Hinton could not help but record the clever exchange in which one of the prisoners quipped that they "had got the joke on Old Pap this time, as they would surely beat him into Kansas City." Another replied that he "wished Old Pap was along with them."[6]

Prisoners of the Confederates were hungrier, more terrified, and continually on the move. Part "of this seething mass of humanity," goaded on by "yells and loudmouthed profanity," Samuel J. Reader thought his captors "more like a motley assemblage of farmers on a big wolf hunt, than soldiers," as they robbed everybody of their hats, overcoats, and pocketbooks. Later, he noticed guards chewing bullets to relieve their thirst and begged for one, after which a Confederate "dropped the bullet he was chewing into his hand, and gave it to me." Under the circumstances, "squeamishness was thrown to the winds." He saw no prisoners shot, although one of the officers "came tearing along at full speed—his black eyes flashing with anger. He shouted as he rode up: 'Shoot them! Kill them! They shoot our boys down in cold blood every time. Serve them as they serve us!'" Several times, Reader heard comments like, "I've seen the Yanks ride up to our wounded as they lay on the ground, and shoot them in cold blood!" The guards seemed to allow them to exhaust themselves with their rants and leave.[7]

As Price himself moved south along the State Line Road with his wagons, Brigadier General M. Jeff Thompson tried to put together something of a rear guard. The Federal advance to New Santa Fe found the Confederate colonel Alonzo W. Slayback "with some of their men briefly barring [the Federals'] way south."[8] However, exhaustion did more to slow the Federals than the small numbers of resisting Confederates in their way.

By midafternoon, Generals Curtis and Alfred Pleasonton converged with their staffs at the farmhouse of a Mr. Thomas along Indian Creek. Although Pleasonton claimed "about 10,000" MSM cavalry, Curtis—with 4,000 volunteers and a KSM of indeterminate size—remained the senior officer and took command. Generals James G. Blunt, George Deitzler, John Sanborn and other commanders turned up, as did Senator Jim Lane and Governor Thomas Carney. They stopped here "for dinner and consultation."[9] Conspicuous by their absence were General William S. Rosecrans of the Department of Missouri and the commander of his large body of infantry, A. J. Smith, supposedly somewhere near Hickman's Mills.

Pleasonton here argued that he should take his forces south from Harrisonville independently. He implied that they would meet northbound troops from Arkansas and the need to keep Missourians near the state for the elections. Curtis insisted "that the success already achieved might not be frittered away in following on a road over which no enemy had retreated." Governor Carney and

General Deitzler insisted on discharging the ill-equipped and minimally paid KSM members back to their home counties. After all, the militia system there had never needed to be more than a largely untried one-size-fits-all arrangement. In the end, Pleasonton deferred and Deitzler sent the KSM home, except for the Fifth, Sixth, and Tenth Regiments from southern Kansas.[10]

More than six hours after Curtis sent his courier to Rosecrans, the head of the Department of Missouri replied from Independence to "repeat my belief expressed in yesterday's dispatch to you that our combined forces can bring Price to grief." He said that the infantry would reach Little Santa Fe the next day. From there, Curtis telegraphed General Henry W. Halleck in Washington that "the pursuit will be renewed at daylight. After four days' obstinate fighting the men and horses are much exhausted and must have a little rest."[11]

A few miles west and south of where the Federal generals ate dinner, their men had several further exchanges of gunfire. Late in the afternoon, Captain Joel Huntoon's company of Colonel Thomas Moonlight's Eleventh Kansas "struck the rear of the enemy and drove him out of Kansas. This was gallantly done and saved that portion of the State from the flames," before continuing on to Aubrey for "a few hours' rest" and forage. Lieutenant Colonel Frederick Benteen's report also implied that his advance continued to encounter the enemy over the rest of the day.[12]

However, Colonel Charles R. Jennison's little brigade engaged in the clearest skirmishing during the day, as it pushed quickly through Little Santa Fe to reach his home in Mound City, near Fort Scott. One of his admirers later wrote that he and his men had "pursued Price, attacking his rear hourly." Around 5 p.m. on Sunday, October 23, Confederates—probably those under Slayback—"advanced on us, opening out with artillery and small-arms, to which we responded with small-arms." After falling back to a strong defensive position on a nearby hill, the Federals "deemed prudent with our small force to retire, which we did, falling back some five miles near Little Santa Fé." They ended the day in camp about a mile south of the rest of the Army of the Border.[13]

Hunger and exhaustion settled the forces around Little Santa Fe. Curtis had sent Major Theodore J. Weed to bring up rations for men and horses, but, even though they were moving day and night, enough of the wagons never quite caught up. Colonel Charles W. Blair's men trickled into camp "about sunset, and stopped to feed, getting the first forage my horses had eaten since we left the Blue." He added that his men had been without rations for two days, so he authorized Hogan's Nineteenth KSM to butcher three or four head of cattle "eaten without bread or salt," though the rest of his brigade had to go hungry.[14]

Notwithstanding Pleasonton's reluctance, he dutifully placed his men behind them, apparently strung out back along Indian Creek. Benteen's had advanced into Kansas, with the Third Iowa Cavalry camping on the state line. However,

Major Samuel S. Curtis stumbled into Sanborn's camp shortly after dark as he moved through Missouri to catch up to his father. There, too, Colonel John F. Philips, trying to sleep with his brigade, complained of stragglers passing through on their way to the Kansas units. Apparently left uninformed about the course of the rest of the battle, Brigadier General John McNeil remained back near Hickman's Mills for the night.[15]

Rosecrans claimed that Smith's infantry had reached that point and "would strike the enemy in flank" the next day. In fact, Smith's men had reached Independence only around 5 p.m.; there he heard from Rosecrans that he would have to move his footsore men into a bizarre "forced march" in the night to get to where Rosecrans had claimed it was. When Rosecrans admitted where his infantry actually was, he added: "Had he been ordered and marched for that point instead of Independence the day before[,] General Smith would have arrived in time to strike the enemy's compact column and train with 9,000 infantry and five batteries."[16] Who but Rosecrans could have given such an order?

Meanwhile, nagging concerns began to keep exhausted men up at night. Wagonmaster R. M. Peck spoke of "jealousies between Generals," and another Union veteran later expressed his confusion about why the commanders did not continue to chase the battered Confederates "instead of waiting 24 hours." From Little Santa Fe on, the veteran wrote, "I saw a great many moves that I thought were blunders."[17]

When the duties of Lieutenant George T. Robinson, a St. Louisan in the Eleventh Kansas Cavalry, brought him to Rosecrans's headquarters, the general imperiously sent for Robinson, then left him waiting as Rosecrans finished his supper. He did not introduce Robinson to any of his staff officers present but asked for "a free statement of what General Curtis had been doing." Robinson reported the efforts of the Army of the Border to hold Price at the Big Blue. Preoccupied with moving Price out of his department, Rosecrans responded to the report by seeking validation from his staff: "Old Curtis appears to be trying to drive Price right back into Missouri." And an underling dutifully agreed that the Kansas commander had gotten things "beautifully muddled up."[18]

"General," Robinson responded reasonably, "you do not suppose that General Curtis would open a clear road for Price to go straight through Kansas." Rosecrans snarled that Robinson knew nothing about the question, and the general's underlings hastened to agree that Curtis had been a "regular old muddle-head" and that his activities indicated that he had been "getting old and childish." Rosecrans justified this with several utterly bizarre assertions about the conduct of the campaign.

In full contradiction of their documented positions, the commander of the Department of Missouri claimed that he had "had the greatest difficulty in getting General Curtis to believe that Price was in Missouri at all." Curtis, complained Rosecrans, had just declared "that the idea of Price, with 3,000 men being in the State of Missouri, was monstrous." "And now, colonel," he said, turning to his aide, "I guess the old man finds that Price is no fiction; that he is a reality, eh?" Another subaltern agreed.

In an obvious attempt to cover his own negligence, Rosecrans insisted that "my own military judgment" had been to move his forces "farther south" to prevent Price's escape. However, Curtis and "the constant cry of Kansas City, Kansas City, induced me to order my troops there, with the beautiful result of losing the whole thing." The documentation unavailable at the time to Lieutenant Robinson or other participants places Rosecrans in a rather poor light.

Finally, Rosecrans described the entire operation of his Kansas comrades as a "border ruffian institution" and asserted that Lane was "actually in command of the whole machine." Robinson sharply noted that Lane had been "at the front and doing his duty as a common soldier as were many other Kansas men, but as to his having command of any portion of the troops it was not so." Rosecrans missed the possible barb about his own absence from the field but insisted that he knew "much better than you possibly can do; I understand and know Jim Lane thoroughly."[19]

To Coldwater Grove and West Point

General Sterling Price insisted on maintaining the 500 wagons and 3,000 head of cattle, though they had dragged down the pace of his Army of Missouri for weeks, but the Confederates got an early start on Monday, October 24. As the Federals camped around Little Santa Fe, the tail of Price's army slept about eight or ten miles to the south. The remnants of units of Jo Shelby's division under Thompson and Slayback had been the last Confederates the Federals had encountered Sunday night. These had apparently continued south, reassembling their scattered members, leaving what the battle had spared behind them, notably Charles Tyler's collection "of conscripts, volunteers and bushwhackers." About five miles beyond camped the advance of Price's army under General John S. Marmaduke that had first disengaged from Sunday's battle and had gotten five miles farther south. From the tracks the Federals knew the Army of Missouri generally moved in columns on either side of the road, with their artillery and wagons in the center.[20] They began this early enough to get several hours ahead of the Federals.

The Federals proved to be less desperately energetic. Before daylight, Lieutenant Josiah M. Hubbard headed south from Little Santa Fe for the Signal Corps and continued past Jennison's men to establish the first forward outpost of the day, atop a church. At 8 p.m., Curtis sent word back to his superiors in Washington that Price had made "rapid progress, but dead horses and debris show his demoralized and destitute condition and my probable success in overhauling him." Up the road, Price's men and the civilians they encountered had a far worse time of it. When the Federals reached the first house over the state line in Kansas, they saw "the malignant fury of the rebel invader." The remains of the fence and outhouse still burned, and their hurried attempt to torch the little dwelling had left scorch marks on the walls and floors. There had been "a perfect saturnalia of destruction" in which the Confederates had taken everything they could and destroyed what they could not take. Women and children were "crazed with terror and grief," and an "old, gray-haired minister of the Gospel lay dead, with white locks reddened by his own blood." The Confederates had also stripped the residents "of nearly every article of clothing on their persons or in the cabin" and capped the visit by shooting one of their own broken-down horses and tumbling the body into the spring "in order to make the water useless."[21]

The dawn was "bright and sufficiently pleasant," as the Union column formed up at Little Santa Fe that Monday. At 8 a.m., as the first of them headed south, Curtis reassured his outposts that he was about to pursue the Confederates with "all my available force." He reorganized the column into two divisions, the Army of the Border under General Blunt and the second under Pleasonton with the cavalry of the Department of Missouri. Major Benjamin S. Jones, an Iowa cavalryman, recalled that "it would have been worse than fanaticism" before then to imagine "the governments of Missouri and Kansas would unite as they did on that day and drive out the defenders of African slavery and the destroyers of the Government, as it was our delight to do." Curtis's son took the general's escort of Coloradoans back to their regiment, which formed the core of James H. Ford's brigade, with that of Moonlight taking of Blunt's advance.[22]

Rosecrans brooded at the further involvement of Pleasonton's horsemen in pressing Confederates, whose danger to his own department seemed to be fading hourly. As Blunt's men headed south, Pleasonton sent one of his staff to inform one of Curtis's that the department troops would take the road from Harrisonville or Pleasant Hill over in Missouri to stay on the flank of the retreating army. Curtis, however, "insisted on the troops keeping on the shortest line," that of the State Line Road. Pleasonton did not have his men on the march until 10 a.m.[23]

At the head of the march, Captain E. W. Kingsbury's three squadrons of Coloradoans reached the Big Blue, where they found that Jennison's brigade had already preceded them. Jennison's men, largely from south Kansas, had a particular concern about getting between their homes and the invaders. They had been fighting the brutal war of reprisals back and forth across the border for the better part of a decade. At the crossing of the Big Blue, Hinton saw "the marks of Colonel Jennison's presence in stark forms of several bushwhacking looking individuals, who had met their fate during the night. Among these was one clothed in a Federal uniform, who, in obedience to general orders, was hung as a spy."[24]

Among Jennison's men rode what there was of Lieutenant Colonel George H. Hoyt's Fifteenth Kansas Cavalry. Although relatively recently organized, years of fighting had hardened the men who had joined it. Much of one company consisted largely of the Lenape (or Delaware) Indians, who had, like most native populations, suffered the most from the advent of the war, which had effectively sanctioned the violent resolution of intertribal rivalries. Confederate officials had entered the Indian Territory three years before with a death list of local Unionists, who had responded in kind, and the result had left the area devastated. Then, too, Hoyt had been John Brown's lawyer after the Harper's Ferry raid.[25] While the pace of Price's retreat might encourage straggling, it could be a perilous undertaking.

The bluecoats spent Monday chasing "a dense moving column of dust some miles to the south" and the debris it left, including abandoned wagons and "hundreds of broken down and abandoned animals." Around noon, they found the limber and caisson of the howitzer the Confederates had captured near Moccabee farm, a good indication of the state of their artillery ammunition. (Among the prisoners, Reader had noticed the abandoned Topeka piece as he had passed the site.) Periodically, the Union advance caught sight of small parties of Price's men rejoining the column from the west. Hinton noted "the charred remains of consumed dwellings, the only standing parts of which were brick chimneys, built according to Southern fashion, on the house's exterior." He found the region "entirely desolate; not with the grand monotony of nature, but with the ruin of civilization and cultivation." The Jayhawkers, the antislavery guerrillas, had "fearfully balanced" those "outrages inflicted upon the Free State settlers of Kansas by citizens of Missouri, for and in behalf of human slavery."[26]

As the afternoon wore on, though, discerning Federals believed they saw signs that they had been gaining on the Confederates, including more of their sick and wounded soldiers. Curtis sent word back to Halleck in Washington that "dead horses and other débris show his demoralized and destitute condition and my probable success in overhauling him." Hinton, too, saw signs that their hard traveling had been "gaining upon the rebel march."[27]

As usual with military operations at the edge of the war, sources remain contradictory about important aspects. Some Federal units functioned by detachment and moved quickly from place to place; the garrisons to the west of the military road at Olathe, Paola, and Mound City noted the Confederates were passing south and shifted their own positions accordingly, some often joining the pursuit. At the same time, Blunt sent bits and pieces of Moonlight's brigade to the west, moving south in advance of the retreating Confederates, just in case they might be needed.[28]

Whatever the distance, afternoon found the bulk of Moonlight's brigade on the line of the military road at Coldwater Grove first, and he reported that they "struck the center of the enemy, skirmished awhile, and held him in check as long as possible." Most sources describe the first major stopping point to the south, Coldwater Grove, as the Federal post thirty to thirty-five miles down State Line Road from Little Santa Fe. Hinton thought most of the army had covered only about fifteen miles that day, but he personally moved from its rear to the front. He became one of the first Union officers to encounter the Confederate treatment of Kansas civilians.[29]

To the south, near the head of the Confederate column, a "stout, healthy looking man" herded along Reader and the other Union prisoners. His habit of swearing recalled in Reader's mind Simon Legree from *Uncle Tom's Cabin.* "At sun-set we came to a heavy body of timber land near a place called 'Trading Post.' Under the trees, lying side by side I saw a number of men—whether corpses or wounded men, it was impossible to tell."[30]

Around the same time—about 6 p.m.—Blunt brought the rear of the Union pursuit into West Point, a deserted and half-burned village near the state line that was roughly midway between Little Santa Fe and Fort Scott. The movement left in the rear Major General James G. Blunt's "division," said to include all the regulars in Kansas, supplemented by the KSM units from southern Kansas. Meanwhile, Moonlight's brigade scurried off the side roads farther west to keep the Confederate patrols from ranging too far from the main column.[31]

At this point, Blunt proposed swinging the Army of the Border west through Kansas to get south of Price's army. With Pleasonton's troops about four miles behind and the still slower supply wagons lagging a bit farther, the movement would get Price's army between them. When Curtis blocked the idea, Blunt reportedly approached Pleasonton with a proposal that he arrest Curtis, take charge, authorize the operation, and secure the crushing of Price's army. One Union account recalled seeing Major Preston B. Plumb at Blunt's headquarters during the discussion. In the end, Pleasonton predictably declined to take the risk, so Blunt, acting on his own, sent Moonlight's brigade to slip around the Confederate flank, ostensibly to protect small Kansas communities to the west, such as Mound City. Moonlight's night march reached Mound City at 2 a.m., having covered sixty-five miles.[32]

As for food, however, circumstances left them few options. "Our trains could not overtake us," reported Curtis, "and we had to pick up forage and food by the way, as occasion offered." They butchered some of the cattle abandoned by the

Confederates that night, roasting the fresh beef over their fires, and often consumed them "without waiting for salt or bread." With darkness, a light but chilling mist began to fall. Blair's brigade of KSM remained still farther to the rear, "having no orders to rest, without fire to dry their drenched garments, and without food. About midnight some fires were lighted, but they were shortly extinguished, under apprehension that our position would be seen through them."[33]

Blunt's scouts began coming back into camp, indicating that the rear of Price's army had already fallen exhausted from their saddles only about eight to ten miles farther. The rear of the Confederate army, at least, had left the State Line Road to raid the well-settled farming communities a few miles west, as well as the large quantity of government hay stacked at the hamlet of Trading Post, just on the Marais des Cygnes river. Some of Hoyt's men, who had been garrisoned there in the summer, knew the dense timber fringing the steep riverbanks. The road from the north passed between two mounds, natural defensive barriers.[34]

Curtis, Pleasonton, and others in the high command traveled between the two divisions, and they had arrived by 8 p.m. Colonel Philips recalled running into the two generals as they were "enjoying a sumptuous supper. It made my hungry palate dilate, but got nothing to eat." Curtis ordered Blunt's diminutive division, part of which had done some skirmishing at Coldwater Grove, to yield the road to Pleasonton's men. Lane also described "the exhaustion of General Blunt's men, and that portion which had fought at Lexington not having tasted food for days." That Pleasonton regularly complained about inaction never kept him from complaining about orders to move into action.[35]

Certainly, Curtis had made many mistakes on his end. He had political reasons for not meeting the Confederates at the Little Blue, and mitigating circumstances explain the collapse of his line along the Big Blue. Now, on Marais des Cygnes, he had little interest in Blunt's proposal to cross behind Price "completely surrounding the rear divisions, compelling their surrender, and the consequent surrender of Price's entire army." Most telling, with the exception of Moonlight's column, sent off on Blunt's orders, the entire Federal pursuit stayed in a single column, moving only as fast as its slowest components.[36]

The Mounds to Fort Scott

The generals also resumed their debate about the mechanics of the pursuit. Blunt argued "with great pertinacity" that the entire column could pass to the west, take a ford upstream from Trading Post, and place itself right in the path of Price's army, forcing it to fight or surrender. Curtis, however, doubted that they could make the march of fifteen miles without the Confederates' discovering it and reacting, but he agreed with Blunt that they should attack immediately in the hope of engaging and pinning the enemy in place. Pleasonton agreed but claimed to be "too sick" to take charge of the night operation and assigned General Sanborn to take his division into the field.[37]

Curtis prepared to call up what few available fresh troops he might have. At midnight, he wrote Colonel Drake at Paola, informing him that the Confederates had retreated south of that town. He still feared an attack on Fort Scott, "but [we] shall press him so hard to-night he will not dare to make the divergence. Try to press provisions to supply us as we go or on our return."[38]

For hours, on and off, Kingsbury's Coloradoans had been in the advance, skirmishing with stragglers and small groups of Confederates, and they seem not to have been aware that Sanborn's men had taken the position immediately behind them. As of 8 p.m., the westerners encountered pickets protecting Price's camps, and moved into action, but Sanborn called them back two hours later. As the rain began falling more heavily and the night became more overcast, Sanborn established a headquarters at the house of Elder John Williams a few miles short of Trading Post, and sent Colonel Joseph J. Gravely's Eight MSM Cavalry to relieve Kingsbury. Meanwhile, Colonel John F. Philips brought up his brigade with Lieutenant Colonel Bazel Lazear's First MSM Cavalry in advance. Amid the thunder and brief, illuminating flashes of lightning, Sanborn decided that nature would do a better job of holding the Confederates in place than his own men.[39]

As they advanced, they encountered the obvious evidence of the Confederates' passing. Price's men had seized "all kinds of clothing," even the flannel from infants, and consumed "every morsel of food, cooked and uncooked," taking along what they could and destroying what they could not. In the *Leavenworth Times*, Hinton reported that the Confederates had murdered seven or eight aged and unarmed men at Trading Post. Three miles north of Trading Post, they had seized Elder Williams, a sixty-year-old preacher who was "indecently mutilated and then hung."[40]

Farther west, the Federals at Mound City, eleven miles west of Trading Post, recovered from a very nervous night. Captain Samuel W. Greer garrisoned the town with a company of the Fifteenth Kansas Cavalry supplemented by three small companies of militia; "exempts and negroes" covered the approaches of the town and loaded the government stores for removal. He had couriers riding south to Fort Scott and north to Paola, and his men exchanged fire with small groups of Confederates venturing near the town. However, messages arrived from Drake at Paola and from Moonlight on the road that they and their men would arrive at Mound City shortly. Around midnight, Moonlight arrived with Lieutenant Colonel Preston B. Plumb's Eleventh Kansas and Captain James H. Young's two companies of the Fifth, about 700 men with four howitzers.[41]

At Fort Scott, Captain David S. Vittum of the Third Wisconsin Cavalry commanded the garrison Blair had left behind. A functionary well integrated into the workings of the base, Vittum had been identified with the efforts of Blair and local contractors such as Alexander McDonald in the roundup of Indian cattle in the territory and its sale to the army as supply. When the Federal Indian units objected to such official rustling, Blair and Vittum had systemically delayed the supply trains those regiments needed.[42]

Civilians and militia prepared Fort Scott "for a desperate resistance." They added rifle pits to the defenses Curtis had raised nearly two years earlier and sandbagged fords over the Marmaton. In addition to 200 men from volunteer regiments, Vittum had four companies, one from the quartermaster's employees, two from the local business community, and another "composed of colored men." In addition, several companies of KSM had arrived on October 22 from Allen County, followed by a battalion from Woodson County.[43]

Just after midnight, the "forty poorly armed citizens" posted to guard the hamlet on the Marmiton found themselves under attack by 150 rebels under a Major I. Piercy. They held briefly, but the attackers overwhelmed and sacked the village, torching the Methodist church and two stores. They also "savagely maltreated and robbed" the widow of a Federal officer before burning her house. They stripped ten prisoners "nearly naked" before marching them out of the village and firing on them, killing six, including Lieutenant Colonel Knowles of the Second Kansas Colored. Word reached Fort Scott, and Vittum sent out what cavalry he had in an attempt to intercept the raiders. He ordered one of the heavy guns to roar its alert at about 1 a.m. on October 24, followed by the drum roll.[44]

Major Milton Burch of the MSM reported a lot of activities in that corner of the state. His men encountered "some 250 rebels in Jasper County near Carthage, under command of Major Piercey, as well as 75 on Butler's Creek, thirty miles south of here." He sent "a spy to Bentonville, Ark. As soon as she returns I will learn the whereabouts of Stand Watie. The rebel force that is in Jasper County is the same force that was in Lawrence County." Burch needed another 150 men to "clean out Piercey and open up communication with Fort Scott."[45]

Rumors raged in all their fury. News of what had been hailed as a victory before Westport seemed to presage an assault on Fort Scott. Stories of artillery firing from the east around noon inspired the idea that General A. J. Smith's infantry had intercepted the Confederates at Pappinsville. Stories also circulated that Generals Douglas H. Cooper and Richard M. Gano would attack the fort with "a large force" coming up from the Indian Territory.[46]

Confederates near Fort Scott met and overran a supply train on Cow Creek that was coming in from Fort Smith. The train lost sixteen killed and several wagons, and a number of refugees were robbed. That evening, the train reached Fort Scott, and its commander, Lieutenant Colonel William T. Campbell of the

Sixth Kansas Cavalry, took charge of the post from Captain Vittum. Shortly after, the fort received dispatches from Blunt and Blair, on their way south and warning of the proximity of Price's army. Another came from Moonlight: "The enemy encamped six miles south-east of Mound City. I cannot reach you early in the morning."[47] In reality, though, Price remained too concerned about his pursuers to worry about Fort Scott.

The Confederate commander made no secret of his fears. Recruits had come into Price's camp reporting that they had "traveled fifteen miles on the route I had traveled, that there was no enemy in my rear." Yet, that night, word came in that Federals had clashed with his pickets. Price consulted Marmaduke, and "we were both of opinion that the enemy were marching upon our right by Mound City on a road parallel to the one on which we were. We were strengthened in that belief by a dispatch which had been captured from the commanding Federal officer at that place to his scouts, stationed near our then encampment, stating that he would be largely re-enforced that night, and that he wanted a sharp lookout [kept] for my army, and to give him the earliest information of the route on which I would travel and the direction."[48]

In short, what Price feared was that the Federals would swing to his south and prevent his continued retreat, the course of action Blunt had proposed and the others had rejected.

11

Judgment Day

The Mounds, Trading Post, Mine Creek, Charlot, and the Marmiton, October 25

On Tuesday, October 25, the armies converged again, roughly fifty-five miles beyond Little Santa Fe, or New Santa Fe, and would do battle at the crossings of rivers and creeks. While some mounted riders could cross all but the deepest places, doing this in large numbers could churn the bottom to a slippery and impassible goo, and the supply wagons or artillery simply had to cross where a stream would be relatively wider, shallower, and have a rocky or gravelly bottom. However, the Federals had tried and failed to protect bridges or fords at both the Little Blue and the Big Blue, with the Confederates failing in the same places (and, arguably, at Brush Creek as well). Neither had the numbers to prevent small groups from crossing upstream and downstream, accumulating the forces needed to turn the defender's flanks. As a result, defenders actually tended to concentrate on the bluffs overlooking the bottomland. On this day, Sterling Price, John S. Marmaduke, and James F. Fagan had no such options.

Participants described it as "one of the most beautiful battles . . . ever fought being on an open smooth prairie." General Alfred Pleasonton, who had fought across the scope of the war and remained little disposed to poetry of expression, called it "the prettiest cavalry fight he ever saw." Captain Dick Hinton believed he had witnessed "a scene worthy of being immortalized in the verse of Tennyson, or by the brush of Horace Vernet," the French painter of military scenes. Its visual promise led, 145 years later, to a documentary produced by the History Channel, *The Lost Battle of the Civil War* (2009), though the state had preserved the site and nobody had ever lost the battle.[1]

THE MOUNDS, THE TRADING POST, AND THE MARAIS DES CYGNES

Price boasted that Kansas would not raise a force large enough to thwart his plans, but Westport reduced the strength of his position to obvious blustering.

156

A number of his commanders had argued for abandoning the massive train of almost 500 wagons and a herd of 3,000 cattle that slowed his retreat south; however, these represented the only tangible success he had to show for the campaign. He left the Arkansans as a rear guard on "the mounds" north of Trading Post. To the south of Trading Post, the wagons had already crossed the Marais des Cygnes, one of a series of rivers and creeks to be forded, but the army had strung out for more than eight miles—a serious problem for later historians, as well, since both sides moved so fast through such unfamiliar territory that they regularly misidentified these streams. Brigadier General William Cabell had about 1,600 men on the steep east mound, with about 300 under Colonel W. F. Slemons under the heavy wooded cover of the west mound a little farther south along the road. Two small guns between them covered the military road.[2]

The Federal advance stumbled in the direction of the Confederates in the rainy darkness. Brigadier General John Sanborn convinced himself that he faced the enemy "in full force, perhaps 10,000 strong, immediately on the high hills in his front." He reined in the "chilled, hungry and tired" advance about half a mile from the timber's edge, just short of the east mound. When his shivering men tried to build fires to keep warm and dry, orders came down to extinguish them. Behind them, by 3 a.m., the exhausted brigades of John F. Philips, Frederick Benteen, and John McNeil tumbled from the saddle.[3]

Back up the road, Major General Samuel R. Curtis strained unsuccessfully to hear the sounds of battle in the cold, rainy night and sent a half-dozen officers forward to find out why. They found General Sanborn wrapped in his blanket, unwilling to attack before daylight, particularly because he lacked the staff to coordinate a movement. Curtis offered his staff to assist and sent up a battery, along with rather unmistakable orders to begin an immediate attack. Colonel Joseph J. Gravely's MSM got to within a hundred yards of the mounds, and some began shooting into the darkness. Meanwhile, Captain Ezra W. Kingsbury's Coloradoans had already pressed the Confederates, while the Fourth Iowa Cavalry of Benteen's brigade had forded upstream to the west and turned up in the rear of the west mound.[4]

Hinton rode up and told Kingsbury that General James G. Blunt's division had been halted, so Kingsbury fell back, met by the Eighth Missouri, which "mistook our men for the rebels." Kingsbury rode forward alone to stop this but had sent an orderly sergeant and four men forward to draw Confederate fire and identify his men to other Union troops. Farther to the rear, Kingsbury met Major Robert H. Hunt with orders to press the advance.[5]

As of 4 a.m., though, Curtis had still heard no artillery, but Captain Hinton and Moses Marcus knew the terrain well enough to creep "through the brush and tall grass half way up the eastern mound, listening to the rebels talk, and ascertaining their numbers." Curtis sent Hunt forward to "ascertain why the artillery had not opened as directed some hours previous." He found that four guns had rolled into position, but the artillerymen were waiting for dawn before opening on the east mound. When they finally did open fire, the guns of Captains Charles H. Thurber and William C. F. Montgomery and Lieutenant Philip Smiley lobbed shells through the gap between the mounds, which had become visible at dawn. They crashed down where the Coloradoans stood. Just before daybreak, the Confederate guns responded.[6] As the early morning light permitted a Federal advance, the Confederates had already tumbled off the remaining mound.

The Federals scampered up the high ground and took advantage of the early light to open a brisk fire on those Confederates trying to form a new line of battle just below the mound to the south. Colonel Charles W. Blair, preoccupied with the safety of Fort Scott, which he had usually commanded, rode far in advance of his men and reached the heights, along with Hinton and the Republican gubernatorial candidate Colonel Samuel J. Crawford. Curtis and Alfred Pleasonton joined them.[7]

Below, the brigades of Sanborn and Benteen took Trading Post with about 100 prisoners and some supplies. At the Marais des Cygnes itself, Confederate officers Colton B. Greene, John Q. Burbridge, and Robert Lawther with John F. Davies rallied a new rear guard with three of H. C. Hynson's Texas guns "on a timbered ravine, running from the main stream." Sanborn reportedly suggested sending the rest of the Colorado Battalion, but Hunt urged using those troops that were already present. Between 8 a.m. and 9 a.m., a bugle call sent Colonel John E. Phelps's Second Arkansas Cavalry, with parts of the Fifth and Eighth MSM Cavalry, past burning ricks of hay and abandoned wagons and into "a spirited musketry engagement." Abandoning their smooth-bore at the Marais des Cygnes, the Confederates fell back with their two rifled guns.[8] Two miles farther south, they deployed again, at a crossroad with routes going east to the state line, west to Mound City, and south to Fort Scott.

The troopers of Philips and Benteen galloped on, as Sanborn's men and horses stopped to feed. Philips's 1,000-man brigade took the center, with Major Henry Hopkins and Captain Patrick Cosgrove of Cloud's Second Kansas Cavalry on the right. To the left, Benteen's brigade filed into line with the Third and Fourth Iowa, the Fourth and Tenth Missouri, and Seventh Indiana Cavalry regiments. Around 11 a.m., they moved to "the brow of a long acclivity which overlooked the creek valley beyond" and saw the open prairie toward the next crossing, where they saw a large line of battle and, in the distance, "a long train and accompanying troops, extending for some miles." Hunt thought the entire Union force hardly "amounted to more than 3,000 or 4,000 men," but the estimate included Sanborn's 500 men back behind off Philips's left. (McNeil's

1,500 men remained far in the rear.)[9] Pleasonton's line likely had about 2,500 men.

The Confederates, on the other hand, had 6,000 to 8,000 prepared to defend the crossing, though their line looked daunting enough for Hinton to estimate twice as many and describe what he saw as "the flower of the rebel army." A farmhouse and fences anchored its right, while a cornfield and a cabin covered the slight swale and a timbered creek bed on the left. Still, to protect the wagons mucking across the ford, marked by "two horseshoe curves," the rebels stood in the valley on the north side, with their backs to the "high banks and deep water" of Mine Creek. Federals quickly saw that "if we succeeded in breaking their centre, there was no possibility of their withdrawing the ten artillery pieces on the left of their line, an error on the part of the rebel General which our officers were not slow to perceive."[10] Price would have been surprised how little their captured wagons concerned the Federals.

As Confederate guns blasted away at the unsupported right of Philips's line, his skirmishers got within 1,000 yards of the enemy, and Hopkins placed his howitzers on the right. "My brigade was precipitated on the enemy's center and left with tremendous energy, when the fighting became general and terrific. The impetuosity of the onset surprised and confounded the enemy. He trembled and wavered and the wild shouts of our soldiers rising above the din of battle told that he gave way. With pistol we dashed into his disorganized ranks and the scenes of death was as terrible as the victory was speedy and glorious."[11]

At one point, the advance faltered. Wounded Major Abial R. Pierce thought "a perfect rout of our line appeared to be almost certain." The Confederates blasted a fire that shuddered and stopped Benteen's line until he ordered "a right half-wheel" that threatened to "cut off the enemy's chance to escape with his artillery." Lazear saw that most of the Confederates had to fight "dismounted on account of being armed with long guns." "The crash of musketry," recalled Blair, who had joined the line, "the scream of shell, the hissing sound of canister and balls, mingled with the shouts of the soldiers and the cries of the wounded" with "walls of fire in front and girdles of steel behind, which marked both lines, formed a scene more easily remembered than described."[12]

As the Union horsemen charged, they galloped past an old woman with several children clinging to her skirts in front of a log cabin. Standing "fearless of the leaden shower which ceaselessly pattered against the cabin wall," she shouted as the bluecoats thundered past: "God bless you boys! Hurra for the Union! Hurra for Kansas! Give it to 'em!" The effect was "like a draught of wine, and with a wild shout the troops cleared the fence, swept over the prairie beyond, and attacked the disordered rebels as they emerged from the timber, capturing a Major and a number of men. Several shells had already fallen in our midst, when it became evident that the left was mistaken for rebels, and it fell back across the prairie to the supports which were coming up."[13]

CHAOS ON MINE CREEK

Almost at the touch, the Confederate line collapsed. Benteen, whose movement actually took longer than most, reported that his men "captured the guns in a shorter space of time than is necessary to record it." "These scenes take longer to describe than to enact," agreed Hinton. A Confederate doctor thought there must have been "desperate fighting" because, he reported, "Price's army demoralized, desertions commenced." Blair described "a fierce hand-to-hand fight, one that surpassed anything for the time it lasted I have ever witnessed.[14]

The speed of it all certainly confused the Union commanders as well. The Confederates were unable to maintain a steady fire, and their responses sputtered into chaos; "it became a hand-to-hand conflict, when the rebel line gave way, retreating in confusion." So quickly did the Union left push to the south side of Mine Creek that Union troops found their own shells still crashing about them. The attackers fell upon the close-packed retreating Confederates with an almost medieval ferocity, one officer claiming, "I cut eight rebels from their horses with my own saber." Several wagons tipped over in the narrow road slowed the pursuit, though Blair saw some Federal squadrons continue on "in almost breathless pursuit." Benteen's men moved so quickly that four shells from a Federal battery landed among them, with Sanborn, Pleasonton, and Major Samuel S. Curtis running into each other on their way to stop the "friendly fire."[15]

Confederate Brigadier General John B. Clark later explained that they had "no time to make any but the most rapid dispositions for battle" against a Union force that he estimated as much larger than it had been. Officers on both sides noted the defenders had "long infantry guns, which they were unable to load on horseback." Greene's mounted regiment in reserve had little time to react to collapse of the Confederate right, when "the first and second lines gave way, and rushing in great disorder ran over and broke the eight right companies of my regiment." "Every effort was made by appeals and threats to retrieve the rout, but it swept in an irresistible mass ungovernable." Greene tried to save two of Williams's guns, but could do nothing with "this panic-stricken mob" that had been his regiment. Charles R. Jennison saw "hundreds of muskets, horse equipments, disabled wagons, &c., encumbered the field, while the number of dead and wounded abandoned by the enemy gave proof that his rout was again complete."[16] Perhaps the first instinct of every experienced soldier in Price's army would have been to reposition himself on the far side of Mine Creek, but reforming after they had gotten there proved to be a different matter.

Marmaduke had begun what became the worst day of his life by clowning on his horse, Miss Mary Price, near the cabin door of a Mrs. Reagins and "promising to ride over any Jayhawkers that got in his way." In the midst of the battle, he stood some of his men dressed in blue uniforms when he saw another, similarly dressed, blazing away at them. He rode up to the assailant, cursing him with orders to stop, only to find Private James Dunleavy of the Third Iowa Cavalry, who waited for him to get close, then leveled his revolver and forced the general to dismount and surrender. Marmaduke asked to be taken to General Pleasonton, and Dunleavy took him to Blair, the first Union officer he saw, and they took him on to a cabin in the rear where the Federal commanders had gathered. After being introduced to Curtis, Dunleavy returned to his regiment; he would later become a recipient of the Congressional Medal of Honor. Marmaduke, meanwhile, found himself back at the home of Mrs. Reagins, who asked, "How are you, General, and how's Miss Mary Price, and where's the Kansas Jayhawkers now?"[17] Marmaduke could do little but tally up the scale of the disaster.

Confederate forces rarely suffered the kinds of losses it had under Marmaduke at Mine Creek. However, confirmation of Price's actual location at this time remains elusive. Accounts place him miles to the south, hurrying the wagons along, but Cabell later informed a Colonel Wheeler that the Confederate commander had been "within a few feet" when Wheeler had been captured "and only escaped by the fleetness of his horse, and a sense of any distinctive dress which could render him a mark."[18] What we know of Price's age and condition raises questions about feats.

Federal accounts reported capturing nine or ten pieces of Confederate artillery, though it is unclear how much ammunition Price had for them. Contrary to his own activities that day, Pleasonton reported himself the advocate of rigorous pursuit and complained that he "with proper support could have rendered our success even more decisive and glorious than it was." Early accounts reported Fagan, the second of Price's three division commanders, killed, but it turned out to have been another person, who also was misidentified as a Brigadier General Graham. Brigadier General William Cabell fell into the hands of the forty-one-year-old New York–born Merritt Young of the Third Iowa Cavalry. Another brigade commander, William F. Slemons, fell into Federal hands, wounded and misreported as dying, but so did Colonels William L. Jeffers, John Waddell, and Lee Crandall and many other officers.[19]

Overall numbers taken remain unclear. Price mentioned only 300 to 400 prisoners, but members of his army talked about losing "one-third of their men" at Mine Creek. Lieutenant Colonel John J. Sears, a Mound City veteran of the Twelfth Kansas—then holding his commission in the Eighteenth USCT—took charge of the prisoners and claimed at least 450 prisoners, including forty-five officers, while other observers thought as many as 200 were killed in the fight-ing. (Some would have realized that the stated Confederate policy toward the USCT would have meant their summary execution of Sears, had matters been reversed.) The St. Louis *Missouri Democrat* later reported the arrival there of "620 of the Rebel prisoners," forty-seven of them officers. Pleasonton claimed 1,000, which General William S. Rosecrans rounded up to "about 2,000," with the Weston *Border Times* reporting as "about 5000 prisoners."[20]

Federals had trouble giving an honest count. Their officers saw large num-bers of these prisoners, "lean, haggard and cadaverous, their cheeks sunken, their forms bowed and their whole appearance wretched in the extreme." They found "quite a number of boys of from fourteen to sixteen, and a few men over fifty." They found the ranks "all clad in rags, some without shoes, some with-out hats, some with greasy blankets or ragged strips of carpeting thrown over their shoulders. The prevailing style was butternut, two or three of the officers only being dressed in what had once been regular rebel uniforms." However, as Philips recalled, they seized many "dressed in our uniform, and in obedience to existing orders from department headquarters, and the usages of war, they were executed instanter, while those taken in Confederate uniform were recognized and treated as prisoners of war." These, with those who had simply left the field and never returned to their commands, surely accounted for much of the dis-crepancy in some Confederate claims that they had lost a third of the army.[21]

The dead and wounded remained uncounted. Federal forces had little time to deal with their own dead and wounded. The army generally left those on the field to the care of citizens. Major Samuel B. Davis scurried from point to point, establishing makeshift hospitals at Trading Post and Mound City before reaching Mine Creek, but much better facilities would be available once Fort Scott had been secured. Dr. A. J. Pierce, returning from Fort Scott to Kansas City, reported scores of Price's men left "lying along the road."[22]

Notwithstanding the victory at Mine Creek, Fort Scott remained vulnerable, with "$4,000,000 worth of public property to be protected or lost," but both Colonel Thomas Moonlight and some of the KSM had already headed toward the fort. During the predawn fighting around Trading Post, Moonlight had reached Mound City to the west. At the start of the campaign, Lieutenant Col-onel Samuel A. Drake and what he had of the Seventeenth Kansas left Mound City to the care of Colonel Potters's Eighteenth KSM and headed for Paola, but Drake and his men made a night march back when the Confederates reached the area. Continuing on to Fort Scott, Drake's men encountered some of Price's men along Sugar Creek, and Moonlight showed up shortly after and reported 800 Confederates that direction, but he had orders from Blunt to reach Fort Scott "and hold the place at all hazards." Among the officers there, First Lieu-tenant William D. Mathews, one of the first African Americans commissioned as an officer, had charge of arming and commanding the blacks brought in by the proclamation of martial law. By the end of the day, Blunt also got word to the fort that Price would probably not be able to attack the installation, "but if he should you must fight him to the last extremity." Meanwhile, it took another fight, but Moonlight's column reached Fort Scott just after midnight.[23]

Back at the main body of troops, Curtis immediately sent his son, Major Curtis, to bring up the fresh troops from the rear. These included not only Blunt's cavalry division but McNeil's brigade. When Pleasonton told General Curtis that McNeil had been unwilling to advance, Curtis sent his aide, Major Chapman S. Charlot, with orders to arrest McNeil "if hesitation was evinced." In reality, the previous night's heavy rain had especially muddied one of the fords, which both armies had just used, and a wagon had mired there and broken down with Blunt and McNeil on the north side. McNeil further noted that he had never received an order to advance and personally "came up on the gallop upon receipt of the order."[24]

In the end, priorities other than getting fresh troops their orders to come up had sidetracked Pleasonton's staff officers. Pleasonton asked Colonel William F. Cloud, a Kansas cavalryman, "to ascertain the road to Fort Scott." Sergeant Amos Peck and a detachment of the Second Kansas Cavalry accompanied Cloud, but getting their bearings in the chaos of the field proved difficult. They encountered Confederate colonel Jeffers near a captured cannon, and he claimed protection for himself and his men. Then Cloud sent to word to Pleasonton that his artillery fire had been landing on Union troops, which Pleasonton denied until Cloud brought in an officer from the detachment that had been under the friendly fire. After this, Pleasonton agreed to stop firing on his own men but complained, "You should carry your colors upon the battle-field."[25] This may have been the second or third such incident in a matter of hours.

While on his errand to the rear to tell McNeil to bring up his troops, Charlot passed Mrs. Reagin's house, where Sears held the Confederate officers taken on the field. There, he found Captain Yates and Major Henry Suess, allegedly sent back with McNeil's orders. Instead, they had stopped to argue with Sears about "General Pleasonton's prisoners." Sears reported that these officers carried orders, not to bring up McNeil but to take the high-ranking Confederates into their custody. Several of these Southern gentlemen had sanctioned the killing of black soldiers, and their white officers may have found Sears an objectionable warden. In any event, Charlot simply reminded them that Curtis had been the senior officer on the field and temporarily resolved matters in favor of Sears. In the end, though, Curtis released the prisoners to Pleasonton's officers, who, wrote Sears, "took them away without any guard, saying they would pledge their honor not to escape. Not having a very [high] appreciation of their honor I required a receipt for them."[26]

THE LITTLE OSAGE, CHARLOT FARM, THE MARMITON, AND FORT SCOTT

Many of those who had fought so long for Fagan and Marmaduke did not simply flee from the field. Veterans believed that, however tempting flight might be, order was the best means of self-preservation. Many who actually managed to make it across Mine Creek found some who had not experienced the fiasco. They threw together a "formidable line of battle . . . on a prairie ridge about one mile to the south." Once the victorious Union horsemen crossed to the south, though, the Confederates ran back in disorder over the ridge into the valley of the Little Osage, roughly two miles to the south of Mine Creek. Blair thought the Confederates "broke and fled before our forces got even within respectable distance."[27]

Price himself hurried back in response to Marmaduke's warning "that the enemy, 3,000 strong, were in sight of his rear, with lines still extending." Fagan had added to Marmaduke's note that he would sustain him, and Price immediately ordered Jo Shelby to take his men "to the rear as rapidly as possible to support Major-Generals Fagan and Marmaduke." Price himself hurried back north "at a gallop" and, past the rear of the train, met what was left of the divisions of Fagan and Marmaduke, which were retreating in utter and indescribable confusion; many had thrown away their arms and were "deaf to all entreaties or commands, and in vain were all efforts to rally them."[28]

Yet, if most Confederates who had been at Mine Creek had no stomach for another fight, neither did many of the Federals. "Half way upon the prairie fresh smoke was rising densely, telling of some new horror," wrote Hinton. In front of one house, he saw "the bloody form of a young man," a member of the Linn County KSM who had rushed ahead of his command to protect his home. There, he had been shot down on the threshold. The Confederates had stripped the house of anything of value and torched the hay and cornstalks "stacked in the barn-yard," while "the adjoining prairie was fast blackening with the flames which ran along its swells."[29]

Preoccupied with Fort Scott, Blair rode far in advance, with Hinton alongside him, taking turns using the spyglass. Behind them, McNeil's brigade turned up, with Sanborn moving up on the right in support. Temporarily assigned to the latter, the 150 members of the Second Kansas Cavalry hurried into a skirmish line. Curtis's Major Thomas I. McKenny ordered them forward, but Pleasonton's Major Suess stopped the advance. By then, Benteen and Philips also awaited orders from Pleasonton, to whom Blair had to explain "the topography of the country, the direction the enemy had taken, my fears for Fort Scott, its situation, amount of stores, &c." At that point, though, Pleasonton "rode forward and very angrily accused McNeil of disobeying his orders to move." Meanwhile, Sanborn's exhausted horses had been on the move since before dawn and simply could not mount another charge; their effort ended "scattered pell-mell over two miles of ground, without order," without commanders, without any point to rally upon but the small squad that had stood the work so well." Major Curtis himself fell asleep as he waited for events to unfold.[30]

Sheer adrenaline must have fueled General Curtis at this point. Given where they were, he felt confident that Fort Scott would be safe. All day, he had ridden through a landscape "graphically marked by the scattered equipments, wagons, guns, utensils, and animals left by the rebels, and the fire and smoke created by their burning of the hay and grain and grass along their route." As they moved toward the Marmiton, he met Jim Lane, who had been working to bring up Blunt's division, a task all the more urgent, given what lay ahead of them.[31]

By 2 p.m., exhausted bluecoats had dragged themselves toward the Marmiton (more regularly later spelled Marmaton), a tributary of the nearby Little Osage. Shelby "had nothing to do all the way to the rear but stand up in his stirrups and swear with every step of his horse," but he got some of his men to the forward slope of a hill, about two miles north of the crossing of the Marmiton at the Charlot family farm, which had a commanding view of the broad open prairie to the north. Brigadier General M. Jeff Thompson had Shelby's original brigade with Smith, Elliott, Gordon, and Williams commanding in the center, protected by a strong stone wall, with a slight rise obscuring Slayback and Erwin, whose men were forming to the left; trees and the undergrowth along a stream protected Thompson's right. Behind them, Fagan had rallied part of his force, and Price "formed the unarmed men, numbering several thousand, in line of battle on the prairie beyond the river." In Marmaduke's absence, Clark took charge of the division, leaving Greene to command Clark's brigade, then reduced to only "about 400 armed men."[32] Some sources credit the Confederates with 8,000 men, with about half armed, though the numbers were actually half that.

Meanwhile, after roughly four hours' march from the rear, McNeil's men arrived and passed to the front through Philips's lines. When Pleasonton ordered him up, with the requisite amount of abuse, McNeil called it "the most joyful news I have heard this day." Blair heard McNeil tell his men that "it made no difference whether there were 1,000 or 10,000 men on that field, he wanted them to ride right over them and saber them down as fast as they came to them." His troops "responded with a yell," their skirmishers advancing "in the face of a galling fire, and the column swept through it like a tornado."[33]

As had been the case through the entire campaign, Major John N. Edwards offered the most fanciful version of events:

> The narrow issue of life or death stood out all dark and barren as a rainy
> sea. The fight was to be made now, and General Price, with the pilot's wary
> eye, saw the storm-cloud sweep down, growing larger and larger and darker

and darker. They came upon me steadily and calm. I waited until they came close enough and gave them volley for volley, shot for shot. For fifteen minutes both lines stood the pelting of the leaden hail without flinching, and the incessant roar of musketry rang out wildly and shrill, all separate sounds blending in a universal crash. The fate of the army hung upon the result, and our very existence tottered and tossed in the smoke of the strife. The red sun looked down upon the scene, and the redder clouds floated away with angry, sullen glare. Slowly, slowly my old brigade was melting away. The high-toned and chivalric Dobbin, formed on my right, stood by me in all that fiery storm, and Elliott's and Gordon's voices sounded high above the rage of the conflict: "My merry men, fight on." All that men could do had been done.

In reality, Shelby's "merry men" lasted only long enough for McNeil's line to organize its advance. Thompson's report indicates that Shelby's lines dissolved about as readily as Marmaduke's and Fagan's had earlier.[34]

Hinton, however, thought McNeil "at least two miles ahead of the next brigade, which was Colonel Benteen's," with Sanborn's and Philips's even farther behind. Except for the small mountain howitzers, the artillery could not keep pace. By 3:00 p.m. Thompson had re-formed his men behind a deep creek just south of the ford. McNeil fought them there for fifteen to twenty minutes, driving them back to a hill about a half-mile away. "Very slowly the army moved away without molestation," Edwards concluded, "and darkness came down alike upon the dying and the dead, and the stars came out, and a weird and dreary silence hushed the air to stillness and repose." As of 3:30 p.m., the head of the Federal pursuit moved along Shiloh Creek, reaching the old Confederate position. McNeil's line continued "about a mile to the top of the hill south of the valley of the Osage." From there, the Union officers could see the Confederates bearing east, which would leave Fort Scott out of danger.[35]

At this point, Jackman's brigade turned up and "saved us," according to Shelby's report, although some of the men led by Fagan and Marmaduke joined in. From behind, though, McNeil's brigade looked "like a pigmy in the face of the rebels, whose flanks extended three-quarters of a mile beyond our own." Pleasonton sent McNeil assurances of support, while Hinton and Crawford got two howitzers into position. Major Suess brought up a couple of Rodman guns, but their crews had been without rations "for three days except one hard cracker to the man." Lieutenant Philip Smiley's section used "double charge of canister" on Shelby's men to push back the Confederate center. Benteen's brigade formed on the Union right, and both "advanced towards the enemy at a walk, all exertions being unavailing to move the horses to either trot or gallop." The Confederates began falling back as "the sun sunk below the horizon."[36]

Benteen and Philips provided enough men for McNeil to present a double line of battle, though Shelby's line seemed four deep and "outflanked me both to the right and to the left." The Federals' horses once more proved unwilling to move at "a trot or a gallop," so they "advanced in line at walk toward the enemy, who continued to retire, gradually massing his flanks upon his center, when their flight became more rapid." Benteen reported he had only "very few rounds per man and my horses [were] completely tired out." Colonel Joseph A. Eppstein thought only the state of their horses "enabled the enemy to make his escape under the cover of the darkness of night and the smoke of prairie fire." Major Henry Hopkins's Kansans reported participating in the action, but Blunt had not yet come up.[37]

As the fighting died, Curtis noticed "a large portion of our forces" moving past the fighting, with Pleasonton citing their need for wood and water. Some pointed out that they could get both by moving forward to the waters being contested at that point. Meanwhile, another courier from McNeil reported "the enemy was flanking him on both sides, which was plainly to be seen, as he was only distant about one mile and a half." To Curtis's astonishment, Pleasonton announced he would take all his men to Fort Scott to secure supplies. Curtis "protested against leaving McNeil and against any loss of distance." Almost on cue, Lieutenant Marshall M. Ehle of the Third Wisconsin—later promoted to captain—arrived from Fort Scott, and reported it was only two and a half rather than the seven miles it actually was, making Pleasonton all the more insistent. Before leaving the field, Curtis repeated his orders for McNeil to hold until reinforced after which he ordered all his troops to turn to Fort Scott.[38]

As the last intact portion of the Confederate army began slipping into the dusk, Pleasonton told Curtis "that Fort Scott was safe and that, so far as he was concerned, the campaign was ended." Curtis insisted that "the pursuit of Price would be continued until he was captured or driven beyond the Arkansas River, and that the troops must not be diverted from this work." He wanted to stay on the field and still hoped for a succession of night marches to get below what was left of the Confederate army and destroy it. Pleasonton then "changed his tune, and said that the men and horses of his division were worn down with fatigue and exposure . . . and that he must move them to Fort Scott to rest and recuperate."[39]

The garrison at Fort Scott welcomed the arrival of the armies. It had already sent the government stores to safety, but the garrison had braced for an attack, turning wagons into barricades. The day had begun at the fort with anxious men and women crowding the rooftops, gazing at the hills north of the city, expecting each moment to see the enemy. At one point, as cavalry approached, they braced for an attack, but the force turned out to be the cavalry from the garrisons in Allen and Woodson Counties that had hurried to help defend the fort. Around noon, they heard the Confederates had crossed the Marais des Cygnes toward them and the telegraph had gone dead. The community had sent most of the women and children to what it deemed safer refuges, and tensions rose. Scouting parties ventured out and returned with three prisoners in the afternoon. Blunt, Cloud, and others sent couriers, but in midafternoon an outpost of "some forty of our citizens, with Col. Perry Fuller at their head" about three miles distant, happily welcomed their former commander, Colonel Charles Blair, who arrived with concrete news.[40]

The KSM seemed to have clearly served its purpose. General William H. M. Fishback reported his command "almost entirely exhausted from fatigue and hunger, some of them fell behind, while others pressed on with me and participated in the fights at the Marais des Cygnes, Mine Creek, Little Osage, and southeast of Fort Scott, all of which were hard-fought battles and victories gained for Kansas." After the night at Fort Scott, Curtis issued General Order No. 57, discharging them.[41]

Back on the field, confusion ruled. The generals intended to send Blunt and his fresh division forward when it arrived, but it reached the field after 5 p.m. with no real orders. Blunt encountered McNeil and learned that Pleasonton had taken his command to Fort Scott. However, frustrated at having missed the action, and "needing subsistence and forage I made a detour to the right, passing through Fort Scott for the purpose of supplying them and be in readiness to follow the pursuit the next morning." His column passed through Fort Scott at midnight. The men of McNeil and Benteen went into camp on the field until they got their rations, but Pleasonton had the supply train sent on to Fort Scott, leaving the famished soldiers "without any food or water or forage for the horses" until the next morning. That night, recalled one veteran, the weather turned "cold enough to freeze quite hard and all the troops and prisoners and captured cannon had passed within 20 feet of me, [but] I knew nothing of it."[42]

The Kansans went out of their way to speak well of their Missouri comrades. Curtis attributed the successes in the field to the rigorous pursuit of Price by Pleasonton and his men, and Curtis praised his counterpart's "great coolness and propriety." However, he, Hinton, and others also praised Pleasonton's brigade commanders, singling out Brigadier General McNeil's "great success and courage." Most important, Curtis wanted desperately to continue pressing forward. Whatever the hardships this imposed on the Federal forces, he pointed out, those the Confederates would face had to be far more daunting.[43]

Pleasonton's behavior continued to be of the sort that had made him enemies in the Army of the Potomac, and neither he nor Rosecrans made much of a secret about their contempt for the Kansas radicals. The *Leavenworth Times* quoted Pleasonton as saying, "If the people of Kansas think they are at all indebted to me, tell them to beat Jim Lane." Pleasonton smoothed it over, and Lane had no wish to pursue conflict with him. More important, Pleasonton insisted on getting custody of the high-ranking Confederates, reportedly ejecting Union officers from the town's hotel to place them there. He then wanted control over all of them, explaining that his Missouri troops— for whom Pleasonton had never been particularly solicitous—had "felt hurt in not being allowed any participation in guarding the prisoners." Curtis handled control over quickly, giving Pleasonton everything he wanted and sending the particularly vociferous John Ritchie of the Second Indian Home Guard home with Colonel Samuel Johnson Crawford, the gubernatorial candidate.[44]

In general, by Mine Creek, the Federals had inverted what usually happened in the Trans-Mississippi war. Here, Confederates, not the Federals, relied heavily on single-shot muskets, while Unionists had learned the hard lessons of the guerrilla war and turned to revolvers and repeating rifles. After this crushing defeat, Price decided not to attack Fort Scott with its 1,000 "negroes under arms." Greene reported crossing the Marmiton at 10 p.m. and invested "one hour to burn the train as directed." Thompson got his brigade over the river somewhat later and camped there, while Greene and others continued on toward Carthage. Thompson described their retreat as "much delayed" by the burning. In part, the speed with which they moved reflected the fact that they did not realize that Jackman's men, not the Federals, had set the wagons on fire. "The Yankees are on us, boys!" they told each other as they scurried along the road to Carthage. "Save yourselves as best you can!"[45]

"I shall pursue no farther," Pleasonton decided, and Rosecrans shared the conclusions with Generals Andrew J. Smith; Edward R. S. Canby, commander in the Trans-Mississippi; and Halleck. Pleasonton reported his activities as though his force had been in the field alone until "my horses were too much exhausted to go into action, and I was compelled to go to the fort for forage." He added that not only had Marmaduke been captured but Fagan had been killed, the Federals had destroyed an army of 25,000, Price had blown up his ammunition train, Price had lost all his artillery or had only one piece left, and the Federals in Missouri "could safely leave General Steele in Arkansas to intercept those that [had escaped] us."[46]

Into the Ozarks

To Newtonia and Beyond, October 26–31

In his telling exchange with Lieutenant George T. Robinson, a Missourian in General Samuel R. Curtis's Army of the Border, General William S. Rosecrans clearly aired ideas and excuses for later use. When Robinson had the temerity to comment on the tardiness of General Alfred Pleasonton's pursuit of the rebels, Rosecrans scorned the idea of their racing to keep up with the action, and his staff exploded with "a bitter feeling" toward Curtis. In reality, though, General Andrew J. Smith had also complained of Pleasonton's unwillingness to press the Confederates and had reportedly even threatened to send him to the rear.[1]

Rosecrans certainly had a distinct view of what needed to be done, even as his Department of Missouri stood apart from the Army of the Border. What existed of cooperation between them had always been tenuous, and it began to shake apart almost as soon as the dust had cleared at Mine Creek. A final attempt to stop Price's retreat came at Newtonia, the regularly contested town on the road from that part of Missouri into Arkansas. So, too, a final series of fights took place in the freezing rains and snow around Fayetteville. The fighting, though, would continue in the absence of the Confederates.

THE VIEW FROM THE DEPARTMENT OF MISSOURI

Pleasonton had persuaded Curtis to spend Tuesday night, October 25, at Fort Scott with the understanding that they would all hit the road at 3 a.m. Wednesday. As the brigades of Colonel Thomas Moonlight and John McNeil arrived, Curtis placed the lot of them into quarters for the night. They gathered the best available horses from the surrounding countryside, as well as the fort's own resources, and corn to keep the men and mounts fed.[2] With enough aggressiveness, Curtis even hoped to get south of Price's army and block its escape.

When the time came to move, though, Pleasonton changed the plans. Colonel John F. Philips, pained by a minor wound in his right eye, "hadn't change of clothes for thirty days" and thought his superiors merely "squabbling over division of spoils and glory of victory." After force-marching his exhausted brigade to and from Lamar, he asked for it to be sent back to their district. Captain George S. Grover and the Warrensburg men did not agree. They had "been in the saddle night and day alike, almost continuously since the 16th of October, with little to eat, and that at rare intervals, many of our best men were worn out, and horses broken down." He hoped Rosecrans would permit a united pursuit that would batter Price's army until it "melted away under such a pursuit, and ceased to exist as an organized body." At the time, Grover asked Charles R. Jennison, James G. Blunt, and Curtis to intervene personally with Rosecrans to permit the Warrensburg outfit to remain with the Kansans. In the end, Grover attributed the decision to Rosecrans's "lack of knowledge of the situation."[3] However, Pleasonton, who was present, concurred, though in a characteristically less than straightforward way.

Pleasonton still assented to sending the brigades of General John B. Sanborn and Colonel Frederick W. Benteen, as well as McNeil's, in pursuit of Price. Although Pleasonton complained of the lack of horses for his artillery, they scrounged enough for Lieutenant Philip Smiley's sections of William C. Montgomery's battery to join the pursuit. Then, backed by a medical certificate, Pleasonton himself claimed that, owing to "a severe fall and exhaustion from my late arduous service, I am unable to move this morning" and needed to get "proper care and attention" back in St. Louis. Although he had every reason to know that Rosecrans himself had already turned back to the city, Pleasonton reassured his comrades that Old Rosy had "left Little Santa Fé yesterday morning to overtake us."[4]

In their defense, Rosecrans and his staff claimed they had to address the ongoing strife that had erupted in the wake of Price's army. Lieutenant Colonel Samuel H. Melcher of the Sixth MSM Cavalry reported "many parties of rebels on Muddy, Clear Fork, Fiefbaux, and Honey Creek" and located "several hundred southwest of Clinton," roughly thirty miles south of Warrensburg. As elsewhere through the entire campaign, the army had left the militia "entirely without orders," but "seventy militia citizens and negroes" had defended Clinton. The *Missouri Democrat* added Clinton to the examples of Pleasant Hill, Warrensburg, and a dozen other places back to Ironton. Melcher organized more and offered to send a thousand "pretty well armed" men to join the pursuit.[5]

Elsewhere in the state, some scattered fighting continued with residual Confederate bands. Federal patrols from Independence dealt with partisans between there and Lexington on October 25 and 26. That second day saw skirmishing around Glasgow and another boat ambushed near Brunswick. Shooting took place again along the Big Blue toward the end of the month, and rumor located residual Confederate forces at Waverly. Federals who had retaken Pilot Knob reported fighting near there on October 26, and their scouts located "several small squads of rebels" south of Paterson with much larger clusters near the Arkansas border. Then, too, "a stray squad" popped up at Tuscumbia in Miller County, and another group skirmished on October 28 at Leasburg. The Thirty-Eighth, Forty-Fifth, and Fifty-Third EMM clashed with guerrillas near Hannibal, Kirksville, Goodland, and reported concentrations at Keytesville and Carrollton. The presence of Erastus Wood with a stranded force of twenty or thirty Confederates near Wentzville created consternation from Middletown to Warrenton, an area unnerved by "Bloody Bill" Anderson's earlier raid to Danville.[6]

Any rumors of Anderson and his band still had the power to terrify Unionists near Bucklin, Paris, Carrollton, and Missouri City, but the Federal mobilizations to deal with Price finally raised the manpower needed to chase down and dissolve these groups. When Anderson and his men did turn up, storming into Albany in Ray County, Lieutenant Colonel S. P. Cox's Thirty-Third EMM not only quickly blasted them back into the brush but happily reported Anderson among the killed. "Six human scalps were found attached to Anderson's bridle and on his body was six revolvers, $300 in gold, $150 in silver, two gold watches." They also retrieved a pocketbook, letters from his wife, two orders from General Price, a lock of his wife's hair, pictures of both Anderson and his wife, and "a small Confederate flag with these words inscribed on it: 'Presented to W. L. Anderson by his friend, F.M.R. Let it not be contaminated by Fed. hands.'"[7]

At Fort Scott, Curtis noted that the delays had ceded an advantage to the Confederates, "who were in even worse shape." However, he lost no time arguing the point, regardless of the absurdity of the position of Rosecrans and Pleasonton. In hindsight, the statewide mobilizations that accompanied the 1864 military campaign delivered a final blow to extensive guerrilla operations, and Rosecrans and Pleasonton seemed to acknowledge this themselves in quickly sending almost all of General Smith's corps on to Tennessee. Tactfully, Curtis asked Rosecrans for permission to use his troops while confiding his "debatable position" to General Henry W. Halleck back in Washington. "The necessity of pushing Price's forces beyond the Arkansas is so obvious," added Curtis, "I have not hesitated to disregard department lines."[8]

At least the drizzling rain stopped on Wednesday, and "the sun presently came out, bright and warm." Famished and fatigued, McNeil's brigade reached Adamson's Ford over the Drywood, eight miles from Fort Scott. Although they "had not been supplied for three days," they took heart from the detritus abandoned by the retreating Confederates. Price's men had taken the time to obstruct the ford and it took several hours to clear it, but McNeil's force did find an abandoned artillery carriage and forty wagons with mess utensils, equipment, small arms and ammunition, as well as a flock of sheep. The Federals continued on to Lamar and camped twenty-seven miles from Fort Scott, at Shanghai, once a flourishing hamlet with stores, a blacksmith shop, and several houses clustered around a sawmill. Secession and war had driven the owner to Illinois, and little remained of the place but its location. As McNeil's tired and hungry men tumbled from the saddles, they expressed "much excitement . . . when it was found that the general subsistence train had not arrived."[9] Blunt's column trailed behind McNeil's, and both officers still believed that the rest of Pleasonton's men would not be far behind.

Perhaps the oddest paradox in all this was that Pleasonton, like Rosecrans, actually blamed Curtis for hobbling an aggressive pursuit of Price's army. Pleasonton claimed that he had captured ten Confederate cannons and taken them to Fort Scott but that "some of the troops of General Curtis' command" had stolen one. In defiance of all geography, he actually reported "all the conflicts and battles that took place between Price's army and my command were in the limits of the State of Missouri" and that "the destruction of Price's army at that time would have been inevitable" after Marais des Cygnes, had Curtis been cooperative. Finally, Pleasonton persuaded Rosecrans to cap one of the most disgracefully inert records of any campaign in the war with an order to reassign all the department's troops to their garrison duties in their Missouri districts.[10]

At this point, the usually thick-skinned Curtis described himself as "astonished and sorely disappointed." He complained of "the erroneous reports circulated in Saint Louis during my pursuit of the enemy concerning my having grasped for these spoils of victory for personal advantages." "I ask for no false plumes, and pluck none from my comrades in arms, for my wearing." So, too, he had every "desire to avoid all reproachful imputations against Generals Rosecrans and Pleasonton, who have acted no doubt upon their best judgment of things as seen at their own standpoints, and I must award to General Pleasonton high commendation for his skill and gallantry on the field." Most important, though, Curtis's abandonment by Rosecrans and Pleasonton left him with "less than 1,000" to follow Blunt's equally small force.[11]

The halt at Fort Scott gave Price's army a roughly eight-hour lead. As the Federals reached Shanghai, the Confederates reached Carthage. They torched what had not been burned earlier, leaving the town "a mass of charred ruins." Perhaps accidentally, they also destroyed and left "the ambulance that contained the medicines belonging to the rebel army, almost entirely consumed by fire; together with abandoned arms, horses, saddles and camp equipage: everything indicating a panic in the rebel ranks, and extreme haste in their endeavor to outstrip their pursuers."[12] Not until 11 a.m. did the exhausted Confederates resume their march.

Blunt goaded his men into an early start, as he had long tended to do. At Coon Creek, they encountered some "nearly starved" KSM prisoners. They reported the Confederates had shot several prisoners in the presence of the provost guard. Most had been "robbed of their clothing, including their shoes." Added Curtis, "All this, however, must not provoke us to acts of barbarity toward our prisoners, but will be a matter of settlement when we secure the commander, which I trust will not be long postponed." However, he also sent Major Thomas I. McKenny to negotiate a release of all prisoners, though he still hoped that Price might surrender his starving army. Early Wednesday afternoon, Blunt reached Carthage only two and a half hours behind Price.[13]

The Federals continued south another five miles. Shortly beyond Carthage, they found Confederates "actually falling dead with starvation in Price's rear." Rumors that Price had been executing prisoners flared to life again as they found the corpse of a black man, "his skull half blown off, evidently by a gun placed so near as to singe the hair in the discharge." (One wonders if the victim had been Samuel Reader's black companion who had been captured on the Big Blue.) The discovery resulted in the "cowardly and dastardly" hanging of a couple of wounded Confederates found at a house outside town, and "instances of barbarous cruelty were not unfrequent" on either side. In one of these, an officer of the Sixteenth Kansas Cavalry approached a prisoner and blew out the man's brains "with the air of a conqueror apparently conscious of having done a heroic act."[14]

That night, Price's army reached the lead mines of Granby. By this point, massive desertions had deflated parts of his army. With fewer and fewer armed Confederates to guard them, prisoners, recruits, and "conscripts" slipped away in disturbingly large numbers. Knowing that nothing lay to the south but picked-over, well-foraged communities, many of the Arkansas conscripts faded beyond the tree line as they neared home. Reader passed his spare quilt to a newly captured German who had joined the prisoners without a coat, was soaked and, "either from the cold or terror, was shaking from head to foot." He had reached the point of asking one of the guards to shoot him before venturing everything on a quick dash into the woods. He understood the irony as he found himself alone and cold at night, trying to find the North star, "the fugitives friend in all ages, past and present." Price later claimed that he left behind many of his own sick and wounded and paroled those prisoners he had "out of humanity," but he had little choice.[15]

NEWTONIA

At midmorning Friday, October 28, Brigadier General M. Jeff Thompson got Jo Shelby's old brigade to Newtonia. The local battalion of the EMM had left its small fort northwest of town for the security of Mount Vernon, where the militiamen drove off Confederate foragers and hunkered down for the rest of the Union army to arrive. Back at Newtonia, First Lieutenant Robert H.

Christian, a recently married German resident and an officer in the Seventh-Sixth EMM detailed to the Seventh Provisional EMM, decided to maintain a small garrison, if only to deter any small guerrilla force that might threaten the town. The militia surrendered to Thompson's advance, which gunned Christian down, scalped him, hacked off his left hand, and warned locals not to retrieve the body. After Thompson arrived, Amanda Ritchey, the daughter of the town founder, appealed to him for the "inhumanly butchered" remains. Meanwhile, the Confederates camped near Big Springs, where they had been in 1862, sending patrols and pickets out the roads to Cassville, Neosho, Granby, and Sarcoxie.[16]

That same morning, the Federal advance got only seven miles beyond the Union camp before finding "the enemy drawn up in battle array at Diamond Prairie." Colonel James H. Ford of the Second Colorado deployed his men and drove the rebels off. By 10 a.m., orders came for McKinney to pack away the white flag. In a few more miles—about five miles short of Granby—Major James Ketner's detachment of the Sixteenth Kansas Cavalry got a clear view of the rear of the Confederate column. Federal skirmishers pushed the Confederates back through Granby. Around 2 p.m., as the rest of Ford's brigade arrived, they approached Newtonia.[17]

Price had reportedly told residents that the Federals "could have all the fighting [they] wanted at Newtonia." Everyone knew that Newtonia would be "the last point on the line of retreat where grain could be obtained"; beyond lay the hunger, exhaustion, and disease of the largely abandoned farms of Arkansas. Blunt's scouts reported a rapid thinning of Confederate ranks, and his forces slipped quickly off the road through the scrub oaks and brush until they came to "the brow of a precipitous bluff, where the road dips into the extensive plain, on which the town of Newtonia is situated." They looked down into the community less than a mile away and saw smoke rising from the steam-powered flouring mill, indicating the army was still at work, while camps stretched two or three miles to the southeast of town. In the distance, they saw part of Price's army trailing off to the south along the Pineville road.[18]

Shortly before 3 p.m., Blunt opted for a blow that Dick Hinton described as "almost unparalleled for audacity during the war." Back up the road, Lieutenant Colonel George H. Hoyt hurried forward what had been Jennison's brigade, but most of the Union forces remained strung out along the road, which left only 900 to 1,000 men in the advance. Confident that reinforcements would come, Blunt ordered his tiny force to attack.[19]

The Confederates probably had, initially, about 2,500 men, but Thompson's command, which had been in the fore while taking the town, had lingered as Price's rear guard. Earlier, Confederate pickets had warned of the Federal approach, but stragglers turned up, reassuring them that they had seen some of those who had formed up begin to turn back into camp. Some Confederates clustered unsuspecting "at the house of a union lady, whose husband was a Captain in the Federal service," making "rude jests and insulting remarks." One began singing, "Hark! I Hear the Feds Coming." Before he had finished the first stanza, a shell from Captain William D. McLain's battery crashed nearby. The Sixteenth Kansas on the left and the Second Colorado on the right swept the Confederates to the southwest. With the first booming of the guns, Thompson's men had run into position near the stone wall bordering Ritchey's cornfield. Shelby decided to throw everything he had out to meet the Federals. Small arms crackled as the Union troops reached the rail fence on one side of a field, and Confederates reached the fence at the south end of the same field. Blunt, "revolver in hand, with the members of his personal staff and volunteer aides, animated the men with his dauntless courage."[20]

Thompson's men held their fire until the Federals were within 500 to 700 yards. McLain's cannons continued to overshoot, while what remained of Confederate captain Richard A. Collins's two-gun battery also opened "with considerable precision into the midst of our troops." Sergeant George Patterson shifted his two howitzers attached to the Fifteenth Kansas "from one point to another . . . and dealt death and destruction in the rebel ranks with every discharge." Those present remembered "the inspiring cheers of the combatants, the constant roar of artillery, and the incessant rattle of fire-arms" with "the clashing of sabres, mingled with the death-cries of the fallen, and the shouts of the officers in giving commands, the galloping to and fro of couriers carrying orders."[21]

More Confederates poured onto the field. Shelby quickly sent Colonel Sidney D. Jackman's men "on foot to co-operate with General Thompson in repelling an attack from the enemy." As Jackman's men arrived, Thompson placed them to cover the artillery and ordered a charge. This was a desperate and dangerous move, given the fragility of the brigade, and threatened to result in the same problem the Federals had faced two days before on the Marmaton. Thompson had Alonzo Slayback to the west on the left, with Major B. Frank Gordon beyond Slayback's men. Two mounted companies under Captains Maurice M. Langhorne and R. H. Adams covered the far right. Thompson got them to the lane between the two fields and stayed at the front, urging the men to go slow. Hinton recalled that "the utmost exertions were made by the leading officers, to bring their men to a charge," but he realized that, if it worked, "so overwhelming was their force, that such an event must have produced disaster to us."[22] While the dismounted Confederates could not effectively charge the mounted Federals, their sheer numbers slowly pushed the Union back.

Few battles became so intense as rapidly, and the officers quickly felt the impact. A ball bored through the rim of one officer's felt hat, and Ketner lost two horses shot from under him. A shell exploding within a few feet temporarily and partially stunned Captain Hinton. Hoyt exposed himself to serious dangers to maintain an unbroken line throughout the battle. As Thompson's men reached the first fence, then jumped the second, and resumed their advance, Union fire mortally wounded Confederate colonel Moses W. Smith of the Eleventh Missouri.[23]

Growing Confederate numbers threatened to overwhelm Blunt's position. Patterson's howitzers checked a particularly threatening move against the Union right, and McLain's battery unlimbered about 500 yards from Ritchey's cornfield to cover the rest of the Union line as it fell back to support the battery. The rapid movement disorganized their ranks, and the Confederates renewed their drive on the Union's flanks, as the Fifteenth and Sixteenth Kansas Cavalry pulled back. On his own initiative, Captain William H. Green responded to Confederate preparations for another charge by sending two Colorado companies into a countercharge that caught the exhausted Confederates by surprise. When sent to the rear with his horse shot through the head and bleeding, a private stayed to take a series of parting shots, expecting his horse to fall momentarily. Another took his mule team with supplies right to the front line.[24]

One of the Colorado regiment's veterans later recalled the "fierce storm of leaden hail from the enemy's guns, that thinned our ranks and stilled the pulsations of many a noble heart." As of 4:30, the sound of gunfire, shouts, cheers, and clashing sabers made clear "the battle was raging in all its fury." By this point, though, some of the Fifteenth and Sixteenth Kansas had begun running out of ammunition, though most stood their ground "without a cartridge to return the galling fire of the enemy."[25]

At least parts of Price's other two divisions also pitched in to the fight. Although he later reported that General James Fagan's men arrived too late, Hinton watched with admiration as one of them, "an officer of splendid proportions, finely mounted on a white horse, who, bareheaded, and sabre in hand, rode furiously up and down the rebel lines, cheering on the men and exposing himself heedlessly to the utmost peril of the strife." At least one commander from General John S. Marmaduke's division also filed a report on its fighting there.[26]

Depending on the source, Blunt either turned the tide on the exhausted Confederates or began preparing a general withdrawal to the bluff, where his men could await reinforcements. At this critical point, Curtis, Sanborn, and Sanborn's staff reached the ridge overlooking the town. With Hinton's assistance, Sanborn got his Sixth MSM Cavalry and the Second Arkansas Cavalry dismounted and into action, even as Smiley's artillery blasted the Confederate center with twenty-two rounds. Blunt's men saw "dense volumes of dust . . . rising from out the forest in our rear, and soon Sanborn's brigade, covered with dust and foam, emerged from the woods, and amid the deafening shouts and wild huzzas of our men, came dashing forward to the rescue, and gallantly bearing down upon the foe, formed on the left, to intercept and repel the column under Shelby." One soldier said, "A grander *sublimer* spectacle was never witnessed, than was exhibited by that band of heroes on that memorable field of Neutonia."[27] As Shelby's men fell back, Blunt's moved forward alongside Sanborn's.

Confederate Edwards called it "one of the quickest, hottest, bloodiest little combats of the Civil War," and James B. Pond, with his battalion of the Third Wisconsin Cavalry, watched what he called "the best fight yet," but both sides claimed victory. "Night closed the contest," wrote Edwards, "and another beautiful victory had crowned the Confederate arms." Price described "a short but obstinate combat" in which the Federals were "repulsed and driven across the prairie three miles with heavy loss." Thompson reported holding his position until the Federals withdrew, after which they "fell back toward our camp, receiving several shots from the enemy's artillery as we retired." One Confederate even called it "an easy fight." However, Curtis described the Confederates as "routed with heavy loss. They now run toward Cassville, where I shall continue after three hours' rest." Nevertheless, Shelby left Lieutenant Colonel William H. Erwin "to watch well the enemy's movements until the next day."[28] The battle ended with the Federals holding the field until about 9 p.m., when they moved into Newtonia for the night.

The battle had ended shortly before sunset, after raging for three hours. Shelby had sought to fight only a rear guard action, and Thompson withdrew the big guns. Thompson later claimed he had ordered a fallback before Sanborn arrived, but Phelps reported the Confederates were disordered, "heedless of the bugle that called to the charge." In this fight, Blunt started with fewer than 1,000, and Union reinforcements brought the total to a bit more than 2,000 (which Price described as 3,000). The Confederates probably never had more than 3,500 to 4,000 on the field (which Federal accounts exaggerated to "a force ten times" theirs).[29]

Blunt described his total losses as 118 killed and wounded with 175 horses killed, while Hinton enumerated 95 wounded, 18 killed, and one missing. Supposedly, the Confederates lost 275 killed and wounded, including two colonels, but they also buried General W. F. Slemons, mortally wounded at Mine Creek three days earlier. Writing in a newspaper rather than one of his more fanciful books, Edwards acknowledged a massive Confederate loss. "Our wounded were removed to a large brick house in Neutonia, that was generously placed at our disposal by the proprietress—a Mrs. Cole, whose endeavors, along with other ladies of the town . . . were taxed to the utmost." He later boasted that only Shelby had pushed the Coloradoans back but "had to give up about eight hundred of his very best in less than hour's fighting to do even that much."[30]

As for casualties, the Confederates had hospitals at the farmhouses of the McClain and the Witherspoon families, but most of those injured in the battle never got there. Confederates left their dead and wounded; in charge of the hospital was "a medical student recruited at Lexington" who was associated with Monroe's Arkansans. When a Confederate surgeon approached under a flag of truce, Curtis sent "such medical stores as humanity demanded should be at his disposal," but nobody seemed to do much serious counting.[31]

The Cold Road to Fayetteville

According to Hinton, Curtis still saw "the surrender of the rebel army" as the main purpose of his campaign and believed it attainable with "efficient co-operation after the battle of Newtonia." After Newtonia, Federals told themselves that the only thing keeping the Confederates together was "the impression that we kill all prisoners," although Curtis's march from Fort Scott had not done everything it could to dispel that. From this point on, both sides faced "a mountainous country very destitute of supplies." A Union spy, "who has been with the Confederates for several days past and during the battle of the 28th, has come in" and confirmed that Price's army would make "as rapidly as possible to Red River." Curtis himself thought it inevitable that, properly pressed, Price's army would fall apart before it got as far as the Arkansas River.[32]

The most serious blow that hit the Federals came after the battle, in the predawn hours of October 29 and from the rear. McNeil got his men into the saddle around 4 a.m. and had marched for two hours before getting his orders to backtrack and continue to Rolla. Without consultation or discussion, Rosecrans recalled his troops, which he would surely not have done without consultation with Pleasonton. Philips had already started back to central Missouri with General E. B. Brown's old brigade, Sanborn's orders took him back to Springfield, and Benteen's were to report back to the Sixteenth Corps.[33]

One could make the strongest case for Sanborn's return to the District of Southwest Missouri, through which Price's army had just passed. Bolstered by the EMM, Lieutenant Colonel John D. Brutsche, with the experienced counterinsurgents of the Sixth and Eighth MSM Cavalry—such as Majors Milton Burch and John R. Kelso and Captain Ozias Ruark—had been monitoring guerrilla activities there. Yet Brutsche reported that "the enemy is devoting all his energies to the single point of getting away without any more fighting, and I think must succeed. He destroys no property, not even public." On the day after Newtonia, Lieutenant Colonel Hugh Cameron, who was with that part of the Second Arkansas Cavalry that Phelps had not taken north with Sanborn, clashed with a large Union force at the Upshaw farm in Barry County, but it, too, had only wanted to get away.[34]

Curtis and Blunt hesitated to continue into Arkansas unsupported. After covering the ten miles to Neosho, they countermarched to Newtonia, where they could more readily get food. Although "the indignation of all was intense," Curtis set the tone by insisting that Rosecrans "could not have known or appreciated the position." Nobody bore more responsibility for any such ignorance than Rosecrans, who had chosen to absent himself from the field and permitted his immediate representative to do likewise without replacing him. Jim Lane spelled it out for even the dullest of Washington officialdom: "Rosecrans and Pleasonton are escorting Marmaduke and Cabell to Saint Louis. Curtis and Blunt are pursuing Price with about 4,000 men. Can they not be re-enforced?"[35]

However, the White House and War Department had never left much doubt about what they wanted done. At one point, a flustered Abraham Lincoln had asked, "While Curtis is fighting Price, have you any idea where the force under Rosecrans is? Or what it is doing?" With the latest news, Major Generals E. R. S. Canby, U. S. Grant, and Halleck all weighed in again, with explicit orders to pursue Price until the large Federal armies positioned in Arkansas. Curtis passed this on to Rosecrans and sent couriers to recall Sanborn, Philips, McNeil and Benteen, but the damage had been done. Philips and McNeil had already covered so much ground that their return would take too much time. While Rosecrans agreed to send Benteen and Sanborn to a rendezvous at Cassville, the latter had already turned back to resume his duties in Springfield.[36]

Even after Curtis conveyed Grant's orders, Sanborn still doubted whether carrying them out would be "legitimate under the circumstances." He believed "Price will be pursued by General Starvation across the river—a most formidable enemy to him." For his part, Curtis understood that Sanborn had responsibility for a chaotic district. Indeed, the same day as Newtonia saw fighting around Dry Wood, Fort Scott, and Cane Creek, the last sputtering into Sunday. Then, too, any assumptions in Washington that the Federals in Arkansas would do anything to meet Price in the desolated northwest corner of the state reflected a real ignorance of how things had functioned there for some time.[37]

For the second time since Mine Creek, dithering in the Union command gave the battered Army of Missouri a major lead on its pursuers, though Price took nothing like a full advantage of the opportunity. The exhaustion of Price's army and the even greater depletion of its forage accounts for much of this tardiness. Local Confederate bands took advantage of Price's presence by threatening the Union garrisons of Brigadier General John M. Thayer at Fort Smith and Colonel La Rue Harrison at Fayetteville.

While Fort Smith represented a bluff, there already existed a serious threat to Fayetteville, where Harrison's First Arkansas Cavalry and about 1,000 militia and volunteers had dug substantial earthworks. While Price campaigned in Missouri, the Confederate colonel William H. Brooks turned up with 300 men and began recruiting (i.e., "conscripting") near Fayetteville. On October 20, Confederate major Buck Brown had attacked Harrison's supply train near Cassville with what the Federals claimed to be 600 men, and the same force later jumped a foraging party under Captain D. C. Hopkins of Curtis's army. During the next few days, Brooks's larger force pressed Fayetteville, which got the erroneous news from Fort Smith that Confederate general Douglas Cooper and an army of 6,000 would be there shortly. On October 25, the same day as Mine Creek, "500 rebels under Brown" attacked Harrison's supply train as it came down from Cassville. After two hours' hard fighting near Bentonville, Harrison gathered "subsistence for a thirty-days' siege" at Fayetteville, which he thought to be "well fortified and intend[ed] to fight it out on this line." Told by the Department of Missouri that the Confederate army "is being dissolved like a mist in the sun," Harrison agreed that he had "deserters by hundreds" turning themselves in at his garrison.[38]

However, even as Rosecrans kept Curtis mired at Newtonia, Brooks got two pieces of artillery onto East Mountain near Fayetteville and began shelling its works. Federal troops under Captains Hopkins and E. B. Harrison pulled their way up the mountainside, at times using bushes, to dislodge the Confederates. There were some modest casualties, and one of the guns burst. Between 10 and 11 a.m., Brooks made his own attack against the Union works on the west side of town. At 11 a.m., the Confederates drove in the pickets and resumed shelling the town. "One shell passed through the wall of Mrs. Steele's house, exploding in the bedroom of her daughter, the wife of a Federal officer, who had but a moment before left the room." Another building, though flying a hospital flag, received shells, "one six pound rifle and one twelve pound howitzer." Harrison reported three attempts to attack the works. From the numbers reported, Brooks lost twelve killed and twenty-five wounded, several mortally, while Brown lost eleven killed and wounded.[39] Harrison's scouts thought they faced "8,000 rebels with two guns," though the actual number of men had been barely large enough to threaten an underfed, underequipped garrison of 1,500, mostly recent recruits or militia.

On Monday, October 31—three days after Newtonia—Curtis resumed his pursuit, heading toward Cassville. Ford, Moonlight, and Hoyt each had fewer than 500 mounted men, so much rested on Benteen's roughly 1,800 veterans, whom Curtis called "the best equipped, disciplined, and commanded force in the field." In Barry County, near the mill at Gadfly, the Federals learned that Price's army had actually taken the Keetsville road toward Pineville and the Arkansas line. Blunt took his men in that direction and Curtis notified Benteen to head that way.[40]

The next two day, the weather and Federal prospects got even worse. On Tuesday, an increasingly persistent and nasty rain pelted their march, but Benteen joined them in the ruins of Keetsville, giving Curtis about 3,000 men who continued through Cross Timbers and the old Pea Ridge battlefield in Arkansas. The heavy rain saturated everybody's blankets. Colonel James H. Ford described himself as "wet as a drowned rat!" When Major James A. Melton showed up with the Cassville garrison—a handful of men from the Second Arkansas Cavalry—it became clear that McNeil would not be coming up. Worse, Rosecrans sent Sanborn to recall Benteen. Curtis finally had enough, countermanding the order and apprising Washington of his action. Meanwhile, Curtis's force could hear the cannons at Fayetteville. Curtis sent them ahead to reinforce the garrison as quickly as possible, but three days of "unremitting rain and snow" capped the bureaucratic delays to strand Curtis near Newtonia.[41]

Curtis's relief column got to Fayetteville on Wednesday between 11 a.m. and noon—although one account states 2 p.m.—killing a rebel lieutenant and two privates and ending a siege that had lasted four hours. Curtis's main body continued on to camp at the old Prairie Grove battlefield. Hinton reported the loss of nine wounded, one mortally out of a garrison of 1,128, including 175 armed citizens, while Confederate casualties had been reported as seventy-five killed and wounded. Hinton thought that without Curtis's timely arrival, Fayetteville would have fallen, and concerted action by Generals Price, Richard M. Gano, and Douglas H. Cooper might have made for the "easy capture of Forts Smith and Gibson." As it was, the demoralized remnants of Thomas R. Freeman's brigade headed east, away from Price's army and back toward their homes, "following down the White River, leaving their broken guns in disgust and probably disbanding near Huntsville." Curtis decided to leave Dodge's Ninth Wisconsin Battery at Fayetteville, while bringing along Harrison with his mounted force of about 300 mounted men of the First Arkansas Cavalry. As night fell, so did the snow, even as far as Springfield, becoming "a severe snow storm" on Thursday. "Camping in mud, rain, and snow at dark on the evening of the 3d at Cross Hollows," wrote Curtis, "I was nearly overcome with fatigue, illness, and the perplexing orders which I have mentioned."[42]

The Confederates suffered severely, but Price decided that, once his army had reached Arkansas, it would be effectively beyond the reach of the jurisdiction-conscious Federals. Price bypassed Cassville to head straight to Pineville and the Arkansas line. Colonel John F. Davies reported that the head of his column camped in the Cherokee Nation as early as October 29, and Price later reported reaching Maysville on October 30 and 31. He later claimed that when the Army of Missouri limped into the area of Maysville, on the border of the Indian

Territory, it detached General John B. Clark's brigade for service in northeast Arkansas.[43]

"Rained all day," noted one Confederate, as his unit trudged into Cane Hill, roughly twenty miles southwest of Fayetteville. He reported it "a remarkable hard trip. Scarcity of forage + rations. Best soldiers regard it as the most difficult campaign of the war." At Cane Hill he "got the first corn for my horse and the first bread for myself since leaving Independence, *Beef without Salt being our only rations.*" "Quite a number of our conscripts absent. A good deal of sickness in the army. Several of our boys left behind. Such are the misfortunes of war. We have endured more than is required of duty, soldiers in the annals of history and just the half is not felt nor told." "This rain reminds you of the children of Israel traversing through the wilderness. But alas! We have no Moses to lead us," wrote Dr. J. H. Baker in his diary. "What is to be the result of this campaign no one can see." The next day, he added, "Low spirits + debility are playing havoc with our men. Many can scarcely go."[44]

Price's later report claimed that Brooks had operated under Fagan at Fayetteville, when his men "closely invested" the Federals there, driving them into their "inner fortification." Price claimed that, while at Cane Hill, he sent more of Fagan's division—with, according to some accounts, Colonel Thomas Freeman of Marmaduke's division and 500 of Shelby's men under Colonel Benjamin Elliott and two of Captain Richard A. Collins guns—to assist Brooks and Brown. Jackman reported Shelby's permitting three colonels "to give their men an opportunity of visiting their friends in Northern Arkansas," adding that "a great many of the men" had already become "insubordinate and were disposed to complain unnecessarily. The Confederate general believed the suffering of his lazy soldiers "was the result of their own inefficiency," since they expected the army to feed them rather than to forage on their own.[45] In fact, of course, officers may have had resources, and telling the private soldier to forage in an area with little or no forage probably contributed to the decision of the men to take off.

Epilogue

Sins of the Fathers

November's Decision

The grubby realities of civil war translated visions of a multiracial community into something like Fort Gibson. "If it was in Kansas, it would be called a city; as is, candor compels us to describe it as an indifferently-third-rate town. It is not quite so large as Pekin, but of similar architecture. Together with its suburbs—Log Town—Mud Town—Skin Town, &c.—it would make quite a figure on the map. Its chief aristocracy is brown camplected [*sic*] men, with white skins, requiring a certificate of moral character, to remain, which accounts for the high order of virtue among that class of our citizens." Not a "city of refuge" but "a Refugee city—the greater part of its denizens being left to the tender mercies of Agents and Providence." War had made it "of greater importance than it is likely to be."[1] On the strength of this community's Indian Brigade rested the last Federal chance to block and capture the shattered remnants of the Army of Missouri.

The last days of the campaign dragged large armies through the darkness and cold of the southern mountains. In the process, the soldiers had a bitter taste of the benign neglect and outright fraud that characterized the government's treatment of the Indians and the Indian soldiers, whose cooperation could have made short work of the remnants of the Confederate army. The campaign closed with an even more nightmarish trek back to where the war seemed to mean something comprehensible to them.

ARKANSAS

According to General John M. Thayer at Fort Smith, the Confederates had sent him notice under a white flag that Sterling Price's army would attack the base, rolling over Fort Gibson along the way. Not a particularly thoughtful or questioning soul, Thayer took the information at face value and opted to curl his lines into the shelter of his fort, although he remained incredulous enough to alert his men to avoid going to "Mackey's Saline for the purpose of manufacturing salt." Thayer lacked any great desire to cooperate in running down the Confederates, partly because General Samuel R. Curtis's emergency mobilization in Kansas had sidetracked mounts at Fort Scott earmarked for Thayer in Arkansas. On Price's side, though, the general claimed that he "received information that the Federal army at Little Rock had been greatly re-enforced by a portion of General Canby's command."[2] Thus, Fort Smith and Little Rock joined Fort Scott, Kansas City, Jefferson City, and St. Louis as Union posts bypassed because supposedly massive Federal armies had materialized.

Years of war had left those remaining in the area "utterly impoverished. Very few persons were at home except women and children. Few of these had food sufficient for the ensuing winter, and barely one was decently clad, while most had not sufficient clothing to hide their nakedness." The passage of two armies through their midst did not help. "Our trail is litterly strewn with broken down horses, mules, wagons + men," wrote one Confederate. "Rations awful short nothing but beef + half rations of that. We are + have been in an awful critical situation." What they could not see was that the Confederates were "nearly exhausted, living on a quarter of a pound of meal a piece per day and abandoning their plunder along the whole route."[3]

The Federals began moving after them again on Saturday, November 5, certain that what was left of Price's army would cross into the Indian Territory near Maysville and attempt to reach the Arkansas River somewhere above Fort Smith. Certainly nobody saw much of the enemy. Moonlight's brigade had veered off toward Bentonville, where it surprised "a small band of guerrillas, killing two in the pursuit." Hoyt's detoured to a flour mill "and drove off a band of rebels who were running the mill." The day ended only eleven miles from Fayetteville, "near the ground occupied by Price's forces the previous night." General James G. Blunt had faced Jo Shelby and other Confederates there, at Prairie Grove, nearly two years before. Blunt himself occupied the house he had used for his conference with the Confederate commanders, and others who had been in the area checked on the well-being of friends they had made locally. "A great many of our regiment," recalled a member of the Eleventh Kansas, "walked around over the battlefield until it was so dark we could not see."[4]

The bluecoats, following in the wake of Price, reported living "mainly on the debris of the retreating army." One soldier described it as "the gloomiest time of my service, being five days without tasting food, except one large burr-oak acorn that I foraged in the Arkansas hills." Dick Hinton noted that long-abandoned cattle provided an abundance of beef, but everything else ran short. Still conspicuous by his absence from the events on which he reported, General

William S. Rosecrans continued to insist that Price's army, "if allowed would almost disintegrate." At Curtis's insistence, Rosecrans claims to have sent the brigades of John B. Sanborn and John McNeil in pursuit, though, in fact, he had not.[5]

On Sunday, November 6, the Union column "drove out some small bands" as they passed through Cane Hill. A bit beyond, Colonel Frederick Benteen's scouts had "several brisk skirmishes with the rebel rear guard," killing half a dozen and losing a bugler. They returned with "an interesting relic," the flag that Quantrill's band had captured a year before when they ambushed Blunt and his escort in the Baxter Springs massacre; the flag was "nearly perfect," though torn to pieces and "packed in an old traveling bag." The town had some huts under construction and other signs that part of the Army of Missouri may have intended to winter there. Federal reports mentioned that they "found forty or fifty prisoners starving and dying," and the Union soldiers paroled "nearly one hundred," including a major, a captain, and a lieutenant. At the approach of the Federals, rumors swept the town of a pursuing force of 30,000. A surgeon had remained behind with the wounded, even though he was told that the Federals would kill him if he was captured, and the Union soldiers went out into the woods to retrieve some of the Confederate wounded who had crawled there for safety.[6]

Realizing that the Confederates had taken the valley of the Sallisaw into the Cherokee Nation, the Federals continued on with what they later called a "midnight march." Native women and children constituted most of the few civilians left to observe their passage. On Monday morning, when the Federals resumed their march, Benteen took the advance, followed by Blunt, with Colonel La Rue Harrison's Arkansans in the rear and Major James Ketner's Sixteenth Kansas Cavalry covering the commissary train. Meanwhile, word finally reached Curtis from the War Department placing him in charge of Rosecrans's troops with orders to pursue Price to the Arkansas River or until they had driven Price into the Federal troops waiting in Arkansas.[7]

What they saw along the trail into the Indian Territory confirmed what the Confederate prisoners at Cane Hill had told them. They made thirty miles that were as "bad as the roads were," with their horses "in bad condition, destitute of corn, and grass poor," passing abandoned "property stolen from the Missouri." Even more than before, the Federals found a course "strewn with arms, half-burned wagons, dead mules, abandoned horses, and all the debris of a routed and demoralized army, including Price's private carriage" and that one piece of artillery. Curtis boasted that Price's men had plundered "the rich products and abundant spoils of the Missouri Valley, but crossed the Arkansas destitute, disarmed, disorganized, and avoiding starvation by eating raw corn and slippery-elm bark." One of Shelby's surgeons reported that the Army of Missouri by that point numbered about 3,500 men.[8]

One of the ministers from Dwight's Mission near Russellville, Arkansas, re-ported "the destitution and demoralization of the rebels was most complete." They marched without any attempt at organization and retained only thirty-two wagons of their vast supply train, with two pieces of artillery.One of the prison-ers, Major James Parrott, had just compiled consolidated returns for the Army of Missouri the previous day, providing the best numbers of any on the cost of the great gamble by the Confederate cause. Parrott frankly told Blunt that, since leaving Lexington, the Army of Missouri had lost 10,056 killed, wounded, or missing. This represented a loss of 83 percent of the last reported 12,176, back when the rebels had entered the state with such high hopes.[9] If one credits Price's army with even a modest number of recruits and conscripts, the proportion of losses was even greater.

THE ORDEAL OF HISTORY

The spectre of race obviously dogged the Confederate forces every step of the way during the campaign. The very idea of armed blacks continually haunted Price and his commanders and surely seemed real enough when Price heard the terrifying rumor that "1,000 negroes under arms" waited for his men behind the defenses of Fort Scott. Race so permeated the thinking of his men that some began to distinguish between whether they were dealing with a "white man or a Yankee," that is, a radical in favor of emancipation. They bluntly told one of the latter who fell into their hands, "You're black as Hell. Hand over that watch and damn quick, too!" Another boasted of "how quick the damned Radical son of a bitch turned black" after being shot.[10] The language inadvertently acknowl-edged an idea of race that had never been a matter of ancestry or skin color but an ideological divide over white supremacy.

Not until the closing years of the war did many adherents of the Union cause begin to transcend the same kind of thinking, which played its role in denying their own forces their last chance to bag what was left of the Army of Missouri and effectively end the Civil War west of the Mississippi. That, however, would have required the War Department to have done only what it had already agreed to do many times for the Indian Brigade at Fort Gibson, one of the most inter-esting organizations of the war. A remarkably successful organization—much more so than the oft-touted little Confederate raiding band of Stand Watie—the brigade had the responsibility of protecting life and property in the Indian Territory. Undersupplied and hungry, they survived in the squalor of a military base surrounded by thousands of refugees, preoccupied with things like getting the bodies of those who had starved or succumbed to disease into "the public burying ground recently staked off by the Indian Authorities."[11]

More than the war put the Indians in this situation. Well-connected businessmen from Fort Scott with ties to Governor Thomas Carney dominated what locals called "the company," a shifting network of entrepreneurs. With the help of Charles W. Blair of Fort Scott and Thayer at Fort Smith, they not only monopolized the trade with the Indians but secured contracts as the exclusive purchaser of whatever the Indians might be able to produce. They capped it all with an extensive business rustling Indian cattle and selling it to the army. If remounted, as it needed to be, the Indian Brigade would protect Indian civilians who were growing crops and raising livestock, so keeping them unmounted would protect both the company and the contractors. Colonel William A. Phillips had taken the issue to the very top, and General U.S. Grant had gone on record for giving the brigade full pay, full rations, and full equipage, including new mounts. When nothing happened anyway, Phillips's Indian troops actually caught government contractors red-handed and killed two when they opened fire. The result landed Phillips under arrest at Fort Smith.

When news arrived of the Confederate disasters in Missouri, the district-level commanders in Arkansas and the Indian Territory rarely even hinted that they sensed an opportunity. Early on, Thayer advised Colonel Stephen H. Wattles at Fort Gibson that he could best prevent an attack by avoiding the Confederates. "If you have a detachment at Mackey's Salt-Works see that it does not remain there too long. It is possible that Price may come by Webber's Falls." This did not extend to allowing Wattles to retain the Second Kansas Colored, which Thayer ordered immediately returned to his base. Thayer had sent the Second Kansas Colored to escort the supply train. General Frederick Steele, in turn, suggested that, should Thayer turn in his direction, he should draw all his outposts "into Fort Smith with all the public property possible."[12]

In short, the interests of the army's local and regional command structure in keeping the Indians—including several thousand veteran Union soldiers—subjugated trumped any interest in stopping any specific Confederate operation. What remained had been a half-starved garrison surrounded by thousands of Indian refugees and military commanders fearful that the Indian soldiers might use whatever mounts they had to protect Indian cattle from government contractors. Thus the army allowed the Indian soldiers to remain without horses, unable to protect any crops, and entirely dependent on the largess of the Office of Indian affairs and licensed government traders. Thayer and the other architects of the Indians' isolation left the brigade incapable of doing anything to stop or slow the passage of the Army of Missouri on Monday and Tuesday, November 7 and 8. Meanwhile, Price's army "cut a new road for more than a mile through an impenetrable canebrake" to reach the locally known ford frequented by Stand Watie's Cherokee raiders.[13]

By some accounts, the Federal advance under Harrison moved only a few hours behind the Confederates as it made its way through the rainy cold of the last twelve miles. They found "the prairie was still burning and his broken-down mules, horses, and baggage were again broadcast over his well-defined way." The first of their men reached the river in time to see a few soaked stragglers clambering up the south bank. A former prisoner of the Confederates told the Federals that most of Price's army had crossed the previous night.[14]

Curtis's men went into camp back on the bluff. They sent patrols across the river. Major Curtis, the general's son, had been "one of those who crossed in pursuit of the enemy." Some accounts report no contact with the last of Price's army, while others say that the Federals fired some shots at Confederate pickets. Then, too, some of the victors of the campaign must have stood swaying with their hunger. One Union soldier remembered, "For seven days I never got a thing to eat but field corn," and that was only the "nubbins the rebels had left," prepared by burning them black and carrying them along to eat on the move.[15]

They knew well that behind them—across the entire Union—voters were going to the polls to decide whether to reelect Lincoln and the Republicans, confirming the emancipationist strategy, or turn to "the rebel-Copperhead-Conservative-McClellan-Vallandigham party." The primary goal of Price's campaign had been to influence the elections in Missouri, particularly by aiding Democratic interest that "constantly represents President Lincoln as a tyrant, a usurper, a revolutionist, a breaker of the Constitution, as fighting against the just rights of the South, and laboring for the overthrow of the rights and liberties of the people." Where it could, the Republican press noted that recruits, such as those General John S. Marmaduke acquired in Franklin County, had recently been involved in Democratic Party meetings. Price himself told one group that the armed secessionists had turned up to protect the rights of Democrats to vote.[16]

The situation melded the Federal military operations with the Republican election campaign and the radical campaign within it. As one Kansas soldier wrote, the military campaign became one "to establish a government untarnished by the blight of slavery, or any of its damnable heresies." The two radical candidates for governor in Missouri and Kansas—Thomas Fletcher and Samuel Crawford—rightly expected victory at the polls. This reflected not only their prominent abolitionist views but their active and prominent role in the military defense of their states.[17]

The exhausted officers and men realized that they would have little use in the future for the artillery ammunition they had dragged with them for hundreds of miles. McClain's Colorado battery fired thirty-four shots, one for each state of the Union. Some described it as sending notice quickly to Forts Smith and Gibson and others as a parting salute to the enemy forces. It certainly conveyed to the enemy that Union forces had plenty more ammunition. Most important, though, the cannons roared an end to a campaign that must have left many of its participants frustrated as well as exhausted and hungry.[18]

Perhaps. But denied a final triumph by their failure to defend their comrades of color, the victorious were left wet and shivering, masters only of the landscape they had helped to devastate, not just through three years of war but through centuries of practiced devastation.

As the day wore on, nature itself seemed to echo the sentiment. As Hinton wrote, the storm that had been brooding all morning in preparation "now broke out in grandeur. The rain poured down in torrents. The forked lightnings flashed, and the thunders rolled heavily and continuously. It was as if the entire aerial artillery, and all voidless forms and forces of the worlds of spirit and space, had been brought together for a grand field day. The scene was truly sublime, vastly magnificent in scale, and wildly tumultuous in its uproar." It brought down trees and created a roaring rush of the river, while "the heavens over head were blacker than fabled Erebus, except when riven by the lurid lightning flame." Hinton also reported: "In the midst of the wild scene, and amid the howling of the storm, half fed and almost worn out, the irrepressible gaiety of conquerors broke jubilantly forth."[19]

In the midst of this chaos, Curtis huddled near a light, scribbling his "congratulatory orders" dissolving his little army. By about 10 p.m., the storm and its clouds had passed. In a very real sense, the military men knew that the election campaign and the military conflict had also moved on to the East. For them it was over. Setting aside the order until morning, the general and his men folded in a well-earned rest.[20]

Long Roads Back

Conspicuous by their absence, of course, were most of the troops of the Department of Missouri, with the exception of Benteen's brigade. That of Colonel John F. Philips had broken down at Fort Scott and returned to the District of Central Missouri. Sanborn had already gotten his troops back to Springfield and the District of Southwest Missouri, from which a second countermarch would have taken too long to matter. On the day the Federal troops reached the Arkansas, McNeil's brigade got his troops to Rolla, Missouri.

Then, too, if the truth be told, Benteen's brigade had been cobbled together from those troops that had been on their way to Tennessee but diverted to chase Price. Appropriately enough, Curtis sent Benteen "by the shortest route and at his own discretion to his proper corps" at Memphis.[21]

Charles R. Jennison's brigade backtracked to Fort Scott by way of Newtonia. "From the difficulty of procuring forage, and the total exhaustion of rations, the march northward was necessarily very much retarded, it requiring eight days to reach Fayetteville." Along the way, guerrillas picked off foraging parties. Before they returned, they claimed a march of "about 1,200 miles, during the most inclement season of the year, without adequate transportation for supplies, subsisting mainly upon the country through which we passed." Although promising an account for the "numberless killed or wounded in action," they never actually set it down.[22]

The brigade of Colorado colonel James H. Ford accompanied Curtis directly back to Fort Scott through Fort Gibson. Contrary to what the soldiers might have expected, they confronted a Federal installation "in almost suffering condition, on account of the scarcity of rations, having been compelled to subsist on quarter rations for the period of nearly three months." Union soldiers passing through found that they, like their Indian comrades, could get bread but only at high price, and they made do with a "burlesque on bread"—beans ground to coarse flour and cakes with a modest amount of corn meal, baked without salt or anything else. "Had with beef and coffee." Curtis knew he had to get his men north without spending any unnecessary time at Fort Scott and sent word for the fort to get supplies sent out to meet them. At Cabin Creek near the border, his men took some solace in finding hickory nuts, and when they saw the supplies coming toward them, they began chanting, "Hard tack. Hard tack." They got to Fort Scott after "thirty-eight days and without change of clothing."[23]

Another column of the pursuers simply went initially into Arkansas. Harrison's small detachment reported to General Steele at Little Rock, but Blunt went to Fort Smith with Moonlight's brigade. The brigade remained there, awaiting supplies before making their way back by way of the Indian Territory, where it performed other functions. "The snow was three or four inches deep," before the unit headed back, reaching Fort Scott in December.[24]

What they experienced had been bad enough for some veterans to argue well into the twentieth century about who had marched the farthest in the long campaign. A member of the Eleventh Kansas claimed his unit had made the war's "longest march," which sparked an exchange in the *National Tribune* early in the twentieth century. One of Benteen's men recalled having been "in the saddle nearly four months before they made a stop of any account." Colonel Lazear fondly remembered having been unable to change clothes for so long that he burned them, as they become "full of gray backs."[25] Yet the hardships recalled just how little those long, hard rides mattered.

"It is now over 43 years since we took part in that terrible raid," recalled one veteran, "and I don't see how anyone could have had a worse time than we did and live." One Union cavalryman recalled stopping with a few members of his company for a memorable meal at an Indian hut near the Arkansas

line, recalling sassafras tea, stone-ground cornbread, and meat, which their sergeant later identified as dog. Worse, the cavalryman recalled, "every day we
were obliged to leave some of our poor dumb friends alone, to be devoured by
wolves or die of starvation. Then was the time that many of the boys put their
arms around their horses necks and cried like children when they kissed the
poor old fellows good-by. There is where a cavalryman appreciates his horse,
having to abandon him to die, with hundreds of dreary miles before him."
Thereafter they could hear the howling of the wolves feasting at night on the
mounts they left behind. "Someone may say, 'Nothing but a poor old horse.'
Well, they have never been situated where their horse was their best friend."[26]

On the other hand, the men returned to find that the campaign had largely
cleaned out what had been the scene of vicious border troubles for years. "At no
time during the war," wrote Hinton, "had South-east Missouri and North-west
Arkansas been so free from bushwhackers."[27] Then, too, they could only guess
the misery of what the Confederates suffered on their way home.

Price acknowledged losing many of their horses for simple want of food,
but he asserted that his men "never approached starvation, nor did they suffer to anything like the extent that other of our soldiers have cheerfully endured without complaint for a much longer time during this war. At all events,
I arrived in the country where forage and subsistence could be obtained in
abundance, bringing with me in safety all the sick and wounded and all my
command with which I entered the Indian country, without a single exception,
except those who voluntarily straggled off and deserted their colors."[28]

His men remembered it a bit differently. Most deserted as the Army of Mis-
souri hurried south, farther from home for the Missouri and Arkansas men.
Desertions stripped all of Price's brigades to the bare bones. As they headed
toward Texas, he sent the brigades of Colonels Thomas H. McCray, Archibald
S. Dobbin, and Thomas R. Freeman "to collect all stragglers and deserters" in
Arkansas. He also authorized Brigadier General William L. Cabell and Colonel
W. F. Slemons to furlough their men. With Colonel Charles H. Tyler's brigade
hurrying ahead toward the Texas line, Price's only two remaining brigades were
one from Shelby's division—under Brigadier General M. Jeff Thompson and
Colonel Sidney D. Jackman—and Colonel Colton Greene's brigade—formerly
John B. Clark's—of Marmaduke's division. Smallpox hit them as they moved
south, and veterans recalled Edwards and other officers who strove to help
them. One man recalled General James F. Fagan's giving his mount to a sick
soldier and walking "along through the mud and rain" on foot. Greene thought
they "endured the severest privations and sufferings during the march through
Indian Territory to Boggy Depot."[29]

"Men are getting demoralized," wrote one Confederate, "and we present a
pitiable, forlorn aspect. G— d— old Price, is the almost constant ejaculation

from men exhausted in both body and spirit." The Indian Territory had been "completely devastated. Where plenty once dwelt, now is nothing but a barren waste." In four days of crossing this "barren waste," he had nothing but acorns until "we at length reach the white settlements, a joyous day to us all." He added that "I have not drawn any from Uncle Jeff since 31st. Aug. 1863."[30]

Even before Price's bedraggled column returned to its lines, the Confederate hierarchy heard of the disaster before it faced the returning army but chose to ignore the realities. Confederates heard of the crushing defeats in Missouri from captured Union dispatches but dismissed them as merely "'thunder,' gotten up for the November election." Declared one Confederate general: "I do not credit the report of General Price's disastrous defeat, &c. Some one would have made his way this far before now if such had been the case."[31]

Confederate self-deception proved remarkable.

At the same time, Rosecrans managed to report on an odd campaign that he essentially commanded. He wrote Washington that he had "returned to Saint Louis to be there during the election, and on the receipt of the news of the enemy having crossed the Arkansas directed the cavalry to repair to their respective districts and Winslow's cavalry to move by the best route and join General Thomas at Nashville."[32] Washington quietly replaced Rosecrans but without any clear and critical breakdown of the campaign.

The condition of the collapsing Trans-Mississippi Confederacy after the campaign had been far too strained to permit any comparable action. However, Missouri governor Thomas Reynolds publicly challenged Price's version, and Price insisted—and got—an interminable and pointless hearing. As the last of the secessionist institutions and leaderships came down about their ears, a handful of officers dutifully allowed Price to document his version of the campaign's history without even trying to vindicate or indict his command of the Army of Missouri.

In the end, the peace that settled over the western border also required peace among the Confederates and peace among the Unionists as well. And that mandated what was, for most whites, a blessed forgetfulness about the real issues and experiences of the Civil War. After 150 years, it seems reasonable to start remembering them.

Notes

Prologue: The Making of a Raid

1. On this earlier phase of the campaign, see Mark A. Lause, *Price's Lost Campaign: The 1864 Invasion of Missouri* (Columbia: University of Missouri Press, 2011).

2. Rick Montgomery, Shirl Kasper, Jean Dodd, and Arthur S. Brisbane, *Kansas City: An American Story* (Kansas City: Kansas City Star Books, 1999), 53; John B. Clark Jr., quoted in "Intercepted Letter," St. Louis *Missouri Democrat*, October 19, 1864, 1.

3. Brig. Gen. Thomas Ewing to Lt. Col. A. G. Hequembourg, October 17, 1864, *The War of the Rebellion; A Compendium of the Official Records of the Union and Confederate Armies, Published Under the direction of the ... Secretary of War ...* 70 vol. in 128 (Washington: Government Printing Office, 1880–1901), hereafter cited as *OR,* 41: (pt. 4), 48; Lazear to Ashley Lazear, August 11, 1864, in "The Civil War Letters of Colonel Bazel F. Lazear," ed. Vivian Kirkpatrick McLarty (Part III) *Missouri Historical Review* [*MHR*], 45: (October 1950), 50. Earlier (Parts I, II), 44: (April, July 1950), 255–72, 387–401.

4. *The Wartime Genesis of Free Labor: The Upper South,* ed. Ira Berlin, Steven F. Miller, Joseph Reidy, and Leslie S. Rowland, series 1, vol. 2 of *Freedom: A Documentary History of Emancipation, 1861–1867, Selected from the Holdings of the National Archives of the United States* (Ser. 1) 2 (New York: Cambridge University Press, 1993): 381, 556, 572, 581–84, 568–69; Zachary J. Lechner, "'Are We Ready for the Conflict?': Black Abolitionist Response to the Kansas Crisis, 1854–1856," *Kansas History,* 31: (Spring 2008), 14–25; Katie H. Armitage, "'Seeking a Home Where He Himself Is Free': African Americans Build a Community in Douglas County, Kansas," *Kansas History,* 31: (Autumn 2008), 154–75; Brent M. S. Campney, "W. B. Townsend and the Struggle against Racist Violence in Kansas," *Kansas History,* 31: (Winter 2008/2009), 260–73.

5. Curtis, *OR,* 41: (pt. 1), 471–72; Special Field Order, October 19, 1864, *OR,* 41: (pt. 4), 117; Maj. C. S. Charlot to Maj. S. S. Curtis, October 19, 1864, *OR,* 41: (pt. 4), 116; Capt. John Willans to Capt. R. D. Mobley, October 21, 1864, *OR,* 41: (pt. 4), 167; Capt. R. S. Rafety to Maj. Gen. S. R. Curtis, October 20, 1864, *OR,* 41: (pt. 4), 149; Capt. R. J. Hinton to Maj. C. S. Charlot, October 20, 1864, *OR,* 41: (pt. 4), 149; Maj. C. S. Charlot to Capt. Rafety, October 20, 1864, *OR,* 41: (pt. 4), 149. "Forward all available troops, including those at Atchison, negroes at fort, and such other troops as General Davies thinks he can spare. Price's entire force is in Lexington. Blunt is falling back in good

order, and I shall stand at every strong point if he comes this way," Curtis to Capt. John Willans, October 20, 1864, *OR,* 41: (pt. 4), 143; John Paul Ringquist, "Color No Longer a Sign of Bondage: Race, Identity and the First Kansas Colored Volunteer Infantry Regiment (1862–1865) (Ph.D. diss., University of Kansas, 2012); Maj. Gen. Samuel R. Curtis, January —, 1865, *OR,* 41: (pt. 1), 473. "A company of colored militia on service here. Do you want them sent to Wyandotte?" "I have been and examined the colored militia command at this place, and find them not in a condition to proceed to Wyandotte, they being over age, invalids, &c. They are engaged at work on the fortifications at this place," Capt. R. D. Mobley to Capt. John Willans, October 21, 1864, *OR,* 41: (pt. 4), 167.

6. Maj. R. H. Hunt to Capt. Willans, October 16, 1864, *OR,* 41: (pt. 4), 15; John Willans to Commanding Officers at Fort Leavenworth and Atchison, October 21, 1864, *OR,* 41: (pt. 4), 167; Roger D. Cunningham, "Douglas's Battery at Fort Leavenworth: The Issue of Black Officers During the Civil War," *Kansas History,* 23: (Winter 2000/2001) 200–17, but see also his *The Black Citizen-Soldiers of Kansas, 1864–1901* (Columbia: University of Missouri Press, 2008). "Information has been received that a number of negroes have deserted from the battery and are coming home. You will cause them to be arrested and will hold them until they can be sent forward," John Willans to Col. Hershfield, October 21, 1864, *OR,* 41: (pt. 4), 168; Paul B. Jenkins, *The Battle of Westport* (Kansas City: Franklin Hudson, 1906), 140, 143.

7. Reader, Autobiography, 3:189, 191, 304.

8. Army of the Border, Special Field Order, October 20, 1864, *OR,* 41: (pt. 4), 144; Wyandot Nation of Kansas, "Wyandotte County Kansas in the Civil War," n.d., http://www.wyandot.org/civilwar.htm; Papers on Historical Algonquian and Iroquois Topics By David A. Ezzo, Michael H. Moskowitz, 89; "Delaware Participation in the American Civil War"; "The Kanza and the Civil War," Friends of the Kaw Heritage, http://www.friendsofkawheritage.org/index.php?news&nid=10.

9. Quoted in Richard Hall, *Patriots in Disguise: Women Warriors of the Civil War* (New York: Marlow, 1994), 167, see also 167–73 enlisted. Notice of Frank Noyes "the captivating courtesan, who formerly consorted with Charley Noyes" dressing in male attire. "In Male Attire," St. Louis *Missouri Democrat,* October 15, 1864, 4. Not published until January 1885 in *Colorado Transcript,* January 14, 1885, the husband of someone he had known in Colorado gave him the diary.

10. Reader, Autobiography, 3: 154, 156, 186–87, 212.

11. "The Times," *Banner of Light,* May 18, 1861, 4. See also "Farming in the West," letter of S.W. Ellis on Child's Plea, *Banner of Light,* May 24, 1862, 6–7. At Kidder, Missouri; Crosby Johnson, *An Illustrated Historical Atlas of Caldwell County, Missouri* (Edwards Brothers, 1876); "The Banner in Kansas," *Banner of Light,* July 9, 1864, 4. See also "A.M." "More Help Is Still the Cry," *Banner of Light,* April 30, 1864, 5; Orlando Durker, "A Plea for Southern Kansas," *Banner of Light,* August 13, 1864, 8. Also "Still another Call," *Banner of Light,* May 14, 1864, 8; Philips, November 7, 1864,. *OR,* 41, 353; Johnson, *An Illustrated Historical Atlas*; Patrick S. Kenney in home guard and joined First MSM Cavalry at nearby Cameron.

12. Jeff R. Bremer, "'A Species of Town-Building Madness': Quindaro and Kansas Territory, 1856–1862," *Kansas History,* 26: (Autumn 2003), 156–71; Larry Schmits,

"Quindaro: Kansas Territorial Free-State Port on the Missouri River," *Missouri Archae-ologist*, 49 (1988), 89–145; "History of Old Quindaro Recalled as School Plans Eightieth Anniversary Fete," *Kansas City Kansan*, May 8, 1938, in *Kansas Historical Quarterly*, 8: (1), (February 1939), archives, KanColl: The Kansas Historical Quarterlies accessed 18 Dec 2008. See also "Quindaro, Kansas on the Underground Railroad," online exhibit of Kansas Collection, Kansas City, Kansas, Library, 2000. See also Marilyn S. Blackwell and Kristen Tegtmeier Oertel, *Frontier Feminist: Clarina Howard Nichols and the Politics of Motherhood* (Lawrence: University Press of Kansas, 2010); John Paul Ringquist, "Color No Longer a Sign of Bondage: Race, Identity, and the First Kansas Colored Volunteer Infantry Regiment (1862–1865)" (Ph.D. diss., University of Kansas, 2012).

13. *The Wartime Genesis of Free Labor*, as *Freedom*, (ser. 1) 2: 589–90.

14. *Freedom*, (ser. 1) 2: 81.

15. Price has received considerable attention from biographers and scholars focused primarily on the early period of the war. See Ralph R. Rea, *Sterling Price, the Lee of the West* (Little Rock, AR: Pioneer Press, 1959); Robert E. Shalhope, *Sterling Price: Portrait of a Southerner*. (Columbia: University of Missouri Press, 1971); and Albert Castel, *General Sterling Price and the Civil War in the West* (Baton Rouge: Louisiana State University Press, 1993). On the numbers, see also Maj. Gen. Samuel R. Curtis, January —, 1865, *OR*, 41: (pt. 1), 479, 517; Jenkins, *Battle of Westport*, 65.

16. Richard J. Hinton, *Rebel Invasion of Missouri and Kansas, and the Campaign of the Army of the Border Against General Sterling Price, in October and November, 1864* (Chicago: Church & Goodman, 1865), 8–9. For a shorter but largely derivative account of the campaign, see Wiley Britton, *The Civil War on the Border*, 2 vols. (New York: G. P. Putnam's Sons, 1890, 1899), 2: 433–518, with the earlier phases in 375–432.

17. George Plattenburg, "John Newman Edwards, Biographical Sketch," in Mary Virginia Plattenburg Edwards, *John N. Edwards: Biography, Memoirs, Reminiscences and Recollections* (Kansas City: Jennie Edwards, 1889), 10–12, 15, 20–22, 24–25; Daniel C. O'Flaherty, *General Jo Shelby: Undefeated Rebel* (1954; reprint, Chapel Hill: University of North Carolina Press, 2000), 5, 11. See also Deryl Sellmeyer, *Jo Shelby's Brigade Iron Brigade* (Gretna, LA: Pelican, 2007), and John H. Eicher and David J. Eicher, *Civil War High Commands* (Stanford, CA: Stanford University Press, 2001).

18. Plattenburg, "John Newman Edwards," 9–10, 16.

19. For his background, see William M. Lamers, *The Edge of Glory: A Biography of General William S. Rosecrans, U.S.A.* (Baton Rouge: Louisiana State University Press, 1961); Rosecrans to Canby, Oct. 5, 1864, *OR*, 41: (pt. 3), 633; Maj. Gen. U. S. Grant to Secretary of War E. M. Stanton, October 11, 1864, *OR*, 41: (pt. 3), 773: "The best general now in Missouri to take that command would be General J. J. Reynolds, if he is there; if not, then Mower would come next. Probably more activity could be insured by sending Sheridan to Missouri, place Meade where Sheridan is, and put Hancock in command of the Army of the Potomac."

20. Col. Charles W. Blair to Maj. Gen. S. R. Curtis, October 10, 1864, *OR*, 41: (pt. 3), 767; Col. C. R. Jennison to Maj. Gen. S. R. Curtis, October 9, 1864, *OR*, 41: (pt. 3), 739; Col. Charles R. Jennison to Col. Charles W. Blair, October 11, 1864, *OR*, 41: (pt. 3), 795–96; Col. Charles R. Jennison to Capt. George S. Hampton, October 13, 1864, *OR*, 41: (pt. 3), 847; Maj. Gen. Samuel R. Curtis, Dept. of Kansas, Fort Leavenworth, January —, 1865,

OR, 41: (pt. 1), 471–72; "Col. Jennison. Some Interesting Incidents of His Adventurous Career in the War," *National Tribune*, July 10, 1884, 8. Rebel Major Bowie and Lieutenant Key have been killed. Colonel Shanks "mortally wounded. "Rebel General Sanwaite [*sic*—Stan Watie]" reported in Tipton yesterday at 8 o'clock with 5, 000 men headed for Boonville. "The Latest News.By telegraph.From Jefferson City.Our Cavalry Skirmishing with the Rebels.Price in California," St. Louis *Missouri Democrat*, October 11, 1864, 1. Raided Lamar, but this was a guerrilla action not directly associated with Price's army, like the "little fight" of October 10 at Thomasville in the Ozarks. October 10, 1864, entry in J. H. Baker Diary, Western Historical Manuscript Collection, University of Missouri–Kansas City.

21. Edwards, "Veteran Sam," in *John N. Edwards*, 166.

22. See Mark A. Lause, *A Secret Society History of the Civil War*.

23. This development was a pivotal feature of the war in the Indian Territory. See Mark A. Lause, *Race and Radicalism in the Union Army* (Urbana: University of Illinois Press, 2009), xxx.

24. Robert Collins, *General James G. Blunt: Tarnished Glory* (Gretna, La.: Pelican, 2005). Robert M. Utley put the cart before the horse in describing Blunt as "a prominent Kansan with little military talent and a penchant for meddling in politics" in *Frontiersmen in Blue: the United States Army and the Indian 1848–1865* (Lincoln: University of Nebraska, 1967), 288, 306; Utley, *Frontiersmen in Blue*, 289, 291, 297–98; Brig. Gen. James H. Carleton to Col. Christopher Carson, October 19, 1864, *OR*, 41: (pt. 4), 121–22. "Cheyennes killed by Captain Nichols on 10th instant near Valley Station had a white woman's scalp, and several bills of lading from men in Saint Joseph to merchants in Denver. They fought to the last. Line safe this side Julesburg," Col. J. M. Chivington to Maj. Gen. S. R. Curtis, October 13, 1864, *OR*, 41: (pt. 3), 851.

25. Maj. Gen. James G. Blunt, commanding First Division, Army of the Border, Dist. of South Kansas, Paola, December 24, 1864, *OR*, 41: (pt. 1), 572; Dept. of Kansas, Special Orders No. 215, October 10, 1864, *OR*, 41: (pt. 3), 764; Maj. Gen. George Sykes to Capt. John Willans, October 25, 1864, *OR*, 41: (pt. 4), 242–43; Hinton, *Rebel Invasion* 9–10, 17; Maj. Gen. S. R. Curtis to Adjutant G. S. Smith, KSM, October 13, 1864, *OR*, 41: (pt. 3), 844. Maj. Samuel B. Davis. I have the honor to report that in compliance with his order I joined Major-General Blunt at Paola, Kans., the 11th ultimo, and Maj. Samuel B. Davis, November 26, 1864, *OR*, 41: (pt. 1), 551; Col. Charles W. Blair, November 26, 1864, *OR*, 41: (pt. 1), 596–97. "General Sykes informs me that Bill Anderson was at Lexington yesterday and Price at Sedalia. Look out for a raid. Every man must have forty rounds of carbine and pistol cartridges each in his box and saddle-bags. Instruct your command on this head," Col. Thomas Moonlight to Lt. Col. Preston B. Plumb, October 9, 1864, *OR*, 41: (pt. 3), 738. Among those brought into the leadership of the army were such officers as Major Henry Almstedt, the former artilleryman who had served with the Marxist forty-eighter Joseph Weydemeyer; the former union printer J. M. Mentzer; xxx. Curtis, *OR*, 41: (pt. 1), 471–72.

26. See John K. Driscoll, *Rogue: A Biography of Civil War General Justus McKinstry* (Jefferson, NC: McFarland, 2005). Michael Thomas Smith's *The Enemy Within: Fears of Corruption in the Civil War North* (Charlottesville: University of Virginia Press, 2011)

focuses on the widespread fears and perceptions of corruption while tending to remain agnostic on the question of what substance fueled those fears.

1. of Liberation and Occupation

1. Gary R. Kremer, "'We Are Living in Very Stirring Times': The Civil War in Jefferson City, Missouri," *MHR*, 106: (January 2012), 69–70. At first, scouts found nothing as far as "a mill four miles from town," though detachments of the Unionist Second Arkansas Cavalry and of the First and Fifth MSM Cavalry did clash independently with the enemy. Lt. Col. Joseph A. Eppstein, November 18, 1864, *OR*, 41: (pt. 1), 382; Col. John E. Phelps, November 2, 1864, *OR*, 41: (pt. 1), 401–2; Col. John F. Philips, November 30, 1864, *OR*, 41: (pt. 1), 354; Col. James McFerran, November 7, 1864, *OR*, 41: (pt. 1), 358, 360; Maj. Gen. Sterling Price, December 28, 1864, *OR*, 41: (pt. 1), 631; Maj. Gen. John B. Clark, Jr., commanding Marmaduke's division CSA, Camp on Red River, Ark., December 19, 1864, *OR*, 41: (pt. 1), 681; Brig. Gen. M. Jeff Thompson, November 24, 1864, *OR*, 41: (pt. 1), 663; Lt. Col. J. F. Davies, December 12, 1864, *OR*, 41: (pt. 1), 696; Brig. Gen. John B. Sanborn, commanding Dist. of Southwest Missouri and Third Brigade, Cavalry Division, *OR*, 41: (pt. 1), 385–86; Maj. Gen. William S. Rosecrans, December 7, 1864, *OR*, 41: (pt. 1), 311.

2. Brig. Gen. Clinton B. Fisk to Hon. James S. Rollins, October 12, 1864, *OR*, 41: (pt. 3), 819. Edward Willis corrected a published statement that Fisk had never left St. Louis nor been in the field. "Random Shots," *National Tribune*, October 4, 1888, 3.

3. Maj. Gen. Alfred Pleasonton, November 30, 1864, *OR*, 41: (pt. 1), 340; Brig. Gen. John B. Sanborn, commanding Dist. of Southwest Missouri and Third Brigade, Cavalry Division, *OR*, 41: (pt. 1), 385–86; A. B. MacDonald, "Interview of A. B. MacDonald of the Kansas City Star with U.S. District Judge John F. Philips and Frank C. Wornall—The Battle of Westport from a Confederate's Standpoint, by Dr. Stephen H. Ragan," *Kansas City Times*, May 30, 1912, in H. H. Crittenden, *The Battle of Westport and National Memorial Park* (Kansas City, MO: Lowell Press, 1938), 35; Philips, Addenda: Itinerary of the District of Central Missouri, commanded by Brig. Gen. Egbert B. Brown, *OR*, 41: (pt. 1), 357; Pleasonton, *OR*, 41: (pt. 3), 757; Hinton, *Rebel Invasion*, 108; Jenkins, *Battle of Westport*, 88. For itineraries of the pursuit, see McFerran, *OR*, 41: (pt. 1), 358, 360; Maj. William B. Mitchell, November 3, 1864, *OR*, 41: (pt. 1), 410; Capt. George M. Houston, November 16, 1864, *OR*, 41: (pt. 1), 381.

4. Brig. Gen. John B. Clark Jr., commanding Marmaduke's division CSA, December 19, 1864, *OR*, 41: (pt. 1), 678; Phelps, *OR*, 41: (pt. 1), 401–402; Col. Colton Greene (3rd Missouri Cavalry), commanding Marmaduke's brigade CSA, December 18, 1864, *OR*, 41: (pt. 1), 688; Mitchell, *OR*, 41: (pt. 1), 410; Hinton, *Rebel Invasion*, 108; Brig. Gen. John B. Sanborn, November 13, 1864, *OR*, 41: (pt. 1), 386; Maj. William Plumb, Sixth Missouri State Militia Cavalry, November 12, 1864. *OR*, s.1, v.41, pt.1, 409; Greene, *OR*, 41: (pt. 1), 688–89; Philips, *OR*, 41: (pt. 1), 354. Gravely's Brigade was not engaged in the battle at California on the evening of October 9, 1864. Col. Joseph J. Gravely, November 15, 1864, *OR*, 41: (pt. 1), 412.

5. Among those with a background in the partisan war were Moses W. Smith, Sidney D. Jackman, De Witt C. Hunter, Alonzo W. Slayback, John T. Coffee, W. O. Coleman,

John A. Schnable, William H. Irwin, and Benjamin Elliott. Brig. Gen. M. Jeff Thompson, commanding Shelby's brigade CSA, Bonham, Texas, November 24, 1864, *OR*, 41: (pt. 1), 663; Brig. Gen. Joseph O. Shelby, December —, 1864, *OR*, 41: (pt. 1), 655. Price said they had orders "to destroy the Pacific Railroad at that place, which he did, destroying track and bridges, &c.," Price, *OR*, 41: (pt. 1), 631. *History of Cole, Moniteau, Morgan, Benton, Miller, Maries and Osage Counties, Missouri* (Chicago: Goodspeed, 1889), 370; Hinton, *Rebel Invasion*, 12–13. See also entry for October 17, 1864, in Baker diary; "The Rebel Raid—Assault upon Jefferson City—Price's March Westward," Jefferson City *Missouri State Times*, October 15, 1864, 2; and "From Jefferson City. Whereabouts of Price," St. Louis *Missouri Democrat*, October 15, 1864, 1.

6. Sanborn, *OR*, 41: (pt. 1), 386–87; reports of Col. John F. Philips, Seventh Missouri State Militia Cavalry, commanding First Brigade, Cavalry Division, to Capt. William T. Kittredge, November 7, 1864, *OR*, 41: (pt. 1), 354; Phelps, *OR*, 41: (pt. 1), 402; Philips, *OR*, 41: (pt. 1), 354–55; McFerran, *OR*, 41: (pt. 1), 358; Eppstein, *OR*, 41: (pt. 1), 382; Capt. William C. F. Montgomery, Battery H, 2nd Missouri Light Artillery, November 15, 1864, *OR*, 41: (pt. 1), 460; Hinton, *Rebel Invasion*, 109; Clark, *OR*, 41: (pt. 1), 678; Col. Robert R. Lawther, December 6, 1864, *OR*, 41: (pt. 1), 698; Davies, *OR*, 41: (pt. 1), 696; Greene, *OR*, 41: (pt. 1), 689; "The Latest News. By telegraph. From Jefferson City," St. Louis *Missouri Democrat*, October 11, 1864, 1.

7. Sanborn, *OR*, 41: (pt. 1), 387; Mitchell, *OR*, 41: (pt. 1), 410; Col. John F. Philips (Seventh Missouri State Militia Cavalry), commanding First Brigade, Cavalry Division, *OR*, 41: (pt. 1), 354–55, with the story, apparently recounted by Lorring.

8. Henry C. Levens and Nathaniel M. Drake, *A History of Cooper County, Missouri. From the First Visit by White Men, in February, 1804, to the 5th day of July, 1876* (St. Louis: Perrin and Smith, 1876), 115–16; James F. Thoma, *This Cruel Unnatural War: The American Civil War in Cooper County, Missouri* (Kingsport TN: James F. Thoma, 2003), xxx.

9. A. W. Reese, Civil War Memoirs, 683, Western Historical Manuscripts Collections, University of Missouri, Columbia (hereafter WHMC); Shelby, *OR*, 41: (pt. 1), 655; Levens and Drake, *A History of Cooper County, Missouri*, 116. See also Price, *OR*, 41: (pt. 1), 631; Thompson, *OR*, 41: (pt. 1), 664; Thoma, *This Cruel Unnatural War*, 120; Robert W. Frizzell, "'Killed By Rebels': A Civil War Massacre and Its Aftermath," *MHR*, 71: (July 1977), 386–90.

10. Brig. Gen. J. O. Shelby to Col. L. A. Maclean, October 9, 1, *OR*, 864, *OR*, 41: (pt. 3), 993; Shelby, *OR*, 41: (pt. 1), 655.

11. Thompson, *OR*, 41: (pt. 1), 664. See also Price, *OR*, 41: (pt. 1), 631; Hinton, *Rebel Invasion*, 110.

12. "The Invasion. Price Makes a Speech at Boonville. Shelby Conscripting. A Militia Captain Hanged. The Raid in Central Missouri," St. Louis *Missouri Democrat*, October 14, 1864, 1; untitled item, *Liberty Tribune*, October 21, 1864, 2; "The Latest News. By telegraph. From Jefferson City. Our Cavalry Skirmishing with the Rebels. . . . Enemy Driven West—Their losses, Etc., Etc.," St. Louis *Missouri Democrat*, October 11, 1864, 1; Price, *OR*, 41: (pt. 1), 631; Thompson, *OR*, 41: (pt. 1), 664; Col. Sidney D. Jackman, November 30, 1864, *OR*, 41: (pt. 1), 673; Clark, *OR*, 41: (pt. 1), 681.

13. Thoma, *This Cruel Unnatural War*, 122–23; "From Boonville," St. Louis *Missouri Democrat*, November 8, 1864, 2; Lazear to Ashley Lazear, October 17, 1864, in "Civil War Letters of Colonel Bazel F. Lazear" (Part III), 53; October 13, 14, 1864, entry in Baker diary, October 12. Reached Huntsville. October 12, 1864, entry in Baker diary.

14. Thomas Reynolds to Maj. Gen. Sterling Price, October 10, 1864, *OR*, 41: (pt. 3), 1000.

15. Price, *OR*, 41: (pt. 1), 632; Edwards, *Noted Guerillas, or the Warfare of the Border* (St. Louis: Bryan, Brand, 1877); Duane Schultz, *Quantrill's War: The Life and Times of William Clarke Quantrill, 1837*–1865 (New York: St. Martin's, 1996); Albert E. Castel and Thomas Goodrich, *Bloody Bill Anderson: The Short, Savage Life of a Civil War Guerilla* (Mechanicsburg, PA: Stackpole Books, 1998); Edward E. Leslie, *The Devil Knows How to Ride: The True Story of William Clarke Quantrill and His Confederate Raiders* (New York: Random House, 1996); Thomas Goodrich, *Bloody Dawn: The Story of the Lawrence Massacre* (Kent, OH: Kent State University Press, 1991); "The Invasion," St. Louis *Missouri Democrat*, October 14, 1864, 1.

16. Shelby, *OR*, 41: (pt. 1), 655–56; "From Boonville," St. Louis *Missouri Democrat*, November 8, 1864, 2. Fisk told Pleasonton that Shelby had hanged the militia officer. Maj. Gen. Alfred Pleasonton to Maj. Gen. William S. Rosecrans, October 12, 1864, *OR*, 41: (pt. 3), 816–17; "The Invasion," St. Louis *Missouri Democrat*, October 14, 1864, 1. Schumaker shot "pierced by seven balls and his throat cut." "From Jefferson City. Whereabouts of Price," St. Louis *Missouri Democrat*, October 15, 1864, 1. While there is no explanation for this particular animosity to Shoemaker, one suspects that that he bore the responsibility for having Confederate sympathizers firing on Confederate soldiers.

17. Thoma, *This Cruel Unnatural War*, 117, 118, 124.

18. S. T. Tracy, operator at Sedalia, to Maj. Gen. William S. Rosecrans, October 11, 1864, *OR*, 41: (pt. 3), 793; T. J. Stiles, *Jesse James: Last Rebel of the Civil War* (New York: Alfred A. Knopf, 2002).

19. Maj. Gen. Alfred Pleasonton to Maj. Gen. William S. Rosecrans, October 11, 1864, *OR*, 41: (pt. 3), 784–85, also noted that the militia had 800 at Sedalia, 300 at Warrensburg, and 300 at Lexington and that he had no contact with Lexington or Boonville; Maj. Gen. Alfred Pleasonton to Maj. Gen. William S. Rosecrans, October 10, 1864, *OR*, 41: (pt. 3), 758–59; William F. Switzler, *Illustrated History of Missouri, From 1541 to 1877* (1879; reprint, New York: Arno, 1975), 271–464; "From Jefferson City," St. Louis *Missouri Democrat*, October 20, 1864, 4; "Price's Great Raid. A Bird's-Eye View. What He was After and What He Was Not After," St. Louis *Missouri Democrat*, October 18, 1864, 2. The reports from Jefferson City, often signed "Waldo," may be by the writer signing as "Gath," as listed in "Civilians at the Battle of Pilot Knob," http://mostateparks. com/sites/default/files/Civilians%20at%20Fort%20Davidson%20updated%202011. pdf. "You say Sanborn is on their left flank. If that is our left flank south of them, all right; if not, wrong," Maj. Gen. William S. Rosecrans to Maj. Gen. Alfred Pleasonton, October 10, 1864, *OR*, 41: (pt. 3), 759.

20. Philips, *OR*, 41: (pt. 1), 355; Thoma, *This Cruel Unnatural War*, 118–20. See also McFerran, *OR*, 41: (pt. 1), 358; Lt. Col. John F. McMahan, November 4, 1864, *OR*, 41: (pt. 1), 407; Mitchell, *OR*, 41: (pt. 1), 410.

21. McFerran, *OR,* 41: (pt. 1), 358; Philips, *OR,* 41: (pt. 1), 355–56.

22. Price, *OR,* 41: (pt. 1), 631–32; Shelby, *OR,* 41: (pt. 1), 656; Jackman, *OR,* 41: (pt. 1), 673–74. See also Col. Colton Greene, December 18, 1864, *OR,* 41: (pt. 1), 689; Davies, *OR,* 41: (pt. 1), 696; Ira M. Mallory, "Missouri Bush & Prairie. Price's Raid," *National Tribune,* September 6, 1900, 8. This represented the third of four articles by Mallory under the general headline "Missouri Bush & Prairie"; the others carried the subheadlines of "Preparing for the Field," "Chasing Guerrillas," and "End of the War and Muster-out," August 23 (pp. 1–2), August 30 (p. 7), and September 13 (pp. 1–2), 1900.

23. Eppstein, *OR,* 41: (pt. 1), 382–83; Jackman, *OR,* 41: (pt. 1), 674; Thoma, *This Cruel Unnatural War,* 121; Hinton, *Rebel Invasion,* 110–11. Jackman elsewhere describes the fight as covering about a mile and a half below the junction of the Tipton road, implying half a mile separated Nichols and Hunter.

24. McMahan, *OR,* 41: (pt. 1), 407; Sanborn, *OR,* 41: (pt. 1), 387; Clark, *OR,* 41: (pt. 1), 681; Gravely, *OR,* 41: (pt. 1), 412; Col. Joseph J. Gravely, November 16, 1864, *OR,* 41: (pt. 1), 414–15; Maj. William Plumb, 6th Missouri State Militia Cavalry, November 12, 1864, *OR,* 41: (pt. 1), 409; Phelps, *OR,* 41: (pt. 1), 402; Mitchell, *OR,* 41: (pt. 1), 410; Sanborn, *OR,* 41: (pt. 1), 387–88; Pleasonton, *OR,* 41: (pt. 3), 816–17. Jefferson City rumors of a fight at Pisgah came by the steamer *Sioux City,* which left JC Thursday morning, they also arrived St. Louis by train from Washington. Rosecrans and party have reached JC by steamer from Washington. "The State Military News. Reported Fighting at Pisgah. Result Not Known. The Telegraph Working to Springfield," St. Louis *Missouri Democrat,* October 15, 1864, 1.

25. Col. S. D. Jackman to Maj. Maclean, October 11, 1864, *OR,* 41: (pt. 3), 1001–1002.

26. Ibid., October 12, 1864, *OR,* 41: (pt. 3), 1006; Greene, *OR,* 41: (pt. 1), 689; Lawther, *OR,* 41: (pt. 1), 698; Shelby, *OR,* 41: (pt. 1), 656; Price, *OR,* 41: (pt. 1), 631–32; Ira M. Mallory, "Missouri Bush & Prairie. Price's Raid," *National Tribune,* September 6, 1900, 8; Pleasonton, *OR,* 41: (pt. 3), 816. See also Robert L. Dyer, "Battle of Wilkin's Bridge," *Boone's Lick Heritage,* 7 (Spring 2000): 10–11.

27. Eppstein, *OR,* 41: (pt. 1), 382–83.

28. Sanborn, *OR,* 41: (pt. 1), 388. "A good many horses were killed and wounded. My own horse was severely shot," Jackman, *OR,* 41: (pt. 1), 674; Shelby, *OR,* 41: (pt. 1), 656. The Federals picked up stragglers from Price's army for days thereafter, eleven on October 13, eight on October 14, and more over the next week or so. Thoma, *This Cruel Unnatural War,* 124–25. "The Missouri Invasion. A Reconnaissance by General Fisk to Boonville. The Rapine on the Banks of the Missouri," St. Louis *Missouri Democrat,* October 24, 1864, 2

29. Col. John V. DuBois to Col. F. D. Callender, October 18, 1864, *OR,* 41: (pt. 4), 77; Jenkins, *Battle of Westport,* 128, 144, and 147. St. Louisans knew one of the key organizers for Price's army, Lachlan Allan MacLean, "clerk in a banking house in this city," the sort of manager to which both armies looked. Their record varied widely, though, on the Confederate side, a lack of resources provided few opportunities for better than abysmal. Maj. Gen. James G. Blunt to Maj. Gen. S. R. Curtis, October 13, 1864, *OR,* 41: (pt. 3), 845; Maj. James Rainsford to Lt. Col. W. H. Stark, October 31, 1864, *OR,*

41: (pt. 4), 354. John Taylor Hughes, *Doniphan's Expedition and the Conquest of New Mexico and California*, 118, 245, 386.

30. Capt. G. W. Yates to Col. C. W. Marsh, October 13, 1864, *OR*, 41: (pt. 3), 837; Rosecrans, *OR*, 41: (pt. 1), 311; Pleasonton, *OR*, 41: (pt. 3), 816.

31. "From the Militia. News from Gen. Pike's Command," St. Louis *Missouri Democrat*, October 13, 1864, 2. Col. Gale based at Pacific. "Price's Great Raid. A bird's-Eye View," St. Louis *Missouri Democrat*, October 18, 1864, 2; "Militia Excitement in Franklin County," St. Louis *Missouri Democrat*, October 22, 1864, 2; "From Southeast Missouri. Fright at Tyler's Mills," St. Louis *Missouri Democrat*, October 9, 1864, 1; "From Southeast Missouri," St. Louis *Missouri Democrat*, October 24, 1864, 1; "From De Soto," St. Louis *Missouri Democrat*, October 15, 1864, 1; Brig. Gen. E. C. Pike to Brig. Gen. Ewing, October 20, 1864, *OR*, 41: (pt. 4), 133.

32. Lt. Col. H. M. Hiller to Brig. Gen. Thomas Ewing, October 13, 1864, *OR*, 41: (pt. 3), 836; Maj. H. H. Williams to Brig. Gen. Thomas Ewing, October 13, 1864, *OR*, 41: (pt. 3), 836, 837; Williams, *OR*, 41: (pt. 3), 887; Brig. Gen. Madison Miller to Brig. Gen. Thomas Ewing, October 17, 1864, *OR*, 41: (pt. 4), 38; Smith, *OR*, 41: (pt. 3), 890; Col. John V. DuBois to Maj. Gen. A. J. Smith, October 18, 1864, *OR*, 41: (pt. 4), 79; Rosecrans, December 7, 1864, *OR*, 41: (pt. 1) 310; Maj. H. H. Williams to Brig. Gen. Thomas Ewing, October 12, 1864, *OR*, 41: (pt. 3), 811; Brig. Gen. Thomas Ewing to Maj. Williams, October 13, 1864, *OR*, 41: (pt. 3), 836; Maj. H. H. Williams to Brig. Gen. Thomas Ewing, October 15, 1864, *OR*, 41: (pt. 3), 887; Thomas Ewing, Jr. to Col. J. V. DuBois, October 16, 1864, *OR*, 41: (pt. 4), 7–8; Rosecrans, December 7, 1864, *OR*, 41: (pt. 1) 310; Maj. H. H. Williams to Brig. Gen. Thomas Ewing, October 12, 1864, *OR*, 41: (pt. 3), 811; Gen. Madison Miller to Brig. Gen. Thomas Ewing, October 15, 1864, *OR*, 41: (pt. 3), 889; District of Rolla, Special Orders No. 162, October 9, 1864, *OR*, 41: (pt. 3), 730; Col. A. Sigel to Capt. Frank Eno, October 29, 1864, *OR*, 41: (pt. 4), 314; Capt. Flanigan to Asst. Quartermaster's office, November 3, 1864, attached as endorsement to Col. A. Sigel to Capt. Frank Eno, October 29, 1864, *OR*, 41: (pt. 4), 315; Maj. Gen. William S. Rosecrans to Col. Hugo Wagelin, October 10, 1864, *OR*, 41: (pt. 3), 754; Maj. Gen. Rosecrans to Col. William Myers at Warrensburg, October 28, 1864, *OR*, 41: (pt. 4), 296; Brig. Gen. Thomas Ewing to Brig. Gen. E. C. Pike, October 17, 1864, *OR*, 41: (pt. 4), 39; M. C. Meigs to Rosecrans, October 12, 1864, *OR*, 41: (pt. 3), 804; Quartermaster General M. C. Meigs to Rosecrans, October 13, 1864, *OR*, 41: (pt. 3), 834; Maj. Gen. William S. Rosecrans to Col. William Myers, October 13, 1864, *OR*, 41: (pt. 3), 834; Maj. Gen. Rosecrans to Col. William Myers at Warrensburg, October 28, 1864, *OR*, 41: (pt. 4), 296; and fourth endorsement by Phil. S. Fox, engineer for reconstruction of railroad bridges on Pacific Railroad, November 5, 1864, attached as endorsement to Col. A. Sigel to Capt. Frank Eno, October 29, 1864, *OR*, 41: (pt. 4), 315; Col. Hugo Wagelin to Maj. Gen. William S. Rosecrans, October 10, 1864, *OR*, 41: (pt. 3), 754; Brig. Gen. E. C. Pike to Brig. Gen. Thomas Ewing, October 29, 1864, *OR*, 41: (pt. 4), 312–13; H. Hannahs to Brig. Gen. E. C. Pike, October 20, 1864, *OR*, 41: (pt. 4), 133; Brig. Gen. E. C. Pike to Brig. Gen. Thomas Ewing, October 29, 1864, *OR*, 41: (pt. 4), 312–13; H. Hannahs to Brig. Gen. E. C. Pike, October 20, 1864, *OR*, 41: (pt. 4), 133.

33. A. J. Smith to Shaw, October 15, 1864, *OR,* 41: (pt. 3), 890; Dubois to Smith, October 18, 1864, *OR,* 41: (pt. 4), 79.

34. Shelby, *OR,* 41: (pt. 1), 656; Clark, *OR,* 41: (pt. 1), 681; Davies, *OR,* 41: (pt. 1), 696; Col. John Q. Burbridge, December 8, 1864, *OR,* 41: (pt. 1), 694; Thompson, *OR,* 41: (pt. 1), 664. "I moved that evening from Boonville to Chouteau Springs on my proposed route, a distance of eleven miles," Price, *OR,* 41: (pt. 1), 632.

35. Brig. Gen. John B. Sanborn to Col. C. W. Marsh, October 13, 1864, *OR,* 41: (pt. 3), 839; Sanborn, *OR,* 41: (pt. 1), 388; Sanborn, *OR,* 41: (pt. 1), 388. See also McFerran, *OR,* 41: (pt. 1), 358; Mitchell, *OR,* 41: (pt. 1), 410; McMahan, *OR,* 41: (pt. 1), 407; Philips, *OR,* 41: (pt. 1), 356; Montgomery, *OR,* 41: (pt. 1), 460; Col. Joseph J. Gravely, November 16, 1864, *OR,* 41: (pt. 1), 415; October 12, 1864, entry in William A. Lyman, Diary, 2. Misc. Mans. 17: #490, WHMC; Hinton, *Rebel Invasion,* 111.

36. Rosecrans quoted in Thomas A. Davies to Maj. Gen. S. R. Curtis, October 13, 1864, *OR,* 41: (pt. 3), 850; Curtis, *OR,* 41: (pt. 1), 472–73.

37. Maj. Gen. William S. Rosecrans, Dept. of the Missouri, St. Louis, December 7, 1864, *OR,* 41: (pt. 1), 311–12; Sanborn, *OR,* 41: (pt. 1), 388; "Gen. Rosecrans in the Field. Arrival of Gen. McNeil. General Pike's Militia at Washington. Movements of Price," St. Louis *Missouri Democrat,* October 13, 1864, 1. On the Miller county EMM, see "The Romance of the Raid," St. Louis *Missouri Democrat,* October 25, 1864, 1, and Clyde Lee Jenkins, *Judge Jenkins' History of Miller County Missouri* (Tuscumbia: Clyde L. Jenkins, 1971), 445, 446–48; "The Invasion," St. Louis *Missouri Democrat,* October 14, 1864, 1.

38. "The Military Situation. Price Retires from Jefferson City," St. Louis *Missouri Republican,* October 11, 1864, 2; "Price's Great Raid. A Bird's-Eye View. What He Was After and What He Was Not After," St. Louis *Missouri Democrat,* October 18, 1864, 2; "From Jefferson City. Pap Price mourning the loss of the Capital. Strength of the Fortifications. Generals Brown, Fisk, Sanborn and McNeil. Pleasanton [*sic*] and the Brigadiers. Rosecrans—His Responsibility," St. Louis *Missouri Democrat,* October 20, 1864, 4.

39. Price, *OR,* 41: (pt. 1), 632–33; Clark, *OR,* 41: (pt. 1), 681; Jackman, *OR,* 41: (pt. 1), 674; Shelby, *OR,* 41: (pt. 1), 656. Brig. Gen. John B. Clark Jr. to Col. Maclean, October 14, 1864, *OR,* 41: (pt. 3), 1010; Col. Maclean to Brig. Gen. John B. Clark Jr., October 14, 1864, *OR,* 41: (pt. 3), 1011; L. A. Maclean to Brig. Gen. John B. Clark, October 15, 1864, *OR,* 41: (pt. 3), 1014.

2. THE RAILROAD

1. "From Jefferson City. Whereabouts of Price," St. Louis *Missouri Democrat,* October 15, 1864, 1.

2. Crittenden, *Battle of Westport and National Memorial Park,* 36.

3. Jenkins, *Battle of Westport,* 81. "Colonel Van Horn I have not seen, but learn that he has about six companies of militia, none yet mustered into the regular service," Lt. Col. W. H. Stark to Maj. Gen. S. R. Curtis, October 11, 1864, *OR,* 41: (pt. 3), 798. Van Horn High School was built on the site of Van Horn's house in Independence, Mis-

souri. Honeywood, in 1955. Truman Road was originally called Van Horn Road in his honor.

4. Col. James H. Ford to Maj. Gen. S. R. Curtis, October 12, 1864, *OR*, 41: (pt. 3), 824; Ford, *OR*, 41: (pt. 1), 606.

5. Maj. Gen. S. R. Curtis to Gov. Thomas Carney, October 10, 1864, *OR*, 41: (pt. 3), 762–63; and Lt. Col. S. H. Melcher to Col. John V. DuBois, October 10, 1864, *OR*, 41: (pt. 3), 755. See also Rosecrans, *OR*, 41: (pt. 1), 312; Rosecrans to Curtis, October 18, 1864, in Curtis, *OR*, 41: (pt. 1), 475.

6. Gov. Thomas Carney to Curtis, with endorsement by Major C. S. Charlot referring to Col. Coates, October 20, 1864, *OR*, 41: (pt. 4), 142; Curtis, *OR*, 41: (pt. 1), 474; Maj. Gen. George W. Deitzler, December 15, 1864, *OR*, 41: (pt. 1), 614–15; MacDonald, "Interview," 35. On October 11, the Army of the Border consisted of the Second Colorado Cavalry, moving from Pleasant Hill to Hickman's Mills; the Eleventh Kansas Cavalry at Paola; the Fifteenth at Mound City; and a detachment of the Sixteenth with the First Colorado and Ninth Wisconsin Batteries. Maj. Chapman S. Charlot, assistant adjutant general, Fort Leavenworth, December 13, 1864, *OR*, 41: (pt. 1), 524.

7. Samuel J. Crawford, *Kansas in the Sixties* (Chicago: A. C. McClurg, 1911), 144.

8. Curtis, *OR*, 41: (pt. 1), 473; Maj. S. S. Curtis to Maj. C. S. Charlot, October 20, 1864, *OR*, 41: (pt. 4), 144; Maj. H. H. Heath to Maj. Gen. S. R. Curtis, October 20, 1864, *OR*, 41: (pt. 4), 148; John Spear to Curtis, October 19, 1864, *OR*, 41: (pt. 4), 120; Maj. Gen. S. R. Curtis to Gen. George Deitzler, October 14, 1864, *OR*, 41: (pt. 3), 872–73; Maj. Gen. S. R. Curtis to Sen. Pomeroy, October 19, 1864, *OR*, 41: (pt. 4), 117; advance from Leavenworth Dist. of North Kansas, Special Orders No. 130, October 22, 1864, *OR*, 41: (pt. 4), 195; Maj. Gen. S. R. Curtis to Maj. Gen. Deitzler, October 21, 1864, *OR*, 41: (pt. 4), 166; Maj. Gen. S. R. Curtis to Maj. Gen. James G. Blunt, October 11, 1864, *OR*, 41: (pt. 3), 794; Curtis, *OR*, 41: (pt. 1), 474.

9. Maj. Thomas I. McKenny, December 1, 1864, *OR*, 41: (pt. 1), 536; Curtis, *OR*, 41: (pt. 1), 473, 474; Curtis, *OR*, 41: (pt. 1), 522; Curtis, *OR*, 41: (pt. 1), 471–72.

10. Blunt, *OR*, 41: (pt. 3), 845; Blunt, *OR*, 41: (pt. 1), 572; Maj. C. S. Charlot to Maj. Gen. James G. Blunt, October 13, 1864, *OR*, 41: (pt. 3), 845–46; Maj. Gen. S. R. Curtis to Capt. John Willans, October 13, 1864, *OR*, 41: (pt. 3), 843; Maj. Gen. S. R. Curtis to Maj. Gen. James G. Blunt, October 14, 1864, *OR*, 41: (pt. 3), 869; Maj. Gen. James G. Blunt to Maj. Gen. S. R. Curtis, October 15, 1864, *OR*, 41: (pt. 3), 896; Maj. Gen. James G. Blunt to Col. Charles R. Jennison, October 13, 1864, *OR*, 41: (pt. 3), 846; Lt. Joseph Mackle to Col. Charles W. Blair, October 13, 1864, *OR*, 41: (pt. 3), 848; Curtis, *OR*, 41: (pt. 1), 471–72. For an odd treatment of Jennison as one of commanders in the field, see "Col. Jennison. Some Interesting Incidents of His Adventurous Career in the War," *National Tribune*, July 10, 1884, 8, which also conflates the fighting during October 21 and 22.

11. First Division, Army of the Border, General Field Orders No. 2, October 15, 1864, *OR*, 41: (pt. 3), 897; Blunt to Curtis, October 16, 1864, *OR*, 41: (pt. 4), 16; Col. Charles R. Jennison, November 23, 1864, *OR*, 41: (pt. 1), 581; Blunt, *OR*, 41: (pt. 1), 572; Fishback, *OR*, 41: (pt. 1), 618–19, 619–20. Jennison's First Brigade had the Fifteenth Kansas Cavalry, a detachment of the Third Wisconsin Cavalry, and five mountain howitzers. Second brigade, The Eleventh Regiment Kansas Volunteer Cavalry; Companies L and

M, Fifth Kansas Volunteer Cavalry; Companies A and D, Sixteenth Kansas Volunteer Cavalry. Four mountain howitzers were in the Eleventh, manned by Company E; and divisional units, while McLain's Independent Battery Colorado Volunteer Artillery, and a section of Second Kansas Battery.Col. Thomas Moonlight, December 15, 1864, *OR*, 41: (pt. 1), 591.

12. Brig. Gen. W. H. M. Fishback, October 28, 1864, *OR*, 41: (pt. 1), 620–21; Blair, October 17, 1864, *OR*, 41: (pt. 4), 57–58; Curtis, *OR*, 41: (pt. 1), 474–75; Blunt, *OR*, 41: (pt. 1), 572–73; Blair, *OR*, 41: (pt. 1), 596–97; Deitzler, *OR*, 41: (pt. 1), 614; Col. James H. Ford, December —, 1864, *OR*, 41: (pt. 1), 606–7; Maj. Robert H. Hunt, November 22, 1864, *OR*, 41: (pt. 1), 543; Deitzler, *OR*, 41: (pt. 1), 615; Curtis, *OR*, 41: (pt. 1), 474–75; Maj. C. S. Charlot to Capt. Ruggles, October 18, 1864, *OR*, 41: (pt. 4), 95; Charlot, *OR*, 41: (pt. 1), 524–25.

13. Col. J. D. Crawford to Brown, Brown to Crawford, October 3, *OR*, s.1, v.41, pt.3, 590–91; Maj. Gen. William S. Rosecrans to Maj. Gen. S. R. Curtis, October 9, 1864, *OR*, 41: (pt. 3), 734.

14. S. T. Tracy to Maj. Gen. S. R. Curtis, October 9, 1864, *OR*, 41: (pt. 3), 741; Maj. Gen. S. R. Curtis to Gov. Thomas Carney, October 9, 1864, *OR*, 41: (pt. 3), 735; "The Capture of Otterville," St. Louis *Missouri Democrat*, October 20, 1864, 1; Brig. Gen. Joseph O. Shelby, December —, 1864, *OR*, 41: (pt. 1), 657. Also see Price, *OR*, 41: (pt. 1), 633.

15. Curtis, *OR*, 41: (pt. 1), 473.

16. Price, *OR*, 41: (pt. 1), 632; Special Orders No. —, October 14, 1864; Price's HQ to Shelby, enclosed with Thompson, *OR*, 41: (pt. 1), 664–65; Col. Maclean to Brig. Gen. Shelby, October 14, 1864, *OR*, 41: (pt. 3), 101; Brig. Gen. M. Jeff Thompson to Maj. Gen. Sterling Price, October 14, 1864, *OR*, 41: (pt. 3), 1011; Brig. Gen. Shelby to Lt. Col. L. A. Maclean, October 14, 1864, *OR*, 41: (pt. 3), 1012.

17. Brig. Gen. M. Jeff Thompson to Maj. Gen. Sterling Price, October 15, 1864, *OR*, 41: (pt. 3), 1013; Capt. J. L. Jenkins to Maj. Gen. Sterling Price, October 17, 1864, *OR*, 41: (pt. 4), 1001.

18. Brig. Gen. M. Jeff. Thompson, October 16, 1864, *OR*, 41: (pt. 4), 1000; "The Capture of Sedalia and Other Matters," St. Louis *Missouri Democrat*, October 24, 1864, 2. "Inquire into the conduct of Crawford in deserting Sedalia. If deserved, arrest him and place a man of head and pluck in command," Col. John V. DuBois to Maj. Gen. Alfred Pleasonton, October 18, 1864, *OR*, 41: (pt. 4), 87.

19. "Getting Out of it," *Sedalia (MO) Weekly Bazoo*, March 21, 1893, 3. On Sparks see McFerran, *OR*, 41: (pt. 1), 360. William Bloess a private of the fortieth EMM promoted to captain Theodore Bloess.

20. Thompson, *OR*, 41: (pt. 4), 1000; Thompson, *OR*, 41: (pt. 1), 665; Shelby, *OR*, 41: (pt. 1), 657. On the post office see "It Moves. The Chequered History of Uncle Sam's Letter Depository in Sedalia. A Roster of the Postmasters—Time Served, Pay Received and Where They Abide," *Sedlia (MO) Weekly Bazoo*, April 12, 1892, 5; "Getting Out of It" (from the St. Louis *Republic*), *Sedalia (MO) Weekly Bazoo*, March 21, 1893, 3.

21. "The Capture of Sedalia and Other Matters," St. Louis *Missouri Democrat*, October 24, 1864, 2; Philips, *OR*, 41: (pt. 1), 356–57.

22. Likely Yarnell B. Blackwell. Thompson, *OR*, 41: (pt. 1), 665; Shelby, *OR*, 41: (pt. 1), 657. On the post office see "It Moves. The Chequered History of Uncle Sam's Letter Depository in Sedalia. A Roster of the Postmasters—Time Served, Pay Received and Where They Abide," *Sedlia Weekly Bazoo*, April 12, 1892, 5; "Getting Out of it," *Sedalia (MO) Weekly Bazoo*, March 21, 1893, 3; "The Deacon's Jargon. Christmas—How Old and How Celebrated in the Days of Washington—The Throngs of People Who Swarmed Sedalia and the Balmy Weather," *Sedalia (MO) Weekly Bazoo*, December 26, 1893, 5.

23. Thompson, *OR*, 41: (pt. 1), 670–71; Price, *OR*, 41: (pt. 1), 633. Three commissioned officers: Capt. O. B. Queen and Lieut. R. T. Berry, Company M, Seventh Cavalry, Missouri State Militia; Lieut. E. Knapp, Seventeenth Illinois Cavalry.

24. "From Sedalia. Its Late Defence and Capture," St. Louis *Missouri Democrat*, November 3, 1864, 2.

25. "Getting Out of It," *Sedalia (MO) Weekly Bazoo*, March 21, 1893, 3; "The Capture of Sedalia and Other Matters," St. Louis *Missouri Democrat*, October 24, 1864, 2.

26. Thompson, *OR*, 41: (pt. 1), 665–66. Thompson reported that his column left Sedalia "just after dark" and "did not travel the usual roads, but took the by-roads, leaving Georgetown to the west, and encamped on Muddy," Thompson, *OR*, 41: (pt. 1), 665; Thompson, *OR*, 41: (pt. 4), 1000; Shelby, *OR*, 41: (pt. 1), 657.

27. "How Warrensburg Was Saved. Exempts, Cripples, Boys and Negroes Armed—They Do Good Service—An Excellent Lesson for All Missouri—Summary Justice to a Traitor," St. Louis *Missouri Democrat*, October 31, 1864, 2; George S. Grover, "The Price Campaign of 1864," *MHR*, 6: (July 1912), 168–69, 170; Bruce Nichols, *Johnson County Missouri in the Civil War* (Independence: Two Trails, 1974), 84. Foster had his own mounted company of the Johnson County Home Guards in 1861. George S. Grover, a private in the 23rd EMM. 1861 George L. Grover in the Johnson County Home Guards.

28. Maj. Martin Anderson, commanding scouts to Maj. Gen. James G. Blunt, October 14, 1864, *OR*, 41: (pt. 3), 870; Major M. Anderson to Blunt, October 16, 1864, *OR*, 41: (pt. 4), 17; Nichols, *Johnson County Missouri*, 84–85. Price moves on Lexington, source from J. T. Tracy, operator at Sedalia. "Highly Important News. Price Moving on Lexington! He has 15, 000 Cavalry!" *Leavenworth Times*, October 12, 1864, 2.

29. Blunt, *OR*, 41: (pt. 1), 573; Lane, *OR*, 41: (pt. 1), 568; Nichols, *Johnson County Missouri*, 84–85; Sergeant Alvin Reavis of the Ninth MSM Cavalry. Foster, of the Seventh Enrolled Missouri Militia.

30. Charlot, OR 41: (pt. 1), 525; Blunt, *OR*, 41: (pt. 1), 573; Lane, *OR*, 41: (pt. 1), 568; Grover, "Price Campaign of 1864," 170.

31. Brig. Gen. Clinton B. Fisk, commanding Dist. of North Missouri, December 8, 1864, *OR*, 41: (pt. 1), 421–22; Pleasonton, *OR*, 41: (pt. 3), 757; "The Raiders. Their Reinforcements. Anderson Approved by Price. Rebel Outrages. Glasgow—Boonville," St. Louis *Missouri Democrat*, October 27, 1864, 1.

32. Brig. Gen. Clinton B. Fisk to Lt. Col. C. W. Marsh, October 12, 1864, *OR*, 41: (pt. 3), 818; Price, *OR*, 41: (pt. 1), 632; Pleasonton, *OR*, 41: (pt. 3), 786. Meeting at Macon to remove the bodies of those killed at Centralia. "The Centralia Victims. Meeting of the Citizens of Shelby and Knox Counties," St. Louis *Missouri Democrat*, October 22, 1864, 2.

33. "From Jefferson City. Pap Price Mourning the Loss of the Capital," St. Louis *Missouri Democrat*, October 20, 1864, 4; "Price's Great Raid. A Bird's-Eye View. What He was After and What He Was Not After," St. Louis *Missouri Democrat*, October 18, 1864, 2; Brig. Gen. Clinton B. Fisk., December 8, 1864, *OR*, 41: (pt. 1), 422, 423, 424; "The Invasion. Price at Boonville. Two Thousand of Shelby's Men Across the Missouri. The Probable Rebel Programme," St. Louis *Missouri Democrat*, October 11, 1864, 4. The Enrolled Missouri Militia of the district responded promptly to the call made upon them, and generally rendered most excellent service in beating back the robber horde. Most of these accounts from JC are by "Waldo" ("Waldo," also "Gath," per "Civilians at the Battle of Pilot Knob," http://mostateparks.com/sites/default/files/Civilians%20 at%20Fort%20Davidson%20updated%202011.pdf.

34. Philips, *OR*, 41: (pt. 1), 356; Phelps, *OR*, 41: (pt. 1), 402; Rosecrans, *OR*, 41: (pt. 1), 312; Maj. Gen. William S. Rosecrans to Maj. Gen. Alfred Pleasonton, October 18, 1864, *OR*, 41: (pt. 4), 85–86; Maj. Gen. William S. Rosecrans to Maj. Gen. Alfred Pleasonton, October 17, 1864, *OR*, 41: (pt. 4), 44; McFerran, *OR*, 41: (pt. 1), 358–59; Mitchell, *OR*, 41: (pt. 1), 410; Eppstein, *OR*, 41: (pt. 1), 383. Sanborn, *OR*, 41: (pt. 1), 388.

35. Col. D. Moore to Gen. A. J. Smith, October 17, 1864, *OR*, 41: (pt. 4), 43; Rosecrans, *OR*, 41: (pt. 1), 312; Montgomery, *OR*, 41: (pt. 1), 460; Rosecrans, *OR*, 41: (pt. 1), 311; Col. John V. DuBois to Commanding Officer at Jefferson City, October 18, 1864, *OR*, 41: (pt. 4), 83; Philips, *OR*, 41: (pt. 1), 356; "Diary of Acting Brig.-Gen. John F. Philips, written in the field and published for the first time by the *Kansas City Star* on the fifty-ninth anniversary of the Battle of Westport" (hereafter Philips diary), in Crittenden, *Battle of Westport and National Memorial Park*, 24. The diary was then in possession of his daughter, Mrs. William M. Fible of Kansas City, Missouri.

36. Col. A. Sigel to Captain Babcocke, October 12, 1864, *OR*, 41: (pt. 3), 817.

37. "Civil War," reprinted from the *Warrenton Journal*, May 1, 1996, http://danville. www2.50megs.com/civilwar.htm; "The Invasion. The Rebels Delaying. Boonville, Glasgow, Lexington. Scout in Randolph and Chariton County. Warrenton Secure. The Raid on Paris. The Outrages at Danville," St. Louis *Missouri Democrat*, October 20, 1864, 1.

38. "Civil War," *Warrenton Journal*, May 1, 1996. Danville became part of Warren County, and this account is partly based on that in *History of St. Charles, Montgomery and Warren Counties* (St. Louis: National Historical, 1885).

39. "Civil War," *Warrenton Journal*, May 1, 1996; "From Missouri," *New York Tribune*, October 21, 1864, 1.

40. "Civil War," *Warrenton Journal*, May 1, 1996; report of Mr. S. A. Thompson, Danville postmaster, to Rosecrans, copies to Fisk, Fletcher, and Col. D. Dyer from Warrensburg, October 27, 1864, *OR*, 41: (pt. 1), 888.

41. "Civil War," *Warrenton Journal*, May 1, 1996; Ewsing, *OR*, 41: (pt. 4), 7; Col. F. Morsey to Capt. Frank Eno, October 15, 1864, *OR*, 41: (pt. 3), 893; Lt. Col. A. G. Hequembourg to Brig. Gen. Thomas Ewing, October 17, 1864, *OR*, 41: (pt. 4), 48; Ewing, *OR*, 41: (pt. 4), 7–8; Col. C. H. Canfield to Capt. Frank Eno, October 20, 1864, *OR*, 41: (pt. 4), 137–38; "The Outrages in Montgomery Co. The Perpetrators Pursued. Thirteen Killed," St. Louis *Missouri Democrat*, October 22, 1864, 1.

42. Maj. Gen. A. J. Smith to Col. Shaw, October 15, 1864, *OR*, 41: (pt. 3), 890; Price, *OR*, 41: (pt. 1), 632; H. Hannahs to Brig. Gen. E. C. Pike, October 17, 1864, *OR*, 41: (pt. 4), 39–40; Brig. Gen. E. C. Pike to Brig. Gen. Thomas Ewing, October 18, 1864, *OR*, 41: (pt. 4), 79; Brig. Gen. Thomas Ewing to Lt. Col. George Klinge, October 17, 1864, *OR*, 41: (pt. 4), 40; Capt. Frank Eno to Col. C. H. Canfield at Wellsville, October 20, 1864, *OR*, 41: (pt. 4), 137; Frank Eno to Gov. Richard Yates of Illinois, October 19, 1864, *OR*, 41: (pt. 4), 108, 109, stating. "Colonel Holmes stopped, with the 250 men I sent up the North Missouri road last evening, at Warrenton, to endeavor to find out if Bill Anderson was in that region; and, if so, to pursue him with that command from there. He reported from Mexico at 7 this morning that he had stopped at Warrenton, and could hear nothing of any rebel force in that region, and therefore went on. I think he should march at once on the force reported at Fayette, and have suggested it to him." "The Invasion. Price at Lexington. Kansas to be Invaded. Capture of Glasgow. Col. Harding and his Command Defeated and Compelled to Surrender. Raid on Ridgely and Smithville. Warrenton Threatened by Bill Anderson," St. Louis *Missouri Democrat*, October 19, 1864, 1; "The Invasion. The Rebels Delaying . . . The Outrages at Danville," St. Louis *Missouri Democrat*, October 20, 1864, 1.

43. Brig. Gen. Clinton B. Fisk to Lt. Col. C. W. Marsh, October 11, 1864, *OR*, 41: (pt. 3), 790–91; Pleasonton, *OR*, 41: (pt. 3), 785–86; Brig. Gen. Clinton B. Fisk., December 8, 1864, *OR*, 41: (pt. 1), 421–22; Special Field Orders No. 2, October 16, 1864, *OR*, 41: (pt. 4), 13. Waldo asks why Fisk not allowed to go on to Glasgow. After capture. They are "Radicals" "and most excellent gentlemen." "Battle of Glasgow. The Rebel forces 8, 000. Shelby's and Marmaduke's Divisions Engaged," St. Louis *Missouri Democrat*, October 24, 1864, 2. Oct. 18. Steamer *Isabella*, correspondent of the *Missouri Democrat*, Waldo Rocheport and Providence." "The Missouri invasion. A reconnaissance by General Fisk to Boonville. The Rapine on the Banks of the Missouri," St. Louis *Missouri Democrat*, October 24, 1864, 2; "The Raiders. Their Reinforcements. Anderson Approved by Price. Rebel outrages. Glasgow—Boonville," St. Louis *Missouri Democrat*, October 27, 1864, 1.

44. Fisk, *OR*, 41: (pt. 1), 421; Capt. J. E. Mayo, Glasgow, to Maj. Gen. William S. Rose-crans, October 11, 1864, *OR*, 41: (pt. 3), 789; Maj. Gen. William S. Rosecrans to Maj. Gen. Alfred Pleasonton, October 11, 1864, *OR*, 41: (pt. 3), 785; Fisk, *OR*, 41: (pt. 1), 424; Maj. Samuel S. Curtis, October 16, 1864, *OR*, s.1, v.41, 531.

3. The River

1. Bill Lay, MMCWRT, "Additional Notes on the Battle of Glasgow October 15, 1864," http://mmcwrt.missouri.org/2000/glasgow3.htm; "The Latest News. By Telegraph. From Jeffeson City. Return of Gen. Fisk. Details of the Fight at Glasgow . . . Response of Rebel Missourians to Price's Call," St. Louis *Missouri Democrat*, October 20, 1864, 1.

2. S. S. Curtis, *OR*, s.1, v.41, 530. Lt. George T. Robinson of Moonlight's Eleventh Kansas Cavalry "proposed to Major-General Curtis to take a small steam ferry-boat down the Missouri River looking for Rosecrans," Lt. George T. Robinson, November 10, 1864, *OR*, 41: (pt. 1), 547. See also Samuel S. Curtis, *A Cruise on the Benton: A Narrative of Combat on the Missouri River in the Civil War* (Waynesboro, VA: M&R

Books, 1967); Col. Chester Harding Jr., November 12, 1864, *OR*, 41: (pt. 1), 434; Bill Lay, MMCWRT, "Additional Notes on the Battle of Glasgow October 15, 1864," http://mmcwrt.missouri.org/2000/glasgow3.htm. *A Sketch of Chester Harding, Artist Drawn by His Own Hand*, ed. Margaret E. White (Boston: Houghton, Mifflin, 1890).

3. Harding, *OR*, 41: (pt. 1), 434–35; Lay, "Additional Notes on the Battle of Glasgow October 15, 1864. Also see Maj. Samuel S. Curtis (2nd Colorado Cavalry), aide-de-camp, *OR*, 41: (pt. 1), 530–32, 532–35; Lay, "Additional Notes on the Battle of Glasgow, October 15, 1864."

4. S. S. Curtis, *OR*, 41: (pt. 1), 530; Harding, *OR*, 41: (pt. 1), 435; Lay, "Additional Notes on the Battle of Glasgow, October 15, 1864."

5. Lay, "Additional Notes on the Battle of Glasgow, October 15, 1864"; misidentified as "John Vince"; S. S. Curtis, *OR*, 41: (pt. 1), 530–31. Bingham had gone to California in 1848 to find gold and in 1852 returned to Arrow Rock, where he joined his brother in manufacturing wagons. Concerned about the safety of its records, the county had organized armed guards only a few weeks earlier; Harding, *OR*, 41: (pt. 1), 435.

6. Harding, *OR*, 41: (pt. 1), 435, 436; Capt. George A. Holloway, October 18, 1864, *OR*, 41: (pt. 1), 430, 431; Fisk, *OR*, 41: (pt. 1), 422. See also Lay, "Additional Notes on the Battle of Glasgow, October 15, 1864." Later claims of 750, 800 and even 900.

7. Harding, *OR*, 41: (pt. 1), 435–36.

8. S. S. Curtis, *OR*, 41: (pt. 1), 531.

9. Lay, "Additional Notes on the Battle of Glasgow, October 15, 1864"; Harding, *OR*, 41: (pt. 1), 436, 437; "Capture of Glasgow," St. Louis *Missouri Democrat*, October 21, 1864, 1; "Battle of Glasgow," St. Louis *Missouri Democrat*, October 24, 1864, 2. A seven-hour fight with a part of Colonel Harding's regiment, Forty-third Missouri Volunteer Infantry, and small detachments of the Ninth Missouri State Militia and Seventeenth Illinois Cavalry, militia not mentioned. Rosecrans, *OR*, 41: (pt. 1), 312.

10. Shelby, *OR*, 41: (pt. 3), 1012; Brig. Gen. Joseph O. Shelby, December —, 1864, *OR*, 41: (pt. 1), 656; Harding, *OR*, 41: (pt. 1), 436; Lay, "Additional Notes on the Battle of Glasgow, October 15, 1864"; "The Invasion," St. Louis *Missouri Democrat*, October 14, 1864, 1; "Battle of Glasgow," St. Louis *Missouri Democrat*, October 24, 1864, 2.

11. Harding, *OR*, 41: (pt. 1), 436; Lt. A. J. Harding to Capt. Frank Eno, October 18, 1864, *OR*, 41: (pt. 4), 91; Clark, *OR*, 41: (pt. 1), 681; Lt. Col. J. F. Davies, December 12, 1864, *OR*, 41: (pt. 1), 696; Lawther, *OR*, 41: (pt. 1), 698.

12. Harding, *OR*, 41: (pt. 1), 436–37; Jackman, *OR*, 41: (pt. 1), 674, 675; Shelby, *OR*, 41: (pt. 1), 656–57; Holloway, *OR*, 41: (pt. 1), 430; "Battle of Glasgow," St. Louis *Missouri Democrat*, October 24, 1864, 2. Captain W. C. P. Carrington killed, Baker's Creek, more commonly known as Champion's Hill, May 16, 1863.

13. Harding, *OR*, 41: (pt. 1), 437; Greene, *OR*, 41: (pt. 1), 689–90; Burbridge, *OR*, 41: (pt. 1), 694.

14. Lawther, *OR*, 41: (pt. 1), 698–99; Harding, *OR*, 41: (pt. 1), 437; Holloway, *OR*, 41: (pt. 1), 430.

15. Harding, *OR*, 41: (pt. 1), 437, 439; Holloway, *OR*, 41: (pt. 1), 430, 431; Jackman, *OR*, 41: (pt. 1), 674–75; "Battle of Glasgow," St. Louis *Missouri Democrat*, October 24, 1864, 2.

16. "The Raiders. Their Reinforcements," St. Louis *Missouri Democrat*, October 27, 1864, 1.

17. Harding, *OR*, 41: (pt. 1), 437–38.

18. Ibid., 438; Holloway, *OR*, 41: (pt. 1), 430–31; Col. Colton Greene, December 18, 1864, *OR*, 41: (pt. 1), 689.

19. Harding, *OR*, 41: (pt. 1), 438; Holloway, *OR*, 41: (pt. 1), 430–31. See also Harding, *OR*, 41: (pt. 1), 439. Col. Green sent compliments to Ewing by one of the paroled officers. "Tell him for me that he fought us bravely, damn him," "Battle of Glasgow," St. Louis *Missouri Democrat*, October 24, 1864, 2.

20. Jackman, *OR*, 41: (pt. 1), 675; Davies, *OR*, 41: (pt. 1), 696; Price, *OR*, 41: (pt. 1), 632; Clark, *OR*, 41: (pt. 1), 686; Greene, *OR*, 41: (pt. 1), 689; Harding, *OR*, 41: (pt. 1), 439. Also see Col. Edwin C. Catherwood, December 2, 1864, *OR*, 41: (pt. 1), 385; Holloway, *OR*, 41: (pt. 1), 431; "The Raiders. Their Reinforcements. Anderson Approved by Price. Rebel Outrages. Glasgow—Boonville," St. Louis *Missouri Democrat*, October 27, 1864, 1; "Battle of Glasgow," St. Louis *Missouri Democrat*, October 24, 1864, 2: Shelby's sharpshooters "successful in killing 2 or 3 men, wounding others, and shooting 1 or 2 officers' horses." See also Lay, "Additional Notes on the Battle of Glasgow, October 15, 1864"; Andrew Dusold with severe head wound.

21. Harding, *OR*, 41: (pt. 1), 439; Holloway, *OR*, 41: (pt. 1), 431; Clark, *OR*, 41: (pt. 1), 682; Burbridge, *OR*, 41: (pt. 1), 694.

22. Burbridge, *OR*, 41: (pt. 1), 694. See also Greene, *OR*, 41: (pt. 1), 690; Lawther, *OR*, 41: (pt. 1), 699; Col. Sidney D. Jackman, November 30, 1864, *OR*, 41: (pt. 1), 675; Davies, *OR*, 41: (pt. 1), 696.

23. "Battle of Glasgow," St. Louis *Missouri Democrat*, October 24, 1864, 2; "From Boonville," St. Louis *Missouri Democrat*, November 8, 1864, 2.

24. Castel and Goodrich, *Bloody Bill Anderson*, 117–22; "The Raiders. Their Reinforcements. Anderson Approved by Price. Rebel Outrages. Glasgow—Boonville," St. Louis *Missouri Democrat*, October 27, 1864, 1; "From Lamine Bridge. Fiendish Atrocities. The Miscreant Anderson at Glasglow," St. Louis *Missouri Democrat*, October 24, 1864, 1; Lawrence O. Christenson, "Carr W. Pritchett and the Civil War Era in Glasgow and Fayette," *MHR*, 103: (October 2008), 46–48.

25. Harding, *OR*, 41: (pt. 1), 438–49; "Battle of Glasgow," St. Louis *Missouri Democrat*, October 24, 1864, 2.

26. Harding, *OR*, 41: (pt. 1), 438; Brig. Gen. Clinton B. Fisk to Capt. W. C. Jones, October 21, 1864, *OR*, 41: (pt. 4), 161–62. See also Holloway, *OR*, 41: (pt. 1), 431; Clark, *OR*, 41: (pt. 1), 686, 687; Fisk, *OR*, 41: (pt. 1), 422–23; U.S. General Fisk to C. S. commander, Boonville, October 17, 1864, enclosure no. 1 with Clark, *OR*, 41: (pt. 1), 685–86.

27. Col. John V. DuBois to officers in charge of flag of truce, October 22, 1864, *OR*, 41: (pt. 4), 185–86; Maj. Gen. W. S. Rosecrans to Maj. Gen. Sterling Price, October 22, 1864, *OR*, 41: (pt. 4), 1011.

28. S. S. Curtis, *OR*, 41: (pt. 1), 531–32.

29. Ibid., 474; Curtis to Gen. Craig at St. Joseph, October 16, 1864, *OR*, 41: (pt. 4), 18–19; Curtis to Gen. Davies, October 16, 1864, *OR*, 41: (pt. 4), 23. See also H. Rudd of Mount Pleasant, Iowa, to Lt. Col. W. H. Stark, forwarded to Maj. Gen. S. R. Curtis,

October 13, 1864, *OR*, 41: (pt. 3), 843; Asst. Provost Marshall J. L. Thompson to Lt. Col. W. H. Stark, October 13, 1864, *OR*, 41: (pt. 3), 843; Lt. A. J. Harding to Capt. Frank Eno, October 14, 1864, *OR*, 41: (pt. 3), 865; Lt. Vance [Sgt. John A. Vance, Glasgow's Company A under Steinmetz], with 69 belonging to the Forty-sixth EMM, "I have been informed, surrendered at Glasgow, but of this I have received no official report," Douglas, *OR*, 41: (pt. 1), 433.

30. Frank Eno for Rosecrans to Brig. Gen. Douglass, October 26, 1864, *OR*, 41: (pt. 4), 253.

31. Pleasonton, *OR*, 41: (pt. 3), 817; Maj. Gen. Sterling Price to the Friends of the Confederacy in Chariton County and Its Neighborhood, October 15, 1864, *OR*, 41: (pt. 3), 1012.

32. Fisk, *OR*, 41: (pt. 1), 424; S. S. Curtis, *OR*, s.1, v.41, 531.

33. Maj. J. Nelson Smith, October 18, 1864, *OR*, 41: (pt. 1), 613.

34. Douglas, *OR*, 41: (pt. 1), 433; Brig. Gen. J. B. Douglass to Maj. Frank S. Bond, October 17, 1864, *OR*, 41: (pt. 4), 47; Brig. Gen. James B. Douglass to Rosecrans, October 16, 1864, *OR*, 41: (pt. 4), 13; Brig. Gen. J. B. Douglass to Maj. Gen. William S. Rosecrans, October 17, 1864, *OR*, 41: (pt. 4), 47; Frank S. Bonds for Rosecrans to Douglass, *OR*, 41: (pt. 4), 13; Fisk, *OR*, 41: (pt. 1), 423; Col. Samuel A. Holmes to Lt. H. Hannahs, October 27, 1864, *OR*, 41: (pt. 4), 276; "The Invasion. The Rebels Delaying . . . The Raid on Paris. The Outrages at Danville," St. Louis *Missouri Democrat*, October 20, 1864, 1.

35. Capt. E. Schelsky, Platte County Guards, to Brig. Gen. Craig, October 26, 1864, *OR*, 41: (pt. 4), 255; Maj. H. Hilliard to Brig. Gen. Craig, October 17, 1864, *OR*, 41: (pt. 4), 50; Lt. A. J. Harding, October 18, 1864, *OR*, 41: (pt. 1), 432; Lt. A. J. Harding to Capt. Frank Eno, October 18, 1864, *OR*, 41: (pt. 4), 91; Maj. H. Hilliard to Brig. Gen. Craig, October 13, 1864, *OR*, 41: (pt. 3), 841; John W. Price of Weston to Capt. John Willans, forwarded to Maj. Gen. S. W. Curtis, October 13, 1864, *OR*, 41: (pt. 3), 844. Harding had transferred from the First Nebraska Cavalry; "The Invasion. Price at Lexington. Kansas to be Invaded . . . Warrenton Threatened by Bill Anderson," St. Louis *Missouri Democrat*, October 19, 1864, 1.

36. Col. J. H. Shanklin to Brig. Gen. James Craig, October 13, 1864, *OR*, 41: (pt. 3), 840–41; Col. J. H. Shanklin to Brig. Gen. Craig, October 14, 1864, *OR*, 41: (pt. 3), 864; Col. J. H. Shanklin to Gen. James Craig, October 16, 1864, *OR*, 41: (pt. 4), 13; Maj. George Deagle, Sixty-fifth Infantry Enrolled Missouri Militia, *OR*, 41: (pt. 1), 443–44. Capts. W. B. Kemper and William G. Garth to Brig. Gen. James Craig, October 14, 1864, *OR*, 41: (pt. 3), 865; Col. J. H. Shanklin to Brig. Gen. Craig, October 17, 1864, *OR*, 41: (pt. 4), 50; Col. J. H. Shanklin to Brig. Gen. Craig, October 17, 1864, *OR*, 41: (pt. 4), 50–51; Shelby, *OR*, 41: (pt. 1), 658; Price, *OR*, 41: (pt. 1), 634. See also Brig. Gen. Craig to Maj. H. Hilliard, October 17, 1864, *OR*, 41: (pt. 4), 50; Col. J. H. Shanklin to Brig. Gen. Craig, October 17, 1864, *OR*, 41: (pt. 4), 51; Col. J. H. Shanklin to Gen. Craig, October 19, 1864, *OR*, 41: (pt. 4), 113; Maj. George Deagle, Sixty-fifth Infantry Enrolled Missouri Militia, *OR*, 41: (pt. 1), 443–44; Fisk, *OR*, 41: (pt. 1), 423. Also August 1, 1862, v. 13. [Cravens in Sixth Missouri Cavalry, others commissioned included D. A. Williams, J. D. Williams, and R. E. Williams].

37. James D. Eads, Company M, First MSM Cavalry, to Capt. Eno, October 17, 1864, *OR*, 41: (pt. 4), 45; Lt. A. J. Harding to Maj. C. S. Charlot, October 18, 1864, *OR*, 41: (pt. 4), 92; A. J. Harding to Maj. Frank Bond, October 19, 1864, *OR*, 41: (pt. 4), 111; Shanklin to Brig. Gen. James Craig, October 20, 1864, *OR*, 41: (pt. 4), 140; Col. J. H. Shanklin to Gen. Craig, October 19, 1864, *OR*, 41: (pt. 4), 113–14; Col. J. H. Shanklin to Gen. Craig, October 19, 1864, *OR*, 41: (pt. 4), 113.

38. Lt. A. J. Harding to Capt. Frank Eno, October 14, 1864, *OR*, 41: (pt. 3), 865; Col. R. J. Eberman to Lt. A. J. Harding, forwarded to Capt. Frank Eno, October 14, 1864, *OR*, 41: (pt. 3), 865; E. J. Crandall to Capt. G. A. Holloway, October 10, 1864, *OR*, 41: (pt. 3), 761; Col. J. H. Shanklin to Brig. Gen. Clinton B. Fisk, October 21, 1864, *OR*, 41: (pt. 4), 162; Brig. Gen. James Craig, EMM, to Brig. Gen. Clinton B. Fisk, October 21, 1864, *OR*, 41: (pt. 4), 162; "The Invasion. The Rebels Delaying . . . The Outrages at Danville," St. Louis *Missouri Democrat*, October 20, 1864, 1; "The Defence of Pleasant Hill. The Right Sort of Loyalty. Another Lesson for the Citizens of Missouri," St. Louis *Missouri Democrat*, November 2, 1864, 2; "The Invasion," St. Louis *Missouri Democrat*, October 14, 1864, 1; "From Chariton County. The Wrongs of Union Citizens," St. Louis *Missouri Democrat*, November 2, 1864, 2; "Story of Vengeance in North Missouri. Reported Killing of Fifteen Citizens. Burning of Property in Milton," St. Louis *Missouri Democrat*, October 22, 1864, 2; "From Northeast Missouri. Rebels in Pike and Ralls County," St. Louis *Missouri Democrat*, October 24, 1864, 1; E. J. Crandall to Capt. G. A. Holloway, October 10, 1864, *OR*, 41: (pt. 3), 761; Mary G. Gordon to Jane Gentry Hudnall, October 7, 1864, Misc. Mans. 12: #576 WHMC; "The Invasion," St. Louis *Missouri Democrat*, October 14, 1864, 1.

39. A. J. Harding, *OR*, 41: (pt. 4), 91; Maj. Frank S. Bond to A. J. Harding, *OR*, 41: (pt. 4), 91; Maj. Gen. S. R. Curtis to Brig. Gen. James Craig, October 18, 1864, *OR*, 41: (pt. 4), 89; Maj. Gen. S. R. Curtis to Brig. Gen. Davies, October 18, 1864, *OR*, 41: (pt. 4), 98; Capt. G. W. McCullough to Brig. Gen. James Craig, October 18, 1864, *OR*, 41: (pt. 4), 90. Stewartsville near St. Joseph. Captain G. W. McCullough and mentions O. C. McDonald of Eighty-Seventh EMM.

40. Brig. Gen. James Craig to Brig. Gen. Clinton B. Fisk, October 18, 1864, *OR*, 41: (pt. 4), 88–89; Col. John V. DuBois to Col. William Forbes, October 17, 1864, *OR*, 41: (pt. 4), 49; Brig. Gen. J. B. Douglass to Maj. Frank Eno, October 9, 1864, *OR*, 41: (pt. 3), 733; Brig. Gen. J. B. Douglass to Col. John V. DuBois, October 17, 1864, *OR*, 41: (pt. 4), 47. Brig. Gen. Thomas Ewing to Maj. F. S. Bond, October 17, 1864, *OR*, 41: (pt. 4), 36. "General Douglass has orders to furnish all assistance and attend to the supplies and communications, but not to command," Maj. F. S. Bond to Brig. Gen.Thomas Ewing, October 17, 1864, *OR*, 41: (pt. 4), 36.

41. Rosecrans, *OR*, 41: (pt. 1), 311.

42. Brig. Gen. John McNeil, November 23, 1864, *OR*, 41: (pt. 1), 371; Henry Dillinberger, "The Big Raid. An Account of How the Rebels Were Driven Out of Missouri," *National Tribune*, May 15, 1890, 3; Brig. Gen. John McNeil, November 23, 1864, *OR*, 41: (pt. 1), 371; Brig. Gen. John McNeil, November 26, 1864, *OR*, 41: (pt. 1), 377.

43. Brig. Gen. John B. Sanborn to John V. DuBois, October 15, 1864, *OR*, 41: (pt. 3), 891; Rosecrans to Pleasonton, October 20, 1864, *OR*, 41: (pt. 4), 135; Rosecrans, *OR*,

41: (pt. 3), 759; Maj. Gen. William S. Rosecrans to Maj. Gen. Alfred Pleasonton, October 9, 1864, *OR*, 41: (pt. 3), 730.

44. L. A. Maclean to Gen. Shelby, October 16, 1864, *OR*, 41: (pt. 4), 1000; "The Invasion. Independence Reoccupied by Union Troops. Price's Advance at Lexington," St. Louis *Missouri Democrat*, October 18, 1864, 1.

4. ARRIVAL OF THE ARMY OF THE BORDER

1. Excerpt from "Reminiscences of the Second" [from Denver *Rocky Mountain News*] in *Soldier's Letters: Second Colorado Cavalry: A Regimental Paper to Accompany the Regiment*, 1: (September 23, 1865), 2, (September 2, 1865), 1; Edwards, "Veteran Sam," in *John N. Edwards*, 165–66. ed. Oliver V. Wallace (August 1864–November 28, 1865, nos. 31–37), quoted in Wood, *Two Civil War Battles*, 125–27.

2. Maj. C. S. Charlot to Gen. James H. Lane, October 9, 1864, *OR*, 41: (pt. 3), 736; Col. James H. Ford to Maj. C. S. Charlot, October 9, 1864, *OR*, 41: (pt. 3), 740; Charlot, *OR*, 41: (pt. 1), 524; Maj. Thomas I. McKenny, December 1, 1864, *OR*, 41: (pt. 1), 536. See also Capt. Edwin I. Meeker, November 22, 1864, *OR*, 41: (pt. 1), 562; Hunt, *OR*, 41: (pt. 1), 542–43; Maj. Gen. S. R. Curtis to Col. James H. Ford, October 11, 1864, *OR*, 41: (pt. 3), 796

3. "Compendium of History," in *Soldier's Letter*, 1: (March 4, 11, 1865), serialized on first page 1.

4. Maj. J. Nelson Smith, October 15, 1864, *OR*, 41: (pt. 1), 611–12; "Compendium of History," in *Soldier's Letter*, 1: (March 18, 1865), 1.

5. "From Lexington, Mo. Ravages of Todd, Pool [xi], and Thrailkill," St. Louis *Missouri Democrat*, October 15, 1864, 4; Capt. James D. Eads, Company M, First MSM Cavalry, commanding post at Lexington, to Maj. Gen. S. R. Curtis, October 12, 1864, *OR*, 41: (pt. 3), 824; Capt. James D. Eads to Capt. Frank Eno, October 15, 1864, *OR*, 41: (pt. 3), 891; Col James H. Ford to Major C. S. Charlot, October 16, 1864, *OR*, 41: (pt. 4), 20; Col James H. Ford to Capt. George S. Hampton, October 16, 1864, *OR*, 41: (pt. 4), 20. Sent toward Lexington five miles but then backtracked. October 16, 1864, entry in Lyman, Diary, 3, Misc. Mans. 17: #490 WHMC. Section on Price's Raid in Lyman's 1931 narrative appended to Lyman, Diary, 21–24. Misc. Mans. 17: #490 WHMC.

6. "Compendium of History," in *Soldier's Letter*, 1: (March 18, 1865), 1.

7. J. N. Smith, *OR*, 41: (pt. 1), 613. Maj. J. Nelson Smith. His (Captain Greene's) report(*) accompanies this and is marked C; also notice(*) marked A, published by Captain Bedinger, C. S. Army, at Lexington, October 14, 1864, and orders(*) marked B, by Capt. George S. Rathbun, same date and army. 613–14. Ford said they killed two on entering the town. Ford, *OR*, 41: (pt. 1), 607. See also Curtis, *OR*, 41: (pt. 1), 474–75; Ford, *OR*, 41: (pt. 1), 607; J. N. Smith, *OR*, 41: (pt. 1), 612–13; Curtis, *OR*, 41: (pt. 4), 117; J. N. Smith, *OR*, 41: (pt. 1), 613; Ford, *OR*, 41: (pt. 1), 607. Col. James H. Ford mistakenly reported that "the brigade books and papers were lost in the evacuation of Independence on the 21st instant, so that the able report of Major Smith cannot be forwarded with this," Ford, *OR*, 41: (pt. 1), 607. Also see Curtis, *OR*, 41: (pt. 1), 474.

8. L. A. Maclean to Maj. Gen. John S. Marmaduke, October 15, 1864, *OR*, 41: (pt. 3), 1013; L. A. Maclean to Brig. Gen. J. O. Shelby, October 15, 1864, *OR*, 41: (pt. 3), 1013–

14; "The Latest. Fighting at the Front. The Prospect," Kansas City *Journal of Commerce*, October 21, 1864, 2.

9. Maj. Gen. James G. Blunt to Maj. Gen. S. R. Curtis, October 17, 1864, *OR*, 41: (pt. 4), 54; Maj. Gen. S. R. Curtis to Gen. Deitzler, October 18, 1864, *OR*, 41: (pt. 4), 96; Rosecrans to Curtis, October 18, 1864, in Curtis, *OR*, 41: (pt. 1), 475; Hon. Samuel C. Pomeroy, December 3, 1864, *OR*, 41: (pt. 1), 570–71; Curtis to Blunt, October 16, 1864, *OR*, 41: (pt. 4), 16; Curtis, *OR*, 41: (pt. 1), 474–75. See also Col. William F. Cloud, November 20, 1864, *OR*, 41: (pt. 1), 558; Samuel J. Reader's Autobiography, transcription of above, by Geo A Root, November 13, 1930, 3:15. Kansas Memory. Kansas Historical Society.

10. Hon. James H. Lane, volunteer aide-de-camp, *OR*, 41: (pt. 1), 567–68. On Lane see Curtis, *OR*, 41: (pt. 1), 471–72; Maj. Gen. S. R. Curtis to James H. Lane, October 11, 1864, *OR*, 41: (pt. 3), 793; Maj. Gen. S. R. Curtis to James H. Lane, October 12, 1864, *OR*, 41: (pt. 3), 821; Jennison, *OR*, 41: (pt. 3), 795.

11. "The Defence of Pleasant Hill. The Right Sort of Loyalty. Another Lesson for the Citizens of Missouri," St. Louis *Missouri Democrat*, November 2, 1864, 2; Major M. Anderson to Blunt, October 16, 1864, *OR*, 41: (pt. 4), 17.

12. J. N. Smith, *OR*, 41: (pt. 1), 613; Nettleton to his sister, December 19, 1864, in Crittenden, *Battle of Westport and National Memorial Park*, 28.

13. Blunt, *OR*, 41: (pt. 4), 54; Maj. Gen. James G. Blunt to Col. J. H. Ford, October 17, 1864, *OR*, 41: (pt. 4), 55; Lane, *OR*, 41: (pt. 1), 568; Moonlight, *OR*, 41: (pt. 1), 591; Maj. Gen. James G. Blunt, December 24, 1864, *OR*, 41: (pt. 1), 573; Hinton, *Rebel Invasion*, 84–85, 88; Moonlight, *OR*, 41: (pt. 1), 592. Blunt, General Field Orders No. 6, October 19, 1864, *OR*, 41: (pt. 4), 118; Jennison, *OR*, 41: (pt. 1), 582; Blunt, *OR*, 41: (pt. 1), 573; Curtis, *OR*, 41: (pt. 1), 475; Moonlight, *OR*, 41: (pt. 1), 591; Grover, "Price Campaign of 1864," 171; "Compendium of History," in *Soldier's Letter*, 1: (March 25, 1865), 1, typographical error "27th." Said to have 1,100 from Hickman's Mills but added a few hundred from the Warrensburg and other militia groups, and the Coloradoans joined them in Lexington.

14. Price, *OR*, 41: (pt. 1), 633; Shelby, *OR*, 41: (pt. 1), 657; Thompson, *OR*, 41: (pt. 1), 665–66.

15. Grover, "Price Campaign of 1864," 171; Blunt, *OR*, 41: (pt. 1), 573; Jennison, *OR*, 41: (pt. 1), 582; Nettleton to his sister, December 19, 1864, in Crittenden, *Battle of Westport and National Memorial Park*, 28; William A. Timbocker, "On Kansas Soil. Exciting Times on the Price Raid Against St. Louis," *National Tribune*, November 21, 1895, 1; A. S. Childers, "Recitals and Reminiscences. Stories Eminently Worth Telling of Experiences and Adventures in the Great National Struggle. Longest March in the War. The 11th Kan. Cav. Claims That It Made it, and Suffered Intense from Cold and Hunger," *National Tribune*, January 31, 1907, 6; Grover, "Price Campaign of 1864," 171; Blunt, *OR*, 41: (pt. 1), 573; Jennison, *OR*, 41: (pt. 1), 582; Nettleton to his sister, December 19, 1864, in Crittenden, *Battle of Westport and National Memorial Park*, 28; Timbocker, "On Kansas Soil"; Childers, "Recitals and Reminiscences"; Not only Hickok (in the Army of the Border) participated in the campaign; so did his friend William F. Cody—the future "Buffalo Bill"— from the Department of Missouri. William F. Cody, *The Life of Buffalo Bill* (1878; reprint, London: 1994), 136–37.

16. Thompson, *OR*, 41: (pt. 1), 666; Shelby, *OR*, 41: (pt. 1), 657; Howard L. Conard, *Encyclopedia of the History of Missouri, A Compendium of History and Biography for Ready Reference. A Memorial and Biographical Record of Kansas City and Jackson County, Mo.* 6 vols. (Chicago: Lewis Publishing, 1896), 259–60, 3:591; claiming 2 p.m. start, Price, *OR*, 41: (pt. 1), 633.

17. Childers, "Recitals and Reminiscences," *National Tribune*, January 31, 1907, 6.

18. Jennison, *OR*, 41: (pt. 1), 582; Blunt, *OR*, 41: (pt. 1), 573; Lane, *OR*, 41: (pt. 1), 568; Jennison, *OR*, 41: (pt. 1), 582; Hinton, *Rebel Invasion*, 85–86. Hinton called the commander of the two Kansas companies "Jack Curtis," but the records give the name as Captain Orren A. Curtis.

19. Childers, "Recitals and Reminiscences," *National Tribune*, January 31, 1907, 6; Blunt, *OR*, 41: (pt. 1), 573–74; Lane, *OR*, 41: (pt. 1), 568; Hinton, *Rebel Invasion*, 87.

20. Hinton, *Rebel Invasion*, 86; Robert Simmons, "The Veteran's Star of Bethlehem," *National Tribune*, April 19, 1883, 7. Looking for other prisoners. "Our destination was Tyler, Texas."

21. Hinton, *Rebel Invasion*, 89; Jenkins, *Battle of Westport*, 55. See also O'Flaherty, *General Jo Shelby*, 134, 135–46, 147–60.

22. Jennison, *OR*, 41: (pt. 1), 582–83; Hinton, *Rebel Invasion*, 89–90.

23. Moonlight, *OR*, 41: (pt. 1), 591–92; Blunt, *OR*, 41: (pt. 1), 574; Hinton, *Rebel Invasion*, 88. 90.

24. Childers, "Recitals and Reminiscences," *National Tribune*, January 31, 1907, 6.

25. Grover, "Price Campaign of 1864," 171–72.

26. Nettleton to his sister, December 19, 1864, in Crittenden, *Battle of Westport and National Memorial Park*, 28; Hinton, *Rebel Invasion*, 86–87; Moonlight, *OR*, 41: (pt. 1), 592. This may have been the bridge that Plumb was sent back to torch. Simpson, March 16, 1910, 7 (stamped numbers different), Plumb Papers, KSHS.

27. Price, *OR*, 41: (pt. 1), 633; Thompson, *OR*, 41: (pt. 1), 666; Davies, *OR*, 41: (pt. 1), 696; Burbridge, *OR*, 41: (pt. 1), 694; October 19, 1864, entry in Baker diary.

28. Grover, "Price Campaign of 1864," 172, 181; Hinton, *Rebel Invasion*, 117.

29. Curtis, *OR*, 41: (pt. 1), 475; Blunt, *OR*, 41: (pt. 1), 574; Hinton, *Rebel Invasion*, 88–89; Shelby, *OR*, 41: (pt. 1), 657.

30. Blunt, *OR*, 41: (pt. 1), 573–74; Lane, *OR*, 41: (pt. 1), 568; Hinton, *Rebel Invasion*, 87, 89–90; Moonlight, *OR*, 41: (pt. 1), 592; Jennison, *OR*, 41: (pt. 1), 582–83. "Latest from the Front! Blunt Driven Out of Lexington! Missouri Under Martial Law! Kansas Militia to Remain on the Border!" Kansas City *Journal of Commerce*, October 20, 1864, 2. Also see "Gen. Price in Saline County, Mo. He Has Been Heavily Reinforced. The Surrender of Glasgow, Mo." "The Invasion. Fighting Near the Border. Blunt Forced form Lexington. He Falls Back to the Little Blue River. Battle on the Big Blue. Price Between Two Fires," St. Louis *Missouri Democrat*, October 22, 1864, 2; "From General Deitzler! Particulars of the Fight! Blunt's Loss Twenty Men! Our Troops Eager for a Fight!," Leavenworth *Daily Times*, October 22, 1864, 2.

31. Maj. Gen. S. R. Curtis to Maj. Gen. Henry W. Halleck, October 20, 1864, *OR*, 41: (pt. 4), 140–41. On casualties see also Davis, *OR*, 41: (pt. 1), 551; "The Latest. Fighting at the Front," Kansas City *Journal of Commerce*, October 21, 1864, 2; "From General Deitzler!," Leavenworth *Daily Times*, October 22, 1864, 2.

32. Blunt, *OR*, 41: (pt. 1), 574; Moonlight, *OR*, 41: (pt. 1), 592; Childers, "Recitals and Reminiscences," *National Tribune*, January 31, 1907, 6; Hinton, *Rebel Invasion*, 90; Grover, "Price Campaign of 1864," 172.

33. McKenny, *OR*, 41: (pt. 1), p. 536; Charlot, *OR*, 41: (pt. 1), 525; Curtis, *OR*, 41: (pt. 1), 475; Curtis to Blunt, October 20, 1864, *OR*, 41: (pt. 4), p. 145, in Curtis, *OR*, 41: (pt. 1), 476; Jenkins, *Battle of Westport*, 36. Curtis's suggestion to leave Moonlight and his Eleventh Kansas on the Little Blue seems even odder, given his explicit concern that "We must not break down our best regiments, Eleventh, Fifteenth, and Sixteenth, and Ford's must have some rest." This was in response to General Blunt's dispatch dated "nine miles east of Independence, 8 a.m. October 20," in which he suggested other arrangements.

34. Curtis to Blunt, October 20, 1864, in Curtis, *OR*, 41: (pt. 1), 476; Jennison, *OR*, 41: (pt. 1), 583; Blunt, *OR*, 41: (pt. 1), 574; Charlot, *OR*, 41: (pt. 1), 525; "Compendium of History," *Soldier's Letter*, 1: (June 10, 1865), 1. Blunt noted that "in consequence of the action of the Governor of Kansas and others of the State authorities he was unable to move the State militia any farther into Missouri." Confirming the order, see Lane, *OR*, 41: (pt. 1), 568.

35. Ford, *OR*, 41: (pt. 1), 607; Charlot, *OR*, 41: (pt. 1), 525; Hinton, *Rebel Invasion*, 93–94; Jenkins, *Battle of Westport*, 56. Sgt. Nettleton, Second Colorado, "rejoined [his] Regiment at Independence on the 20th," Nettleton in Crittenden, *Battle of Westport and National Memorial Park*, 28–29. Also see McKenny, *OR*, 41: (pt. 1), 536.

36. H. G. Ward, "Price's Raid. How Major Smith of the Independent Colorado Met His Death," *National Tribune*, March 29, 1883, 3.

37. Ewing to Rosecrans, October 21, 1864, *OR*, 41: (pt. 4), 156; Deitzler, *OR*, 41: (pt. 1), 615; Curtis, *OR*, 41: (pt. 1), 478; Blair, *OR*, 41: (pt. 1), 597; Blair to Curtis, in Curtis, *OR*, 41: (pt. 1), 482; Pomeroy, *OR*, 41: (pt. 1), 571; Brig. Gen. Thomas A. Davies to Curtis, October 19, 1864, *OR*, 41: (pt. 4), 121; Jenkins, *Battle of Westport*, 56.

38. Philips diary in Crittenden, *Battle of Westport and National Memorial Park*, 24–25; Major W. D. McDonald to Brig. Gen. James Craig, October 20, 1864, *OR*, 41: (pt. 4), 140. Rumor that Blunt had lost artillery at Lexington. Exaggerated report in St. Joseph *Herald*. "The Invasion. Fighting Near the Border. Blunt Forced from Lexington. He Falls Back to the Little Blue River. Battle on the Big Blue. Price Between Two Fires," St. Louis *Missouri Democrat*, October 24, 1864, 1.

39. Montgomery, *OR*, 41: (pt. 1), 460; Maj. Emory S. Foster to Maj. Gen. S. R. Curtis, October 18, 1864, *OR*, 41: (pt. 4), 98; Hinton, *Rebel Invasion*, 114.

40. Curtis, *OR*, 41: (pt. 1), 485; Curtis to Rosecrans, telegraph, October 21, 1864, in Curtis, *OR*, 41: (pt. 1), 479; "The Latest. Fighting at the Front," Kansas City *Journal of Commerce*, October 21, 1864, 2.

41. Curtis, *OR*, 41: (pt. 1), 476; Rosecrans, *OR*, 41: (pt. 1), 312; Rosecrans to A. J. Smith, October 20, 1864, *OR*, 41: (pt. 4), 134; Rosecrans, *OR*, 41: (pt. 1), 312; Pleasonton, *OR*, 41: (pt. 1), 340; Brig. Gen. John McNeil, November 23, 1864, *OR*, 41: (pt. 1), 371; Eppstein, *OR*, 41: (pt. 1), 383; Houston, *OR*, 41: (pt. 1), 381; Philips, *OR*, 41: (pt. 1), 357; Philips diary in Crittenden, *Battle of Westport and National Memorial Park*, 24. See also McFerran, *OR*, 41: (pt. 1), 359; Hinton, *Rebel Invasion*, 114. Moved to within "about 10 miles" of Lexington, put into camp, then roused after dark and moved on

"expecting to have a fight, but had a few shots & captured 15 prisoners," October 20, 1864, entry in Lyman diary, 3, Misc. Mans. 17: #490 WHMC.

42. Sanborn, *OR*, 41: (pt. 1), 388–89; Phelps, *OR*, 41: (pt. 1), 402–03; report of Maj. William Plumb, Sixth Missouri State Militia Cavalry, November 12, 1864, *OR*, 41: (pt. 1), 409; Hinton, *Rebel Invasion*, 111–13; Mitchell, *OR*, 41: (pt. 1), 410; Gravely, *OR*, 41: (pt. 1), 412; Pleasonton to Rosecrans, October 19, 1864, *OR*, 41: (pt. 4), 110; Rosecrans to Curtis, October 20, 1864, *OR*, 41: (pt. 4), 141; Rosecrans, *OR*, 41: (pt. 1), 312; Rosecrans, *OR*, 41: (pt. 1), 313; "Latest from the Front!" Kansas City *Journal of Commerce*, October 20, 1864, 2. When Ewing passed Rosecrans information on Curtis's numbers directly from Kansas allegedly totaling "2, 000 cavalry volunteers and 1, 000 cavalry militia and 6, 000 infantry militia," Rosecrans dismissed the information as "mistaken." Ewing, *OR*, 41: (pt. 4), 36; Maj. F. S. Bond to Brig. Gen. Thomas Ewing, October 17, 1864, *OR*, 41: (pt. 4), 36.

43. Blunt to Curtis, October 20, 1864, *OR*, 41: (pt. 4), 145; Hinton, *Rebel Invasion*, 91.

44. Brig. Gen. Egbert B. Brown, November 3, 1864, *OR*, 41: (pt. 1), 348; Hinton, *Rebel Invasion*, 113–14. Drew rations for another four days, moved to Milford Mills. October 19, 1864, entry in Lyman diary, 3, Misc. Mans. 17: #490 WHMC. Colonel Edward F. Winslow's brigade of regular cavalry from Maj. Gen. A. J. Smith's command arrived in the field. It had moved by boat from St. Louis to Jefferson City and covered "thirty miles per diem, to Wellington." It formed Pleasonton's fourth brigade, and he himself joined his troopers at Dunksburg on Thursday. Winsolow, *OR*, 41: (pt. 1), 329; Maj. Gen. Alfred Pleasonton to Maj. Frank S. Bond, October 18, 1864, *OR*, 41: (pt. 4), 84; Pleasonton, *OR*, 41: (pt. 1), 340; Rosecrans, *OR*, 41: (pt. 1), 312.

45. Fisk, *OR*, 41: (pt. 1), 423; Clinton B. Fisk, U.S. Army, commanding District of North Missouri, *OR*, 41: (pt. 1), 423; "The Latest News. By Telegraph. From Jefferson City. Return of Gen. Fisk. Details of the Fight at Glasgow . . . Response of Rebel Missourians to Price's Call," St. Louis *Missouri Democrat*, October 20, 1864, 1.

46. "The Invasion. Independence Reoccupied by Union Troops. Price's Advance at Lexington," St. Louis *Missouri Democrat*, October 18, 1864, 1; "The Raiders. Their Reinforcements. Anderson Approved by Price. Rebel Outrages. Glasgow—Boonville," St. Louis *Missouri Democrat*, October 27, 1864, 1.

47. Maj. Gen. James F. Fagan to Lt. Col. L. A. Maclean, October 18, 1864, *OR*, 41: (pt. 4), 1003; W. B. Welch, chief surgeon of the division, to Capt. John King at division headquarters, included with Fagan, *OR*, 41: (pt. 4), 1003–04; Col. Arch. S. Dobbin to Maj. John King to Capt. John King, October 18, 1864, *OR*, 41: (pt. 4), 1004; October 20, 1864, entry in Baker diary; William G. Hazen to Alexander R. Hazen, December 21, 1864, Misc. Mans. 2: #44. WHMC.

48. "The Capture of Fry and Glathart. Statement of Mr. Samuel Fry" [from *State Journal*], Kansas *Daily Tribune*, October 25, 1864, 2.

49. Maj. Gen. Sterling Price, November 2, 1864, *OR*, 41: (pt. 1), 624; Price, *OR*, 41: (pt. 1), 633; Thompson, *OR*, 41: (pt. 1), 666.

5. From the Little Blue to the Big Blue

1. See Paul Kirkman, *The Battle of Westport: Missouri's Great Confederate Raid* (Charleston, SC: History Press, 2011), 83–92. Also see "Fight on the Little Blue" [from

Kansas City Journal], *Liberty Tribune*, October 28, 1864, 2; "The Fighting in Missouri. The Situation to the 23d," St. Louis *Missouri Democrat*, October 25, 1864, 2; "Glorious News. Our Last Dispatches Confirmed," St. Louis *Missouri Democrat*, October 28, 1864, 1. On the weather, see Reader, Autobiography, 17.

2. Moonlight, *OR*, 41: (pt. 1), 592, 593; Jenkins, *Battle of Westport*, 57; Moonlight, *OR*, 41: (pt. 1), 592; Hinton, *Rebel Invasion*, 93, 94; "Compendium of History," in *Soldier's Letter*, 1: (March 25, 1865), 1, typographical error "27th."; S. R. Curtis, *OR*, 41: (pt. 1), 477–78.

3. Moonlight, *OR*, 41: (pt. 1), 592, 593; Timbocker, "On Kansas Soil," *National Tribune*, November 21, 1895, 1; Hinton, *Rebel Invasion*, 92–93; Jenkins, *Battle of Westport*, 57; Childers, "Recitals and Reminiscences," *National Tribune*, January 31, 1907, 6; Hinton, *Rebel Invasion*, 90. Marmaduke reports that his Engineer Company under Captain James T. Hogane saved the bridge.

4. Greene, *OR*, 41: (pt. 1), 690; Davies, *OR*, 41: (pt. 1), 696; Price, *OR*, 41: (pt. 1), 633. Lawther claimed a loss of only "1 man killed, 1 officer and 12 men wounded, and 6 men captured," Lawther, *OR*, 41: (pt. 1), 699. Greene. "credit is due to Capt. Charles K. Polk of Company B, who held the enemy in check on my left. Sergeant Woolsey, Company G, was conspicuous for gallantry during the action, and Private Shepherd, Company F, deserves especial notice for rallying his company and leading a charge against the battery. I now marched to Independence and was ordered to picket the approaches to that town from the south and west." Jenkins, *Battle of Westport*, 56–57.

5. Moonlight, *OR*, 41: (pt. 1), 592; Hinton, *Rebel Invasion*, 95; Simpson, March 16, 1910, 7, 8, mistook the officer as Colonel H. M. McGee, though he said that he met them by chance in a St. Louis hotel in 1877. Plumb Papers, KSHS.

6. Price, *OR*, 41: (pt. 1), 633–34; Thompson, *OR*, 41: (pt. 1), 666; and, Jenkins, *Battle of Westport*, 61. Shelby's Report, 657) Nichols broke the Union line in his front and drove it back. (Jackman's report, 675).

7. Timbocker, "On Kansas Soil," *National Tribune*, November 21, 1895, 1; Moonlight, *OR*, 41: (pt. 1), 593; Hinton, *Rebel Invasion*, 95; and, Jenkins, *Battle of Westport*, 58. Moonlight, *OR*, 41: (pt. 1), 592–93; Hunt, *OR*, 41: (pt. 1), 544; Ford, *OR*, 41: (pt. 1), 607; Curtis, *OR*, 41: (pt. 1), 477; Hinton, *Rebel Invasion*, 97–98, 99, 100. consisted of 900 men with roughly four hundred each in the Second Colorado and Sixteenth Kansas Cavalry, and the rest manning half a dozen guns in a Colorado Battery. Captain Nelson Gregg got "a severe gunshot wound in the right arm which is likely to disable him for life." A Captain G. L. Grove (not found in military service files), only twenty-three years old, later collapsed from overexertion and died at Westport a few days later.

8. Jennison, *OR*, 41: (pt. 1), 583–84, 590; Curtis, *OR*, 41: (pt. 1), 477; Hinton, *Rebel Invasion*; and, Jenkins, *Battle of Westport*, 57, 58, 61; Maj. Gen. S. R. Curtis to Maj. Gen. Henry W. Halleck (same to Pleasonton), October 21, 1864, *OR*, 41: (pt. 4), 163; Timbocker, "On Kansas Soil," *National Tribune*, November 21, 1895, 1. See also Meeker, *OR*, 41: (pt. 1), 562, 563–64.

9. Curtis, *OR*, 41: (pt. 1), 476, 478; Lane, *OR*, 41: (pt. 1), 568; Timbocker, "On Kansas Soil," *National Tribune*, November 21, 1895, 1; Lane, *OR*, 41: (pt. 1), 568–69; Curtis, *OR*, 41: (pt. 1), 476; Jenkins, *Battle of Westport*, T 56, 58; Hinton, *Rebel Invasion*, 94. Curtis called his artillery to the front "as he had determined to feel the enemy on the Little Blue," McKenny, *OR*, 41: (pt. 1), 536–37; Hunt, *OR*, 41: (pt. 1), 543; Curtis, *OR*,

41: (pt. 1), 476–77; Hinton, *Rebel Invasion*, 95–96, 96–97, 98, 100; Curtis, *OR*, 41: (pt. 1), 478; Lane, *OR*, 41: (pt. 1), 568–69; "Fight on the Little Blue! Major Smith, of the 2d Colorado, Killed!" Kansas City *Journal of Commerce*, October 22, 1864, 2. Fifteen of the forty mounted men with Curtis lost their horses to the heavy fire. "Colonel Walker is the man to command the Sixteenth in the field. The regiment will move down to Olathe soon, and I will see what can be done. The following is part of General Orders, No. 55," Curtis, *OR*, 41: (pt. 3), 793.

10. Moonlight, *OR*, 41: (pt. 1), 592–93; Hunt, *OR*, 41: (pt. 1), 544; Ford, *OR*, 41: (pt. 1), 607; Curtis, *OR*, 41: (pt. 1), 477; Hinton, *Rebel Invasion*, 97–98, 99, 100. Ford, *OR*, 41: (pt. 1), 607; Nettleton to his sister, December 19, 1864, in Crittenden, *Battle of Westport and National Memorial Park*, 29; Hunt, *OR*, 41: (pt. 1), 543; Jenkins, *Battle of Westport*, 57. Kansas militia, under Captain McDowell, reported for duty and did good service in guarding and delivering the ammunition supplies, Curtis, *OR*, 41: (pt. 1), 478.

11. Lane, *OR*, 41: (pt. 1), 568–69; Grover, "Price Campaign of 1864," 173–74; Curtis, *OR*, 41: (pt. 1), 478; Jenkins, *Battle of Westport*, 58, 61; Hinton, *Rebel Invasion*, 98.

12. A. C. Jones, "The Boy-Inspector of Cavalry," *National Tribune*, January 25, 1883, 2; George West letter in "The Second Colorado. Some Further Reminiscences of a Famous Cavalry Regiment," *National Tribune*, February 22, 1883, 3; H. G. Ward, "Price's Raid. How Major Smith of the Independent Colorado Met His Death," *National Tribune*, March 29, 1883, 3; Hinton, *Rebel Invasion*, 97, 330; Grover, "Price Campaign of 1864," 172–73; "Compendium of History," in *Soldier's Letter*, 1: (April 3, 1865), 1, interspersed with parenthetic exuberant bursts of joy that Richmond had fallen. Clark, 683. On Smith's death, see also Curtis, *OR*, 41: (pt. 1), 474–75; Ford, *OR*, 41: (pt. 1), 608; and Jenkins, *Battle of Westport*, 57–58. Ford mistakenly assumed "the brigade books and papers were lost in the evacuation of Independence on the 21st instant, so that the able report of Major Smith cannot be forwarded with this." Ford, *OR*, 41: (pt. 1), 607.

13. Brig. Gen. Joseph O. Shelby, December —, 1864, *OR*, 41: (pt. 1), 657–58; Jackman, *OR*, 41: (pt. 1), 675; Price, *OR*, 41: (pt. 1), 634; "Compendium of History," in *Soldier's Letter*, 1: (April 3, 1865), 1.

14. Hunt, *OR*, 41: (pt. 1), 543; "Compendium of History," *Soldier's Letter*, 1: (June 3, 1865), 1.

15. Ford, *OR*, 41: (pt. 1), 607–08; statement of Benjamin F. Simpson, 8, 9, Plumb Papers, KSHS; "Fight on the Little Blue! Major Smith, of the 2d Colorado, Killed!" Kansas City *Journal of Commerce*, October 22, 1864, 2; Hinton, *Rebel Invasion*, 101. Shelby pursued with Thompson's Iron Brigade. (Price's Report in *OR* Vol. 41, Part 1, 634).

16. Curtis, *OR*, 41: (pt. 1), 476; Grover, "Price Campaign of 1864," 173–74; Timbocker, "On Kansas Soil," *National Tribune*, November 21, 1895, 1.

17. Hunt, *OR*, 41: (pt. 1), 543–44; Hinton, *Rebel Invasion*, 101.

18. Statement of Benjamin F. Simpson, 8, 9.

19. Maj. Gen. S. R. Curtis to Maj. Gen. James G. Blunt, October 21, 1864, *OR*, 41: (pt. 4), 165; Statement of Benjamin F. Simpson, 9–10.

20. Lane, *OR*, 41: (pt. 1), 568–69; Jenkins, *Battle of Westport*, 58, 61; Hinton, *Rebel Invasion*, 99, 101; Statement of Benjamin F. Simpson, 10, 16.

21. Davis, *OR*, 41: (pt. 1), 551; "Compendium of History," *Soldier's Letter*, 1: (June 3, 1865), 1.

22. Statement of Benjamin F. Simpson, 10.

23. Curtis, *OR*, 41: (pt. 1), 478; Moonlight, *OR*, 41: (pt. 1), 593; Sheffield Ingalls, *History of Atchison County, Kansas* (Lawrence, KS: Standard, 1916), 459; Jenkins, *Battle of Westport*, 61. Jennison claimed to have commanded "Col. Jennison. Some Interesting Incidents of His Adventurous Career in the War," *National Tribune*, July 10, 1884, 8; Jenkins, *Battle of Westport*, 61. Also see Ford, *OR*, 41: (pt. 1), 608; Hinton, *Rebel Invasion*, 102, 103, 104; Jenkins, *Battle of Westport*, 61.

24. Grover, " Price Campaign of 1864," 174–75; Hinton, *Rebel Invasion*, 99, 105; Jenkins, *Battle of Westport*, 73. "The occasional story that Major Smith and George Todd killed each other simultaneously is unworthy of consideration." Prisoners Jerry Glathart and Samuel Fry later said that Todd had led the charge against Smith's command. Ward, "Price's Raid. How Major Smith of the Independent Colorado Met His Death," *National Tribune*, March 29, 1883, 3; Maj. Gen. S. R. Curtis to Mrs. Curtis, October 22, 1864, *OR*, 41: (pt. 4), 190.

25. Grover, "Price Campaign of 1864," 173, 181; "Compendium of History," *Soldier's Letter*, 1: (June 3, 1865), 1. Back to Independence, as troops filed through, "Hurrah for the Second Colorado, and the Old Flag!" People generally recorded the wounding of officers. Hinton, *Rebel Invasion*, 103. Grover, "Price Campaign of 1864," 180–81, reports several officers from Warrensburg had been taken in the September 1861 capture of Lexington by Price.

26. Thompson, *OR*, 41: (pt. 1), 666; Moonlight, *OR*, 41: (pt. 1), 593. Jennison claimed to have commanded "The overwhelming force compelled him to retreat, but he fought every step and made a stand on the Little Blue, bringing on a general engagement." "Col. Jennison. Some Interesting Incidents of His Adventurous Career in the War," *National Tribune*, July 10, 1884, 8.

27. McKenny, *OR*, 41: (pt. 1), 537; Col. C. R. Jennison to Capt. George S. Hampton, October 22, 1864, *OR*, 41: (pt. 4), 192.

28. Hinton, *Rebel Invasion*, 103; diary of Sgt. Francis M. Gordon, WHMC-KC; Simpson, 16.

29. "Fight on the Little Blue! Major Smith, of the 2d Colorado, Killed!" Kansas City *Journal of Commerce*, October 22, 1864, 2; "From Kansas City. Glorious News from Our Army. Price's Army Routed," St. Louis *Missouri Democrat*, October 24, 1864, 1; Hinton, *Rebel Invasion*, 103; Jennison, *OR*, 41: (pt. 1), 583–84, 590; Curtis, *OR*, 41: (pt. 1), 477; Hinton, *Rebel Invasion*; Jenkins, *Battle of Westport*, 57, 58, 61; Maj. Gen. S. R. Curtis to Maj. Gen. Henry W. Halleck (same to Pleasonton), October 21, 1864, *OR*, 41: (pt. 4), 163; Timbocker, "On Kansas Soil," *National Tribune*, November 21, 1895, 1. On the day, see also Meeker, *OR*, 41: (pt. 1), 562, 563–64.

30. Hinton, *Rebel Invasion*, 103; "The Capture of Fry and Glathart. Statement of Mr. Samuel Fry" [from *State Journal*], Kansas *Daily Tribune*, October 25, 1864, 2. Rumored capture of Jerry Glathart and Sam Fry of Lawrence. "Fight on the Little Blue! Major Smith, of the 2d Colorado, Killed!" Kansas City *Journal of Commerce*, October 22, 1864, 2; "Battle of Westport," Kansas City *Journal of Commerce*, October 24, 1864, 2, reprinted as "Battle of Westport. Signal Rout of Price! Details of the Engagement," St. Louis *Missouri Democrat*, October 31, 1864, 3. Marmaduke's losses were one man killed, one officer and twelve men wounded, and six men captured. Lawther, *OR*, 41: (pt. 1), 699.

31. Curtis, *OR*, 41: (pt. 1), 479; Jenkins, *Battle of Westport*, 66, 67–69. Price later reported that he had "determined to advance on the Santa Fé road." Price, *OR*, 41: (pt. 1), 634. "Numerically superior Federal force entrenched on the opposite side of the stream whose natural situation made it difficult to cross without hindrance," Jenkins, *Battle of Westport*, 68.

32. John Edwards Hicks, "Battle Cast Pall over Westport," in *The Battle of Westport*, ed. Westport Historical Society (Kansas City: Westport Historical Society, 1996), 27; Fuller to his father, October 24, 1864, in Julia Greene, Papers of the Rev. Jonathan B. Fuller, D.D.—A Selection of Documents (submitted by Larry G. Gray, winter 1993), 43–44, WHMC-KC. Thought attack was but a feint while Price moved the main body southwest "I am furthermore persuaded that if Pleasanton [*sic*] has not threatened their rear, those rascals might have amused us rather more than would have been pleasant." Fuller to his father, October 24, 1864, in Greene, Fuller Papers, 43.

33. Curtis, *OR*, 41: (pt. 1), 478–479; Maj. Gen. S. R. Curtis to Maj. Gen. Henry W. Halleck (same to Pleasonton), October 21, 1864, *OR*, 41: (pt. 4), 163; Moonlight, *OR*, 41: (pt. 1), 592; Hunt, *OR*, 41: (pt. 1), 544; "The Fighting in Missouri," St. Louis *Missouri Democrat*, October 25, 1864, 2. Last reports that Curtis had swung back from the Big Blue. "The Invasion," St. Louis *Missouri Democrat*, October 24, 1864, 1; Hinton, *Rebel Invasion*, 105.

34. Curtis, *OR*, 41: (pt. 1), 479; Blair, *OR*, 41: (pt. 1), 597; "The Latest News. Price Forcing the Passage of the Blue! He Is Advancing upon Independence! Our Forces Slowly Falling Back! Captains McLain and Gregg Wounded! Let Every Man Turn Out! Rally! Men of Kansas, and Hurl Back the Invader! To Arms! To Arms! Victory or Death!" Leavenworth *Daily Times*, October 22, 1864, 2; Jenkins, *Battle of Westport*, 62. Estimates of Price's army ranged as high as 37,000. Curtis estimated that he had raised "altogether, to about 15,000," but this number surely included everything he hoped he had behind him in Kansas City and back in Kansas. Curtis, *OR*, 41: (pt. 1), 479; Blair, *OR*, 41: (pt. 1), 597; Deitzler, *OR*, 41: (pt. 1), 615; "Compendium of History," in *Soldier's Letter*, 1: (June 10, 1865), 1. 35. "Compendium of History," in *Soldier's Letter*, 1: (June 17, 1865), 1; Hinton, *Rebel Invasion*, 123; letter to editor dated October 20 from soldier in Twenty-first Regiment, KSM, Kansas *Daily Times*, October 22, 1864, 2.

36. Price, *OR*, 41: (pt. 1), 634.

37. Curtis, *OR*, 41: (pt. 1), 479; Blair, *OR*, 41: (pt. 1), 597: "thus arranged, resolved to check or defeat the long continued progress of Price's army of 30, 000. For his officers and men, taken prisoners, generally reported the enemy's force at from 25,000 to 37,000, and boasted of constant accessions by volunteering and conscription," Jenkins, *Battle of Westport*, 65; Blair, *OR*, 41: (pt. 1), 597–98; Blair to Curtis, in Curtis, *OR*, 41: (pt. 1), 482. [T] he men "supped, slept, and breakfasted next morning, their horses, together with all the transportation, having been sent back to Kansas City to avoid unnecessary incumbrances." "At this place I found Colonel Blair in command of the Fifth, Sixth, and Tenth Regiments Kansas State Militia and Captain McLain's Colorado battery. I immediately gave the necessary orders to erect fortifications and place the troops in position," Deitzler, *OR*, 41: (pt. 1), 615.

38. Curtis, *OR*, 41: (pt. 1), 479; Deitzler, *OR*, 41: (pt. 1), 615; Hinton, *Rebel Invasion*, 122–23; Jenkins, *Battle of Westport*, 66, 67–68, 68–69. Price later reported that he had

"determined to advance on the Santa Fé road." Price, *OR*, 41: (pt. 1), 634; "numerically superior Federal force entrenched on the opposite side of the stream whose natural situation made it difficult to cross without hindrance."

39. Often mistakenly called the Second Kansas Colored State Militia; [James Rafferty said to have died January 1, 1863 at Fayetteville AR].

40. Hinton, *Rebel Invasion*, 123–24.

41. Curtis was roughly where Fifteenth Street would extend to the river. Jenkins, *Battle of Westport*, 62, 65.

42. Simpson, 10–11; Hinton, *Rebel Invasion*, 123–24.

43. Hinton, *Rebel Invasion*, 124, 150. Roughly an estenstion of Sixty-first street. For description of the ford, see Crittenden, *Battle of Westport and National Memorial Park*, 37; Jenkins, *Battle of Westport*, 116.

44. Hinton, *Rebel Invasion*, 124–25; Jennison, 2 Moonlight, 3 Blair, 4 Ford. Blunt, *OR*, 41: (pt. 1), 575; Moonlight, *OR*, 41: (pt. 1), 593, quoted in Curtis, *OR*, 41: (pt. 1), 481; Ford, *OR*, 41: (pt. 1), 608.

45. I. Bonebrake, "Recollections of the Second Day's Fight in the Battle of Westport," in Westport Historical Society, *Battle of Westport*, 31, excerpt from Westport, 1812–1912 (Kansas City: Franklin Hudson, 1912), 71–74. Reader recorded seven companies of his own Second KSM, five of the Third, one of the Nineteenth, and the twenty-four-pound brass howitzer of Burns Battery, Reader, Autobiography, 3:19, 22, 24, 37, 35, 51, 53.

46. Reader, Autobiography, 3:31, 43, 200–201.

47. Deitzler, *OR*, 41: (pt. 1), 615; Hinton, *Rebel Invasion*, 125, 126–27. This was likely James T. Burnes of the Fifteenth Missouri Cavalry, then a militia unit. Deitzler's report conveys rumors, and probably neither the Confederate force nor the Missouri militia wasanywhere close to that size. The latter probably consisted of Lt. Jacob Axline's Independent Company EMM, which had served earlier at Hickman's Mill, though not noted as officially in service at this point.

48. Davis, *OR*, 41: (pt. 1), 551; McKenny, *OR*, 41: (pt. 1), 537; Robinson, *OR*, 41: (pt. 1), 546; Robinson to Coates, October 11, included in Robinson, *OR*, 41: (pt. 1), 550; Pomeroy, *OR*, 41: (pt. 1), 571; Curtis, *OR*, 41: (pt. 1), 485; Jenkins, *Battle of Westport*, 56, 62–65. On the KSM, see also Hinton, *Rebel Invasion*, 92, 126, 158; Pomeroy, *OR*, 41: (pt. 1), 571; Fishback, *OR*, 41: (pt. 1), 621; Price, *OR*, 41: (pt. 1), 624; Orange Warner letter in "The Second Colorado," *National Tribune*, February 22, 1883, 3.

49. Quoted in Hall, *Patriots in Disguise*, 167; also see 167–73.

50. Curtis, *OR*, 41: (pt. 1), 485; Curtis to Rosecrans, telegraph, October 21, 1864, in Curtis, *OR*, 41: (pt. 1), 479; Maj. Gen. S. R. Curtis to Maj. Gen. William S. Rosecrans, October 21, 1864, *OR*, 41: (pt. 4), 164; Curtis, *OR*, 41: (pt. 1), 485; Rosecrans, *OR*, 41: (pt. 1), 313; Curtis to Rosecrans, telegraph, October 21, 1864, in Curtis, *OR*, 41: (pt. 1), 479; Rosecrans, *OR*, 41: (pt. 1), 313; Rosecrans to Pleasonton, October 21, 1864, *OR*, 41: (pt. 4), 158.

51. Pleasonton to Rosecrans, October 21, 1864, *OR*, 41: (pt. 4), 157–58; Rosecrans to Curtis, telegraph, October 21, 1864, in Curtis, *OR*, 41: (pt. 1), 479; October 21, 1864, entry in Lyman diary, 4. Misc. Mans. 17: #490 WHMC. Described as "three days of severe skirmishing, followed by two days of hard fighting." Lexington review. Night retreat "resting briefly at Napoleon City" fourteen miles west of Lexington. "The Fighting in

Missouri," St. Louis *Missouri Democrat*, October 25, 1864, 2; Rosecrans, *OR*, 41: (pt. 1), 312. See also Houston, *OR*, 41: (pt. 1), 381; Mitchell, *OR*, 41: (pt. 1), 410; Phelps, *OR*, 41: (pt. 1), 403; McFerran, *OR*, 41: (pt. 1), 359; Maj. Frank S. Bonds to Maj. Gen. Pleasonton, October 22, 1864, *OR*, 41: (pt. 4), 182. Kansas City's postmaster reported Confederates had taken Sibley, eight miles below Independence, "and [are] driving our troops." "Look out for a 'big time' this way soon." "Additional" under "Price's Whole Army at Independence. A Battle Yesterday afternoon. Capts. McLain & Gregg Wounded. Gen. Curtis Fortifying at Kansas City. Kansans to the Rescue," Kansas *Daily Times*, October 22, 1864, 2; "Fight on the Little Blue! Major Smith, of the 2d Colorado, Killed!" Kansas City *Journal of Commerce*, October 22, 1864, 2.

52. Pleasonton to A. J. Smith, October 21, 1864, *OR*, 41: (pt. 4), 159.

6. The Big Blue and the Reprise

1. Curtis, *OR*, 41: (pt. 1), 484; Maj. Chapman S. Charlot, December 13, 1864, *OR*, 41: (pt. 1), 526; Curtis, *OR*, 41: (pt. 1), 479. See also Kirkman, *Battle of Westport: Missouri's Great Confederate Raid*, 93–102.

2. Reader, Autobiography, 33; Hinton, *Rebel Invasion*, 125. Reader recorded seven companies of his own Second KSM, five of the Third, one of the Nineteenth, and the twenty-four-pound brass howitzer of Burns Battery. Reader, Autobiography, 3:19, 22, 24, 37.

3. Quoted in Jenkins, *Battle of Westport*, 64, but see also 62, 65; Curtis, *OR*, 41: (pt. 1), 484; Capt. Edwin I. Meeker, November 23, 1864, *OR*, 41: (pt. 1), 564; Charlot, *OR*, 41: (pt. 1), 526; Hinton, *Rebel Invasion*, 127; Jenkins, *Battle of Westport*, 65–66; Curtis to Grant, October 22, 1864, in Curtis, *OR*, 41: (pt. 1), 479; Blunt to Curtis, in Curtis, *OR*, 41: (pt. 1), 480; Deitzler, *OR*, 41: (pt. 1), 615. The advance cut off two companies of the Fifteenth Kansas Cavalry that were scouting to the east of the Big Blue; one rode through by way of Hickman's Mill. Hinton, *Rebel Invasion*, 128–29; "Compendium of History," in *Soldier's Letter*, 1: (June 10, 1865), 1.

4. Jennison, *OR*, 41: (pt. 4), 191; C. R. Jennison to Maj. Gen. James G. Blunt, October 22 [note: item was printed with the pages of correspondence for October 21], 1864, *OR*, 41: (pt. 4), 165; Hinton, *Rebel Invasion*, 125, 298. For claims about Brown's Ford, see "Col. Jennison. Some Interesting Incidents of His Adventurous Career in the War," *National Tribune*, July 10, 1884, 8, and "The Invasion," St. Louis *Missouri Democrat*, October 24, 1864, 1.

5. Jennison, *OR*, 41: (pt. 1), 584, also quoted in Curtis, *OR*, 41: (pt. 1), 481; Thompson, *OR*, 41: (pt. 1), 666; Ford, *OR*, 41: (pt. 1), 608; Blunt, *OR*, 41: (pt. 1), 575; McKenny, *OR*, 41: (pt. 1), 537; Maj. T. I. McKenny to Curtis, in Curtis, *OR*, 41: (pt. 1), 483; Charlot, *OR*, 41: (pt. 1), 526; Hinton, *Rebel Invasion*, 129–30; Blair, *OR*, 41: (pt. 1), 598, quoted Blair to Curtis, in Curtis, *OR*, 41: (pt. 1), 482; Deitzler, *OR*, 41: (pt. 1), 615; Maj. Gen. Deitzler to Curtis, in Curtis, *OR*, 41: (pt. 1), 480; Jenkins, *Battle of Westport*, 66–67, 68.

6. Thompson, *OR*, 41: (pt. 1), 666; Shelby, *OR*, 41: (pt. 1), 658; Stephen H. Ragan, "The Battle of Westport," talk given to Daughters of the Confederacy, October 23, 1910, in Crittenden, *Battle of Westport and National Memorial Park*, 55; Price, *OR*, 41: (pt. 1), 634; October 22, 1864, entry in Baker diary.

7. Blunt, *OR*, 41: (pt. 1), 575, quoted in Curtis, *OR*, 41: (pt. 1), 480; Jennison, *OR*, 41: (pt. 1), 584, quoted in Curtis, *OR*, 41: (pt. 1), 481; Moonlight, *OR*, 41: (pt. 1), 593; McKenny, *OR*, 41: (pt. 1), 537; Grover, "Price Campaign of 1864," 174–75; Hinton, *Rebel Invasion*, 132. Blunt said he sent Moonlight after hearing artillery around 1 p.m.

8. Moonlight, *OR*, 41: (pt. 1), 594; "Compendium of History," in *Soldier's Letter*, 1: (June 10, 1865), 1. John M. Woodward of the Eleventh Kansas.

9. Curtis, *OR*, 41: (pt. 1), 479–80; Ford, *OR*, 41: (pt. 1), 608; Curtis, *OR*, 41: (pt. 1), 480–81; Jennison, *OR*, 41: (pt. 1), 584, quoted in Curtis, *OR*, 41: (pt. 1), 481; Col. Charles W. Blair, November 25, 1864, *OR*, 41: (pt. 1), 597–98; Blair to Curtis, in Curtis, *OR*, 41: (pt. 1), 482; Deitzler, *OR*, 41: (pt. 1), 615, quoted in Curtis, *OR*, 41: (pt. 1), 480; Fishback, *OR*, 41: (pt. 1), 621.

10. Blair, *OR*, 41: (pt. 1), 597–98; Hinton, *Rebel Invasion*, 144–45.

11. Maj. Gen. S. R. Curtis to Brig. Gen. Grant, October 22, 1864, *OR*, 41: (pt. 4), 192; Jenkins, *Battle of Westport*, 74; Curtis, *OR*, 41: (pt. 1), 481.

12. Reader, Autobiography, 3:28, 39, 45.

13. Hinton, *Rebel Invasion*, 133–34; "Battle of Westport. Old Price Defeated. He Is Fleeing South," Kansas City *Journal of Commerce*, October 24, 1864, 2, reprinted as "Battle of Westport," St. Louis *Missouri Democrat*, October 31, 1864, 3; Hinton, *Rebel Invasion*, 135–36; Reader, Autobiography, 3:63, 65, 71, 74, 76, 78, 80–81, 90. Veale also said to have theoretically about seven hundred men. See also James W. Steele, *The Battle of the Blue of the Second Regiment K.S.M. October 22, 1864: The Fight, the Captivity, the Escape, as Remembered by Survivors and Commemorated by the Gage Monument at Topeka, Kansas* (Chicago: D. H. Christophel, 1896); Reader, Autobiography, 3:92, 94–95, 96, 102, 104, 108, 110; Maj. Gen. Deitzler to Curtis, in Curtis, *OR*, 41: (pt. 1), 481; Curtis, *OR*, 41: (pt. 1), 480; Maj. Gen. Deitzler to Curtis, in Curtis, *OR*, 41: (pt. 1), 481; Curtis, *OR*, 41: (pt. 1), 480; Jackman, *OR*, 41: (pt. 1), 675; Jenkins, *Battle of Westport*, 74–75, 78; Ragan, "Battle of Westport," 55–56.

14. Jackman, *OR*, 41: (pt. 1), 675; Reader, Autobiography, 3:116, 118, 120; Jenkins, *Battle of Westport*, 74–75, 78; Reader, Autobiography, 3:122, 124, 134; Ragan, "Battle of Westport," 55–56; Price, *OR*, 41: (pt. 1), 634–35; "Casualties in the Topeka Regiment," Leavenworth *Daily Times*, October 26, 1864, 2; Hinton, *Rebel Invasion*, 139–41, 142–43. Two flags captured.

15. Bonebrake, "Recollections of the Second Day's Fight," Steele, *Battle of the Blue*, 87, 102, 89, 105.

16. Lt. Cyrus M. Roberts, December 15, 1864, *OR*, 41: (pt. 1), 566–67, quoted in Curtis, *OR*, 41: (pt. 1), 483–84; Hinton, *Rebel Invasion*, 137–38; Jenkins, *Battle of Westport*, 74–75 and 77.

17. Deitzler, *OR*, 41: (pt. 1), 616; Roberts, *OR*, 41: (pt. 1), 567; Curtis, *OR*, 41: (pt. 1), 484; Jenkins, *Battle of Westport*, 80.

18. Hinton, *Rebel Invasion*, 139–43; Jenkins, *Battle of Westport*, 80; "Statements of Wounded Men," Kansas City *Journal of Commerce*, October 28, 1864, 2; Reader, Autobiography, 3:172; Fuller to his father, October 24, 1864, in Greene, Fuller Papers, 43–44.

19. Maj. Gen. Pleasonton, *OR*, 41: (pt. 4), 182; Pleasonton, *OR*, 41: (pt. 1), 340; Pleasonton to Rosecrans, October 22, 1864, *OR*, 41: (pt. 4), 183; McNeil, *OR*, 41: (pt. 1), 371–72; Col. John V. DuBois to Maj. Gen. A. J. Smith, October 22, 1864, *OR*, 41: (pt. 4),

181; Montgomery, *OR*, 41: (pt. 1), 460; Eppstein, *OR*, 41: (pt. 1), 383; Rosecrans, *OR*, 41: (pt. 1), 312–13; Hinton, *Rebel Invasion*, 114–15. Eppstein, "Casualties in my command: 1 killed, 1 severely wounded, since died." In the chaos, McNeil could not find Maj. George Houston, in temporary command of the Thirteenth Missouri Cavalry. Probably Sunday, October 23, but mistyped as "Sunday, October 2." W. T. Foster diary, 1864–1865 (C0450), WHMC.

20. S. S. Harris, "The Fight at Independence. A Woman's Prompt Action Aided the Union Charging Column," *National Tribune*, April 14, 1898, 2. Confederate Arkansans "formed splendidly for they were a part of Hindman's command and were well disciplined men and good soldiers," Simpson, March 16, 1910, 7.

21. Price, *OR*, 41: (pt. 1), 635; Clark, *OR*, 41: (pt. 1), 683–84, 685; Greene, *OR*, 41: (pt. 1), 690; Lawther, *OR*, 41: (pt. 1), 699.

22. Harris, "Fight at Independence," *National Tribune*, April 14, 1898, 2; Pleasonton, *OR*, 41: (pt. 1), 340; McNeil, *OR*, 41: (pt. 1), 371–72; Montgomery, *OR*, 41: (pt. 1), 460; Eppstein, *OR*, 41: (pt. 1), 383; Rosecrans, *OR*, 41: (pt. 1), 312–13; McMahan, *OR*, 41: (pt. 1), 407; Maj. William Plumb, Nov. 12, 1864, *OR*, 41: (pt. 1), 409; Mitchell, *OR*, 41: (pt. 1), 410–11; Gravely, *OR*, 41: (pt. 1), 412; Pleasonton, *OR*, 41: (pt. 1), 340; Rosecrans, *OR*, 41: (pt. 1), 313; Jenkins, 69, 71; Philips in Crittenden, *Battle of Westport and National Memorial Park*, 25. Eppstein, "Casualties in my command: 1 killed, 1 severely wounded, since died." A detachment of the Second Missouri Cavalry came into the fight after thirty-five miles on the road. Houston, *OR*, 41: (pt. 1), 381.

23. Hinton, *Rebel Invasion*, 117–19; Steele, *Battle of the Blue*, 34.

24. Phelps, *OR*, 41: (pt. 1), 403; McNeil, *OR*, 41: (pt. 1), 371–72; Jenkins, *Battle of Westport*, 69–70. Col. Edwin C. Catherwood in McNeil's. At the battle of Independence—Officers wounded, 4; enlisted men wounded, 7. Catherwood, *OR*, 41: (pt. 1), 385; Ira M. Mallory, "Missouri Bush & Prairie. Price's Raid," *National Tribune*, September 6, 1900, 8; McNeil, *OR*, 41: (pt. 1), 371–72; Jenkins, *Battle of Westport*, 69–70; Col. Edwin C. Catherwood in McNeil's. At the battle of Independence—Officers wounded, 4; enlisted men wounded, 7;Catherwood, *OR*, 41: (pt. 1), 385.

25. Pleasonton, *OR*, 41: (pt. 4), 183–84; S. S. Harris, "The Fight at Independence," *National Tribune*, April 14, 1898, 2; McNeil, *OR*, 41: (pt. 1), 371–72; Jenkins, *Battle of Westport*, 69–70. Col. Edwin C. Catherwood in McNeil's. At the battle of Independence—Officers wounded, 4; enlisted men wounded, 7. Catherwood, *OR*, 41: (pt. 1), 385; Mallory, "Missouri Bush & Prairie. Price's Raid," *National Tribune*, September 6, 1900, 8. After a day in Confederate hands, Independence experienced a second battle and a Federal reoccupation. The ladies of the town cheered the Union successes from the gallery above the square. Jenkins, *Battle of Westport*, 71.

26. Rosecrans, *OR*, 41: (pt. 1), 313; Pleasonton to Rosecrans, October 22, 1864, *OR*, 41: (pt. 4), 184–85; Phelps, *OR*, 41: (pt. 1), 403; Jenkins, *Battle of Westport*, 71, 72. "Fierce fight just west of town. Lieutenant Mullins shot in bowels mortally. Rebel Colonel Young killed by Crittenden's command. Colonel Beeman, rebel, killed. Captain Davidson wounded," Philips in Crittenden, *Battle of Westport and National Memorial Park*, 25; McNeil, *OR*, 41: (pt. 1), 371; Jenkins, *Battle of Westport*, 70–77, 96; Hinton, *Rebel Invasion*, 115; October 22, 1864, entry in Lyman diary, 4, Misc. Mans. 17: #490 WHMC; Sanborn, *OR*, 41: (pt. 1), 389.

27. Greene, *OR*, 41: (pt. 1), 690; Capt. Benjamin S. Johnson, December 21, 1864, *OR*, 41: (pt. 1), 693; Jenkins, *Battle of Westport*, 69, 71–72, 73–74, 78–79; Crittenden, *Battle of Westport and National Memorial Park*, 34. Pleasonton, *OR*, 41: (pt. 4), 183. Col. Colton B. Greene had turned his Third Missouri Cavalry over to Capt. Benjamin S. Johnson, who formed "at sunrise on the bank of Big Blue River as infantry." These supported Pratt's guns and pressed on the Big Blue, but the unit's reported losses was three killed and seven wounded the day before at the Little Blue.

28. Maj. Gen. Alfred Pleasonton, November 1, 1864, *OR*, 41: (pt. 1), 336–37, 340. On the casualties see Brown, *OR*, 41: (pt. 1), 346–47, 349; Brig. Gen. Egbert B. Brown, October 24, 1864, *OR*, 41: (pt. 1), 347; McFerran, *OR*, 41: (pt. 1), 360; McFerran, *OR*, 41: (pt. 1), 359; Philips in Crittenden, *Battle of Westport and National Memorial Park*, 25; McFerran, *OR*, 41: (pt. 1), 359; Jenkins, *Battle of Westport*, 82.

29. Hinton, *Rebel Invasion*, 150, 115–16; Maj. Gen. John S. Marmaduke to Lt. Col. Maclean, October 22, 1864, *OR*, 41: (pt. 4), 1012; MacDonald, "Interview," 38; Jenkins, *Battle of Westport*, 81–82; Davies, *OR*, 41: (pt. 1), 696; McFerran, *OR*, 41: (pt. 1), 359–60; Burbridge, *OR*, 41: (pt. 1), 694: "Our loss was heavy, but especially in the regiment of the gallant Jeffers." Federals stopped only at 2 a.m. Clark, *OR*, 41: (pt. 1), 683–84. Price's reported, erroneously. Price, *OR*, 41: (pt. 1), 635. Lawther claimed absurdly that two men were wounded at the crossing of the Big Blue. Lawther, *OR*, 41: (pt. 1), 699.

30. Winslow, *OR*, 41: (pt. 1), 328, 329: "A portion only of the First Brigade joined me on the march, the Second New Jersey and Nineteenth Pennsylvania Regiments having fallen to the rear by orders from Major-General Pleasonton"; Maj. Benjamin S. Jones, 3rd Iowa Cavalry, November 28, 1864, *OR*, 41: (pt. 1), 334; Maj. Gen. Alfred Pleasonton, November 1, 1864, *OR*, 41: (pt. 1), 337, 340; Mary B. Townsend, "The Third Iowa Cavalry in Sterling Price's 1864 Missouri Raid," *MHR*, 105: (October 2010), 50; Jenkins, *Battle of Westport*, 82; Crittenden, *Battle of Westport and National Memorial Park*, 37.

31. Winslow, *OR*, 41: (pt. 1), 330; Brown, *OR*, 41: (pt. 1), 347; Jenkins, *Battle of Westport*, 82; McFerran, *OR*, 41: (pt. 1), 360; Philips diary in Crittenden, *Battle of Westport and National Memorial Park*, 25. Philips recalled "General Brown tried to snub me by throwing me in rear and giving advance to McFerran." west of Independence, Lt. Mullins "shot in the bowels mortally" Confederate Colonels Young, Beeman killed and Davidson wounded.

32. Price, *OR*, 41: (pt. 1), 635; Pleasonton, *OR*, 41: (pt. 1), 313; Price, *OR*, 41: (pt. 1), 635; Maj. Gen. Alfred Pleasonton, commanding Provisional Cavalry Division, Warrensburg, November 1, 1864, *OR*, 41: (pt. 1), 337; Pleasonton, *OR*, 41: (pt. 1), 340; Davis, *OR*, 41: (pt. 1), 55; McNeil, *OR*, 41: (pt. 1), 372; Crittenden, *Battle of Westport and National Memorial Park*, 39; Hinton, *Rebel Invasion*, 116–17.

33. Maj. T. I. McKenny to Curtis, in Curtis, *OR*, 41: (pt. 1), 483; Price, *OR*, 41: (pt. 1), 634; Jackman, *OR*, 41: (pt. 1), 675–76.

34. Price, *OR*, 41: (pt. 1), 635; Thompson, *OR*, 41: (pt. 1), 666–67; Maj. T. I. McKenny to Curtis, in Curtis, *OR*, 41: (pt. 1), 483; Price, *OR*, 41: (pt. 1), 634; Jackman, *OR*, 41: (pt. 1), 675–76; quoted in Hall, *Patriots in Disguise*, 167–68, 168–70, 170–73.

35. Hicks, "Battle Cast Pall over Westport," 26, 29, 30.

36. Addenda to Blunt, December 24 1864, *OR*, 41: (pt. 1), 580, in Curtis, *OR*, 41: (pt. 1), 480; Jennison, *OR*, 41: (pt. 1), 584–85, quoted in Curtis, *OR*, 41: (pt. 1), 481;

Jenkins, *Battle of Westport*, 74, 77–78; McKenny, *OR*, 41: (pt. 1), 537, also quoted in Curtis, *OR*, 41: (pt. 1), 482–83; Moonlight, *OR*, 41: (pt. 1), 593, quoted in Curtis, *OR*, 41: (pt. 1), 481–82; Lane, *OR*, 41: (pt. 1), 569; Hunt, *OR*, 41: (pt. 1), 544; Hinton, *Rebel Invasion*, 130–31, 131–32; Moonlight, *OR*, 41: (pt. 1), 593; Lane, *OR*, 41: (pt. 1), 569; Hunt, *OR*, 41: (pt. 1), 544; Maj. Hunt to Curtis, in Curtis, *OR*, 41: (pt. 1), 483; S. S. Curtis, *OR*, 41: (pt. 1), 533.

37. McKenny, *OR*, 41: (pt. 1), 538, and Maj. T. I. McKenny to Curtis, in Curtis, *OR*, 41: (pt. 1), 483; Cloud, *OR*, 41: (pt. 1), 55; Blunt, *OR*, 41: (pt. 1), 575; Blunt to Curtis, in Curtis, *OR*, 41: (pt. 1), 486; Childers, "Recitals and Reminiscences," *National Tribune*, January 31, 1907, 6; Meeker, *OR*, 41: (pt. 1), 564; Maj. Theodore J. Weed, December 1, 1864, *OR*, 41: (pt. 1), 555; Blair, *OR*, 41: (pt. 1), 597–98; Maj. Gen. S. R. Curtis to Lt. Col. Stark, October 22, 1864, *OR*, 41: (pt. 4), 193; Col. Thomas Moonlight to Maj. Gen. S. R. Curtis, October 22, 1864, *OR*, 41: (pt. 4), 192; S. S. Curtis, *OR*, 41: (pt. 1), 532–33; Curtis, *OR*, 41: (pt. 1), 484–85; H. H. Heath to Maj. Gen. S. R. Curtis, October 22, 1864, *OR*, 41: (pt. 4), 189; Jenkins, *Battle of Westport*, 86; Hinton, *Rebel Invasion*, 132, 143–44, 145–46.

38. Jenkins, *Battle of Westport*, 80–81; Fuller to his father, October 24, 1864, in Greene, Fuller Papers, 40, 41; "Battle of Westport," Kansas City *Journal of Commerce*, October 24, 1864, 2, reprinted as "Battle of Westport," St. Louis *Missouri Democrat*, October 31, 1864, 3; McKenny, *OR*, 41: (pt. 1), 537–38.

39. Blair, *OR*, 41: (pt. 1), 598; Deitzler, *OR*, 41: (pt. 1), 616; Curtis, *OR*, 41: (pt. 1), 485; Hinton, *Rebel Invasion*, 144–46; Moonlight, *OR*, 41: (pt. 1), 593; Pomeroy, *OR*, 41: (pt. 1), 571; Curtis, *OR*, 41: (pt. 1), 485; Simpson, 11; Jennison, *OR*, 41: (pt. 4), 191; Jennison, *OR*, 41: (pt. 1), 585; Curtis, *OR*, 41: (pt. 1), 480; Hinton, *Rebel Invasion*, 143, 144, 149–50; Sundown Curtis heard from Pleasonton. "The Fighting in Missouri," St. Louis *Missouri Democrat*, October 25, 1864, 2; Curtis, *OR*, 41: (pt. 1), 484; Charlot, *OR*, 41: (pt. 1), 526; Robinson, *OR*, 41: (pt. 1), 546–47; Lane, *OR*, 41: (pt. 1), 569

40. Grover, "Price Campaign of 1864," 175; Jennison to Curtis, in Curtis, *OR*, 41: (pt. 1), 480, 481; Deitzler, *OR*, 41: (pt. 1), 616; Lane, *OR*, 41: (pt. 1), 569; Charlot, *OR*, 41: (pt. 1), 526; McKenny, *OR*, 41: (pt. 1), 537.

41. Jenkins, *Battle of Westport*, 72–73; Deitzler, *OR*, 41: (pt. 1), 616; Jackman, *OR*, 41: (pt. 1), 676; "Battle of Westport," Kansas City *Journal of Commerce*, October 24, 1864, 2, reprinted as "Battle of Westport," St. Louis *Missouri Democrat*, October 31, 1864, 3. Big Blue "where a great many of our brave boys lie buried under those old oak trees." Henry Dillinberger, "The Big Raid. An Account of How the Rebels Were Driven Out of Missouri," *National Tribune*, May 15, 1890, 3. Loss "not so heavy on our side." Rebel lost "suffered terribly." "From Kansas City," St. Louis *Missouri Democrat*, October 24, 1864, 1; Jenkins, *Battle of Westport*, 80; Ragan, "Battle of Westport," 55–56; Childers, "Recitals and Reminiscences," *National Tribune*, January 31, 1907, 6.

42. Nettleton to his sister, December 19, 1864, in Crittenden, *Battle of Westport and National Memorial Park*, 29; Davis, *OR*, 41: (pt. 1), 551; Curtis, *OR*, 41: (pt. 1), 484.

43. Ragan, "Battle of Westport," 55–56; Price, *OR*, 41: (pt. 1), 635; Crittenden, *Battle of Westport and National Memorial Park*, 37; Jenkins, *Battle of Westport*, 79. Definitively ascertained that Price Saturday night at widow Marsha's about nine miles from West-

port. "Large quantities of beef and other stores were left by him at that place." Some forty wounded found there. Shelby wounded. "At first they talked of taking him into Mr. Wornell's house, but thought it a little too risky and took him further to the rear." "Price's Headquarters on Sunday," Kansas City *Journal of Commerce*, October 26, 1864, 2.

44. Crawford, *Kansas in the Sixties*, 148–49; Simpson, 11, 12.

45. Crawford, *Kansas in the Sixties*, 149–50; Bonebrake, "Recollections of the Second Day's Fight," 34–35.

46. Rosecrans to Curtis, October 22, 1864, *OR*, 41: (pt. 4), 185; Rosecrans to Pleasonton, October 22, 1864, *OR*, 41: (pt. 4), 184.

7. Brush Creek

1. *History of Saline County, Missouri, Carefully Written and Compiled from the Most Authentic Official and Private Sources* (St. Louis: Missouri Historical Co., 1881), 310; Hinton, *OR*, 149–50, 151; Jenkins, *Battle of Westport*, 81, 89–91; MacDonald, "Interview," 33.

2. Maj. Gen. Sterling Price, November 18, 1864, *OR*, 41: (pt. 1), 635; Ragan, "Battle of Westport," 56–57; Jenkins, *Battle of Westport*, 90–91; "Battle of Westport" [from Kansas City *Journal*], *Liberty Tribune*, October 28, 1864, 2. See also *Liberty Tribune*, October 23, 1864; "A Crushing Day for Price! Retreating South in Great Disorder! Price Abandons His Plunder! Narrow Escape of Mound City! Price Loses His Last Battery!" Leavenworth *Daily Times*, October 26, 1864, 2; Kirkman, *Battle of Westport: Missouri's Great Confederate Raid*, 103–109.

3. McKenny, *OR*, 41: (pt. 1), 538; Blunt, *OR*, 41: (pt. 1), 576; Blair, *OR*, 41: (pt. 1), 598; Jenkins, *Battle of Westport*, 81, 85, 89. Jenkins, *Battle of Westport*, 81, 85; Hinton, *OR*, 153, 163. Blunt, *OR*, 41: (pt. 1), 576, Blunt to Curtis, in Curtis, *OR*, 41: (pt. 1), 486–87.

4. Charlot, *OR*, 41: (pt. 1), 527; Hinton, *OR*, 152–54; Simpson, 12, 13.

5. Curtis, *OR*, 41: (pt. 1), 485; S. S. Curtis, *OR*, 41: (pt. 1), 533; Curtis, *OR*, 41: (pt. 1), 485; Weed, *OR*, 41: (pt. 1), 555; Meeker, November 22, 23, 1864, *OR*, 41: (pt. 1), 562, 564; Robinson, *OR*, 41: (pt. 1), 546; and, Jenkins, *Battle of Westport*, 95. Col. S. J. Crawford Hinton, *OR*, 149, 157–58; Simpson, 12. The Nineteenth KSM dismounted and slid to the right under Curtis's direction. Hinton, *OR*, 160.

6. Curtis, *OR*, 41: (pt. 1), 485; Fishback, *OR*, 41: (pt. 1), 621; Jennison, *OR*, 41: (pt. 1), 585; Jenkins, *Battle of Westport*, 89, 91, 95–96; Blunt, *OR*, 41: (pt. 1), 575–76; and, Jackman, *OR*, 41: (pt. 1), 676; Fuller to his father, October 24, 1864, in Greene, Fuller Papers, 41–42; Hinton, *OR*, 155, 155–56; Blair, *OR*, 41: (pt. 1), 598, and Blair to Curtis, in Curtis, *OR*, 41: (pt. 1), 490; Henry J. Vivian, "Personal Reminiscence of Major H. J. Vivian of the Last Day of the Battle of Westport," in Westport Historical Society, *Battle of Westport*, 36–37, excerpt from Westport, 1812–1912 (Kansas City: Franklin Hudson Publishing Company, 1912), 69–70, the Federals had access to the road to Wornall's.

7. Moonlight, *OR*, 41: (pt. 1), 594, Moonlight to Curtis, in Curtis, *OR*, 41: (pt. 1), 489; Blunt to Curtis, in Curtis, *OR*, 41: (pt. 1), 486; Moonlight, *OR*, 41: (pt. 1), 593–94; Jenkins, *Battle of Westport*, 81, 85–8x; Blair, *OR*, 41: (pt. 1), 598; Blair to Curtis, in Curtis, *OR*, 41: (pt. 1), 490; Blunt to Curtis, in Curtis, *OR*, 41: (pt. 1), 487; Blair, *OR*, 41: (pt. 1),

598–99; Lane, *OR*, 41: (pt. 1), 569; Hinton, *OR*, 160. Blair's brigade—the Fourth, Fifth, Sixth, Tenth, and Nineteenth KSM, with Dodge's and Minor's black artillerymen—extended Jennison's left. Jenkins, *Battle of Westport*, 81, 85; Hinton, *OR*, 152, 153, 154–58, 159, 163.

8. Ford, *OR*, 41: (pt. 1), 608–609, and Ford to Curtis, in Curtis, *OR*, 41: (pt. 1), 488; Hinton, *OR*, 158; Thompson, *OR*, 41: (pt. 1), 667; Vivian, "Personal Reminiscence," 36–37.

9. Shelby, *OR*, 41: (pt. 1), 658; Thompson, *OR*, 41: (pt. 1), 667; Nettleton and Ragan, "The Battle of Westport," 29, 56; Blunt, *OR*, 41: (pt. 1), 576, 578–79; Blunt to Curtis, in Curtis, *OR*, 41: (pt. 1), 487, 490; McKenny, *OR*, 41: (pt. 1), 538; "Battle of Westport," Kansas City *Journal of Commerce*, October 24, 1864, 2, reprinted as "Battle of Westport," St. Louis *Missouri Democrat*, October 31, 1864, 3; Jenkins, *Battle of Westport*, 91–92, 106; Hinton, *OR*, 158–59, 159–60.

10. Hunt, *OR*, 41: (pt. 1), 544; Jenkins, *Battle of Westport*, 140, 143–44; Hinton, *OR*, 162; Shelby, *OR*, 41: (pt. 1), 658. Federal officers found it to be an imitation Parrott, cast in a Confederate foundry in Texas.

11. MacDonald, "Interview," 51.

12. Price, *OR*, 41: (pt. 1), 635; Hinton, *OR*, 277; Jenkins, *Battle of Westport*, 92; Ragan, "Battle of Westport," 56.

13. Blunt, *OR*, 41: (pt. 1), 575–76; Jennison, *OR*, 41: (pt. 1), 585, and Jennison to Curtis, in Curtis, *OR*, 41: (pt. 1), 488; Dietzler, *OR*, 41: (pt. 1), 616, and Deitzler to Curtis, in Curtis, *OR*, 41: (pt. 1), 487; Jenkins, *Battle of Westport*, 92, 95, 103.

14. Dietzler, *OR*, 41: (pt. 1), 616–17, and Deitzler to Curtis, in Curtis, *OR*, 41: (pt. 1), 487; "Col. Jennison. Some Interesting Incidents of His Adventurous Career in the War," *National Tribune*, July 10, 1884, 8.

15. Jennison, *OR*, 41: (pt. 1), 585, and Jennison to Curtis in Curtis, *OR*, 41: (pt. 1), 488; Timbocker, "On Kansas Soil," *National Tribune*, November 21, 1895, 1; Hinton, *OR*, 156; Jenkins, *Battle of Westport*, 92.

16. Simpson, 12–13.

17. Maj. Gen. S. R. Curtis to Maj. Gen. Henry W. Halleck, October 23, 1864, *OR*, 41: (pt. 4), 208.

18. Grover, "Price Campaign of 1864," 175–76; "From Kansas City," St. Louis *Missouri Democrat*, October 24, 1864, 1.

19. Dietzler, *OR*, 41: (pt. 1), 616–17, and Deitzler to Curtis, in Curtis, *OR*, 41: (pt. 1), 487; Fishback to Curtis, in Curtis, *OR*, 41: (pt. 1), 489; Hinton, *OR*, 158.

20. Weed, *OR*, 41: (pt. 1), 555.

21. Curtis, *OR*, 41: (pt. 1), 486, 488; Hinton, *OR*, 158, 161; and, Jenkins, *Battle of Westport*, 105; Fred L. Lee, "George Thoman, Westport Farmer," in Westport Historical Society, *Battle of Westport*, 45–46. Curtis described Thoman as seventy-five, but the Thoman in the essay was forty-five.

22. Weed, *OR*, 41: (pt. 1), 555; Curtis, *OR*, 41: (pt. 1), 486. Curtis last saw Thoman "sunk down with delight and exhaustion when he saw the success of our guns," Jenkins, *Battle of Westport*, 103–105, 106. Curtis, *OR*, 41: (pt. 1), 485–86.

23. Blair, *OR*, 41: (pt. 1), 598, 599, and Blair to Curtis, in Curtis, *OR*, 41: (pt. 1), 490; Hinton, *OR*, 157, 163; Curtis, *OR*, 41: (pt. 1), 485–86; Hinton, *OR*, 157, 158–59.

24. Dietzler, *OR*, 41: (pt. 1), 617; Fishback, *OR*, 41: (pt. 1), 621, and Fishback to Curtis, in Curtis, *OR*, 41: (pt. 1), 489.

25. McKenny, *OR*, 41: (pt. 1), 538; Capt. Hezekiah F. Douglass of Leavenworth, Kansas, and 2nd Lt. Minor held commissions dated February 1865, and the latter died in March. A Patrick Minor. Enlisted as a Private (date unknown). "G" Co. US CT 2nd Infantry.

26. Ford to Curtis, in Curtis, *OR*, 41: (pt. 1), 488; Curtis to Brig. Gen. T. A. Davies, October 23, 1864, *OR*, 41: (pt. 4), 211; Jenkins, *Battle of Westport*, 89–90, 106; Hinton, *OR,* 154, 155, 160, 165.

27. Ford, *OR*, 41: (pt. 1), 608, 609, Ford to Curtis, in Curtis, *OR*, 41: (pt. 1), 487–88; Thompson, *OR*, 41: (pt. 1), 667; Blair, *OR*, 41: (pt. 1), 599; "Compendium of History," in *Soldier's Letter*, 1: (June 17, 1865), 1; Hinton, *OR*, 156, 160–61, 163; Jenkins, *Battle of Westport*, 109–10; Nettleton, in Crittenden, *The Battle of Westport*, 29; Hinton, *OR*, 157, 161, 164. Simpson house was at 53rd Street site of McLain's battery clash. Reports of McGhee's death may have come from reports of a dead Confederate officer around whom "the rebels had built a little pen of rails," "Battle of Westport," Kansas City *Journal of Commerce*, October 24, 1864, 2, reprinted as "Battle of Westport," St. Louis *Missouri Democrat*, October 31, 1864, 3; Gordon diary, WHMC-KC; "Compendium of History," in *Soldier's Letter*, 1: (June 24, 1865), 1. "At the southeast corner of Fifty-fourth Street and Wornall Road, where you see the clump of green cedars, stood the house of Ben Simpson, that was riddled with shot and shell by the batteries on the Country Club house site," MacDonald, "Interview," 33.

28. MacDonald, "Interview," 33, 34, 49, 50; "Battle of Westport," Kansas City *Journal of Commerce*, October 24, 1864, 2, reprinted as "Battle of Westport," St. Louis *Missouri Democrat*, October 31, 1864, 3.

29. Curtis, *OR*, 41: (pt. 1), 486; Hinton, *OR*, 158, 163; Jenkins, *Battle of Westport*, 105. Jenkins located the positions in terms of the Country Club grounds of the 1920s, which became Jacob L. Loose Park. In today's terms, the firing became steady from a line running from west of the park to the east across the UMKC campus almost to Troost Avenue. The three Confederate Parrott guns fired from the southeastern end of the park; McLain's Federal battery was at the northeastern end of the park at Wornall Road. Jenkins, *Battle of Westport*, 106, 109.

30. Hunt, *OR*, 41: (pt. 1), 544; Jenkins, *Battle of Westport*, 140, 143; Philips in Crittenden, *Battle of Westport and National Memorial Park*, 26.

31. Curtis, *OR*, 41: (pt. 1), 486; Weed, *OR*, 41: (pt. 1), 555; Bonebrake, "Recollections of the Second Day's Fight," 35.

32. Jennison, *OR*, 41: (pt. 1), 585–86, 586–87, and Jennison to Curtis, in Curtis, *OR*, 41: (pt. 1), 486, 488–89; Hinton, *OR*, 161–63, 165; and, Jenkins, *Battle of Westport*, 110.

33. Cloud, *OR*, 41: (pt. 1), 558; Curtis, *OR*, 41: (pt. 1), 485, 486; S. S. Curtis, *OR*, 41: (pt. 1), 533, quoted in Major Curtis to Curtis, in Curtis, *OR*, 41: (pt. 1), 490; Hinton, *OR*, 154.

34. Hinton, *OR,* 161–63, 163–64, 164–65; and, Jenkins, *Battle of Westport*, 110; "the remains of a rebel cannon, broken to pieces by a shot form one of our guns," the pieces lay among scattered bodies, saddles, blankets, horses, "Battle of Westport," Kansas City *Journal of Commerce*, October 24, 1864, 2, reprinted as "Battle of Westport," St. Louis *Missouri Democrat*, October 31, 1864, 3.

35. Simpson, 13, 15.

36. Curtis to Brig. Gen. T. A. Davies, October 23, 1864, *OR*, 41: (pt. 4), 211; Hinton, *OR*, 166–67.

37. Rosecrans, *OR*, 41: (pt. 4), 184–85; DuBois, *OR*, 41: (pt. 4), 181; Rosecrans to A. J. Smith, October 22, 1864, *OR*, 41: (pt. 4), 181; Rosecrans to Maj. Gen. Canby, October 22, 1864, *OR*, 41: (pt. 4), 178.

8. Byram's Ford Through Bloody Hill

1. Jenkins, *Battle of Westport*, 121. "Where the herd of cows is grazing, is Bloody Hill. That hill is the field of the Battle of the Blue," MacDonald, "Interview," 32.

2. MacDonald, "Interview," 38. "The severest and most important actions of the conflict were those conducted at the crossing of the Big Blue," Jenkins, *Battle of Westport*, 110, 115; Hinton, *Rebel Invasion*, 164; Jones, *OR*, 41: (pt. 1), 334; Winslow, *OR*, 41: (pt. 1), 329–30; Kirkman, *Battle of Westport: Missouri's Great Confederate Raid*, 111–16.

3. Pleasonton, *OR*, 41: (pt. 1), 337; Brown, *OR*, 41: (pt. 1), 348, 349; Brown, *OR*, 41: (pt. 1), 348–49; Jenkins, *Battle of Westport*, 86; Sanborn, *OR*, 41: (pt. 1), 389–90. "When Pleasonton in position, charge sounded and the whole line moved forward quickly, crossed [probably said "across"] Brush Creek and advanced on the rebels," Simpson, 13.

4. Winslow, *OR*, 41: (pt. 1), 328 or 330; Crittenden, *Battle of Westport and National Memorial Park*, 37, and MacDonald, "Interview," 39; Hinton, *Rebel Invasion*, 169; Montgomery, *OR*, 41: (pt. 1), 460. Jenkins accurately placed this confrontation at about 8 a.m., but he recounts it in that part of his book covering events near dawn. Jenkins, *Battle of Westport*, 86. He also describes (82, 96) "several vain attempts" to force a crossing and blames Brown for giving the Confederates time to deploy three of their remaining six-rifled Parrott guns.

5. Winslow, *OR*, 41: (pt. 1), 328 or 330; Clark, *OR*, 41: (pt. 1), 684; Davies, *OR*, 41: (pt. 1), 696; Jenkins, *Battle of Westport*, 81, 91.

6. "Compendium of History," in *Soldier's Letter*, 1: (June 17, 1865), 1; "Gen. Brown Under Arrest," Kansas City *Journal of Commerce*, October 26, 1864, 2; Brown, *OR*, 41: (pt. 1), 348. Afterward General Brown was court-martialled at St. Louis on charges brought by General Pleasonton, for Brown's conduct on this occasion, but he was acquitted. Hinton, *Rebel Invasion*, 169n.

7. Philips in Crittenden, *Battle of Westport and National Memorial Park*, 25, and in MacDonald, "Interview," 39–40. See also Jenkins, *Battle of Westport*, 87–88, and Clark, 44.

8. Hinton, *Rebel Invasion*, 168. For another view see McFerran, *OR*, 41: (pt. 1), 360. Philips suspected Brown had become timid, writing, "A short time previously he had been wounded in the left arm and the bone had been taken out so that the arm hung limp. That experience seemed to have sapped his nerve," but this had occurred almost two years previously, and he had shown little timidity in the interim. MacDonald, "Interview," 39. Jenkins, *Battle of Westport*, 86–87; Pleasonton, *OR*, 41: (pt. 1), 337. See also Winslow, *OR*, 41: (pt. 1), 330.

9. MacDonald, "Interview," 40; Jenkins, *Battle of Westport*, 88.

10. Col. John F. Philips, November 7, 1864, *OR*, 41: (pt. 1), 350; Pleasonton, *OR*, 41: (pt. 1), 337, 341; Hinton, *Rebel Invasion*, 169–70; Jenkins, *Battle of Westport*, 41, 89, 96, 101, 115, 116; Maj. George W. Kelly, November 3, 1864, *OR*, 41: (pt. 1), 363, 364; Lt. Col. Bazel F. Lazear, November 5, 1864, *OR*, 41: (pt. 1), 360, 361.

11. Jenkins, *Battle of Westport*, 41, 96, 101, 121, 122, 127, and Philips diary, 25; Crittenden, *Battle of Westport and National Memorial Park*, 41, 43; *OR*, 7: 31Philips, *OR*, 41: (pt. 1), 350–51; Lazear, *OR*, 41: (pt. 1), 360, 361; Hinton, *Rebel Invasion*, 170, 171. Philips did not return to the battle site until 1912 when the old man retraced his steps with A. B. McDonald. MacDonald, "Interview," 26.

12. "Majors Mullins and Neill, of the First, ever fought with distinguished heroism and made for themselves a name not soon to be forgotten,"J. F. Philips. "Captain Missemer of the Fourth Cavalry Missouri State Militia who commanded his regiment at the battle of the Osage, is commended for his bravery and judgment,"Philips, *OR*, 41: (pt. 1), 353. Hinton, *Rebel Invasion*, 170–72.

13. Pleasonton, *OR*, 41: (pt. 1), 341; Jenkins, *Battle of Westport*, 116, 128; MacDonald, "Interview," 31–32.

14. Philips, *OR*, 41: (pt. 1), 351; Jenkins, *Battle of Westport*, 121–22; Crittenden, *Battle of Westport and National Memorial Park*, 42. Jenkins muddled this account of what happened with Brown.

15. Jenkins, *Battle of Westport*, 127; Crittenden, *Battle of Westport and National Memorial Park*, 43, and Philips diary, 26. Second Lt. Columbus Dale, Fourth MSM Cavalry, died of wounds suffered at Big Blue, October 24. OAR, VII, 19. Of Crittenden, Philips reports: "At the battle of the Osage he dashed into the midst of a party of twelve rebels, killed 4 and took the other 8 prisoners," Philips, *OR*, 41: (pt. 1), 353.

16. Winslow, *OR*, 41: (pt. 1), 328, 330; Townsend, "Third Iowa Cavalry," 50.

17. Jenkins, *Battle of Westport*, 121, 122, 127; Diary in Crittenden, *Battle of Westport and National Memorial Park*, 26; Hinton, *Rebel Invasion*, 171; Winslow, *OR*, 41: (pt. 1), 328, 330; Jenkins, *Battle of Westport*, 122, 127; Hinton, *Rebel Invasion*, 170–72; 1st Lt. Clifford Thomson, on behalf of Pleasonton, to Rosecrans, *OR*, 41: (pt. 4), 204.

18. Sanborn, *OR*, 41: (pt. 1), 389–90; Gravely, *OR*, 41: (pt. 1), 412–13; Phelps, *OR*, 41: (pt. 1), 403–04; Hinton, *Rebel Invasion*, 171.

19. Hinton, *Rebel Invasion*, 171, 172–73; Jones, *OR*, 41: (pt. 1), 334; Lt. Col. Frederick W. Benteen, *OR*, 41: (pt. 1), 330, 33; Jenkins, *Battle of Westport*, 122, 127–128.

20. "From Kansas City," St. Louis *Missouri Democrat*, October 24, 1864, 1; "A Fighting Family,"Milwaukee *Sunday Telegraphy, Corning (NY) Journal*, September 8, 1881, 1.

21. Philips diary, 26; Jenkins, *Battle of Westport*, 128.

22. Jenkins, *Battle of Westport*, 96, 121, 128; Price, *OR*, 41: (pt. 1), 635; Montgomery, *OR*, 41: (pt. 1), 460; Crittenden, *Battle of Westport and National Memorial Park*, 42, 43; Hinton, *Rebel Invasion*, 170, 172. Hardest hit, Philips, diary, 26; *OR*, 7: 18, 19, 27. Crittenden led the second of "two gallant charges" but it, too, failed.

23. Jenkins, *Battle of Westport*, 115; Crittenden, *Battle of Westport and National Memorial Park*, 32; MacDonald, "Interview," 32.

24. Lt. Col. Frederick W. Benteen, *OR*, 41: (pt. 1), 331; Sanborn, *OR*, 41: (pt. 1), 389–90.

25. Philips, *OR*, 41: (pt. 1), 351; Hinton, *Rebel Invasion*, 172–73; Crittenden, *Battle of Westport and National Memorial Park*, 33–34.

26. Clark, *OR*, 41: (pt. 1), 684. This is now Swope Parkway, up to the grove of trees at Sixty-third and Walnut Streets, once the site of the Hinkle farm, itself east and a little south of the Wornall home at Sixty-first Street Terrace and Wornall Road. Mac-Donald, "Interview," 32. "On the 23d had 2 men wounded, and the enemy succeeded in capturing Lieutenant-Colonel Young and Captain Davidson, of my regiment, both brave, gallant officers," Lawther, *OR*, 41: (pt. 1), 699. Kelly thought they had driven the Confederates from the hill around 10 a.m., though it actually was closer to 11 a.m. Maj. George W. Kelly, November 3, 1864, *OR*, 41: (pt. 1), 363; Hinton, *Rebel Invasion*, 173. This Confederate rear guard formed on the north—south line of present-day Elm-wood Avenue; Jenkins, *Battle of Westport*, 137.

27. Hinton, *Rebel Invasion*, 163.

28. Fishback, *OR*, 41: (pt. 1), 621, quoted in Curtis, *OR*, 41: (pt. 1), 489; Curtis, *OR*, 41: (pt. 1), 486; Charlot, *OR*, 41: (pt. 1), 526; Jenkins, *Battle of Westport*, 137–38.

29. Curtis, *OR*, 41: (pt. 4), 208.

30. First Lt. Clifford Thomson, on behalf of Pleasonton, to Rosecrans, *OR*, 41: (pt. 4), 204.

31. McNeil, *OR*, 41: (pt. 1), 372; Eppstein, *OR*, 41: (pt. 1), 383; Hinton, *Rebel Invasion*, 177–78; Jenkins, *Battle of Westport*, 101; October 23, 1864, entry in Lymandiary, 4, Misc. Mans. 17: #490 WHMC; Pleasonton, *OR*, 41: (pt. 1), 337, 341; McNeil, *OR*, 41: (pt. 1), 372; McNeil, *OR*, 41: (pt. 1), 372; Crittenden, *Battle of Westport and National Memorial Park*, 39; Jenkins, *Battle of Westport*, 79, 86; Hinton, *Rebel Invasion*, 168; 115–16, 117. Kansas accounts to run an hour behind those with clocks set in Missouri. McNeil cited Lieut. E. O. Manning, Eighty-first U.S. Colored Troops, for his assiduous attention to duty, and his conduct in the face of the enemy. McNeil, November 23, 1864, *OR*, 41: (pt. 1), 373.

32. Price, *OR*, 41: (pt. 1), 636; Hinton, *Rebel Invasion*, 177.

33. Clark, *OR*, 41: (pt. 1), 684; Marmaduke quoted in Pleasonton, *OR*, 41: (pt. 1), 337; Jenkins, *Battle of Westport*, 101–2; on McNeil's fears, MacDonald, "Interview," 39.

34. McNeil, *OR*, 41: (pt. 1), 372; Burbridge, *OR*, 41: (pt. 1), 694.

35. Hinton, *Rebel Invasion*, 177–78.

36. Townsend, "Third Iowa Cavalry," 50–51; Maj. Gen. Rosecrans to Maj. Gen. Canby, October 24, 1864, *OR*, 41: (pt. 4), 220; Hinton, *Rebel Invasion*, 133.

37. Price, *OR*, 41: (pt. 1), 635–36; Jenkins, *Battle of Westport*, 147.

38. "From Kansas City," St. Louis *Missouri Democrat*, October 24, 1864, 1; Grover, "Price Campaign of 1864," 175.

9. Across the Prairie to Indian Creek

1. Shelby, *OR*, 41: (pt. 1), 658; October 23, 1864, entry in Baker diary; W. M. Price, aide-de-camp to Marmaduke, to Lt. Col. Maclean, October 23, 1864, *OR*, 41: (pt. 4), 1012; Thompson, *OR*, 41: (pt. 1), 667; MacDonald, "Interview," 33. See also Kirkman, *Battle of Westport: Missouri's Great Confederate Raid*, 116–17.

2. Edwards, *Shelby and His Men; or, the War in the West* (Cincinnati: Miami Printing, 1867); Ragan, "Battle of Westport," 57.

3. Thompson, *OR*, 41: (pt. 1), 667; MacDonald, "Interview," 33.

4. Vivian, "Personal Reminiscence," 37. This essay says that they waited until 4:30, which would have been impossible, and almost surely reflects an error in transcribing or typesetting what Vivian had written by hand to describe events that apparently occurred at about 11:30 at the latest.

5. McKenny, *OR*, 41: (pt. 1), 538; Simpson, 14, 15, mentions telling the boy's father later in the day; Childers, "Recitals and Reminiscences," *National Tribune*, January 31, 1907, 6; Robinson, *OR*, 41: (pt. 1), 546; Blunt, *OR*, 41: (pt. 1), 576; MacDonald, "Interview," 50.

6. Deitzler to Curtis, in Curtis, *OR,* 41: (pt. 1), 487; Blunt, *OR,* 41: (pt. 1), 576; Fishback, *OR*, 41: (pt. 1), 621, quoted in Curtis, *OR,* 41: (pt. 1), 489; Hinton, *Rebel Invasion*, 166, 174; Nettleton in Crittenden, *The Battle of Westport*, 29; Grover, "Price Campaign of 1864," 176.

7. Sanborn, *OR*, 41: (pt. 1), 389–90; Pleasonton, *OR*, 41: (pt. 1), 337; Rosecrans, *OR*, 41: (pt. 1), 313; McMahan, *OR*, 41: (pt. 1), 407; Hinton, *Rebel Invasion*, 173–74; Philips, *OR*, 41: (pt. 1), 351; McMahan, *OR*, 41: (pt. 1), 407; Philips, in Crittenden, *Battle of Westport and National Memorial Park*, 25, 26.

8. Benteen, *OR*, 41: (pt. 1), 331; Hinton, *Rebel Invasion*, 173–75.

9. Jackman, *OR*, 41: (pt. 1), 676, 678. Major Edwards wrote Shelby's report, which began with Jackman's dismounting "with almost the forlorn determination of Cortez, who burnt his ships, resolved to conquer or die." One might expect the next line to read that Jackman's men shot their horses or took some comparable action, Edwards adds, Shelby, *OR*, 41: (pt. 1), 658, 659.

10. Jackman, *OR*, 41: (pt. 1), 676; Shelby, *OR*, 41: (pt. 1), 658, 659; Deitzler to Curtis, in Curtis, *OR*, 41: (pt. 1), 487; "The Battle-Field and the Hospital," Leavenworth *Daily Times*, October 26, 1864, 2.

11. Montgomery, *OR*, 41: (pt. 1), 460; Philips, in Crittenden, *Battle of Westport and National Memorial Park*, 26; Hinton, *Rebel Invasion*, 166, 174; Price, *OR*, 41: (pt. 1), 636; Philips, *OR*, 41: (pt. 1), 351; Sanborn, *OR*, 41: (pt. 1), 389–90; McMahan, *OR*, 41: (pt. 1), 407; Fuller to his father, October 24, 1864, in Greene, Fuller Papers, 42; Hinton, *Rebel Invasion*, 166–67.

12. Gravely, *OR*, 41: (pt. 1), 413.

13. Shelby, *OR*, 41: (pt. 1), 659.

14. Hicks, "Battle Cast Pall over Westport," 29; Hinton, *Rebel Invasion*, 133; Jenkins, *Battle of Westport*, 139.

15. Shelby, *OR*, 41: (pt. 1), 659; McKenny, *OR*, 41: (pt. 1), 538; Curtis, *OR*, 41: (pt. 1), 486; Charlot, *OR*, 41: (pt. 1), 526–27; Pleasonton, *OR*, 41: (pt. 1), 337; Rosecrans, *OR*, 41: (pt. 1), 313; Maj. Gen. S. R. Curtis to Maj. Gen. Rosecrans, October 23, 1864, *OR*, 41: (pt. 4), 208; Price, *OR*, 41: (pt. 1), 636; Thompson, *OR*, 41: (pt. 1), 667; Hinton, *Rebel Invasion*, 166; Nettleton to his sister, December 19, 1864, in Crittenden, *Battle of Westport and National Memorial Park*, 29. Major Weed described this as "three miles south of the timber," Weed, *OR*, 41: (pt. 1) 555. Shelby, *OR*, 41: (pt. 1), 659.

16. Shelby, *OR*, 41: (pt. 1), 659; Blunt, *OR*, 41: (pt. 1), 576.

17. Thompson, *OR*, 41: (pt. 1), 667–68; Shelby, *OR*, 41: (pt. 1), 659; Jenkins, *Battle of Westport*, 147. Marmaduke's men fell back to Sixty-third and Walnut Streets in the front of Hinkle's grove; Shelby's position had been at Sixty-third and the Paseo.

18. Shelby, *OR*, 41: (pt. 1), 659; Crittenden, *Battle of Westport and National Memorial Park*, 33–34; Price, *OR*, 41: (pt. 1), 636; Hinton, *Rebel Invasion*, 166. Final stand at site of Forest Hill Cemetery, 6900 Troost. Then had a stone wall running west to the state line. Pleasonton allowed his cavalry to pursue the latter, recalling them at about 1 pm.[?]

19. Simpson, 14, 15. This almost certainly was the John Majors farm, about four miles southeast of Westport. Jenkins describes an east-west Confederate line roughly along the present-day Sixty-third Street, and places this "at almost exactly 1 o'clock," in *Battle of Westport*, 139–40.

20. Grover, "Price Campaign of 1864," 176; Philips, *OR*, 41: (pt. 1), 351; Jones, *OR*, 41: (pt. 1), 334–35. Jenkins also seems to have muddled what had happened with Winslow. Jenkins, *Battle of Westport*, 121–22.

21. Deitzler, *OR*, 41: (pt. 1), 617; Deitzler to Curtis, in Curtis, *OR*, 41: (pt. 1), 487; Lane, *OR*, 41: (pt. 1), 569; Blair, *OR*, 41: (pt. 1), 599; Hinton, *Rebel Invasion*, 165–66, 298.

22. Charlot, *OR*, 41: (pt. 1), 526–27; Pleasonton to Rosecrans, *OR*, 41: (pt. 4), 203–204; Hinton, *Rebel Invasion*, 173–75. Kansas City spread south over most of these fields, and later accounts of the battle located these positions with modern street maps. After Thompson's charge, the stone wall to which some of them withdrew is said to have been near the Confederate memorial in Forest Hill Cemetery.

23. Grover, "Price Campaign of 1864," 176; Deitzler to Curtis, in Curtis, *OR*, 41: (pt. 1), 487; Weed, *OR*, 41: (pt. 1), 555; Phelps, *OR*, 41: (pt. 1), 404; Blair to Curtis, in Curtis, *OR*, 41: (pt. 1), 490. See also "'Old Pap' on the Skeddadle! The Kansas Militia Will Fight," Kansas *Daily Tribune*, October 25, 1864, 2.

24. Curtis, *OR*, 41: (pt. 4), 208; Major Curtis to Curtis, in Curtis, *OR*, 41: (pt. 1), 490–91; Fishback, *OR*, 41: (pt. 1), 621. See, for example, "The Battle of Sunday," Leavenworth *Daily Times*, October 26, 1864, 2; "Price Repulsed near Kansas City and Again at Westport." Brig. Gen. James Craig to Col. Shanklin, October 24, 1864, *OR*, 41: (pt. 4), 228.

25. Edwards, *Shelby and His Men*; Ragan, "Battle of Westport," 60. Ragan read this paper "at a meeting of Stonewall Jackson Chapter U.C.V., Kansas City, Mo., on the anniversary of the Battle of Westport, October 23, 1910," doing so as a "lieutenant-colonel and assistant surgeon" General Missouri Division, U.C.V. [1–9].

26. Blunt, *OR*, 41: (pt. 1), 576; "Compendium of History," in *Soldier's Letter*, 1: (June 17, 1865), 1.

27. Jennison, *OR*, 41: (pt. 1), 587; McKenny, *OR*, 41: (pt. 1), 538; Ford to Curtis, in Curtis, *OR*, 41: (pt. 1), 488; Ford, *OR*, 41: (pt. 1), 609; Pleasonton, *OR*, 41: (pt. 1), 337; Rosecrans, *OR*, 41: (pt. 1), 313; "Compendium of History," in *Soldier's Letter*, 1: (June 17, 1865), 1; Price, *OR*, 41: (pt. 1), 636; Hinton, *Rebel Invasion*, 175.

28. "Our Report," Leavenworth *Daily Times*, October 26, 1864, 2; Fuller to his father, October 24, 1864, in Greene, Fuller Papers, 42; Curtis, *OR*, 41: (pt. 1), 491; "Battle of Westport," Kansas City *Journal of Commerce*, October 24, 1864, 2, reprinted as "Battle of Westport," St. Louis *Missouri Democrat*, October 31, 1864, 3; carved by owner John Murdock, Company B, 15th Arkansas., "A Relic," Kansas City *Journal of Commerce*, October 26, 1864, 2. Not in Civil War database.

29. Pleasonton to Rosecrans, *OR*, 41: (pt. 4), 205–206. See also McMahan, *OR*, 41: (pt. 1), 407.

30. Curtis, *OR*, 41: (pt. 4), 208; Fuller to his father, October 24, 1864, in Greene, Fuller Papers, 43–44; "From Kansas City," St. Louis *Missouri Democrat*, October 24, 1864, 1.

31. Jackman, *OR*, 41: (pt. 1), 676. Also note Maurice Moulson Langhorne in *A Memorial and Biographical Record of Kansas City and Jackson County, Mo.* (Chicago: Lewis, 1896), 259–60. The fairly common estimate of 1,000 also appears in Mark A. Plummer, "Missouri and Kansas and the Capture of General Marmaduke," *MHR*, 59: (October 1964), 95–96.

32. Hicks, "Battle Cast Pall over Westport," 30.

33. "Battle of Westport," Kansas City *Journal of Commerce*, October 24, 1864, 2, reprinted as "Battle of Westport," St. Louis *Missouri Democrat*, October 31, 1864, 3.

34. Fuller to his father, October 24, 1864, in Greene, Fuller Papers, 43–44.

35. "The Prisoners," Kansas City *Journal of Commerce*, October 26, 1864, 2; "The Battle-Field and the Hospital," Leavenworth *Daily Times*, October 26, 1864, 2.

36. "Battle of Westport," Kansas City *Journal of Commerce*, October 24, 1864, 2, reprinted as "Battle of Westport," St. Louis *Missouri Democrat*, October 31, 1864, 3, quoted in Hinton, *Rebel Invasion*, 180; "The Prisoners," Kansas City *Journal of Commerce*, October 26, 1864, 2.

37. "List of Wounded Men Received at Kansas City General Hospital Since October 20th [*sic*] 1864," Kansas City *Journal of Commerce*, October 28, 1864, 2; "The Battle-Field and the Hospital," Leavenworth *Daily Times*, October 26, 1864, 2..

38. "The Battle-Field and the Hospital," Leavenworth *Daily Times*, October 26, 1864, 2; MacDonald, "Interview," 51; mother of G. Van Millett, artist; "Battle-Field and the Hospital," 2; Hicks, "Battle Cast Pall over Westport," 30.

39. Rosecrans, *OR*, 41: (pt. 4), 181; Rosecrans to Maj. Gen. Canby, October 22, 1864, *OR*, 41: (pt. 4), 178; Rosecrans to Pleasonton, October 23, 1864, *OR*, 41: (pt. 4), 203; Major Gen. A. J. Smith to Rosecrans, October 23, 1864, *OR*, 41: (pt. 4), 202; Rosecrans to Major Gen. A. J. Smith, October 23, 1864, *OR*, 41: (pt. 4), 202.

40. Rosecrans to Pleasonton, October 23, 1864, *OR*, 41: (pt. 4), 205; Smith to Rosecrans, *OR*, 41: (pt. 4), 202; Rosecrans to Smith, October 23, 1864, *OR*, 41: (pt. 4), 203; Rosecrans to A. J. Smith, October 25, 1864, *OR*, 41: (pt. 4), 237.

41. McNeil, *OR*, 41: (pt. 1), 372; S. S. Curtis, *OR*, 41: (pt. 1), 533, quoted in Major Curtis to Curtis, in Curtis, *OR*, 41: (pt. 1), 490; Price, *OR*, 41: (pt. 1), 635; Hinton, *Rebel Invasion*, 178. See also Davies, *OR*, 41: (pt. 1), 696.

42. Brig. Gen. McNeil to Rosecrans, October 24, 1864, *OR*, 41: (pt. 4), 224–25.

43. Maj. Gen. Rosecrans to Maj. Gen. S. R. Curtis, October 23, 1864, *OR*, 41: (pt. 4), 209; Rosecrans to Pleasonton, October 23, 1864, *OR*, 41: (pt. 4), 205; Rosecrans, *OR*, 41: (pt. 1), 313; Rosecrans to Pleasonton, October 23, 1864, *OR*, 41: (pt. 4), 205–206.

44. Pleasonton to Rosecrans, October 23, 1864, *OR*, 41: (pt. 4), 203–04; Rosecrans, *OR*, 41: (pt. 1), 313; Maj. Frank S. Bond to Mr. Crain, telegraph operator, October 23, 1864, *OR*, 41: (pt. 4), 201.

45. Pleasonton to Rosecrans, *OR*, 41: (pt. 4), 203–204.

46. Pleasonton to Rosecrans, *OR*, 41: (pt. 4), 205.

47. Maj. Gen. Rosecrans to Maj. Gen. S. R. Curtis, October 23, 1864, *OR*, 41: (pt. 4), 209.

48. Hinton, *Rebel Invasion*, 165–66.

10. FLIGHT AND PURSUIT

1. Hinton, *Rebel Invasion*, 240.

2. Little Santa Fe, or New Santa Fe, was located at what is now 122nd and State Line Road in Leawood, Kansas, according to the U.S. Geological Survey.

3. Curtis, *OR*, 41: (pt. 1), 491; Deitzler, *OR*, 41: (pt. 1), 617; MacDonald, "Interview," 50.

4. Hinton, *Rebel Invasion*, 179–80. A little cemetery at Fifty-first and Troost Avenue had likely burials with others on the W. B. Clark farm south of Forest Hill Cemetery, to which many Confederate remains would later be removed and a monument placed over them by the Daughters of the Confederacy. MacDonald, "Interview," 50

5. Davis, *OR*, 41: (pt. 1), 551–52; Pomeroy, *OR*, 41: (pt. 1), 571; Hinton, *Rebel Invasion*, 181–82; MacDonald, "Interview," 50, 51.

6. Hinton, *Rebel Invasion*, 180–81: "They seem to belong to a different race from ours, and most certainly an inferior one."

7. Reader, Autobiography, 3:160, 167, 184, 189, 254, 264.

8. Thompson, *OR*, 41: (pt. 1), 668. The Coloradoans credited Price with great skill in managing the retreat. "Compendium of History," in *Soldier's Letter*, 1: (June 24, 1865), 1. For those involved, these rearguard skirmishes could seem to be a "desperate engagement," from October 24, 1864, entry in Baker diary.

9. Pleasonton, *OR*, 41: (pt. 1), 341; Maj. R. H. Hunt to Capt. Willans, October 24, 1864, *OR*, 41: (pt. 4), 230; Curtis, *OR*, 41: (pt. 1), 491; McKenny, *OR*, 41: (pt. 1), 538.

10. Lane, *OR*, 41: (pt. 1), 569; Curtis, *OR*, 41: (pt. 1), 486; Pleasonton, *OR*, 41: (pt. 1), 337; Weed, *OR*, 41: (pt. 1), 555–56; Deitzler to Curtis, in Curtis, *OR*, 41: (pt. 1), 487; Curtis, *OR*, 41: (pt. 1), 491; Curtis, *OR*, 41: (pt. 1), 522; Deitzler, *OR*, 41: (pt. 1), 617; Hinton, *Rebel Invasion*, 175–76.

11. Curtis, *OR*, 41: (pt. 1), 492. Based ultimately on department sources, Hinton thought the force pursuing Price to be "about 10, 000 men, with three field batteries, and two of mountain howitzers," and Rosecrans and A. J. Smith seemed to be near Independence. See *Rebel Invasion*, 184.

12. Moonlight, *OR*, 41: (pt. 1), 594; Benteen, *OR*, 41: (pt. 1), 331; Hinton, *Rebel Invasion*, 178–79. Blunt's Second Brigade bivouacked for the night six miles south of the main body at Little Santa Fe. Blunt, *OR*, 41: (pt. 1), 576.

13. Curtis, *OR*, 41: (pt. 1), 489; McKenny, *OR*, 41: (pt. 1), 538; Ford, *OR*, 41: (pt. 1), 609; "Col. Jennison. Some Interesting Incidents of His Adventurous Career in the War," *National Tribune*, July 10, 1884, 8; Thompson, *OR*, 41: (pt. 1), 668; Ford, *OR*, 41: (pt. 1), 609; Jennison, *OR*, 41: (pt. 1), 587.

14. Weed, *OR*, 41: (pt. 1), 557; Blair, *OR*, 41: (pt. 1), 599. See also Cloud, *OR*, 41: (pt. 1), 558; Hunt, *OR*, 41: (pt. 1), 544; Hinton, *Rebel Invasion*, 176–77.

15. S. S. Curtis, *OR*, 41: (pt. 1), 534; Sanborn, *OR*, 41: (pt. 1), 390; Phelps, *OR*, 41: (pt. 1), 404. See also McNeil, *OR*, 41: (pt. 1), 372; Jones, *OR*, 41: (pt. 1), 335; Benteen, *OR*, 41: (pt. 1), 331; Mitchell, *OR*, 41: (pt. 1), 411; Philipsin Crittenden, *Battle of Westport and National Memorial Park*, 26.

16. Rosecrans, *OR*, 41: (pt. 1), 313. As early as Sunday, Rosecrans acknowledged that the only possible use of Smith's infantry at this point would be "in case of possible reverse to us or re-enforcements which were constantly reported on their way to meet the enemy."

17. Childers, "Recitals and Reminiscences," *National Tribune*, January 31, 1907, 6.

18. Conversation reported by Robinson, *OR*, 41: (pt. 1), 547–48.

19. As a final shot, Rosecrans noted that Robinson had become "not as much of a Fremont man as when you were on his staff." Robinson agreed and left

20. Hinton, *Rebel Invasion*, 183. See also Clark, *OR*, 41: (pt. 1), 684; Thompson, *OR*, 41: (pt. 1), 668. Continued to retreat that night until 1 o'clock. See also October 24. Dan Smith, "The Battle of Mine Creek and Events Leading to that Battle," 5–6, in Smith, Dan, Misc. Mans. KSHS.

21. Meeker, *OR*, 41: (pt. 1), 563 or 564; Curtis, *OR*, 41: (pt. 1), 493; Hinton, *Rebel Invasion*, 189–90.

22. Curtis, *OR*, 41: (pt. 1), 492; Curtis to Col. J. A. Keeler (Olathe), Col. S. A. Drake (Paola), Capt M. H. Insley (Fort Scott), October 23, 1864, *OR*, 41: (pt. 4), 210; Maj. Gen. S. R. Curtis to Maj. Gen. Rosecrans, October 24, 1864, *OR*, 41: (pt. 4), 229; Hopkins, *OR*, 41: (pt. 1), 560; Charlot, *OR*, 41: (pt. 1), 527; Jones, *OR*, 41: (pt. 1), 335; Hinton, *Rebel Invasion*, 184; Rosecrans, *OR*, 41: (pt. 1), 313; Reader, Autobiography, 269.

23. Weed, *OR*, 41: (pt. 1), 555; Hunt, *OR*, 41: (pt. 1), 544. See also Eppstein, *OR*, 41: (pt. 1), 383; Houston, *OR*, 41: (pt. 1), 381; Philips in Crittenden, *Battle of Westport and National Memorial Park*, 26. Philips reported his men reached Little Santa Fe at daylight.

24. Hinton, *Rebel Invasion*, 184–85; Ford, *OR*, 41: (pt. 1), 609. Mound City. Smith, "Battle of Mine Creek," 11.

25. Lause, "Race and Radicalism in the Union Army," 73–74, 80, 81–82, 88–89.

26. Hinton, *Rebel Invasion*, 185, 186–87; Reader, Autobiography, 3:273. Reader described the season as "dry and most of the small streams were dried up, causing us great suffering from thirst," particularly with the day "rather warm and the roads dusty" (3:254).

27. Maj. Gen. S. R. Curtis to Maj. Gen. Halleck, October 24, 1864, *OR*, 41: (pt. 4), 229; Hinton, *Rebel Invasion*, 187.

28. Hinton, *Rebel Invasion*, 186, 190; McKenny, *OR*, 41: (pt. 1), 538; Blunt, *OR*, 41: (pt. 1), 576; J. A. Keeler to Curtis, October 23, 1864, *OR*, 41: (pt. 4), 210; Col. S. A. Drake (Paola) to Curtis, October 23, 1864, *OR*, 41: (pt. 4), 210.

29. Moonlight, *OR*, 41: (pt. 1), 594; Blunt, *OR*, 41: (pt. 1), 579. Coldwater Grove is described as fifteen miles from Santa Fe, but Wiki article on "Coldwater Grove's Post" says it was more than thirty miles away, giving as its source Clarence W. Long, *The Prelude: A History of the Border* (N.p.: Clarence W. Long, 1990), 95–96; William C. Pollard Jr., "Forts and Military Posts in Kansas: 1854–1865" (Ph.D. diss., Faith Baptist College

and Seminary, 1997), 28, copy in Kansas State Historical Society, Topeka. This longer distance also jibes with the location of the present Coldwater Road, which is nearly fifteen miles east of Paola, Kansas (Coldwater Road off 319th and 327th Streets below Louisburg, Kansas). For an earlier action at the post, see September 1863, 22. Hinton reported being with Lieutenant Colonel Wheeler of the Thirteenth and a Captain Young of the Fifth Kansas as they were approaching the first house over the line, where they "rendered the bereaved woman what assistance and consolation they could."

30. Reader, Autobiography, 3:197, 199, 233–34, 282.

31. Hinton, *Rebel Invasion*, 183, 185–86. "Moonlight's command, that took the right-hand road at Little Santa Fe, which goes to Mound City," McKenny, *OR*, 41: (pt. 1), 538. The US Geographical Survey locates West Point near the present Drexel, Missouri. Note: "West Point" may also be near "West Line" in Cass County, Missouri.

32. Blunt, *OR*, 41: (pt. 1), 576, 579; See also Ford, *OR*, 41: (pt. 1), 609; Blair, *OR*, 41: (pt. 1), 599; Moonlight, *OR*, 41: (pt. 1), 594; Simpson, 14, 15–16. Other sources indicate that the brigade had already been detached for "the protection of Olathe, Paola, Mound City, and Fort Scott, on the Kansas border," Lane, *OR*, 41: (pt. 1), 569.

33. Curtis, *OR*, 41: (pt. 1), 493; Hinton, *Rebel Invasion*, 188, 194.

34. Blunt, *OR*, 41: (pt. 1), 576; Hinton, *Rebel Invasion*, 188; Trading Post. Smith, "Battle of Mine Creek," 6–8.

35. Curtis, *OR*, 41: (pt. 1), 493, 495; Maj. Samuel S. Curtis, Second Colorado Cavalry, aide-de-camp, *OR*, 41: (pt. 1), 534; McKenny, *OR*, 41: (pt. 1), 538; Rosecrans, *OR*, 41: (pt. 1), 313; Philips diary, 26; Pleasonton, *OR*, 41: (pt. 1), 337; Pleasonton, *OR*, 41: (pt. 1), 341; Lane, *OR*, 41: (pt. 1), 569.

36. "Compendium of History," in *Soldier's Letter*, 1: (October 7, 1865), 1; Marais des Cygnes; Smith, "Battle of Mine Creek," 10–11.

37. Mitchell, *OR*, 41: (pt. 1), 411; McMahan, *OR*, 41: (pt. 1), 407; Maj. William Plumb, Sixth Missouri State Militia Cavalry, November 12, 1864, *OR*, 41: (pt. 1), 409; Hinton, *Rebel Invasion*, 188–89; Smith, "Battle of Mine Creek," 8–10. About fifty miles to Trading Post. October 24, 1864, entry in Lyman diary, 4. Misc. Mans. 17: #490 WHMC; Simpson, 14.

38. Curtis, *OR*, 41: (pt. 1), 493.

39. Pleasonton, *OR*, 41: (pt. 1), 337; Pleasonton, *OR*, 41: (pt. 1), 341; Hinton, *Rebel Invasion*, 189, 193–94, 197, 198, 348; Curtis, *OR*, 41: (pt. 1), 493–94; Sanborn, *OR*, 41: (pt. 1), 390–91; Gravely, *OR*, 41: (pt. 1), 413; Philips, *OR*, 41: (pt. 1), 351–52; "Compendium of History," in *Soldier's Letter*, 1: (July 8, 1865), 1; Ford, *OR*, 41: (pt. 1), 609. Nettleton wrote, "We saw no more of them (though we marched night and day) till we got to them at midnight on the Marais des Cygnes," Nettleton to his sister, December 19, 1864, in Crittenden, *Battle of Westport and National Memorial Park*, 29.

40. Hinton, *Rebel Invasion*, 190–91.

41. Hinton, *Rebel Invasion*, 191–93, 223. The Kansas cavalry units present had a James E. Greer in the Eleventh and a Samuel W. Greer in the Fifteenth. Samuel Tucker, "Price Raid through Linn County, Kansas, October 24, 25, 1864" (1958).

42. Anderson to Phillips, July 19, 1864, *OR*, 41 (pt 2): 265; Britton, UIB, 432, 430; Daniel H. Ross to Ross, July 7, 1864, PCJR, 2: 597. See also Phillips to Herron, Janu-

ary 16, 1865, *OR*, 48 (pt 1): 542–43; Cunningham, *General Stand Watie's Confederate Indians*, 183..

43. Hinton, *Rebel Invasion*, 243–44, 240–41.

44. Hinton, *Rebel Invasion*, 241–43; Brig. Gen. Jno. B. Scott, KSM, to Deitzler, October 23, 1864, *OR*, 41: (pt. 4), 210. This was likely the Major Piercy with Stand Watie and others skirmishing near Enterprise, Missouri, on August 18, 1864, *Branded as Rebels*, 347. 45. Maj. Milton Burch to Col. J. D. Brutsche, October 10, 1864, *OR*, 41: (pt. 3), 760; Lt. Col. J. D. Brutsche to Major Burch, October 23, 1864, *OR*, 41: (pt. 4), 207; Col. Milton Burch to Col. J. D. Brutsche, October 24, 1864, *OR*, 41: (pt. 4), 226.

46. Hinton, *Rebel Invasion*, 243.

47. Ibid., 238, 242–45; Curtis, *OR*, 41: (pt. 1), 522.

48. Price, *OR*, 41: (pt. 1), 636; Greene, *OR*, 41: (pt. 1), 691.

11. JUDGMENT DAY

1. Hinton, *Rebel Invasion*, 210, 211–12, quotation, 209; Benteen, *OR*, 41: (pt. 1), 332; Lazear to Ashley Lazear, November 7, 1864, in "Civil War Letters of Colonel Bazel F. Lazear" (Part III), 58.

2. Hinton, *Rebel Invasion*, 198, 277; Price, *OR*, 41: (pt. 1), 636.

3. McNeil, *OR*, 41: (pt. 1), 372; Benteen, *OR*, 41: (pt. 1), 331; McKenny, *OR*, 41: (pt. 1), 538–39; Philips, *OR*, 41: (pt. 1), 351; Curtis, *OR*, 41: (pt. 1), 495; Philips, in Crittenden, *Battle of Westport and National Memorial Park*, 26–27.

4. Gravely, *OR*, 41: (pt. 1), 413; Curtis, *OR*, 41: (pt. 1), 494; Kelly, *OR*, 41: (pt. 1), 363; Hinton, *Rebel Invasion*, 189, 190, 194, 198–99, 200, 217, 348–49; Sanborn, *OR*, 41: (pt. 1), 391; Maj. William Plumb, November 12, 1864, *OR*, 41: (pt. 1), 409; "Compendium of History," in *Soldier's Letter*, 1: (July 1, 1865), 1. The Fourth Iowa Cavalry hit the southernmost or west mound from an unexpected direction and quickly drove the Confederates away.

5. "Compendium of History," in *Soldier's Letter*, 1: (July 1, 1865), 1.

6. Weed, *OR*, 41: (pt. 1), 556; Kelly, *OR*, 41: (pt. 1), 363; Hinton, *Rebel Invasion*, 198, 200–202, 349; Maj. Robert H. Hunt, November 22, 1864, *OR*, 41: (pt. 1), 544–45; Weed, *OR*, 41: (pt. 1), 556; Capt. William C. F. Montgomery, November 15, 1864, *OR*, 41: (pt. 1), 460; Lane, *OR*, 41: (pt. 1), 569–70. Compare the role accorded the other men in the reports of Rosecrans, *OR*, 41: (pt. 1), 313–14, and Curtis, *OR*, 41: (pt. 1), 493, 495. These were the guns of Montgomery, *OR*, 41: (pt. 1), 460.

7. Hinton, *Rebel Invasion*, 200, 202; Blair, *OR*, 41: (pt. 1), 599–600; Col. Charles W. Blair, January 1, 1865, *OR*, 41: (pt. 1), 601; Curtis, *OR*, 41: (pt. 1), 494.

8. Hinton, *Rebel Invasion*, 202–205, 205; Curtis, *OR*, 41: (pt. 1), 495; Sanborn, *OR*, 41: (pt. 1), 391–92; Hunt, *OR*, 41: (pt. 1), 544–45; Eppstein, *OR*, 41: (pt. 1), 383; Phelps, *OR*, 41: (pt. 1), 404–405; Greene, *OR*, 41: (pt. 1), 691; Lawther, *OR*, 41: (pt. 1), 699; Burbridge, *OR*, 41: (pt. 1), 694; Davies, *OR*, 41: (pt. 1), 696–97; "Compendium of History," in *Soldier's Letter*, 1: (July 8, 1865, and July 15, 1865), 1. Also see Col. Charles W. Blair, January 1, 1865, *OR*, 41: (pt. 1), 601–02. J. F. Davies reported being attacked "about 9 o'clock, but Pratt's [Hynson's] battery did such good execution that the enemy were

compelled to fall back. Blunt led out at daylight & pitched into the rebs at the crossing of the Marais des Cygnes, got that good to Mine Creek." October 25, 1864, entry in Lyman diary, 4–5. Misc. Mans. 17: #490 WHMC

9. Maj. Henry Hopkins, November 26, 1864, *OR*, 41: (pt. 1), 560; Philips, in Crittenden, *Battle of Westport and National Memorial Park*, 26–27; Kelly, *OR*, 41: (pt. 1), 363; Lazear, *OR*, 41: (pt. 1), 361; Benteen, *OR*, 41: (pt. 1), 331–32; Jones, *OR*, 41: (pt. 1), 335; Mitchell, *OR*, 41: (pt. 1), 411; Hinton, *Rebel Invasion*, 207–208; Philips, *OR*, 41: (pt. 1), 352; Lazear, *OR*, 41: (pt. 1), 361; Pleasonton, *OR*, 41: (pt. 1), 337–38; Curtis, *OR*, 41: (pt. 1), 500; Maj. S. S. Curtis, quoted in Curtis, *OR*, 41: (pt. 1), 501; Weed, *OR*, 41: (pt. 1), 556; Blair, *OR*, 41: (pt. 1), 602; Philips, *OR*, 41: (pt. 1), 352; Kelly, *OR*, 41: (pt. 1), 363; Maj. Robert H. Hunt, November 22, 1864, *OR*, 41: (pt. 1), 545; Kelly, *OR*, 41: (pt. 1), 364.

10. Hinton, *Rebel Invasion*, 205–207; Simpson, 14–15; Smith, "Battle of Mine Creek," 11–15. Victory oddly ascribed to "Crawford's regiment."

11. Philips, in Crittenden, *Battle of Westport and National Memorial Park*, 26–27; Hinton, *Rebel Invasion*, 207–208; Philips, *OR*, 41: (pt. 1), 352; Lazear, *OR*, 41: (pt. 1), 361; Pleasonton, *OR*, 41: (pt. 1), 337–38; Curtis, *OR*, 41: (pt. 1), 500; Hopkins, *OR*, 41: (pt. 1), 560; Maj. S. S. Curtis, quoted in Curtis, *OR*, 41: (pt. 1), 501; Weed, *OR*, 41: (pt. 1), 556; Blair, *OR*, 41: (pt. 1), 602; Philips, *OR*, 41: (pt. 1), 352; Hunt, *OR*, 41: (pt. 1), 545. So many officers fell that several sergeants had to lead companies. Kelly, *OR*, 41: (pt. 1), 364.

12. S. S. Curtis, *OR*, 41: (pt. 1), 534; Blair, *OR*, 41: (pt. 1), 602. "Total—wounded, 27; missing, 1. Loss in horses in engagement in 23d and 25th, 21 killed and 55 wounded, and equipments lost," Lazear, *OR*, 41: (pt. 1), 361. Mullins killed at Independence, Barcley badly wounded at the Blue. "Our loss in men will be about fifty or more killed and wounded." Suspected his brigade hit the hardest. Lazear to Ashley Lazear, November 2, 1864, in "Civil War Letters of Colonel Bazel F. Lazear" (Part III), 56; Hinton, *Rebel Invasion*, 208–10, 348; Benteen, *OR*, 41: (pt. 1), 332; Maj. Abial R. Pierce, October 27, 1864, *OR*, 41: (pt. 1), 336. Lieutenant Curtiss of the Fourth Iowa Cavalry was instantly killed while gallantly encouraging on his men, and Lieut. B. Armbrust, Company A, Fourth Cavalry Missouri Volunteers, was wounded in the bridle-arm while bravely charging at the head of his company.

13. Hinton, *Rebel Invasion*, 211.

14. Ibid.,, quotation, 209; Benteen, *OR*, 41: (pt. 1), 332; Lazear to Ashley Lazear, November 7, 1864, in "Civil War Letters of Colonel Bazel F. Lazear" (Part III), 58; October 25, 1864, entry in Baker diary; Grover, "Price Campaign of 1864," 176.

15. Pierce, *OR*, 41: (pt. 1), 336; Hunt, *OR*, 41: (pt. 1), 545; Benteen, *OR*, 41: (pt. 1), 332; S. S. Curtis, *OR*, 41: (pt. 1), 534; Hinton, *Rebel Invasion*, 213; Blair, *OR*, 41: (pt. 1), 603.

16. Clark, *OR*, 41: (pt. 1), 684–85; Greene, *OR*, 41: (pt. 1), 691; Burbridge, *OR*, 41: (pt. 1), 694; Jennison, *OR*, 41: (pt. 1), 587.

17. Curtis, *OR*, 41: (pt. 1), 497–98; Blair, *OR*, 41: (pt. 1), 603–604, quoted in Curtis, *OR*, 41: (pt. 1), 498–99; Hinton, *Rebel Invasion*, 212–15; Thomas J. Bryant, "The Capture of General Marmaduke by James Dunlay, an Iowa Private Cavalryman," *Iowa Journal of History and Politics*, 11: (April 1913), 248–57; "Compendium of History," in *Soldier's Letter*, 1: (July 15, 22, 1865), both 1; Plummer, "Missouri and Kansas," 90–91, 93–94.

18. Price, *OR*, 41: (pt. 1), 624; Price, *OR*, 41: (pt. 1), 637; Hinton, *Rebel Invasion*, 213.

19. Philips, *OR*, 41: (pt. 1), 352; Philips, Addenda: Itinerary of the District of Central Missouri, commanded by Brig. Gen. Egbert B. Brown, *OR*, 41: (pt. 1), 357–58; Pleasonton, *OR*, 41: (pt. 1), 337–38, 341; Pleasonton to Rosecrans, October 25, 1864, *OR*, 41: (pt. 4), 238; Frank Eno to Brig. Gen. Douglass, October 27, 1864, *OR*, 41: (pt. 4), 284. See also Jones, *OR*, 41: (pt. 1), 335; Pierce, *OR*, 41: (pt. 1), 336, Pierce of Fourth Iowa Cavalry to Maj. Gen. Curtis, October 27, 1864, *OR*, 41: (pt. 4), 289–90; Pleasonton to Rosecrans, October 25, 1864, *OR*, 41: (pt. 4), 238; Hinton, *Rebel Invasion*, 212. For the one-third estimate, see *History of Saline County*, 310. Hinton, *Rebel Invasion*, 212, 213, 215.There was a Col. Robert H. Graham of Texas but no indication he had been on this campaign.

20. Price, *OR*, 41: (pt. 1), 624, 637; Weed, *OR*, 41: (pt. 1), 557; Hinton, *Rebel Invasion*, 212–13, 215. See also Lane, *OR*, 41: (pt. 1), 570; Nettleton to his sister, December 19, 1864, in Crittenden, *Battle of Westport and National Memorial Park*, 29; Rosecrans, *OR*, 41: (pt. 1), 313–14; Charlot, *OR*, 41: (pt. 1), 527; "About 5000 prisoners have been captured . . . much of Price's plunder retaken, and the balance destroyed by himself to prevent it from falling into our hands," "The News," Weston, *Border Times*, October 28, 1864, 2.

21. Philips, *OR*, 41: (pt. 1), 352; "Arrival of Rebel Prisoners. Their Forlorn Appearance—How They Were Captured, and What They Say," St. Louis *Missouri Democrat*, November 5, 1864, 5. The latter mentions many officers and reports that many prisoners "claim that they were unwilling conscripts." Aware of the orders to shoot Confederates taken in Federal blue, Reader thought "of the fellow who took my coat, and that he might sometime come to grief with his plunder. But the rule seemed a hard one nevertheless," Reader, Autobiography, 3:214, 216.

22. Davis, *OR*, 41: (pt. 1), 552; "Just from the Front!! Complete Rout of General Price," Kansas City *Journal of Commerce*, October 28, 1864, 2. See also Ira M. Mallory, "Missouri Bush & Prairie. Price's Raid," *National Tribune*, September 6, 1900, 8.

23. Hinton, *Rebel Invasion*, 223–24, 241; Capt. M. H. Insley to Maj. S. S. Curtis, October 20, 1864, *OR*, 41: (pt. 4), 150; Blunt to Capt. M. H. Insley at Fort Scott, October 23, 1864, *OR*, 41: (pt. 4), 209; Col. Thomas Moonlight, December 15, 1864, *OR*, 41: (pt. 1), 594; Blair, *OR*, 41: (pt. 1), 604; Col. Moonlight to S. R. Curtis, October 25, 1864, *OR*, 41: (pt. 4), 243; Hinton, *Rebel Invasion*, 223–246. Some miles off, they saw "a heavy volume of smoke . . . rising from a dense body of timber, which was known to be in the vicinity of Fort Lincoln," Hinton, *Rebel Invasion*, 222–23. Manlove, a member of the militia under Captain Greer, was killed, and Mr. Williams was severely wounded, during this fight.

24. Curtis, *OR*, 41: (pt. 1), 495–96; Curtis, *OR*, 41: (pt. 1), 500; Hinton, *Rebel Invasion*, 216.

25. Col. William F. Cloud, November 20, 1864, *OR*, 41: (pt. 1), 558–59; Pierce, *OR*, 41: (pt. 1), 336; Hinton, *Rebel Invasion*, 211, 348–50.

26. Charlot, *OR*, 41: Curtis, *OR*, 41: (pt. 1), 496; (pt. 1), 527; Lt. Col. J. J. Sears to Maj. C. S. Charlot, October 27, 1864, *OR*, 41: (pt. 4), 288; Hinton, *Rebel Invasion*, 216. Pleasonton had sent the order through Major Suess, who had evidently been sidetracked into an argument about whether Pleasonton or Curtis should have control of the prisoners. Hinton, *Rebel Invasion*, 229. McKenny told McNeil to move forward around

daylight. McNeil, *OR*, 41: (pt. 1), 372. Suess of Seventh MSM Cavalry. Possibly Capt. John W. Yates.

27. Blair, *OR*, 41: (pt. 1), 605–606; Hinton, *Rebel Invasion*, 215–16.

28. Price, *OR*, 41: (pt. 1), 637.

29. Hinton, *Rebel Invasion*, 222.

30. McKenny, *OR*, 41: (pt. 1), 539; Sanborn, *OR*, 41: (pt. 1), 392; Phelps, *OR*, 41: (pt. 1), 404–05; S. S. Curtis, *OR*, 41: (pt. 1), 534–35; Blair, *OR*, 41: (pt. 1), 604–605; Hinton, *Rebel Invasion*, 220–22, 227–30. Little Osage. Another fight. "Compendium of History," in *Soldier's Letter*, 1: (July 22, 1865), 1.

31. Curtis, *OR,* 41: (pt. 1), 502.

32. Price, *OR*, 41: (pt. 1), 637; Shelby, *OR*, 41: (pt. 1), 659–60; Vivian, "Personal Reminiscence," 37. See also Davies, *OR*, 41: (pt. 1), 696–97; Greene, *OR*, 41: (pt. 1), 691. Price orders Oct. 25. "Colonel Tyler's brigade will march on the right flank of the train in rear of the brigade of Major-General Fagan's division," Army of Missouri, General Orders No. 22, October 25, 1864, *OR*, 41: (pt. 4), 1013.

33. Brig. Gen. John McNeil, November 23, 1864, *OR*, 41: (pt. 1), 372–73; Curtis, *OR*, 41: (pt. 1), 497; McKenny, *OR*, 41: (pt. 1), 539; Cloud to Curtis, quoted in Curtis, *OR*, 41: (pt. 1), 499–500; Curtis, *OR*, 41: (pt. 1), 496–97; Blair, *OR*, 41: (pt. 1), 605; Hinton, *Rebel Invasion*, 230–31. Eppstein's Fifth MSM Cavalry dismounted and advanced as skirmishers. Major Hopkins and Captain Cosgrove, both Kansans, advanced with Colonel Cloud's Second Kansas Cavalry and took the skirmish line before Sanborn's brigade, where Phelps's Arkansans joined them. Eppstein, *OR*, 41: (pt. 1), 383–84; Hinton, *Rebel Invasion*, 226–228, 232, 350–51.

34. Shelby, *OR*, 41: (pt. 1), 660.

35. Edwards, "Veteran Sam," in *John N. Edwards*, 166; Shelby, *OR*, 41: (pt. 1), 660–61; Thompson, *OR,* 41: (pt. 1), 668–69; Cloud, *OR*, 41: (pt. 1), 559; Brig. Gen. John McNeil, November 23, 1864, *OR*, 41: (pt. 1), 372–73; McMahan, *OR*, 41: (pt. 1), 407–408; Hinton, *Rebel Invasion*, 225–26, 231–33. "All ran, yet none were frightened," noted Thompson, "and as there was no discipline I found a quiet voice and ordinary remark attracted more attention than the vehement language and orders that some use." Fires set by the retreating Confederates began spreading north across the fields over which they had fought along Mine Creek and the Little Osage, "burning the bodies of their wounded and charring the remains of their dead." Hinton noted "charred bodies," and later a Confederate prisoner who asked whether his brother had been captured received papers taken from the brother's burned corpse.

36. Thompson, *OR*, 41: (pt. 1), 668; Shelby, *OR*, 41: (pt. 1), 660; Jackman, *OR*, 41: (pt. 1), 676–77, claimed also that he merely "sustained a loss of 4 killed and 10 wounded"; Hinton, *Rebel Invasion*, 233–35; Curtis, *OR*, 41: (pt. 1), 503; Montgomery, *OR*, 41: (pt. 1), 461; Mitchell, *OR*, 41: (pt. 1), 411; Blair, *OR*, 41: (pt. 1), 604; Hunt, *OR*, 41: (pt. 1), 545; McKenny, *OR*, 41: (pt. 1), 539; Montgomery, *OR*, 41: (pt. 1), 460–61.

37. Curtis, *OR*, 41: (pt. 1), 502–503; Brig. Gen. John McNeil, November 23, 1864, *OR*, 41: (pt. 1), 373; Eppstein, *OR*, 41: (pt. 1), 384; Benteen, *OR*, 41: (pt. 1), 332–33; Hopkins, *OR*, 41: (pt. 1), 560.

38. Curtis, *OR*, 41: (pt. 1), 502; McKenny, *OR*, 41: (pt. 1), 540; Curtis to Pleasonton, October 26, 1864, 6 pm. Inclosure with Pleasonton, *OR*, 41: (pt. 1), 339–40; Pleasonton,

OR, 41: (pt. 1), 341; Phelps, *OR,* 41: (pt. 1), 405; S. S. Curtis, *OR,* 41: (pt. 1), 535; Hinton, *Rebel Invasion*, 235–37; Hon. James H. Lane, *OR,* 41: (pt. 1), 570.

39. Mitchell, *OR,* 41: (pt. 1), 411; Weed, *OR,* 41: (pt. 1), 557; Curtis, *OR,* 41: (pt. 1), 503; S. S. Curtis, *OR,* 41: (pt. 1), 534; Hunt, *OR,* 41: (pt. 1), 545; Thompson, *OR,* 41: (pt. 1), 669. "Half-loaded wagons to feed my troops. I think I have all of Price's cannon but three, and thousands of his arms are scattered along the road. I shall proceed in the pursuit with all the forces I can keep on the way," Curtis, *OR,* 41: (pt. 1), 504. Hinton believed it "the golden occasion to once more precipitate a ruinous flight upon the invaders," Hinton, *Rebel Invasion*, 235.

40. Blair, *OR,* 41: (pt. 1), 606; Hinton, *Rebel Invasion*, 245–47. Fort Scott report on battle. "From Fort Scott. The Battle on the 25th," St. Louis *Missouri Democrat*, November 2, 1864, 1.

41. Fishback, *OR,* 41: (pt. 1), 621–22; Curtis, *OR,* 41: (pt. 1), 504; Fishback, *OR,* 41: (pt. 1), 622; Hinton, *Rebel Invasion*, 248–49, 247, 250, 251–52, 351. Hinton quotes Lane on 253.

42. Jones, *OR,* 41: (pt. 1), 335; S. S. Curtis, *OR,* 41: (pt. 1), 535; Blunt, *OR,* 41: (pt. 1), 576–77; S. S. Curtis, *OR,* 41: (pt. 1), 535. Also see Ford, *OR,* 41: (pt. 1), 609; Childers, "Recitals and Reminiscences,". *National Tribune*, January 31, 1907, 6; Hinton, *Rebel Invasion*, 237–38.

43. Curtis, *OR,* 41: (pt. 1), 501–502; S. R. Curtis to Henry W. Halleck, October 25, 1864, *OR,* 41: (pt. 4), 242; Hinton, *Rebel Invasion*, 184. Half a dozen guns and five colonels. Also see Brig. Gen. Thomas Ewing Jr. to Col. S. A. Holmes, October 28, 1864, *OR,* 41: (pt. 4), 298. The charge of Mine Creek was directed by Maj. General Curtis through his staff officers, Colonels Crawford, Blair, Cloud, Volunteer Aide-de-Camp, Major Weed, and Captain Hinton of General Blunt's staff, "who charged with the extreme left of your brigade through the corn field, and endeavored to attack the enemy as he was emerging in disorder from the timber south of the corn field, which effort was defeated by the shell from our own guns," Hinton, *Rebel Invasion*, 349–50.

44. "General Pleasanton [*sic*] and General Lane," St. Louis *Missouri Democrat*, November 5, 1864, 2; Plummer, "Missouri and Kansas," 99–101; Curtis to Pleasonton, October 26, 1864, 6 pm. Inclosure with Maj. Gen. Alfred Pleasonton, commanding Provisional Cavalry Division, *OR,* 41: (pt. 1), 339–40; Curtis to Pleasonton, October 27, 1864, *OR,* 41: (pt. 4), 287; Curtis, *OR,* 41: (pt. 1), 505–507; Philips, *OR,* 41: (pt. 1), 352–53; Philips, in Crittenden, *Battle of Westport and National Memorial Park*, 27; Charlot, *OR,* 41: (pt. 1), 527; Pleasonton to Curtis, October 27, 1864, *OR,* 41: (pt. 4), 286; Hinton, *Rebel Invasion*, 253–54, 261; Cloud, *OR,* 41: (pt. 1), 558. See also Lazear, *OR,* 41: (pt. 1), 361; Plummer, "Missouri and Kansas," 102.

45. Price, *OR,* 41: (pt. 1), 636–37; Thompson, *OR,* 41: (pt. 1), 669; Greene, *OR,* 41: (pt. 1), 691, 692; Thompson, *OR,* 41: (pt. 1), 669; Shelby, *OR,* 41: (pt. 1), 661; "Compendium of History," in *Soldier's Letter*, 1: (July 15, 1865), 1; Hinton, *Rebel Invasion*, 216–17, 238–39.

46. Pleasonton, *OR,* 41: (pt. 1), 338; Maj. Gen. Pleasonton to Maj. Gen. S. R. Curtis, October 27, 1864, *OR,* 41: (pt. 4), 286; Pleasonton to Rosecrans, October 27, 1864, *OR,* 41: (pt. 4), 274; Rosecrans to Maj. Gen. Alfred Pleasonton, October 27, 1864, *OR,* 41: (pt. 4), 278; Rosecrans to Maj. Gen. A. J. Smith, October 27, 1864, *OR,* 41: (pt. 4), 277;

Rosecrans to Halleck, October 27, 1864, *OR*, 41: (pt. 4), 275; Hinton, *Rebel Invasion*, 213. For little or no mention of the Army of the Border see also Pleasonton, *OR*, 41: (pt. 1), 341; Pleasonton to Rosecrans, October 27, 1864, *OR*, 41: (pt. 4), 274; Henry Dillinberger, "The Big Raid. An Account of How the Rebels Were Driven Out of Missouri," *National Tribune*, May 15, 1890, 3. See also the appeal to break off the pursuit, Col. Jno. F. Philips to Maj. Gen. S. R. Curtis, October 27, 1864, *OR*, 41: (pt. 4), 279.

12. INTO THE OZARKS

1. Robinson, *OR*, 41: (pt. 1), 548, 549–50. See also S. S. Curtis, *OR*, 41: (pt. 1), 534; Hinton, *Rebel Invasion*, 255–57. Also present from the Indian Brigade was Ellithorpe of the Leavenworth Conservative.

2. Maj. Gen. S. R. Curtis to Maj. Gen. Henry W. Halleck, October 27, 1864, *OR*, 41: (pt. 4), 285; Curtis to Pleasonton, October 26, 1864, *OR*, 41: (pt. 1), 339–40; Curtis, *OR*, 41: (pt. 1), 510; Blunt, *OR*, 41: (pt. 1), 578; Brig. Gen. John McNeil, November 25, 1864, *OR*, 41: (pt. 1), 374; Hinton, *Rebel Invasion*, 276; Maj. S. S. Curtis to Blunt, October 27, 1864, *OR*, 41: (pt. 4), 287. See also Hunt, *OR*, 41: (pt. 1), 545–46; Charlot, *OR*, 41: (pt. 1), 528; Ford, *OR*, 41: (pt. 1), 609; Jennison, *OR*, 41: (pt. 1), 587; Moonlight, *OR*, 41: (pt. 1), 594; McKenny, *OR*, 41: (pt. 1), 540; Blunt, *OR*, 41: (pt. 1), 577; Lane, *OR*, 41: (pt. 1), 570; Hinton, *Rebel Invasion*, 259–60; Larry Wood, *The Two Civil War Battles of Newtonia* (Charleston, SC: History Press, 2010), 113. William F. Cloud later returned to Fort Scott to prepare to escort a train to Fort Smith. Cloud, *OR*, 41: (pt. 1), 559; "Compendium of History," in *Soldier's Letter*, 1: (July 22, 1865), 1. Also see Curtis, *OR*, 41: (pt. 1), 504. After Mine Creek. "Price Still Retreating," *Liberty Tribune*, October 28, 1864, 2. Resupplying Pleasonton's cavalry with horses. Maj. Gen. Rosecrans to Maj. Gen. S. R. Curtis, October 23, 1864, *OR*, 41: (pt. 4), 209; Rosecrans to Pleasonton, October 23, 1864, *OR*, 41: (pt. 4), 205.

3. Philips, *OR*, 41: (pt. 1), 352–53; Philips in Crittenden, *Battle of Westport and National Memorial Park*, 27; Grover, "Price Campaign of 1864," 176–79; Hinton, *Rebel Invasion*, 261; Wood, *Two Civil War Battles*, 113.

4. Maj. Gen. Pleasonton to Maj. Gen. S. R. Curtis, October 27, 1864, *OR*, 41: (pt. 4), 286; McNeil, *OR*, 41: (pt. 1), 374; Sanborn, *OR*, 41: (pt. 1), 392; Curtis, *OR*, 41: (pt. 1), 505; Wood, *Two Civil War Battles*, 113. See also Houston, *OR*, 41: (pt. 1), 381; Kelly, *OR*, 41: (pt. 1), 363; Phelps, *OR*, 41: (pt. 1), 405; Mitchell, *OR*, 41: (pt. 1), 411; Montgomery, *OR*, 41: (pt. 1), 461; Benteen, *OR*, 41: (pt. 1), 333. See also Maj. Jones, *OR*, 41: (pt. 1), 335; Pleasonton, *OR*, 41: (pt. 1), 338, 339, 342, November 30, 1864, *OR*, 41: (pt. 1), 342. See also Lazear, *OR*, 41: (pt. 1), 361; Hopkins, *OR*, 41: (pt. 1), 560; Curtis, *OR*, 41: (pt. 1), 504; Maj. Gen. Pleasonton to Maj. Gen. S. R. Curtis, October 27, 1864, *OR*, 41: (pt. 4), 286; Rosecrans, *OR*, 41: (pt. 1), 314; Rosecrans, *OR*, 41: (pt. 1), 314. "Spring Grove" probably meant the location near present-day Windsor in Henry County, roughly fifty miles east, back toward St. Louis.

5. Report of Lt. Col. Samuel H. Melcher, Sixth Missouri State Militia Cavalry, October 27, 1864, *OR*, 41: (pt. 1), 892–93; "From Sedalia. Guerillas in Clinton County. 250 Attack Clinton. 70 Militia Repulse Them," St. Louis *Missouri Democrat*, October 28, 1864, 1.

6. This description is based on the extensive but spotty references in the *OR* as well as "Story of Vengeance in North Missouri" (from *Missouri Democrat*), *Liberty Tribune*, October 28, 1864, 2; "The Capture of Sedalia and Other Matters," St. Louis *Missouri Democrat*, October 24, 1864, 2; *History of Cole, Moniteau . . . Counties*, 556; "Pursuit of Price. Part Taken by the 16th Army Corps," St. Louis *Missouri Democrat*, November 5, 1864, 2; "Arrival of Major Generals Rosecrans and Smith," St. Louis *Missouri Democrat*, November 5, 1864, 2.

7. Col. J. H. Shanklin to Brig. Gen. Craig, October 27, 1864, *OR*, 41: (pt. 4), 284; Col. J. H. Shanklin to Gen. Craig at Carrollton, October 28, 1864, *OR*, 41: (pt. 4), 301; Brig. Gen. Craig to Lt. Col. Stark, October 26, 1864, *OR*, 41: (pt. 4), 258; Major L. C. Pace to Major Rainford, October 26, 1864, *OR*, 41: (pt. 4), 258; Lewis C. Pace, future leader of Nebraska Greenback Party; Holmes, *OR*, 41: (pt. 4), 276; E. J. Crandall to Gen. Craig, October 24, 1864, *OR*, 41: (pt. 4), 227; repeating the Anderson story, Lt. Col. F. M. Jackson to Col. J. H. Shanklin at Chillicothe, October 25, 1864, *OR*, 41: (pt. 4), 24; "Bill Anderson. His Death Put Beyond Doubt. His Commission from the Rebel Price," St. Louis *Missouri Democrat*, November 3, 1864, 1; "Bill Anderson Killed!" Kansas City *Journal of Commerce*, October 28, 1864, 2, and also *Liberty Tribune*, November 4, 1864, 2; Fisk, *OR*, 41: (pt. 1), 423–24. See also Col. J. H. Shanklin to Brig. Gen. Craig, October 29, 1864, *OR*, 41: (pt. 4), 317–18; Capt. Frank Eno to Brig. Gen. Douglass, October 29, 1864, *OR*, 41: (pt. 4), 316; Wiley Britton, "Bill Anderson. The Gerrillas [*sic*] Whose Name Was a Terror in Missouri," *National Tribune*, July 31, 1890, 1; E. A. Proctor, "Killing of Bill Anderson. A Comrade Who Says That Soldiers and Citizens Dispatched Him," *National Tribune*, October 25, 1900, 3; Brig. Gen. James Craig to Capt. Frank Eno, October 30, 1864, *OR*, 41: (pt. 4), 334; Rainsford, *OR*, 41: (pt. 4), 354; "Civil War," Warrenton *Journal*, May 1, 1996.

8. Curtis, *OR*, 41: (pt. 1), 504–505; Pleasonton, *OR*, 41: (pt. 1), 338; Pleasonton in Enclosure, October 26, 1864; Maj. Gen. Alfred Pleasonton, commanding Provisional Cavalry Division, *OR*, 41: (pt. 1), 339, November 30, 1864, *OR*, 41: (pt. 1), 342.

9. Curtis, *OR*, 41: (pt. 1), 505; Charlot, *OR*, 41: (pt. 1), 527; Meeker, *OR*, 41: (pt. 1), 563 or 564; Reader, Autobiography, 3:346; Hinton, *Rebel Invasion*, 238–39, 260, 262; Wood, *Two Civil War Battles*, 113. See also History of Vernon County, 1887, 814, 815, 817; "Compendium of History," in *Soldier's Letter*, 1: (July 22, 1865), 1. See also "The Pursuit of Price," St. Louis *Missouri Democrat*, October 28, 1864, 1.

10. Pleasonton, *OR*, 41: (pt. 1), 341–42; Addenda, Pleasonton to Capt. Frank Eno, December 10, 1864, *OR*, 41: (pt. 1), 342–43; Rosecrans, *OR*, 41: (pt. 1), 314; Hinton, *Rebel Invasion*, 254–55; Curtis, *OR*, 41: (pt. 1), 510–11; Pleasonton, *OR*, 41: (pt. 1), 338; Philips, in Crittenden, *Battle of Westport and National Memorial Park*, 28.

11. Maj. Gen. S. R. Curtis to Maj. Gen. Henry W. Halleck, October 30, 1864, *OR*, 41: (pt. 4), 331; Curtis, *OR*, 41: (pt. 1), 504, 506; McKenny, *OR*, 41: (pt. 1), 540.

12. Hinton, *Rebel Invasion*, 262; Wood, *Two Civil War Battles*, 113; "Marched sixty-one miles." "I don't know that a longer march graces modern history + fatal day to horse flesh," October 26, 1864, entry in Baker diary.

13. Curtis to Pleasonton, October 27, 1864, *OR*, 41: (pt. 4), 286–87; Hinton, *Rebel Invasion*, 261; Wood, *Two Civil War Battles*, 114.

14. Curtis to Halleck, October 30, 1864, *OR*, 41: (pt. 4), 331; Curtis, *OR*, 41: (pt. 1), 507; Hinton, *Rebel Invasion*, 261, 262; Wood, *Two Civil War Battles*, 114–16; "Compendium

of History," in *Soldier's Letter*, 1: (July 29, 1865), 1. Nathaniel C. Credit and Ira G. Robinson were captains discharged or dismissed after the campaign.

15. Price, *OR*, 41: (pt. 1), 637; Wood, *Two Civil War Battles*, 114–15, 115–16; Reader, *Autobiography*, 3:293, 311–12, 324, 326, 340, 342, 358. The Connecticut man the Confederates had conscripted, Donald M. Palmer, also escaped at this point. See his *Four Weeks in the Rebel Army* (New London, CT, 1865). "Of the Shawnee County militia, one hundred have come in paroled," Hinton, *Rebel Invasion*, 278.

16. Davies, *OR*, 41: (pt. 1), 697; Price, *OR*, 41: (pt. 1), 637–38; Thompson, *OR*, 41: (pt. 1), 669; *OR*, 7: 46; Hinton, *Rebel Invasion*, 273; Wood, *Two Civil War Battles*, 116–17, 118. Price also indicated that the defenders of Newtonia has slipped away, noting that Shelby's men pursued and failed to catch them. Price, *OR*, 41: (pt. 1), 637; "From the Southwest. Price Below Newtonia. A Fight There," St. Louis *Missouri Democrat*, November 5, 1864, 1. Christian in the service files, though sometimes name is Christenson.

17. Curtis, *OR*, 41: (pt. 1), 507; Hinton, *Rebel Invasion*, 262–63; Wood, *Two Civil War Battles*, 116; "Compendium of History," in *Soldier's Letter*, 1: (July 29, 1865), 1. See also *Goodspeed's History of Newton, Lawrence, Barry and McDonald Counties, Missouri* (Chicago: Goodspeed, 1888).

18. Hinton, *Rebel Invasion*, 264, 265; Wood, *Two Civil War Battles*, 118–19; Curtis, *OR*, 41: (pt. 1), 507–08. See also Houston, *OR*, 41: (pt. 1), 381; Jennison, *OR*, 41: (pt. 1), 587–88; Hunt, *OR*, 41: (pt. 1), 546; October 28, 1864, entry in Baker diary. Blunt is quoted in Curtis, *OR*, 41: (pt. 1), 508–509.

19. Jennison, *OR*, 41: (pt. 1), 588, 590; Hinton, *Rebel Invasion*, 265–67, 273, 274; Wood, *Two Civil War Battles*, 120. A Colorado writer had not entirely exaggerated when he wrote of hurling 900 men against 10,000. See "Compendium of History," in *Soldier's Letter*, 1: (August 26, 1865), 1.

20. "Compendium of History," in *Soldier's Letter*, 1: (August 26, 1865), 1; Hinton, *Rebel Invasion*, 265–66, 267, 271–72, 273, including Jennison's report; Ford, *OR*, 41: (pt. 1), 609–10, quoted in Curtis, *OR*, 41: (pt. 1), 509; Hinton, *Rebel Invasion*, 265, 267–68; Wood, *Two Civil War Battles*, 118, 119–20, 120–22.

21. Wood, *Two Civil War Battles*, 122–23; "Compendium of History," in *Soldier's Letter*, 1: (August 5 and 26, 1865), both on 1; "Compendium of History," in *Soldier's Letter*, 1: (July 22, 1865), 1.

22. Jackman, *OR*, 41: (pt. 1), 677; Shelby, *OR*, s.1, v.41, pt.1, 661; Wood, *Two Civil War Battles*, 122, 124; Curtis, *OR*, 41: (pt. 1), 509; Hinton, *Rebel Invasion*, 272–73. Observers praised both colonels, Ford and Burris. Quoted on Hoyt, Hinton, *Rebel Invasion*, 274. "I desire to mention Lieut. Jos. Mackle, A. A. A. G., 1st Brigade, and Lieutenant W. H. Bisbee," quoted in Hinton, *Rebel Invasion*, 274. Hinton, *Rebel Invasion*, 269. He left the regiments of Hunter and Nichols of Jackman's brigade to support the battery but threw those of Schnable, Coleman, and Shaw into the line.

23. Wood, *Two Civil War Battles*, 124.

24. Ibid., 124–25; Hinton, *Rebel Invasion*, 269; "Compendium of History," in *Soldier's Letter*, 1: (September 2, 1865), 1. Three times Confederates were goaded to charge but driven back. During the hottest part, enemy guns "silenced by our batteries," "Compendium of History," in *Soldier's Letter*, 1: (August 5, 1865), 1.

25. "Compendium of History," in *Soldier's Letter: Second Colorado Cavalry: A Regimental Paper to Accompany the Regiment,*ed. Oliver V. Wallace (August 1864–November 28, 1865, nos. 31–37), quoted in Wood, *Two Civil War Battles,* 125–27.

26. Price, *OR,* 41: (pt. 1), 638; Lawther, *OR,* 41: (pt. 1), 699. See also Clark, *OR,* 41: (pt. 1), 685; Davies, *OR,* 41: (pt. 1), 697; Hinton, *Rebel Invasion,* 269; Wood, *Two Civil War Battles,* 128–29. "Colonel Reefe received many complimentary volleys from our line, but seemed to bear a charmed life," Hinton, *Rebel Invasion,* 269.

27. Charlot, *OR,* 41: (pt. 1), 528, quoted in Curtis, *OR,* 41: (pt. 1), 509; Hinton, *Rebel Invasion,* 270. See also Nettleton, in Crittenden, *Battle of Westport and National Memorial Park,* 29; Plumb, *OR,* 41: (pt. 1), 409; Mitchell, *OR,* 41: (pt. 1), 411; Halleck to Curtis, October 28, 1864, *OR,* 41: (pt. 4), 302; Hinton, *Rebel Invasion,* 270–71. See also McMahan, *OR,* 41: (pt. 1), 408; Gravely, *OR,* 41: (pt. 1), 413; Rosecrans to Curtis, October 30, 1864, *OR,* 41: (pt. 4), 332; Hinton, *Rebel Invasion,* 268–69; Wood, *Two Civil War Battles,* 127. The "coolness and self-possession" Lieutenant John Crites. Hinton, *Rebel Invasion,* 275; "Compendium of History," in *Soldier's Letter,* 1: (August 5, 1865), 1, and *Soldier's Letter,* 1: (August 12, 1865), 1.

28. Curtis, *OR,* 41: (pt. 1), 510; Sanborn to Rosecrans, October 30, 1864, *OR,* 41: (pt. 4), 333–34; Wood, *Two Civil War Battles,* 129–30; Thompson, *OR,* 41: (pt. 1), 669; Price, *OR,* 41: (pt. 1), 638; October 27, 1864, entry in Baker diary. Also see Price, *OR,* 41: (pt. 1), 624; Shelby, *OR,* s.1, v.41, pt.1, 661; Edwards, "Veteran Sam," in *John N. Edwards,* 166; Blair to Brig. Gen. Thomas A. Davies, October 31, 1864, *OR,* 41: (pt. 4), 356. "We retreated by the way of Carthage and Newtonia, at which place we had the last fight, driving back and completely routing them," William G. Hazen to Alexander R. Hazen, December 21, 1864. Misc. Mans. 2: #44. WHMC.

29. Price, *OR,* 41: (pt. 1), 638; Hinton, *Rebel Invasion,* 298; Wood, *Two Civil War Battles,* 127–29.

30. Hinton, *Rebel Invasion,* 272; "Compendium of History," in *Soldier's Letter,* 1: (August 19, 1865), 1; Edwards, "Veteran Sam," in *John N. Edwards,* 166. 15th Kansas, ten killed, twenty-nine wounded and one missing; 16th Kansas, two killed and thirteen wounded; 3rd Wisconsin (Lieutenant Pond commanding) eleven wounded; 2d Colorado Battery, one killed, five wounded. Also see *OR,* s.1, v.41, pt.1. Also: 8, 13, 22.

31. Price, *OR,* 41: (pt. 1), 638; Davis, *OR,* 41: (pt. 1), 552–53; Hinton, *Rebel Invasion,* 275; Wood, *Two Civil War Battles,* 124.

32. Curtis, *OR,* 41: (pt. 1), 510; Curtis, *OR,* 41: (pt. 1), 513; Hinton, *Rebel Invasion,* 275–77.

33. Curtis, *OR,* 41: (pt. 1), 511; McNeil, *OR,* 41: (pt. 1), 374; Lt. Col. Frederick Benteen to Maj. Gen. S. R. Curtis, October 29, 1864, *OR,* 41: (pt. 4), 318–19. See also Kelly, *OR,* 41: (pt. 1), 363; Eppstein, *OR,* 41: (pt. 1), 384; McMahan, *OR,* 41: (pt. 1), 408; Philips, in Crittenden, *Battle of Westport and National Memorial Park,* 28; Hinton, *Rebel Invasion,* 276, 277–78.

34. Lt. Col. J. D. Brutsche to Maj. Melton, October 14, 1864, *OR,* 41: (pt. 3), 859; Maj. Milton Burch to Col. J. D. Brutsche, October 19, 1864, *OR,* 41: (pt. 4), 112; Lt. Col. J. D. Brutsche to Col. J. V. DuBois, October 22, 1864, *OR,* 41: (pt. 4), 186; Department of Southwest Missouri, Special Orders No. 286, October 25, 1864, *OR,* 41: (pt. 4), 239–40; Lt. Col. J. D. Brutsche to Major Cosgrove at Lebanon, October 25, 1864, *OR,* 41: (pt. 4),

240; Lt. Col. J. D. Brutsche to Lt. Col. Hugh Cameron, October 25, 1864, *OR*, 41: (pt. 4), 240; Lt. Col. J. D. Brutsche to Major Cosgrove at Lebanon, October 25, 1864, *OR*, 41: (pt. 4), 240; Brig. Gen. John B. Sanborn to Maj. Gen. William S. Rosecrans, October 31, 1864, *OR*, 41: (pt. 4), 351; Lt. Col. J. D. Brutsche to Col. J. Darr, Jr., October 27, 1864, *OR*, 41: (pt. 4), 279; Lt. Col. J. D. Brutsche to Maj. Melton, October 27, 1864, *OR*, 41: (pt. 4), 281; Lt. Col. Hugh Cameron, 2nd Arkansas Cavalry, *OR*, 41: (pt. 1), 406–407; Maj. Samuel Montgomery, Sixth Missouri Cavalry, *OR*, 41: (pt. 1), 455–57; Sanborn, *OR*, 41: (pt. 1), 385–96. See also Lt. Col. J. D. Brutsche to Col. Harrison, October 27, 1864, *OR*, 41: (pt. 4), 281–82; *Goodspeed's History of Newton, Lawrence . . . Counties*; Lt. Col. Hugh Cameron at Cassville, later at Springfield. Plum, *Military Telegraph during the Civil War*, 2:221.

35. Curtis, *OR*, 41: (pt. 1), 511; Moonlight, *OR*, 41: (pt. 1), 594–95; Ford, *OR*, 41: (pt. 1), 610; Jennison, *OR*, 41: (pt. 1), 588; J. H. Lane to General Davies, October 28, 1864, *OR*, 41: (pt. 4), 302; McKenny, *OR*, 41: (pt. 1), 540–41; Hunt, *OR*, 41: (pt. 1), 546; Charlot, *OR*, 41: (pt. 1), 528; Hinton, *Rebel Invasion*, 277; Curtis, *OR*, 41: (pt. 1), 513; Curtis, *OR*, 41: (pt. 1), 522; Maj. Gen. James G. Blunt, December 24, 1864, *OR*, 41: (pt. 1), 578; Ford, *OR*, 41: (pt. 1), 610; Hunt, *OR*, 41: (pt. 1), 546; Houston, *OR*, 41: (pt. 1), 381; Mitchell, *OR*, 41: (pt. 1), 411; Lane to Secretary of War Stanton, October 29, 1864, *OR*, 41: (pt. 4), 319; Hinton, *Rebel Invasion*, 275, 279–80. One Coloradoan generously concluded that "Rosecranz [*sic*] was ignorant of the true state of the campaign," "Compendium of History," in *Soldier's Letter*, 1: (September 2, 1865), 1.

36. Abraham Lincoln to John G. Nicolay, Oct. 21, 1864, in *The Collected Works of Abraham Lincoln*, ed. Roy P. Basler, 9 vols. (New Brunswick, NJ: Rutgers University Press, 1953), 8:57; J. F. Bennett to Capt. Joseph T. Foster, First Iowa Cavalry, October 25, 1864, *OR*, 41: (pt. 4), 238; Maj. Gen. E. R. S. Canby to Maj. Gen. C. C. Washburn, October 14, 1864, *OR*, 41: (pt. 3), 859; Maj. Gen. E. R. S. Canby to Rosecrans, October 15, 1864, *OR*, 41: (pt. 3), 885; Maj. Gen. H. W. Halleck to Rosecrans, October 24, 1864, *OR*, 41: (pt. 4), 219–20; Col. John V. DuBois to Maj. Gen. A. J. Smith, October 28, 1864, *OR*, 41: (pt. 4), 299; Curtis, *OR*, 41: (pt. 1), 511–13; Maj. Gen. Rosecrans to Maj. Gen. Henry W. Halleck, October 31, 1864, *OR*, 41: (pt. 4), 343; Sanborn to Rosecrans, October 31, 1864, *OR*, 41: (pt. 4), 350–51. See also Charlot, *OR*, 41: (pt. 1), 528–29; Hinton, *Rebel Invasion*, 278; Maj. C. S. Charlot to Lt. Col. Charles W. Blair, October 30, 1864, *OR*, 41: (pt. 4), 335–36; Maj. Gen. S. R. Curtis to Maj. Gen. H. W. Halleck, October 28, 1864, *OR*, 41: (pt. 4), 301; Col. Charles W. Blair to Maj. Gen. William S. Rosecrans, October 31, 1864, *OR*, 41: (pt. 4), 355; McNeil, *OR*, 41: (pt. 1), 374. See also Houston, *OR*, 41: (pt. 1), 381. Washington hostile about Rosecrans. Plummer, "Missouri and Kansas," 102–103.

37. Sanborn to Rosecrans, October 30, 1864, *OR*, 41: (pt. 4), 334; Phelps, *OR*, 41: (pt. 1), 406; Curtis, *OR*, 41: (pt. 1), 513; Curtis, *OR*, 41: (pt. 1), 514; 22, 13, 30/34; February 14, 1862, 8; Hinton, *Rebel Invasion*, 280, quote on 281.

38. Hinton, *Rebel Invasion*, 283–84; M. LaRue Harrison to Col. Stephen H. Wattles, October 27, 1864, *OR*, 41: (pt. 4), 273; Col. M. LaRue Harrison to Col. J. D. Brutsche, October 24, 1864, *OR*, 41: (pt. 4), 226; Col. M. LaRue Harrison to Col. Stephen H. Wattles, October 29, 1864, enclosed with Brig. Gen. Douglas H. Cooper to Capt. M. L. Bell, November 7, 1864, enclosed with M. L. Bell to Brig. Gen. W. R. Boggs, November 9, 1864, *OR*, 41: (pt. 4), 1041; Jones, *OR*, 41: (pt. 1), 335; Col. M. LaRue Harrison to Col.

Stephen H. Wattles, October 27, 1864, enclosed with Brig. Gen. Douglas H. Cooper to Capt. M. L. Bell, November 7, 1864, enclosed with M. L. Bell to Brig. Gen. W. R. Boggs, November 9, 1864, *OR*, 41: (pt. 4), 1040–41. See also Kim Allen Scott, "The Civil War in a Bottle: Battle at Fayetteville, Arkansas," *Arkansas Historical Quarterly*, 54: (Autumn, 1995), 239–68.

39. Hinton, *Rebel Invasion*, 283–85; Daniel E. Sutherland, "1864: 'A Strange, Wild Time,'" *Rugged and Sublime: The Civil War in Arkansas*, ed. Mark K. Christ (Little Rock: Department of Arkansas Heritage, 1994), 149–50, 167; Hinton, *Rebel Invasion*, 286–87; Shelby, *OR*, s.1, v.41, pt.1, 661; McKenny, *OR*, 41: (pt. 1), 541; "Account of Siege of Fayetteville, Ark Nov. 1864," from the *Missouri Democrat*, and posted at http://history-sites.com

40. Ford, *OR*, 41: (pt. 1), 610; Curtis, *OR*, 41: (pt. 1), 514; Curtis, *OR*, 41: (pt. 1), 522; Jennison, *OR*, 41: (pt. 1), 588; Mitchell, *OR*, 41: (pt. 1), 411; Hunt, *OR*, 41: (pt. 1), 546; Charlot, *OR*, 41: (pt. 1), 529; Hinton, *Rebel Invasion*, 280, 282.

41. Hunt, *OR*, 41: (pt. 1), 546; Charlot, *OR*, 41: (pt. 1), 529; McKenny, *OR*, 41: (pt. 1), 541; Meeker, *OR*, 41: (pt. 1), 564; Curtis, *OR*, 41: (pt. 1), 513–15, 523; Hinton, *Rebel Invasion*, 282–83; "Compendium of History," in *Soldier's Letter*, 1: (September 2, 9, 16, 1865), 1.

42. "Compendium of History," in *Soldier's Letter*, 1: (September 23, 1865), 1; Curtis, *OR*, 41: (pt. 1), 515; Charlot, *OR*, 41: (pt. 1), 529; Hunt, *OR*, 41: (pt. 1), 546; Ford, *OR*, 41: (pt. 1), 610; McKenny, *OR*, 41: (pt. 1), 541; Hinton, *Rebel Invasion*, 281–82, 287; November 3, 1864, entry in Lyman diary, 6. Misc. Mans. 17: #490 WHMC; Curtis, *OR*, 41: (pt. 1), 514; Curtis, *OR*, 41: (pt. 1), 522; Jennison, *OR*, 41: (pt. 1), 588; Mitchell, *OR*, 41: (pt. 1), 411; Hunt, *OR*, 41: (pt. 1), 546; Charlot, *OR*, 41: (pt. 1), 529; Hinton, *Rebel Invasion*, 280, 282; Curtis, *OR*, 41: (pt. 1), 515; Charlot, *OR*, 41: (pt. 1), 529; Hinton, *Rebel Invasion*, 283.

43. Price, *OR*, 41: (pt. 1), 638; Clark, *OR*, 41: (pt. 1), 685; Davies, *OR*, 41: (pt. 1), 697; Price, *OR*, 41: (pt. 1), 637–38; Thompson, *OR*, 41: (pt. 1), 669–70. The *Galveston News* published a brief excerpt from the diary of an officer in Fagan's division. Hinton, *Rebel Invasion*, 295.

44. October 31, 1864, entry in Baker diary; William G. Hazen to Alexander R. Hazen, December 21, 1864. Misc. Mans. 2: #44. WHMC; entry under November 3–4, 1864, in Baker diary, November 5, 1864 in Baker diary.

45. Price, *OR*, 41: (pt. 1), 623; Maj. Gen. Sterling Price, November 18, 1864, *OR*, 41: (pt. 1), 624; Price, *OR*, 41: (pt. 1), 638; Shelby, *OR*, 41: (pt. 1), 661; Jackman, *OR*, 41: (pt. 1), 677.

Epilogue: Sins of the Fathers

1. "Fort Gibson," *Cherokee Tomahawk*, March 13, 1865, 1.

2. Lt. Col. Owen A. Bassett to Col. S. H. Wattles, October 9, 1864, *OR*, 41: (pt. 3), 724; Brig. Gen. John M. Thayer to Col. S. H. Wattles, October 11, 1864, *OR*, 41: (pt. 3), 779; Charlot, *OR*, 41: (pt. 4), 116; Price, *OR*, 41: (pt. 1), 638 or 637–38. This represented a continuation of the departmental turf battles that plagued the Federal response from the outset. Arkansas commanders kept for nine days Union infantry originally intended

to chase Price north into Missouri. See "Price's Great Raid. A Bird's-Eye View. What He Was After and What He Was Not After," St. Louis *Missouri Democrat*, October 18, 1864, 2.

3. W. F. Burnett, "The Price Raid," *National Tribune*, August 29, 1907, 6; Hinton, *Rebel Invasion*, 288, 289; "Compendium of History," in *Soldier's Letter*, 1: (July 22, 1865), 1; November 1–6, 1864, entries in Baker diary; "Just from the Front!!," Kansas City *Journal of Commerce*, October 28, 1864, 2. W. F. Burnett, "The Price Raid," *National Tribune*, August 29, 1907, 6; Hinton, *Rebel Invasion*, 288, 289.

4. Hinton, *Rebel Invasion*, 287–89; Curtis, *OR*, 41: (pt. 1), 516; Jennison, *OR*, 41: (pt. 1), 588–89; Hunt, *OR*, 41: (pt. 1), 546; Charlot, *OR*, 41: (pt. 1), 529; McKenny, *OR*, 41: (pt. 1), 541; Childers, "Recitals and Reminiscences," *National Tribune*, January 31, 1907, 6. "Had met the McClellan family in the hospital at Cane Hill after the earlier battle, had sons in the Confederate army. On the 5th of November Lieutenant Quinby, acting signal officer, was detailed by your order to proceed to Saint Louis on special duty," Meeker, *OR*, 41: (pt. 1), 564.

5. Rosecrans, *OR*, 41: (pt. 1), 314; W. F. Burnett, "The Price Raid," *National Tribune*, August 29, 1907, 6; Hinton, *Rebel Invasion*, 288, 289.

6. Hunt, *OR*, 41: (pt. 1), 546; Charlot, *OR*, 41: (pt. 1), 529; McKenny, *OR*, 41: (pt. 1), 541; Hinton, *Rebel Invasion*, 289–90; "Compendium of History," in *Soldier's Letter*, 1: (September 23, 1865), 1.

7. Curtis, *OR*, 41: (pt. 1), 516–17, 519; Hunt, *OR*, 41: (pt. 1), 546; Charlot, *OR*, 41: (pt. 1), 529–30; McKenny, *OR*, 41: (pt. 1), 541; Hinton, *Rebel Invasion*, 290–91; Jenkins, *Battle of Westport*, 101.

8. Curtis, *OR*, 41: (pt. 1), 516–17, 518; Charlot, *OR*, 41: (pt. 1), 529; November 6, 1864, entry in Baker diary.

9. Hinton, *Rebel Invasion*, 294. Complete composition of Price's army. "From Warrensburg—the Wisconsin and Illinois Soldiers—Treatment of Bushwhackers—Communications Re-established," St. Louis *Missouri Democrat*, November 2, 1864, 2.

10. Price, *OR*, 41: (pt. 1), 636–37; "The Raiders. Their Reinforcements," St. Louis *Missouri Democrat*, October 27, 1864, 1; "From Boonville," St. Louis *Missouri Democrat*, November 8, 1864, 2; quoted in Michael B. Dougan, *Confederate Arkansas: The People and Policies of a Frontier State in Wartime* (Tuscaloosa: University of Alabama Press, 1976), 111.

11. General Orders No. 8, First Lieutenant William Gallaher by order of Phillips, February 25, 1865 Fort Gibson, *Cherokee Tomahawk*, March 13, 1865, 4. See also, "A. C. Ellithorp to Conservative." "The Pursuit of Price," St. Louis *Missouri Democrat*, October 28, 1864, 1.

12. Col. Stephen H. Wattles, to Brig. Gen. John M. Thayer, November 2, 1864, enclosed with Brig. Gen. Douglas H. Cooper to Capt. M. L. Bell, November 7, 1864, enclosed with M. L. Bell to Brig. Gen. W. R. Boggs, November 9, 1864, *OR*, 41: (pt. 4), 1040; Brig. Gen. John M. Thayer to Col. S. H. Wattles, October 18, 1864, *OR*, 41: (pt. 4), 74; Brig. Gen. John M. Thayer to Col. S. H. Wattles, October 27, 1864, *OR*, 41: (pt. 4), 272; Maj. Gen. F. Steele to Brig. Gen. John M. Thayer, October 29, 1864, *OR*, 41: (pt. 4), 308. "General Cooper has notified me that his train under flag of truce will not reach North Fork Town until November 3. You will therefore be governed accordingly. This will probably make it safe for you to keep the detachment at Mackey's Lick for a week into November, and also to

send out detachments for corn. No later information," Brig. Gen. John M. Thayer to Col. S. H. Wattles, October 29, 1864, *OR*, 41: (pt. 4), 309. Rosecrans to Canby, "No doubt you will have ordered Steele to do what he can to hurt Price on his return." Rosecrans to Maj. Gen. Canby, October 22, 1864, *OR*, 41: (pt. 4), 178.

13. Charlot, *OR*, 41: (pt. 1), 529.

14. November 8, 1864, entry in Lyman diary, 6. Misc. Mans. 17: #490 WHMC; "Compendium of History," in *Soldier's Letter*, 1: (October 21, 1865), 1; Meeker, *OR*, 41: (pt. 1), 563; Charlot, *OR*, 41: (pt. 1), 529; McKenny, *OR*, 41: (pt. 1), 541.

15. November 6, 1864, entry in Baker diary; Charlot, *OR*, 41: (pt. 1), 529; Meeker, *OR*, 41: (pt. 1), 563; McKenny, *OR*, 41: (pt. 1), 541; S. S. Curtis, *OR*, 41: (pt. 1), 534; Ira M. Mallory, "Missouri Bush & Prairie. Price's Raid," *National Tribune*, September 6, 1900, 8.

16. "From Lexington, Mo. Ravages of Todd, Pool [xi], and Thrailkill," St. Louis *Missouri Democrat*, October 15, 1864, 4; "The Raid. From Franklin County. Murder of Citizens by Rebels. The Damage at Washington. A Horrible Outrage. Tom Price's Men Going to Sterling," St. Louis *Missouri Democrat*, October 14, 1864, 2; "The Lesson of Price's Invasion," Kansas City *Journal of Commerce*, October 28, 1864, 2.

17. Letter to editor from a soldier in Twenty-first Regiment, KSM, *Kansas Daily Times*, October 22, 1864, 2. See also A. J. Harding to Brig. Gen. Clinton B. Fisk, October 27, 1864, *OR*, 41: (pt. 4), 283; "Union Rally," St. Louis *Missouri Democrat*, November 2, 1864, 1; "Important Address to the German Radicals of St. Louis by Leading German Citizens," St. Louis *Missouri Democrat*, November 3, 1864, 2; "Mississippi County Meeting and Nomination," St. Louis *Missouri Democrat*, November 4, 1864, 1; Men of Fletcher's regiment organizing a convention at Rolla to cover nominations for St. Francois county. St. Louis *Missouri Democrat*, October 24, 1864, 1; "Col. Fletcher for Lincoln," Weston *Border Times*, November 4, 1864, 2. The St. Joseph Union printer N. T. Doan called to order. "Radical Ratification Meeting in 'Old Grundy,'" St. Louis *Missouri Democrat*, October 13, 1864, 2. John Wolff. See also "An Ordinance to Enable Citizens of This State in the Military Service of the United States or the State of Missouri to Vote," October 12, 1864, *OR*, 41: (pt. 3), 808.

18. "I have got everything satisfactory with the county committees above, but Shanklin, aided by Craig, is trying to make trouble with Grundy County. I am compelled, during your absence, to do some things my judgment condemns. A report has been very industriously circulated here that you were under arrest for cowardice, but the publication in the city papers of the Democrat's correspondence dispelled the bad effect. I am most unpleasantly situated while Craig is in command, but have adhered to your instructions,"Hinton, *Rebel Invasion*, 293. Hunt, *OR*, 41: (pt. 1), 546; Ford, *OR*, 41: (pt. 1), 610; Meeker, *OR*, 41: (pt. 1), 564; Hinton, *Rebel Invasion*, 291; Curtis, *OR*, 41: (pt. 1), 517; Jennison, *OR*, 41: (pt. 1), 589; Maj. Gen. James G. Blunt, December 24, 1864, *OR*, 41: (pt. 1), 578; Hinton, *Rebel Invasion*, 292–93; Nettleton to his sister, December 19, 1864, in Crittenden, *Battle of Westport and National Memorial Park*, 29–30; Charlot, *OR*, 41: (pt. 1), 529.

19. Hinton, *Rebel Invasion*, 293–94, 297.

20. Ibid.; McKenny, *OR*, 41: (pt. 1), 541–42; Charlot, *OR*, 41: (pt. 1), 529; Ford, *OR*, 41: (pt. 1), 610.

21. Brig. Gen. John B. Sanborn, November 13, 1864, *OR*, 41: (pt. 1), 395–96; "Compendium of History," in *Soldier's Letter*, 1: (October 21, 1865), 1; Charlot, *OR*, 41: (pt. 1), 529.

22. Jennison, *OR*, 41: (pt. 1), 589; "Compendium of History," in *Soldier's Letter*, 1: (October 21, 1865), 1; Charlot, *OR*, 41: (pt. 1), 529.

23. "Compendium of History," in *Soldier's Letter*, 1: (October 21, 28, 1865), both 1; Charlot, *OR*, 41: (pt. 1), 529; Nettleton to his sister, December 19, 1864, in Crittenden, *Battle of Westport and National Memorial Park*, 30; McKenny, *OR*, 41: (pt. 1), 542.

24. Curtis, *OR*, 41: (pt. 1), 518; "Compendium of History," in *Soldier's Letter*, 1: (October 21, 1865), 1; Charlot, *OR*, 41: (pt. 1), 529; Moonlight, *OR*, 41: (pt. 1), 595; Charlot, *OR*, 41: (pt. 1), 529; McKenny, *OR*, 41: (pt. 1), 541; Childers, "Recitals and Reminiscences," *National Tribune*, January 31, 1907, 6.

25. Childers, "Recitals and Reminiscences," *National Tribune*, January 31, 1907, 6; Jasper Malone, "The Longest March," *National Tribune*, April 4, 1907, 4; W. H. Rickman, "That Longest March," *National Tribune*, April 4, 1907, 4; W. F. Burnett, "Price's Raid," *National Tribune*, May 9, 1907, 6; J. F. Ward, "That Longest March. A Reply to the Strictures on the 11th Kan. Cav. And Col. Moonlight," *National Tribune*, May 23, 1907, 6; W. F. Burnett, "The Price Raid," *National Tribune*, August 29, 1907, 6; Lazear to Ashley Lazear, November 2, 1864, in "The Civil War Letters of Colonel Bazel F. Lazear" (Part III), 56; Meeker, *OR*, 41: (pt. 1), 563. "The distance traversed, going and returning, including the various marches and countermarches of headquarters of the Army of the Border, is about 850 miles," Curtis, *OR*, 41: (pt. 1), 519.

26. W. F. Burnett, "Price's Raid," *National Tribune*, May 9, 1907, 6; Henry Dillinberger, "The Big Raid. An Account of How the Rebels Were Driven Out of Missouri," *National Tribune*, May 15, 1890, 3.

27. Hinton, *Rebel Invasion*, 287–88.

28. Price, *OR*, 41: (pt. 1), 639; October 29, 1864, entry in Baker diary.

29. Maj. Gen. Sterling Price, November 18, 1864, *OR*, 41: (pt. 1), 624–25; Price, *OR*, 41: (pt. 1), 639. The *Galveston News* published a brief excerpt from the diary of an officer in Fagan's division. Hinton, *Rebel Invasion*, 295; Shelby, *OR*, 41: (pt. 1), 659; Greene, *OR*, 41: (pt. 1), 692; Burbridge, *OR*, 41: (pt. 1), 694–65.

30. William G. Hazen to Alexander R. Hazen, December 21, 1864. Misc. Manuscripts WHMC, UMC.

31. Brig. Gen. Douglas H. Cooper to Capt. M. L. Bell, November 7, 1864, enclosed with M. L. Bell to Brig. Gen. W. R. Boggs, November 9, 1864, *OR*, 41: (pt. 4), 1040.

32. Rosecrans, *OR*, 41: (pt. 1), 315.

Index